A CHAIN ACROSS THE AGES

FORTY CENTURIES OF PRAYER, 2000 B.C.—A.D. 1941

COMPILED AND ARRANGED FOR DAILY USE BY
SELINA FITZHERBERT FOX, M.B.E., M.D., B.S.

WITH INDEX OF SUBJECTS AND AUTHORS

LONDON
JOHN MURRAY, ALBEMARLE STREET, W.

FIRST EDITION . . . . . *January,* 1913
Reprinted . . . . *March,* 1913
Reprinted . . . . *May,* 1913
Reprinted . . . . *March,* 1915
CHEAPER EDITION . . . . *October,* 1915
Reprinted . . . . *July,* 1916
Reprinted . . . . *December,* 1918
Reprinted . . . . *September,* 1920
THIRD EDITION ENLARGED . . *June,* 1923
FOURTH EDITION . . . . . *July,* 1925
Reprinted . . . . *January,* 1927
FIFTH EDITION . . . . . . *June,* 1928
Reprinted . . . . . . *February,* 1930
Reprinted . . . . *June,* 1933
Reprinted . . . . . . *September,* 1936
SIXTH EDITION . . . . . . *June,* 1941
Reprinted . . . . . . *April,* 1944
Reprinted . . . . . . *November,* 1947

To those who in the past, have "cried unto the Lord,"

To those who in the present, "call upon the God of their fathers,"

To those who in the time to come, will pray to Him "Who heareth us always,"

I DEDICATE THIS BOOK.

IT is good for me to draw near to God, since my whole perfection, both natural and moral, consists in my union with Him.

It is good for me, indeed the best thing I can do, to hold me fast by my God, to unite myself to Him by as many ties and bands as I can, by all the cords and chains of love and by every link of that chain, to make this union as close and as strong as is possible, and so to draw near to Him, and fasten myself upon Him by the most cleaving love, that He may reward my imperfect union here with a perfect and everlasting one hereafter.

(John Norris, A.D. 1657–1711.)

THE COMPILER'S PREFACE
TO THE SIXTH EDITION.

IN 1913—twenty-eight years ago—the "Chain of Prayer" was first published, and ever since that date its output has steadily increased.

Letters and messages of appreciation have been received from all parts of the world, bearing testimony to the help, comfort and inspiration derived from use of the book.

The moving words and expressions of gratitude which have come in throughout these years have been a real joy, and surely enabled one to take heart and courage again, in realizing that prayer—the habit of daily prayer—has not died out, as one has been urged by many to believe. The demand for a book of this character goes far to refute such belief.

Among the alterations and additions in this new Edition will be found the completion of the four weeks of prayers for use at eventide. A large number of letters asked that at least a month's prayers should be given for evening worship.

Other prayers have been added to help to meet various events in human life, both personal and national, but none of the old familiar petitions have been removed except where inadvertently a prayer had been inserted twice. As several writers of letters have said: "There seem few events which cannot now be met by some appropriate and uplifting petition." Great care has been taken in checking, as far as possible, the dates of the various authors and sources from which the prayers have been taken. To simplify matters, it has been arranged to state at the end of each prayer, whenever obtainable, the name and date of birth of the author, and in the index to give the date of birth and death. In a few cases, however, the two dates could not be ascertained.

It has been thought better to classify all the Liturgies from which prayers have been selected under the broad term "The Centuries A.D.," instead of trying to allocate them to any particular century.

An interesting Note on Ancient Liturgies which explains the reason for this alteration has been kindly contributed by Mr. F. C. Eeles, O.B.E., D.Litt. My gratitude to him must be recorded for the invaluable help he has so generously given.

COMPILER'S PREFACE

I also wish to thank Miss Emily L. Cashel for her painstaking research for Authors and dates. Her accurate work in connection with the new Index of " Authors and Sources " of the prayers has been of the greatest help to me, in my effort to bring the book up to date.

I cannot close this Preface without including the Printers. The way they have fitted in the prayers I was anxious to include has immensely lightened my task. I am sincerely grateful for their untiring courtesy.

With the outbreak of war everything around us seemed to be shaken to its very foundations. The widespread attitude that had been taken up of trying to leave God out of account in human thought, human calculation and affairs, was no less rudely shaken. Events occurred in our National and personal lives which proclaimed aloud "God reigneth." He was speaking to the hearts of men in no uncertain words, and saying in terms that could not be misunderstood: "Without ME ye can do nothing."

The cry that has been uttered down through the ages, in man's dire necessity and distress, came again from fearful and stricken hearts: "O God, hear my prayer."

The unfailing response was there: "Then shall ye call upon ME, and ye shall go and pray unto ME, and I will hearken unto you."

The fact of the continuity of a chain of prayer with its links unbroken throughout the centuries may perhaps help some to fulfil the conditions: "Call, Go and pray." The result will bring the assurance to us that He is ever ready to hearken. "Prove Me now herewith, saith the Lord of Hosts, if I will not open you the windows of heaven, and pour you out a blessing, that there shall not be room enough to receive it."

So again this little book of prayers and praises is sent out with the fervent hope that it may be the means of helping many to a "closer walk with God."

SELINA F. FOX.

May, 1941.

PREFACE

THIS collection of prayers was originally made with no thought further than that of meeting a difficulty experienced in finding a book suited to the particular needs of morning and evening prayers in our own household. In consequence, however, of frequent requests to make the compilation more generally known, the idea of publication gradually developed.

The prayers have been gathered from widely different sources, and were often met with in the course of everyday reading or contributed by friends. They have consequently been, in some cases, most difficult to retrace, and in several instances it has proved impossible to determine their origin, though every effort has been made to give author and date to every one in the collection.

It has been no easy task to select the prayers from the large number at one's disposal, and were it not for the size of the book, they could well have been arranged for a year instead of for only six months. The primary object, that of making the book really useful in the home, has above all been kept in view; for this reason many old prayers, though of great interest and quaint in their language, have been omitted, and others retained which seemed more appropriate to the needs of our modern life. In this way numbers of different authors have of necessity been excluded, so that the book can in no way be called—nor indeed does it aim at being—a comprehensive anthology from all the available writers throughout the centuries.

The work of finding and verifying the source, together with the more difficult task of selection, has been lightened by the ever-ready and untiring help and sympathy of my friend, the late Mrs. W. Elliot Graham, who throughout has done so much not only to guide my endeavours, but to facilitate the labour of research.

I wish to express my sincere thanks to all who have in so many ways assisted me; my special thanks are due to the authors and publishers who have so readily given me not only their permission to use copyright material, but have also suggested possible sources from whence other prayers could be gleaned. The following is an alphabetical list of those who have so kindly helped me:

Messrs. George Allen and Co., for prayers from "Before the Throne," by Rev. William Bellars. Messrs. H. R. Allenson, Ltd., for a prayer by Rev. J. R. Miller, from "Great Souls at

Prayer," by Mrs. Mary Tileston. The Association for Promoting Christian Knowledge, Dublin, for prayers from "Family Prayers of the Church of Ireland." Messrs. Bell and Sons, for prayers from "A Book of Family Prayer," by Rev. Ernest Hawkins. The Church of England Zenana Missionary Society, for a prayer used by the Society. The Church Missionary Society, for prayers used by the Society. The Hon. Mrs. Gell, for prayers from "The Cloud of Witness," published by Mr. H. Frowde. Miss Georgina A. Gollock, for the prayer, "The Church's Approach to the Nations." General E. E. Goulaeff, for prayers of Father John of the Russian Church, from "My Life in Christ," published by Messrs. Cassell and Co., Ltd. Rev. John Hunter, D.D., for prayers from "Devotional Services," published by Messrs. J. M. Dent and Co. Canon J. O. Johnston, for prayers from the Cuddesdon "Manual of Missionary Intercession." Messrs. Kegan Paul, Trench, Trübner and Co., for prayers from "A Collection of Prayers," by George Dawson. Messrs. Longmans, Green and Co., for prayers from "Private Prayers," by Rev. E. B. Pusey; "Family Prayers," by Rev. A. F. Thornhill; "The Treasury of Devotion"; "Manual of Prayers," by Rev. W. E. Scudamore; "Family Prayers," by Dean Goulburn; "Suggestions on Prayer," by Miss L. H. M. Soulsby; and "Private Prayers," by Bishop Ashton Oxenden. Messrs. Macmillan and Co., for prayers from "Prayers for Family Use," by Bishop Brooke Foss Westcott. Bishop Handley C. G. Moule, for the use of his prayers. Also for the generous permission given by the Rev. James Ferguson, D.D., to include several prayers from his book "Prayers for Common Worship," published by Messrs. Allenson & Co. Messrs. A. R. Mowbray and Co., for prayers from "Sursum Corda." The National Council of the Evangelical Free Churches, for prayers from "Yet Another Day," by Rev. J. H. Jowett. Messrs. Nisbet and Co., for prayers from "Readings for the Sick," by Rev. F. P. Wickham; "Prayers for Busy Homes," O. H. C.; "The Churchman's Book of Family Prayers," by Bishop Boyd Carpenter. Sir Isaac Pitman and Son, for prayers from "Prayers of Archbishop Benson." Society for Promoting Christian Knowledge, for prayers by Miss Christina G. Rossetti; "Daily Services," by Rev. H. Stobart; "Prayers for Working Men," by Rev. H. W. Turner. Society of St. John the Evangelist, for prayers from "The Intercessory Manual," by Rev. R. M. Benson, published by Messrs. Longmans, Green and Co. My thanks are due also to the Trustees of the will of the late Dr. James Martineau for their kind permission to include several prayers from "Home Prayers," published in 1891, three prayers of which have been slightly altered. Rev. A. F. Thornhill, for

prayers from "Family Prayers," published by Messrs. Longmans, Green and Co. Messrs. Wells Gardner, Darton and Co.,
for prayers from "Family Prayers," by Bishop Walsham How;
"Household Prayers," by Rev. L. Tuttiett; "Words for the
Weary," by Rev. E. H. Sharpe. Messrs. J. Whitaker and Sons,
for prayers from "The Narrow Way." I must further acknowledge my indebtedness to the book of "Ancient Collects," by
Dr. William Bright; to Canon Christopher Wordsworth, for his
translation of St. Dunstan's "Kyrie Rex Splendens." I must
also record my thanks to Mrs. Wordsworth for the prayer by
the late Bishop Wordsworth; to the late Professor Knight and
Messrs. Dent and Sons for the use of prayers from "Prayers
Ancient and Modern"; and also to the Rev. Canon Girdlestone,
for his kindness in giving me the approximate dates of the
writers in the centuries B.C.

If, owing to the way in which the work was originally begun,
any copyright may have been unknowingly infringed, I can only
express my sincere regrets and apologies.

SELINA F. FOX.

January, 1913.

SUPPLEMENTARY ACKNOWLEDGEMENTS

IT has not been possible to trace the authors of several of
the additional prayers, but my thanks are due to: The
Rev. E. A. L. Clarke for prayers taken from his invaluable
collection "The People's Missal"; the Industrial Christian
Fellowship for two prayers; the Students' Christian Movement
for prayers from their collection "Prayers for Students"; and
to the Bishop of Bombay for permission to include one prayer
from "Devotions for the Period of Reconstruction," compiled
by him.

SELINA F. FOX.
BERMONDSEY MEDICAL MISSION,
44, GRANGE ROAD,
LONDON, S.E.I.

June, 1923.

CONTENTS

CONTENTS

THE CHAIN ACROSS THE CENTURIES

CENTURIES B.C.

TWENTIETH TO EIGHTEENTH CENTURIES.

Abraham.   Jacob.

FIFTEENTH CENTURY.

Moses.   Aaron.

ELEVENTH CENTURY.

David.   Solomon.

EIGHTH CENTURY.

Isaiah.   Hezekiah.

SEVENTH CENTURY.

Manasseh.   Daniel.

SIXTH CENTURY.

Baruch.   Ezra.

FIFTH CENTURY.

Nehemiah.   Pericles.

CENTURIES A.D.

FIRST CENTURY.

OUR LORD AND SAVIOUR   St. John.
   JESUS CHRIST.   St. Jude.
St. Clement of Rome.   St. Paul.
St. James.   St. Peter.
                                  St. Luke

Bishop Polycarp.

SECOND AND THIRD CENTURIES.

Bishop Irenæus.   Emperor Constantine the Great.

FOURTH CENTURY.

St. Ambrose.   St. Cyril.
St. Augustine.   St. Ephraim the Syrian.
St. Basil.   St. Hilary.
St. Chrysostom.   St. Nerses of Clajes.
            Bishop Serapion.

FIFTH CENTURY.

St. Gelasius.   St. Leo.
St. Bridget.   St. Patrick.

THE CHAIN ACROSS THE CENTURIES

SIXTH CENTURY.

St. Gregory.

St. Columba.
Mohammed.

SEVENTH CENTURY.
The Venerable Bede.

EIGHTH CENTURY.

Albinus Flaccus Alcuinus.
King Charlemagne.

Archbishop Egbert.

NINTH CENTURY.

King Alfred.
John Scotus Erigena.

St. Dionysius.
Bishop Ædelwald.

TENTH CENTURY.

St. Æthelwold.
King Canute.

Archbishop Dunstan.
Earl Brihtnoth.

ELEVENTH CENTURY.

St. Anselm.   St. Bernard.   Bishop Leofric.

TWELFTH CENTURY.

Pope Innocent III.   St. Francis of Assisi.
Archdeacon Dan Jeremy.

THIRTEENTH CENTURY.

St. Thomas Aquinas.
Archbishop Thomas Brad-
    wardine.

St. Richard, Bp. of Chichester.
Richard de Hampole Rolle.

FOURTEENTH CENTURY.

St. Thomas à Kempis.
Raymond Jordanus.
St. Bernardine.
Lady Juliana of Norwich.

Laurence Minot.
Most noble Order of the Garter.
Ludolphus of Saxony.
John Tauler.

FIFTEENTH CENTURY.

Dean Colet.
Vittoria Colonna.
Archbishop Cranmer.
Desiderius Erasmus.
King Henry VI.
Archbishop Hermann.

Ignatius Loyola.
Martin Luther.
Philip Melanchthon.
Sir Thomas More.
Girolamo Savonarola.
Ludovicus Vives.

THE CHAIN ACROSS THE CENTURIES

SIXTEENTH CENTURY.

Rev. Bernhard Albrecht.
Bishop Andrewes.
Rev. Johann Arndt.
General Lord Astley.
Francis Bacon.
Rev. T. Becon.
Jakob Boehme.
John Calvin.
Bishop Cosin.
Sir Francis Drake.
Edward VI. Primer.
Queen Elizabeth.
Rev. Joachim Embden.
Rev. Nicholas Ferrar.
Lady Jane Grey.
Archbishop Grindal.
Bishop Hall.

Archbishop Hamilton.
King Henry VIII.
Rev. George Herbert.
Rev. John Knox.
Archbishop Laud.
Rabbi of Lissa.
John Norden.
Ludovicus Palma.
Archbishop Matthew Parker.
Bishop James Pilkington.
Bishop Ridley.
Scottish Psalter.
Rev. Richard Sibbes.
Dr. Sutton.
Archbishop Whitgift.
Richard Zouche.

SEVENTEENTH CENTURY.

Dean Lancelot Addison.
Rev. Gottfried Arnold.
Rev. Dr. Isaac Barrow.
Rev. Richard Baxter.
Dean Brevint.
Dr. Brough.
Bishop Gilbert Burnet.
Bishop Joseph Butler.
King Charles I.
Rev. Jeremiah Dyke.
John Evelyn.
Archbishop Fénélon.
Bishop Gunning.
Bishop John Hacket.
Sir Matthew Hale.
Dr. Henry Hammond.
Rev. Matthew Henry.
Bishop George Hickes.
Charles How.
Rev. Benjamin Jenks.
Bishop Ken.

Rev. John Kettlewell.
Archdeacon Edward Lake.
Archbishop Leighton.
John Milton.
Robert Nelson.
Rev. John Norris.
Bishop Simon Patrick.
Bishop John Pearson.
Archdeacon Johann Quirsfeld.
Bishop Reynolds.
Melchior Ritter.
Bishop Sanderson.
Bishop Sherlock.
Bishop Sparrow.
Bishop Nathaniel Spinckes.
Bishop Jeremy Taylor.
Archbishop John Tillotson.
Dr. Henry Vaughan.
Bishop Wilson.
Rev. W. Wollaston.

EIGHTEENTH CENTURY.

American Prayer Book.
Dr. Thomas Arnold.
Ludwig von Beethoven.
Rev. Edward Bickersteth.
Rev. William Blake.

Bishop Blomfield.
Baron Christian Bunsen.
Dr. Chalmers.
Rev. William E. Channing.
Earl of Clarendon.

xv

THE CHAIN ACROSS THE CENTURIES

Princess Elizabeth.
Mrs. Maria Hare.
Bishop Reginald Heber.
Dr. Samuel Johnson.
Rev. Henry Martyn.
Lord Nelson.
Non-Juror's Prayer Book.
Rev. Sir J. E. Phillips.

Rev. Martin J. Routh.
Rev. Michael Sailer.
Rev. C. Simeon.
Gerhard Tersteegen.
Rev. S. Weiss.
Rev. John Wesley.
Henry Kirke White.

NINETEENTH AND TWENTIETH CENTURIES.

Preb. Hon. James Adderley.
Dean Henry Alford.
Bishop Anderson.
Bishop Armstrong.
Rev. Isaac Ashe.
Judge Sir C. Bailhache.
Rev. W. Bellars.
Archbishop Benson.
Rev. R. M. Benson.
Rev. Eugène Bersier.
Bishop Bickersteth.
Bishop Blunt.
Bishop Brent.
William Bright.
Bishop Phillips Brooks.
Rev. James Burns.
Dean Butler.
Rev. G. Calthrop.
Bishop Boyd Carpenter.
Rev. T. T. Carter.
Rev. C. J. N. Child.
Rev. E. A. L. Clarke.
Rev. Robert Collyer.
Preb. Berdmore Compton.
Bishop George Cotton.
Archbishop Crozier.
Archbishop R. Davidson.
Rev. George Dawson.
Canon P. Dearmer.
Rev. Thomas Dee.
Rev. Dr. Digby.
Rev. F. W. Drake.
Dr. F. C. Eeles.
Rev. Rufus Ellis.
S. T. Fraser.
Rev. Dr. James Ferguson.

Rev. Henry Wilder Foote.
Rev. Thomas Furlong.
The Hon. Mrs. Lyttelton Gell.
Rev. Steven Gladstone.
W. E. Gladstone.
Miss Georgina A. Gollock.
Dean Goulburn.
Bishop Grafton.
Rev. W. Graham.
Rev. Samuel Green.
Canon Ernest Hawkins.
Rev. Fitz-Henry Hele.
Canon H. Scott Holland.
Bishop Hornby.
Rev. F. J. A. Hort.
Bishop Walsham How.
Rev. Dr. John Hunter.
Rev. A. L. Illingworth.
Rev. E. D. Jarvis.
Father John, Russian Church.
J. L. Johnston.
Rev. J. H. Jowett.
Bishop King.
Rev. Charles Kingsley.
Professor Knight.
Canon Henry Parry Liddon.
George, 4th Lord Lyttelton.
S. B. Macey.
Rev. A. W. Markby.
Rev. Charles Marriott.
Catherine Marsh.
Chief Justice Martin.
Rev. James Martineau.
Rev. F. Denison Maurice.
Rev. A. McCheane.
Dr. Norman McLeod.

ANCIENT LITURGIES

IN the case of the earlier forms of prayer it is very seldom possible to give dates with any degree of accuracy. Ancient liturgies are composite structures built up little by little in the course of many years. It is sometimes possible to say that a particular form goes back to a certain century, but this is no proof that it did not exist much earlier. On the other hand, the traditional ascription of certain liturgies to particular saints does not mean that they were written by those saints in the form in which we have them now. The utmost that can be said in many cases is that the oldest parts of them represent the traditional use of the churches with which those great names were traditionally associated. Thus, the liturgy known as that of St. James comes to us in a form used in the fourth century; some of it may be earlier, to what extent or how much earlier no one can say. The liturgy of St. Basil was probably rearranged by him; that of St. Chrysostom, closely akin to it, is no doubt to some extent an abridgment of it in which he had a share. But what is called in the Anglican Prayer Book "A Prayer of St. Chrysostom" must not be regarded as actually written by him; it is only one of many prayers in the liturgy which goes by his name and which now contains elements of many different dates. So too in the Latin rites, collects which can be traced back to Mss. of the Sacramentaries or books of prayers known by the names of St. Leo or St. Gregory must not be regarded as having been written by those saints or even as having been in existence in their time.

Very often the same prayer has been altered at some later date, though it still retains its ancient beginning or much of its original wording.

In the Anglican Prayer Book there are many collects translated from the older Latin service books. Some were altered, while retaining a good deal of the original. Other collects in the English Prayer Book are known to have been actually written in 1549 or 1662, while the Scottish, American, or the revised English rites contain prayers of much more recent origin. It is therefore possible to give more or less exact dates for some of these later prayers in a way that is out of the question for those which have come down the centuries from earlier times.

FRANCIS C. EELES.

THE CENTURIES A.D.

Liturgies throughout the Centuries from which prayers have been selected.

It is impossible in the space available here to provide an adequate bibliography of all the sources used. Enough to say that they include, among the more ancient, firstly, liturgies of the principal oriental groups, those of St. Basil and St. Chrysostom used by the Orthodox churches of Greece, Russia, the Middle East and the Balkan countries; the African or Alexandrian family of which that of St. Mark may be regarded as the prototype, and the far eastern Persian or Nestorian, a variety of which has survived in India.

Then come the older western rites, the Roman and the local rites largely derived from it, like those of our own mediæval service books of Sarum or Salisbury use, the immediate source of the reformed English services. The short and terse collects of the authentic Roman tradition are found in the Sacramentaries, as they are called, associated with the names of SS. Leo, Gelasius and Gregory.

And then there are the older books of Gallican or non-Roman type represented now by the Mozarabic rite in Spain.

Later on come the reformed rites, whether Anglican or Lutheran, and in particular the different editions of the English Prayer Book, chiefly 1549, 1662, and 1928, with the other Anglican forms developed since the eighteenth century, first by the Non-jurors, then by the Scottish Episcopal Church and her daughter church in the United States.

In our own time the return to the use of liturgical forms by non-episcopalians has added to the sources on which we have been able to draw, apart altogether from the multitude of prayers written for private use by various persons.

For a collection of this kind, limitations of space and considerations of convenience and purpose have made it necessary to make use of the shorter forms, and to avoid the longer ones and those connected with the administration of the Sacraments.

FOREWORD

SO long as human life has existed, so ancient is the desire to pray to Him, Who under different names, different symbols and figures, has been recognized as God or the Supreme Being. Often mistily beheld, never fully comprehended, always feared, and sometimes loved, He has been sought and worshipped.

In the following collection of prayers forty centuries have been traversed, and through all, the same words of praise, the same songs of thanksgiving, the same deep soul-longings, have been uttered and poured forth at the feet of Him Who has seemed so far off, and yet Who has ever been, and is, so inexpressibly near.

In this twentieth century it has been said, and observation makes the statement appear correct, that personal prayer is being forgotten and family worship omitted; that to a great extent God is no longer acknowledged as FIRST amidst all human circumstances, nor man's absolute dependence upon Him recognized. Again, we hear that it is only by some appalling disaster or great upheaval that man is forced to own the existence and presence of such a Being. "When Thy judgments are in the earth, the inhabitants of the world will learn righteousness" (Isa. xxvi. 9).

In man's dire necessity he still instinctively turns to God in prayer and supplication.

The Divine in the human heart *will* assert itself at such times. It is there; it may be latent, but it exists, and it needs assisting and helping in its development and growth.

This book has been compiled to meet this need. The "chain of prayer" has been made from the widest sources, and gathered from twenty centuries B.C. "across the ages" to the present time.

No two prayers are the same. They have been so arranged that subjects of diverse interest have been included for every day, extending over a period of six months.

FOREWORD

Some of the intercessions for our King, Queen Elizabeth, and Country, including those more usually known, together with the Benedictions, will be found at the end of the volume. Prayers have also been added to meet the needs of the many and varied circumstances of life, and the special seasons of the Christian year. These latter may be used or omitted at discretion. It is hoped by this arrangement that the book may reach a wider circle, and be helpful to people of all schools of thought.

This collection of praises, thanksgivings, and supplications is sent out with the earnest hope that it may be the means of making prayer a greater reality in daily life, and that this power which has been placed in our hands may be more used.

May the book bring many into closer union with Christ, Who was essentially the Man of Prayer, and be the means of enabling lives to be lived in the more conscious influence and presence of the Holy Spirit.

MORNING PRAYERS.

"After this Manner Pray Ye."

OUR Father, Which art in Heaven, Hallowed be Thy Name. Thy kingdom come. Thy will be done, in earth as it is in heaven. Give us this day our daily bread. And forgive us our trespasses, As we forgive them that trespass against us. And lead us not into temptation; But deliver us from evil: For Thine is the kingdom, The power, and the glory, For ever and ever. Amen.   *(Our Lord's Prayer, A.D. 31, St. Matthew vi. 9.)*

Ascription.

ALMIGHTY God, Whose glory the heavens are telling, the earth His power, and the sea His might, and Whose greatness all feeling and thinking creatures everywhere herald; to Thee belongeth glory, honour, might, greatness and magnificence now and for ever, to the ages of ages, through Jesus Christ our Lord. Amen.   *(Liturgy of St. James.)*

The Consecration of Sunday.

O LORD, our heavenly Father, at the beginning of another week we come to Thee for help and light. Grant, we beseech Thee, that we may hallow this day of rest to Thy service, and find in Thee all peace and strength. Quicken our devotion that we may serve Thee in spirit and in truth, and lay a good foundation for our coming work. Be with us in all the public services of Thy day, that we may join in them with heart and soul, and receive the blessing which Thou hast promised to all who sincerely pray to Thee and faithfully hear Thy word. This we ask for the sake of Jesus Christ our Lord. Amen.   *(Bishop Westcott, A.D. 1825.)*

"Do This in Remembrance of Me."

GRANT, O Lord, we beseech Thee, unto Thy Servants who shall this day commemorate in the Holy Sacrament the precious death of Thy dear Son, and receive the blessed communion of His Body and Blood, that they may approach Thy holy Table with true repentance, faith, thankfulness and charity; and being filled with Thy grace, and heavenly benediction, may obtain remission of their sins and all other benefits of His Passion, through the same Jesus Christ our Lord. Amen.   *(Rev. W. E. Scudamore, A.D. 1813.)*

For Absent Friends.

O GOD, Who art everywhere present, look down with Thy mercy upon those who are absent from among us. Give Thy holy angels charge over them, and grant that they may be kept safe in body, soul and spirit, and presented faultless before the presence of Thy glory with exceeding joy; through Jesus Christ our Lord. Amen.   *(Rev. R. M. Benson, A.D. 1824.)*

For Assistance in Daily Work.

O GOD, Who knowest that we are not sufficient of ourselves to think anything as of ourselves, but that all our sufficiency is of Thee, assist us with Thy grace in all the work which we are to undertake this week. Direct us in it by Thy wisdom, support us by Thy power, that doing our duty diligently, we may bring it to a good end, so that it may be profitable to our souls, and tend to the greater glory of Thy Name; through Jesus Christ our Lord. Amen.   (*Treasure of Devotion*, A.D. 1872.)

Assurance of God's Care.

O LORD, Father everlasting, in Whom is all we need or can desire; our hearts take comfort in the very thought of Thee; we have rest in the remembrance that we are Thine.
                              (*S. T. Fraser, Twentieth Century.*)

For Recollectedness.

O HEAVENLY Father, in Whom we live and move and have our being, we humbly pray Thee so to guide and govern us by Thy Holy Spirit, that in all the cares and occupations of our daily life we may never forget Thee, but remember that we are ever walking in Thy sight; for Thine own Name's sake. Amen.
                              (*From an Ancient Collect.*)

General Intercession.

L OOK in mercy, O Lord, on all around us. Bless this parish and neighbourhood in which we live. Bless our King and Country. Guide our rulers, that everything may be ordered according to Thy will for Thy glory and the welfare of all men. Give us peace and such prosperity as may be good for us. Look in mercy upon all the sins and misery of men, and help us in some way to minister to their needs, and make known among us the saving power of Thy gospel; through Jesus Christ our Lord. Amen.   (*Rev. A. F. Thornhill, Nineteenth Century.*)

For God's Guidance.

I NTO Thy hands, O Lord, we commend our spirits, souls and bodies, for Thou hast created and redeemed them, O Lord God Almighty. Guide us and all whom we love this day with Thine eye, and kindle Thy light in our hearts, that Thy godly knowledge increasing in us more and more, we may always be found to walk and live after Thy will and pleasure; through Jesus Christ our Lord. Amen.   (*From an Ancient Collect.*)

For the Presence of the Holy Spirit.

O OUR Father, may the influence and presence of Thy Holy Spirit abide with us to-day. May every week be as a long sabbath of unbroken holiness. May every task be sanctified; for the sake of Jesus Christ our Lord and Saviour. Amen.
                              (*Rev. J. H. Jowett*, A.D. 1864.)

Prayer for Forgiveness.

O LORD, our God, great, eternal, wonderful in glory, Who keepest covenant and promise for those that love Thee with their whole heart, Who art the life of all, the help of those that flee unto Thee, the hope of those who cry unto Thee. Cleanse us from our sins, and from every thought displeasing to Thy goodness, cleanse our souls and bodies, our hearts and consciences that with a pure heart and a clear mind, with perfect love and calm hope, we may venture confidently and fearlessly to pray unto Thee, through Jesus Christ our Lord. Amen.

(Coptic Liturgy of St. Basil.)

Supplication.

A LMIGHTY God, we invoke Thee, the fountain of everlasting Light, and entreat Thee to send forth Thy truth into our hearts, and to pour upon us the glory of Thy brightness; through Jesus Christ our Lord. Amen.   *(Sarum Breviary.)*

Prayer for Family and Friends.

A LMIGHTY God, we beseech Thee to look upon this household. Grant that every member of it may be taught and guided of Thee. Bless the relations and friends of each of us. Thou knowest their several necessities. Prosper, we beseech Thee, every effort at home and abroad to advance Thy kingdom; through Jesus Christ our Lord. Amen.

(Archbishop Tait, A.D. 1811.)

For Bishops and Pastors.

O LORD God of hosts, fill, we beseech Thee, all those whom Thou hast set as Pastors over Thy sheep, with righteousness and true holiness, that by their faith and piety they may overcome the wicked one, and save the Lord's flock from the danger of his assaults; through Jesus Christ our Lord. Amen.

(Gothic Missal.)

"None of Self and All of Thee."

O SAVIOUR, pour upon us Thy Spirit of meekness and love. Annihilate selfhood in us. Be Thou all our life. Guide Thou our hand which trembles exceedingly, upon the Rock of Ages. Amen.   *(Rev. William Blake, A.D. 1773.)*

For Guidance and Protection.

B E Thou, O Lord, our protection, Who art our redemption; direct our minds by Thy gracious Presence, and watch over our paths with guiding love; that among the snares which lie hidden in the path wherein we walk, we may so press onwards with hearts fixed on Thee, that by the track of faith we may come to be where Thou wouldest have us; through Jesus Christ our Lord. Amen.   *(Mozarabic Liturgy.)*

For Divine Control.

O LORD God, King of heaven and earth, may it please Thee this day to order and to hallow, to rule and to govern, our hearts and our bodies, our thoughts, our works, and our words, according to Thy commandments, that we, being helped by Thee, may here and for ever be delivered and saved; through Jesus Christ our Lord. Amen.   (*Roman Breviary.*)

For Self-Control.

PRESERVE us this day from the temptations of the world, the flesh, and the devil. Suffer us not to fall into idle habits, and if diligent in business, suffer not our hearts to be so engrossed but that we may serve Thee, the Lord; and grant that Thy presence may be with us, giving us peace in our souls all the day long; through Jesus Christ our Lord. Amen.

(*Rev. Thomas Furlong, Nineteenth Century.*)

An Intercession.

O GOD, the Giver of every good gift, we pray for our kindred and friends, and for all who are dear to us, that they may be preserved outwardly in their bodies and inwardly in their souls, and that doing Thy will and rejoicing in Thy mercy and love here, they may be partakers of Thy joy hereafter. O God, Thou Who art the Strength of the weak, the Refuge of the distressed, the Comforter of the sorrowful, we pray Thee to have compassion on those who are worn with toil; to bless and support all aged persons; to defend and bless all little children; to protect all who travel by land, sea, or air; to comfort all who are suffering in body or in mind; to extend Thy mercy to all who are oppressed, especially those who are "persecuted for righteousness' sake"; to deliver the tempted, and to bring back all who have wandered from Thy way. Hear us, O heavenly Father, on behalf of all men; for the sake of Jesus Christ, our Lord and Saviour. Amen. (*Rev. Dr. J. Hunter*, A.D. 1849, *adapted.*)

Prayer for the King.

WE pray Thee, that Thou wouldest keep our Sovereign in perpetual peace, strength, and righteousness. Be Thou, O Lord, his defence, and give him the victory over all his enemies; that we also, in the tranquillity of his days, may lead a quiet and peaceable life in all godliness and honesty; through Jesus Christ our Lord. Amen.   (*Liturgy of the Greek Church.*)

For Light.

INCLINE, O Lord, Thy merciful ears, and illuminate the darkness of our hearts by the light of Thy visitation; through Jesus Christ our Lord. Amen.

(*Gelasian Sacramentary.*)

For Repentance and Dedication.

O MERCIFUL God, Who hast preserved us from the dangers of the night, unto Thee and to Thy Service do we offer and give up our souls and bodies, for Thou art their Maker and Preserver. We confess that they are unfit to be offered to Thee, by reason of the many sins whereby we have stained them. Yet have mercy upon us, most merciful Father. Grant us true repentance, and may the love of Jesus Christ cleanse us from all sin, for His name's sake. Amen. (*Rev. H. Stobart, 19th Century.*)

For Confidence.

O LORD Jesus Christ, Who art the Way, the Truth, and the Life, we pray Thee suffer us not to stray from Thee, Who art the Way, nor to distrust Thee, Who art the Truth, nor to rest in any other thing than Thee, Who art the Life. Teach us by Thy Holy Spirit what to believe, what to do, and wherein to take our rest. For Thine own name's sake we ask it. Amen.
(*Desiderius Erasmus*, A.D. 1467.)

General Intercession.

HAVE mercy, we beseech Thee, O Lord, on all mankind. Make Thy way known upon earth, Thy saving health among all nations. Bring into Thy fold Thine ancient people Israel. Bless, guide, and govern by Thy Spirit Thy whole Church, heal its divisions, cleanse it from all corruptions, and make it fruitful unto all good works. Have mercy on the people of this land, and pour forth largely Thy blessing on all the colonies and dependencies of it. Bless our King and Government, the Parliament of our Nation, and the Councils of our Church, and grant that all laws made by them may work for righteousness and peace. Bless this place in which we live with a spirit of charity and godliness. Bless our own household and all its absent members. Bless all who are near and dear to us wheresoever they are. Bless the poor and the afflicted, the sorrowing and the perplexed. To each and all of us grant that which Thou knowest to be best; through Jesus Christ our Lord. Amen.   (*Source not found.*)

For Guidance.

O GOD, forasmuch as without Thee we are not able to please Thee, mercifully grant that Thy Holy Spirit may in all things direct and rule our hearts; through Jesus Christ our Lord. Amen. (*Gelasian Sacramentary: B. of C.P.*, A.D. 1549.)

Commendation.

MAY God the Father bless us; May Christ take care of us; The Holy Ghost enlighten us all the days of our life. The Lord be our Defender and Keeper of body and soul, both now and for ever, to the ages of ages. Amen.
(*Ædelwald. Saxon Bishop, Ninth Century*, A.D.)

"For a Time of Refreshing from the Presence of the Lord."

WE beseech Thee, Almighty God, to behold our prayers, and to pour out upon us Thy loving tenderness; that we who are afflicted by reason of our sins, may be refreshed by the coming of our Saviour; through the same Jesus Christ our Lord.   Amen.
                                    (*Gelasian Sacramentary.*)

For a Realization of God's Good Providence.

O THOU Eternal, in Whose appointment our life standeth. Thou hast committed our work to us, and we would commit our cares to Thee. May we feel that we are not our own, and that Thou wilt heed our wants, while we are intent upon Thy will. May we never dwell carelessly or say in our hearts: "I am here, and there is none over me," nor anxiously as though our path were hid; but with a mind simply fixed upon our trust, and choosing nothing but the dispositions of Thy Providence. More and more fill us with that pity for others' troubles, which comes from forgetfulness of our own, and the glad hope of the children of eternity. And unto Thee, the Beginning and the End, Lord of the living, Refuge of the dying, be thanks and praise for ever. Amen.
                          (*James Martineau, Published* A.D., 1891.)

For the Ministry.

O LORD, we beseech Thee to raise up for the work of the ministry faithful and able men, counting it all joy to spend and be spent for the sake of Thy dear Son, and for the souls for which He shed His most precious blood upon the cross, and we pray Thee to fit them for their holy function by Thy bountiful grace and heavenly benediction; through Jesus Christ our Lord, Who liveth and reigneth with Thee and the Holy Ghost, one God, world without end. Amen.
                          (*Archbishop E. W. Benson,* A.D. 1829.)

For Humility.

O GOD, give us humility and meekness, make us long-suffering and gentle, help us ever to esteem others better than ourselves, and so, O Lord, teach us thus to follow more closely in the steps of our Divine Master, Jesus Christ our Lord.   Amen.
                                    (*Twentieth Century.*)

For Holiness.

PRESERVE, O Lord, and deepen our trust in Thee, increase our confidence in Thy love, wisdom, and justice; that so we may not live without God in the world.   Direct our thoughts and words aright this day; may integrity and uprightness preserve us, and be expressed in everything that we do; through Jesus Christ our Lord. Amen. (*Professor Knight, Nineteenth Century.*)

For Divine Guidance in Prayer.

LORD, we know not what we ought to ask of Thee; Thou only knowest what we need; Thou lovest us better than we know how to love ourselves. O Father! give to us, Thy children, that which we ourselves know not how to ask. We would have no other desire than to accomplish Thy will. Teach us to pray. Pray Thyself in us; for Christ's sake. Amen.

(François de la Mothe Fénélon, A.D. 1651.)

A Prayer for To-day.

ALMIGHTY God, we bless and praise Thee that we have wakened to the light of another earthly day; and now we will think of what a day should be. Our days are Thine, let them be spent for Thee. Our days are few, let them be spent with care. There are dark days behind us, forgive their sinfulness; there may be dark days before us, strengthen us for their trials. We pray Thee to shine on this day, the day which we may call our own. Lord, we go to our daily work, help us to take pleasure therein. Show us clearly what our duty is, help us to be faithful in doing it. Let all we do be well done, fit for Thine eye to see. Give us strength to do, patience to bear, let our courage never fail. When we cannot love our work, let us think of it as Thy task, and by our true love to Thee make unlovely things shine in the light of Thy great love; through Jesus Christ our Lord. Amen. *(Rev. George Dawson, A.D. 1821.)*

Intercession for the King, and All in Authority.

BLESS, O Lord, we beseech Thee, our King and Parliament, our Judges and Magistrates, our Municipalities and Councils, and all who bear any office and rule in the State. Save our nation from the sins that most easily beset it. Raise the drunkard, lift up the fallen. Lighten the lot of the poor, open the hearts of the wealthy. Bless every effort for the well-being of our people. Prosper the work of Thy Church, that we may live godly, righteous, and sober lives, to the glory of Thy Holy Name; through Jesus Christ our Lord. Amen.

(Rev. W. E. Scudamore, A.D. 1813.)

For All Men Everywhere.

WE pray for our dear Native Country, and for all Nations. That the faith of Christ may liberate the peoples from fear and distrust, and the Cross of Christ everywhere give victory and peace, to the glory of Thy Holy Name. Amen.

(Rev. James Ferguson, D.D., A.D. 1873.)

For Love.

ALMIGHTY and everlasting God, preserve the works of Thy mercy, and pour into our hearts the sweetness of Thy most holy love, and of entire devotion to Thy holy will; through Jesus Christ our Lord. Amen. *(Rev. Rowland Williams, A.D. 1818.)*

Thanksgiving for Sunday.

O GOD, glory be to Thy Name for this day. Make it a day of reverent joy, and holy gladness of heart, and so bring home to us the greatness of our spiritual mercies in Christ, that we may be filled with love and praise, and evermore give thanks unto Thee; through Jesus Christ our Lord. Amen.

(Bishop Walsham How, A.D. 1823.)

For Growth in Grace and Stability.

GIVE us grace, O our God, to listen to Thy call, to obey Thy voice, and to follow Thy guiding. Thou leadest us to pleasures that never fade, to riches which no moth nor rust can corrupt or destroy. Unsearchable riches are in Thy hand, O give us grace to know Thy value of them and to covet them. Thou leadest us to fountains of living water, suffer us not to wander or turn aside till we attain unto the pleasures which are at Thy right hand for evermore. Establish, settle, strengthen us, that our goodness may not be like the early dew, which passeth away, but make us steadfast, immovable, always abounding in the work of the Lord, forasmuch as we know that our labour is not in vain in the Lord. Grant this, we beseech Thee, for Thy dear Son, Jesus Christ's sake. Amen.

(Ludovicus Vives, A.D. 1492.)

Intercession for All Men.

BLESS, O Lord, we beseech Thee, all our relations and friends. Have mercy on all who are sick, comfort all who are in pain, anxiety, or sorrow. Awake all who are careless about eternal things. Bless the children, and keep them in innocency of life. Bless all who are young and in health, that they may give the days of their strength to Thee. Comfort the aged and infirm, that Thy peace may rest upon them. Bless this our family and household, that we may all seek to help and not to hinder one another in the fear and love of Thy Holy Name; through Jesus Christ our Lord. Amen.

(Rev. A. F. Thornhill, Nineteenth Century.)

For the Ministry.

BLESS, we beseech Thee, O Lord, Thy whole clergy and ministers, that they may handle Thy holy things with holiness, and be pleasing to Thee, Who art our High Priest for ever; for Thine honour and glory, both now and evermore. Amen.

(Prof. William Bright, A.D. 1824.)

A Prayer for To-day.

IN this hour of this day, fill us, O Lord, with Thy mercy, that rejoicing throughout the whole day, we may take delight in Thy praise; through Jesus Christ our Lord. Amen.

(Sarum Breviary.)

Prayer for Steadfastness.

GRANT, O Lord, that as we go forth once more to our daily labour we may remember the truths that we learnt, and may carry out the resolutions we made on Thy holy day. Keep us from our besetting sins, and strengthen us to do Thy holy will, that we may never forget Whose we are and Whom we serve; through Jesus Christ our Lord. Amen.

(Bishop Walsham How, A.D. 1823.)

"In the World, yet not of the World."

O LORD, Who hast promised a blessing to those who first seek Thy kingdom and righteousness, enlighten, we pray Thee, our hearts, that we be not entangled among the things of this world. Teach us, as those who are risen with Thee, so to set our affection on things above, that our life even now may be truly hid with Thee, O Christ, in God. Show us, O Lord, the path of life, the fulness of joy in Thy holy presence, the eternal pleasures at Thy right hand, that we may set Thee alway before us, and have no good beyond Thee, the true portion of our inheritance and our God; through Jesus Christ our Lord. Amen.

(Col. iii. 1--3; Ps. xvi., adapted.)

For Sovereign Rulers and their Kingdoms.

O GOD of infinite mercy, remember all Sovereign Rulers; preserve their persons in health and honour, their crowns in wealth and dignity, their kingdoms in peace and plenty, the churches under their protection in piety and knowledge, and a strict and holy religion. Keep them perpetually in Thy fear and favour, and crown them with glory and immortality; through Jesus Christ our Lord. Amen.

(Bishop Jeremy Taylor, A.D. 1613.)

For our Friends.

BE gracious, O Lord, to all our friends and acquaintances; those whom we shall meet this day; and grant that our intercourse in this world, whether for business or pleasure, may be hallowed by the Presence, and prospered through the intercession of Thy Son, Jesus Christ our Lord. Amen.

(Rev. R. M. Benson, A.D. 1824.)

For Trust.

WHAT is before us, we know not, whether we shall live or die; but this we know, that all things are ordered and sure. Everything is ordered with unerring wisdom and unbounded love, by Thee, our God, Who art love. Grant us in all things to see Thy hand; through Jesus Christ our Lord. Amen.

(Rev. C. Simeon, A.D. 1759.)

For Consecration.

PRESERVE us blameless, O Lord, in our goings out and comings in this day. Fill us with the simplicity of a Divine purpose, that we may be inwardly at one with Thy holy will, and lifted above vain wishes of our own. Set free from every detaining desire or reluctance, may we heartily surrender all our powers to the work which Thou hast given us to do; rejoicing in any toil, and fainting under no hardness that may befall us as good soldiers of Jesus Christ, and counting it as our crown of blessing, if we may join the company of the faithful who have kept Thy Name, and witnessed to Thy kingdom in every age. Prepare us to seek our rest, not in outward ease, but in inward devotedness, only fulfil to us the word of the Chief of Saints, leave us His peace while we remain here, and then receive us unto Thyself to mingle with the mighty company of our fore-runners; through Jesus Christ our Lord. Amen.

(*James Martineau, Published* A.D., 1891.)

For All who are Distressed in Mind, Body, or Estate.

O LORD, Who dost not willingly afflict the children of men, behold from Thy holy habitation of Heaven the multitude of miserable souls and lives amongst us, and have mercy upon us. Have mercy on all ignorant souls, and instruct them; on all deluded minds, and enlighten them. Have mercy on all broken hearts, and heal them; all struggling with temptation, and rescue them; all that are fallen from Thee, and raise them; all that stand with Thee, and confirm them. O blessed Jesus, that didst shed Thy blood for our souls to save them, shed Thy Holy Spirit on all, and heal them; for Thy pity's sake. Amen.

(*Dr. Brough*, A.D. 1671.)

For the Universal Church.

GRACIOUS Father, we humbly beseech Thee for Thy Universal Church. Fill it with all truth, in all truth with all peace. Where it is corrupt, purge it; and where it is in error, direct it; where it is superstitious, rectify it; where anything is amiss, reform it,; where it is right, strengthen and confirm it; where it is in want, furnish it; where it is divided and rent asunder, make up the breaches thereof, O Thou holy One of Israel; for the sake of Jesus Christ our Lord and Saviour. Amen.

(*Archbishop Laud*, A.D. 1573.)

For Unworldliness.

ALMIGHTY God, Who by Thy Divine Power hast given unto us all things that pertain unto life and godliness, grant that we fail not of Thine exceeding great and precious promises, but, escaping the corruption that is in the world, may be made partakers of the Divine Nature; through the knowledge of Him Who hath called us by glory and virtue, Thy Son Jesus Christ our Lord. Amen. (*St. Peter*, A.D. 66, *adapted from 2 Peter* i.)

PRAYER FOR GUIDANCE

GRANT to us, Lord, we beseech Thee, the spirit to think and do always such things as be rightful; that we, who cannot do anything that is good without Thee, may by Thee be enabled to live according to Thy will; through Jesus Christ our Lord. Amen.   (*Leonine Sacramentary: Book of Common Prayer,* A.D. 1549.)

FOR ALL NATIONS.

O THOU in Whose hand are the hearts of Thy creatures, shed abroad Thy peace upon the world. By the might of Thy Holy Spirit quench the pride, and anger, and greediness which cause man to strive against man, and people against people. Lead all nations in the ways of mutual help and goodwill, and hasten the time when the earth shall confess Thee indeed for its Saviour and King, and no evil deeds of man shall defile Thy glorious creation; through Jesus Christ our Lord.   Amen.

(*Source not found.*)

FOR OUR SAILORS AND SOLDIERS.

BLESS, O Lord, our sailors and soldiers, of whatever rank or quality.   Grant that in the midst of every temptation which besets them they may fight manfully against the world, the flesh, and the devil; and, resisting all evil by the spirit of Thy ghostly strength, may acquire true courage in the victory of faith.   Prosper them in the maintenance of our country's honour, and keep them safe from enemies spiritual and temporal, that they may glorify Thee upon the earth, until they are called to rest in the triumph of Thy glory; through Jesus Christ our Lord. Amen.   (*Rev. R. M. Benson,* A.D. 1824.)

PRAYER FOR RENEWED ZEAL.

O MOST merciful Father, we confess that we have done little to forward Thy kingdom in the world, and to advance Thy glory.   We would humble ourselves before Thee for our past neglects, and seek for Thy forgiveness.   Pardon our shortcomings.   Give us greater zeal for Thy glory.   Make us more ready and more diligent by our prayers, by our alms, and by our examples, to spread abroad the knowledge of Thy truth, and to enlarge the boundaries of Thy Kingdom.   May the love of Christ constrain us, and may we do all to Thy glory; through Jesus Christ our Lord.   Amen. (*Bishop Walsham How,* A.D. 1823.)

A PETITION.

O GOD, Author of Eternal Light, do Thou shed forth continual day upon us who watch for Thee, that our lips may praise Thee, our life may bless Thee, our meditations may glorify Thee; through Jesus Christ our Lord.   Amen.

(*An Ancient Collect.*)

For Grace and Christ's Companionship.

WE yield Thee hearty thanks, O Lord our God, for Thy great goodness to us. Mercifully assist us in every duty each one of us has to do, and vouchsafe to be our Companion every day, from morning to night, and night to morning; that we may love Thy presence and walk in it vigilantly, and, being delivered from all errors and adversities, may joyfully serve Thee in all godly quietness, and grant us Thy peace all the days of our life, through Jesus Christ our Lord.   Amen.

(Rev. James Skinner, A.D. 1818.)

For Devotion to God and His Service.

O OUR God, we believe in Thee, we hope in Thee, and we love Thee, because Thou hast created us, redeemed us, and dost sanctify us.   Increase our faith, strengthen our hope, and deepen our love, that giving up ourselves wholly to Thy will, we may serve Thee faithfully all the rest of our life.   And finally we pray, that we may be found worthy through Thy grace to inherit Life Eternal; through Jesus Christ our Lord.   Amen.

(The Narrow Way, A.D. 1869.)

A Prayer for All Men.

O GOD, we pray Thee to have mercy upon all men.   Bless Thy holy Church throughout the world.   Bless that portion of it to which we belong.   Bless all Thy ministering servants. Bless, we beseech Thee, our King and all in authority under him. We pray also for our own relations, all the absent members of our respective families, our friends and benefactors.   We beseech Thee to hear us on behalf of the poor, the sick, and the distressed; to each and all, grant, O Lord, that which Thou knowest to be best; through Jesus Christ our Lord.   Amen.

(Rev. H. Stobart, Nineteenth Century.)

For Converts (Missionary Work).

REMEMBER, O Lord, all who in heathen lands are under instruction for Holy Baptism; have mercy upon them and confirm them in the faith; remove all the remains of idolatry and superstition from their hearts, that being devoted to Thy law, Thy precepts, Thy fear, Thy truths, and Thy commandments, they may grow to a firm knowledge of the word in which they have been instructed, and may be found worthy to be made an habitation of the Holy Ghost, by the laver of regeneration, for the remission of their sins, through Jesus Christ our Lord. Amen.   *(Basilian Liturgy.)*

For Guidance.

GRANT that no word may fall from me against my will unfit for the present need.   *(Pericles, B.C. 499.)*

MEMORIAL OF CHRIST'S PASSION.

O LORD Jesus Christ, Who for the redemption of mankind
didst vouchsafe to die upon the Cross, that the whole world,
which lay in darkness, might be enlightened. We beseech Thee
pour such light into our souls and bodies that we may be enabled
to attain to that light which is eternal, and through the merits
of Thy Passion may after death joyfully enter within the gates
of Paradise, Who, with the Father and the Holy Ghost, livest
and reignest, One God, world without end. Amen. (*Anon.*)

INTERCESSION FOR MISSIONS.

O GOD, Who hast made of one blood all nations of men for to
dwell on the face of the whole earth, and didst send Thy
blessed Son to preach peace to them that are far off, and to
them that are nigh; grant that all the peoples of the world may
feel after Thee and find Thee; and hasten, O Lord, the fulfilment
of Thy promise to pour out Thy Spirit upon all flesh; through
Jesus Christ our Lord. Amen. (*G. Cotton, Bp. Calcutta,* A.D. 1813.)

FOR GRACE, CONSTANCY, AND KNOWLEDGE.

G RANT us, we beseech Thee, Almighty and most merciful
God, fervently to desire, wisely to search out, and perfectly
to fulfil, all that is well-pleasing unto Thee this day. Order
Thou our worldly condition to the glory of Thy Name; and, of all
that Thou requirest us to do, grant us the knowledge, the desire,
and the ability, that we may so fulfil it as we ought; and may
our path to Thee, we pray, be safe, straightforward, and perfect
to the end. Give us, O Lord, a steadfast heart, which no unworthy affection may drag downwards; give us an unconquered
heart, which no tribulation can wear out; give us an upright
heart, which no unworthy purpose may tempt aside. Bestow
upon us also, O Lord our God, understanding to know Thee,
diligence to seek Thee, wisdom to find Thee, and a faithfulness
that may finally embrace Thee; through Jesus Christ our Lord.
Amen.   (*St. Thomas Aquinas,* A.D. 1225.)

"CONQUERORS THROUGH HIM WHO LOVED US."

N OW, O God, our Saviour, we entreat Thee, subdue our
iniquities. Only Thine Almighty arm can vanquish them.
We look to Thee for victory. Fight for us, fight in us, that we
may be more than conquerors, through Him who loved us, even
Jesus Christ, our only Lord and Saviour. Amen.
                              (*Rev. Ed. Bickersteth,* A.D. 1786.)

PERSEVERANCE.

O LORD GOD, when thou givest to thy servants to endeavour
any great matter, grant us also to know that it is not the
beginning, but the continuing of the same, until it be thoroughly
finished, which yieldeth the true glory; through him that for the
finishing of thy work laid down his life, our Redeemer, Jesus
Christ. Amen. (*Sir Francis Drake,* A.D. 1541). (*On the day
he sailed into Cadiz,* 1587.)

FOR ACCEPTABLE WORSHIP.

O LORD God, most high, Who humblest Thyself to behold the things in the heavens, Who art most awful in power and majesty, and glory inconceivable. Fill us, we pray Thee, with the most humble reverence of Thyself, and for all that belongs to Thy Holy Name, Thy House, Thy worship, Thy Word, and Thy sacraments; that so we may be prepared to rejoice in Thy Presence on the morrow, and with the hosts of Thy redeemed in that terrible day of Thy righteous judgments, through Jesus Christ our Lord. Amen.

(Prebendary Berdmore Compton, Nineteenth Century.)

A PRAYER FOR INDIA.

O LORD Jesus Christ, Who (as at this time) didst burst the prison-house of the grave, and open to all that believe in Thy Name the gate of a glorious resurrection, let the light of Thy truth, we beseech Thee, shine on all that dwell in darkness. Have mercy on the great land of India. Bless all the rulers and peoples of that land. Bless, guide, and enlighten all who are inquiring after truth, and hasten the time, if it be Thy gracious will, when the knowledge of Thy Name shall cover the world as the waters cover the sea; for Thine honour and glory. Amen. *(Reginald Heber, Bishop of Calcutta, A.D. 1783.)*

FOR THE KING AND COUNTRY.

B LESS, we beseech Thee, merciful Lord, our Country, and all its colonies and dependencies. Give Thine abundant grace to our King, and to all who bear office throughout the realm, that in all things we may be governed righteously and in Thy fear, and grant to us, not only such outward prosperity as is according to Thy will, but, above all things, such virtue and true religion that Thy Holy Name may be ever glorified in the midst of us; through Jesus Christ our Lord. Amen.

(Rev. W. Bellars, Nineteenth Century.)

FAMILY AND HOUSEHOLD.

V ISIT we beseech Thee most gracious Father, this family and household with Thy protection. Let Thy blessing descend and rest on all who belong to it. Guide us here, and hereafter bring us to Thy glory; through Jesus Christ our Lord. Amen.

(Bishop John Ryle, A.D. 1816.)

FOR THE INFLUENCE OF THE HOLY SPIRIT.

S O fill us with Thy Spirit, O Lord, that we, passing from one thing to another, may go from strength to strength, everywhere full of Thy praise, everywhere full of Thy work, finding the joy of the Lord to be our strength, until the time when the work of this world shall close, and the weary hours shall come to an end, and darkness shall come, and our eyes shall rest for awhile, then give us an abundant entrance into life eternal; through Jesus Christ our Lord. Amen.

(Rev. George Dawson, A.D. 1821.)

For the Hallowing of Sunday.

ALMIGHTY God, Who after the creation of the world didst rest from all Thy works and sanctify a day of rest for Thy creatures, grant to us, we beseech Thee, that, putting away from us all earthly cares and anxieties, we may this day worthily approach the services of Thy sanctuary. But grant also that, being under grace and under law to Christ, we may be enabled to hallow all our days by living in Thy constant fear and love, and may in Thy peace enjoy a perpetual sabbath of the soul; through Jesus Christ our Lord. Amen.   (*Source unknown.*)

For Enlightened Minds.

O LORD Heavenly Father, in Whom is the fulness of light and wisdom; enlighten our minds by Thy Holy Spirit, and give us grace to receive Thy Word with reverence and humility, without which no man can understand Thy Truth. For Christ's sake. Amen.   (*John Calvin*, A.D. 1509.)

Prayer for the Parish.

ALMIGHTY and everlasting God, Who dost govern all things in heaven and earth, mercifully hear our prayers, and grant to this parish (and place in which we live) all things needful for its spiritual welfare. Strengthen and confirm the faithful, visit and relieve the sick, turn and soften the wicked, arouse the careless, recover the fallen, restore the penitent. Remove all hindrances, we beseech Thee, to the advancement of Thy truth, and bring us all to be of one heart and mind in Jesus Christ, to the honour and glory of Thy Name, through the same Jesus Christ our Lord. Amen.

(*William J. Butler, Dean of Lincoln*, A.D. 1818.)

For All for Whom we ought to Pray.

WE call to mind, O God, before Thy throne of grace, all those whom Thou hast given to be near and dear to us, and all for whom we are especially bound to pray, beseeching Thee to remember them all for good, and to fulfil, as may be expedient for them, all their desires and wants. We commend to Thee any who may have wronged us, whether by word or deed, beseeching Thee to forgive them and us all our sins, and to bring us to Thy heavenly kingdom, through Jesus Christ our Lord. Amen.   (*Bishop Hamilton*, A.D. 1561.)

Intercession for the Jews.

LOOK down in compassion, O Lord Christ, upon Thine own people, the Jews, in all parts of the world. Open their hearts to receive Thee, their true Messiah and Saviour. Forgive those who have persecuted them. Help us to care for them, and ever to pray for the peace of Jerusalem, for Thy sake, Who art both the Light to lighten the Gentiles and also the Glory of Thy people Israel. Amen.

(*Rev. A. F. Thornhill, Nineteenth Century.*)

Prayer for Pardon.

O LORD Jesus Christ, Who didst give Thy Life for us that
we might receive pardon and peace; mercifully cleanse us
from all sin, and evermore keep us in Thy favour and love, Who
livest and reignest with the Father and the Holy Spirit, ever
one God, world without end.   Amen.

(From an Ancient Collect.)

For Heavenly-Mindedness.

GRANT us, O Lord, not to mind earthly things, but to love
things heavenly; and even now, while we are placed among
things that are passing away, to cleave to those that shall abide;
through Jesus Christ our Lord.

(Leonine Sacramentary.)

For the Nation and All those in Authority.

O GOD, our refuge and strength, Who orderest all things in
heaven and earth; look down with Thy mercy upon us as
a nation.   Remember not our iniquities, nor the iniquities of
our forefathers, neither take Thou vengeance of our sins.   Pour
out upon us, and on all the people of this land, the spirit of
grace and supplication, and join us together in piety, loyalty,
and brotherly love.   Direct the counsels and strengthen the
hands of all in authority for the repression of crime and outrage,
the maintenance of order and law, and of public peace and safety;
so that, leading quiet lives in all godliness and honesty, we may
be Thy people, and Thou mayest vouchsafe to be our God, and
that we may bless and glorify Thee, our Defender and Deliverer;
through Jesus Christ our Lord.   Amen.

(Rev. H. Stobart's Collection, Nineteenth Century.)

For All Teachers and the Work of Education.

DIRECT, O Lord, the work of education, and guide all those
to whom Thou hast entrusted it, that in their various stations
they may do Thee hearty service; and, when their task is completed, they may render up their account with joy; through
Jesus Christ our Lord.   Amen.

(Manual of the Guild of St. Peter, Nineteenth Century.)

For Mission Hospitals, Patients, and Workers.

O LORD, let Thy perpetual Providence guide and direct the
conduct of all mission hospitals, that doctors and nurses,
together with the patients committed to their charge, may be
brought, through contact with the mystery of suffering, into
union with Thee, where alone it is solved.   For Thy Name's
sake.   Amen.   *(Sursum Corda, A.D. 1898.)*

For Daily Guidance by the Holy Spirit.

ALMIGHTY Lord our God, direct our steps this day into the way of peace, and strengthen our hearts to obey Thy commandments; may the Dayspring visit us from on high, and give light to those who sit in darkness and the shadow of death, that they may adore Thee for Thy mercy, follow Thee for Thy truth, desire Thee for Thy sweetness, Who art the blessed Lord God of Israel, both now and evermore.   Amen.

(An Ancient Collect.)

For Christian Graces.

O LORD, long-suffering and abundant in goodness and truth, fill us, we beseech Thee, with graces. Make us long-suffering and patient, cordial and sympathizing, kind and good. Teach us to hold and speak the truth in love, and to show mercy that we may obtain mercy; through Jesus Christ our Lord. Amen.   *(Christina G. Rossetti, A.D. 1830.)*

A Prayer for Ourselves and Others.

MOST merciful and gracious Lord God, Who art revealed to us as the Hearer of prayer, and hast commanded Thy people to come into Thy presence and pour out their hearts before Thee; enable us, we beseech Thee, to draw near to Thee at the beginning of this day, and send Thy Holy Spirit to help our infirmities.   We pray Thee to fit us for the duties of the day, to arm us to meet any trial.   Help us to be in Thy fear all the day long, and as Thy servants, be always watchful, with our loins girt about and our lamps burning.   We commend to Thy care and keeping all Thy people everywhere.   We pray for our Sovereign Lord the King; may his throne be established in righteousness.   Bless all the members of the Royal Family. Give our senators wisdom, and so guide their deliberations that all that is done in this great Empire may be done to Thy praise and glory, in the extension of our Redeemer's kingdom; for the sake of Jesus Christ our Lord.   Amen.

(Rev. G. Calthrop, Nineteenth Century.)

For Joyful Service.

LET us serve God and be cheerful for His honour and glory. Amen.   *(Bishop Hacket, A.D. 1592.)*

For Love and Perseverance.

O BLESSED Lord, we beseech Thee to pour down upon us such grace as may not only cleanse this life of ours, but beautify it a little, if it be Thy will, before we go hence and are no more seen.   Grant that we may love Thee with all our heart, and soul, and mind, and strength, and our neighbour as ourself, and that we may persevere unto the end; through Jesus Christ our Lord.   Amen.   *(Rev. James Skinner, A.D. 1818.)*

For Daily Grace.

O GOD, purify our hearts that we may entirely love Thee, and rejoice in being beloved by Thee. May we never sink into an undue love of anything here below, nor be immoderately oppressed with the cares of this life; but teach us ever to "abhor that which is evil, and cleave to that which is good." May we use this world as not abusing it. May we be endowed with true humility of spirit, and never be allowed to think more highly of ourselves than we ought to think. Make us kindly affectioned one to another with brotherly love, delighting to do good, and ever showing all meekness to all men. May we rejoice to owe no man anything, but to love one another. Make us so happy that we may be able to love our enemies, to bless those that curse us, to do good to them that hate us, to rejoice with them that do rejoice, and to weep with them that weep. And help us to pray always, and not faint, in everything giving thanks, offering up the sacrifice of praise continually; possessing our souls in patience, and learning in whatsoever state we are therewith to be content; for the sake of Jesus Christ, our Lord and Master. Amen.   (*Rev. Fielding Ould*, A.D. 1864.)

For the Lonely.

O GOD of love, Who art in all places and times, pour the balm of Thy comfort upon every lonely heart. Have pity upon those who are bereft of human love, and on those to whom it has never come. Be unto them a strong consolation, and in the end give them fulness of joy, for the sake of Jesus Christ, Thy Son, our Lord. Amen.   (*Anon.*, A.D. 1888.)

For our Country.

O FATHER Almighty, Who, rejoicing in all Thy works, yet especially lovest the home of Thy glory, and teachest Thy servants also to seek in particular the peace of the cities in which they are called to dwell, have mercy on this our beloved land, in which our fathers have lived and died; vouchsafe to cleanse it more and more from all that is evil or displeasing to Thee, and grant that it may never cease to be one of the tranquil abodes of Thy Church, and fruitful to Thee in all good works. Endue all those who are in authority over it with wise hearts and a true regard for it; have compassion on its toiling multitudes in all their manifold orders and estates. Give us always, if it be good for us, health, and might, and a prosperous commerce; friendship and honour among the nations: and a forward place in the midst of those who are called to do great things for Thee. We pray Thee for His sake Who wept for the faithless city of the children of His people, and Who died for all the earth, even Jesus Christ our Lord. Amen.

(*Daily Services, Rev. H. Stobart, Nineteenth Century.*)

For Forgiveness and Mercy.

ALMIGHTY and merciful God, the Fountain of all goodness, Who knowest the thoughts of our hearts, we confess unto Thee that we have sinned against Thee, and done evil in Thy sight. Wash us, we beseech Thee, from the stains of our past sins, and give us grace and power to put away all hurtful things, so that, being delivered from the bondage of sin, we may bring forth worthy fruits of repentance. O Eternal Light, shine into our hearts. O Eternal Goodness, deliver us from evil. O Eternal Power, be Thou our support. Eternal Wisdom, scatter the darkness of our ignorance. Eternal Pity, have mercy upon us. Grant unto us, that with all our hearts, and minds, and strength, we may evermore seek Thy face; and finally, bring us, in Thine infinite mercy, to Thy holy presence. So strengthen our weakness, that, following in the footsteps of Thy blessed Son, we may obtain Thy mercy, and enter into Thy promised joy; through the same Jesus Christ, our only Saviour and Redeemer. Amen.   (*A. F. Alcuinus*, A.D. 735.)

For Steadfastness.

O GOD, Who hast promised that they who endure to the end shall be saved, give us grace to persevere in Thy holy service all our days, that we may reach the end of our faith, even the salvation of our soul; through Jesus Christ our Lord. Amen.
                              (*The Narrow Way*, A.D. 1869.)

For Consistent Lives in our Countrymen Abroad.

O LORD Jesus Christ, Who hast commanded us by Thy Apostles to walk worthy of the vocation wherewith we are called, and as we have each received Thy gifts, so to minister the same one to another, grant to all who are called by Thy Holy Name, and especially to our fellow-countrymen who sojourn in distant lands, that they may show forth Thy praises. Who hast called them out of darkness into marvellous light. Preserve them, we beseech Thee, from the sin of offending Thy little ones who believe in Thee, and from causing Thy word to be blasphemed among the heathen. Make them as the salt of the earth, and as a light in the world; that so, beholding their good works, and won by their holy lives, multitudes may be turned to Thy truth to glorify Thee in the day of visitation, Who art our Saviour and our God, blessed for ever. Amen.
(*Society for the Propagation of the Gospel*, A.D. 1701.)

Supplication for All Men.

BLESS, we beseech Thee, all whom we should remember before Thee; and do for us, for the good of our relations and friends, for the welfare of our King and our country, and for the increase of Thy true religion, abundantly above all that we may ask or think; for the sake of Jesus Christ our Lord. Amen.
                              (*"By a Clergyman,"* A.D. 1845.)

REPRISALS.

O ALMIGHTY God, help us to put away all bitterness and wrath, and evil-speaking, with all malice. May we possess our souls in patience, however we are tempted and provoked, and not be overcome with evil, but overcome evil with good. Enable us, O God of patience, to bear one another's burdens, and to forbear one another in love. Oh, teach and help us all to live in peace, and to love in truth, following peace with all men, and walking in love, as Christ loved us, of Whom let us learn such meekness and lowliness of heart, that in Him we may find rest for our souls. Subdue all bitter resentments in our minds, and let the law of kindness be in our tongues, and a meek and quiet spirit in all our lives. Make us so gentle and peaceable, that we may be followers of Thee, as dear children, that Thou, the God of peace, mayest dwell with us for evermore; to the honour and glory of Thy great Name. Amen.

(Rev. Benjamin Jenks, A.D. 1646.)

FOR ALL IN AUTHORITY.

O GOD, Who gavest Thy Holy Spirit to the elders of Thy people Israel, give wisdom to all bodies of men unto whom Thou hast entrusted the government of Thy servants, especially to the Parliament of our realm, the ministers of the Crown, and the convocations and gatherings of the Church, that they may faithfully execute what Thy Divine Providence hast ordained, for the good of the world, and the extension of Thy kingdom; through Jesus Christ our Lord. Amen.

(Sursum Corda, A.D. 1898.)

FOR FRIENDS AND RELATIONS.

HAVE mercy, O Lord, upon all those whom Thou has associated with us in the bonds of friendship and kindredship, and grant that they, with us, may be so perfectly conformed to Thy Holy Will, that being cleansed from all sin, we may be found worthy, by the inspiration of Thy love, to be partakers together of the blessedness of Thy heavenly kingdom; through Jesus Christ our Lord. Amen.   *(Gallican Sacramentary.)*

FOR SPIRITUAL LIGHT.

A LMIGHTY God, in Whom is no darkness at all, grant us Thy light perpetually, and when we cannot see the way before us, may we continue to put our trust in Thee, that so being guided and guarded, we may be kept from falling this day, and finally, by Thy mercy, enter into our rest; through Jesus Christ our Lord. Amen.   *(Professor Knight, Nineteenth Century.)*

For Holiness.

SEND down, O Lord, the Spirit of power into our hearts, and enable us to subdue all unruly passions, to mortify all lusts and desires, and to deny ourselves; that what Thou determinest may be our choice, and Thy will be the rule of all our actions, through Jesus Christ our Lord. Amen.

(Bishop Sparrow, A.D. 1612.)

For Perseverance.

ALMIGHTY God, to Whom all things belong, Whose is light and darkness, Whose is good and evil. Master of all things, Lord of all. Who hast so ordered it, that life from the beginning shall be a struggle throughout the course, and even to the end; so guide and order that struggle within us, that at last what is good in us may conquer, and all evil be overcome, that all things may be brought into harmony, and God may be all in all. So do Thou guide and govern us, that every day whatsoever betide us, some gain to better things, some more blessed joy in higher things, may be ours, that so we, though but weaklings, may yet, God-guided, go from strength to strength, until at last, delivered from that burden of the flesh, through which comes so much struggling, we may enter into the land of harmony and of eternal peace. Hear us, of Thy mercy; through Jesus Christ our Lord. Amen.   *(Rev. George Dawson, A.D. 1821.)*

For the King and All in Authority.

O GOD, Who hast taught us to make supplications unto Thee for Kings and all who are in authority, look mercifully upon all such for whom we are bound to pray, and grant that, under their governance, we may lead a quiet and peaceable life in all godliness and honesty; through Jesus Christ our Lord. Amen.

(1 Tim. ii. 2; St. Paul, First Century.)

For the Children of our Nation.

O LORD Jesus Christ, we beseech Thee, by the innocence and obedience of Thy holy childhood, and by Thy reverence and love for little children, do Thou guard the children of our land, do Thou preserve their innocence, strengthen them when ready to slip, recover the wandering, and remove all that may hinder them from being brought up in Thy faith and love; Who livest and reignest, One God, world without end. Amen.

(Rev. S. Gladstone, A.D. 1844.)

For Likeness to Christ.

LORD Jesus, by the indwelling of Thy most Holy Spirit, purge our eyes to discern and contemplate Thee until we attain to see as Thou seest, judge as Thou judgest, choose as Thou choosest, and having sought and found Thee, to behold Thee for ever and ever. We ask this for Thy Name's sake. Amen.

(Christina G. Rossetti, A.D. 1830.)

For a Sunday Blessing.

WE praise Thee, O Lord our God, for this Thy holy day. Grant that it may be to us a day of rest from worldly toil, and care. Refresh our souls with Thy heavenly gifts. Enable us to worship Thee in Thy house of prayer, in spirit, and in truth. Bless the ministers of Thy Church, especially those who labour in this place; make Thy Word in their mouth powerful to the conversion of sinners, and to the building up of Thy people in the faith of Thy blessed Son. Grant that all who confess Thy holy name may be of one heart, and of one soul, united in one holy bond of truth and peace, of faith and love, and may with one mind and one mouth glorify Thee; through Jesus Christ our Lord. Amen. (*Canon E. Hawkins*, A.D. 1802.)

A Prayer for Missionaries.

O MOST merciful Saviour and Redeemer, Who wouldst not that any should perish, but that all men should be saved, and come to the knowledge of the truth; fulfil Thy gracious promise to be present with those who are gone forth in Thy Name to preach the Gospel of Salvation in distant lands. Be with them in all perils by land or by water, in sickness and distress, in weariness and painfulness, in disappointment and persecution. Bless them, we beseech Thee, with Thy continual favour, and send Thy Holy Spirit to guide them into all truth. O Lord, let Thy ministers be clothed with righteousness, and grant that Thy word spoken by their mouth may never be spoken in vain. Endue them with power from on high; and so prosper Thy work in their hands, that the fulness of the Gentiles may be gathered in, and all Israel be saved. Hear us, O Lord, for Thy mercy's sake; and grant that all who are called by Thy Name may be one in Thee, and may abound more and more in prayers, and in free-will offerings for the extension of Thy Kingdom throughout the world, to Thy honour and glory. Who liveth and reigneth with the Father and the Holy Ghost, ever one God, world without end. Amen.

(*Society for the Propagation of the Gospel*, A.D. 1701.)

For Illumination.

SHINE into our hearts, O loving Master, by the pure light of the knowledge of Thyself, and open the eyes of our mind to the contemplation of Thy teaching, and put into us the fear of Thy blessed commandments; that trampling down all that is worldly, we may follow a spiritual life, thinking and doing all things according to Thy good pleasure. For Thou art our sanctification, and our illumination, and to Thee we render glory, Father, Son, and Holy Spirit, now and ever, and unto ages of ages. Amen.

(*Eastern Church Liturgy : Daybreak Office.*)

For Light.

O LORD, Who hast brought us through the darkness of night to the light of the morning, and Who by Thy Holy Spirit dost illumine the darkness of ignorance and sin; we beseech Thee, of Thy loving-kindness, to pour Thy holy light into our souls, that we may ever be devoted to Thee by Whose wisdom we were created, by Whose mercy we were redeemed, and by Whose Providence we are governed; to the honour and glory of Thy great Name. Amen.   (*Book of Hours*, A.D. 1864.)

For the Guidance of the Holy Spirit.

ALMIGHTY God, the Giver of all good things, without Whose help all labour is ineffectual, and without Whose grace all wisdom is folly, grant, we beseech Thee, that in all our under-takings, Thy Holy Spirit may not be withheld from us: but that we may promote Thy glory, and the salvation both of ourselves and others. Grant this, O Lord, for the sake of Jesus Christ our Lord. Amen.   (*Dr. Samuel Johnson*, A.D. 1709.)

For the King and his People.

ALMIGHTY God, Whose kingdom is everlasting, and power infinite; have mercy upon the whole Church; and so rule the heart of Thy chosen servant George our King and Governor, that he (knowing Whose minister he is) may above all things seek Thy honour and glory; and that we, and all his subjects (duly considering whose authority he hath), may faithfully serve, honour, and humbly obey him, in Thee, and for Thee, according to Thy blessed word and ordinance; through Jesus Christ our Lord, Who with Thee, and the Holy Ghost liveth and reigneth ever one God, world without end. Amen.

(*Archbishop Cranmer*, A.D. 1489.)

For Missionaries and their Work.

O GOD, Who by Thy Son Jesus Christ has commanded us to go into all the world and preach the Gospel to every creature, make us faithful and obedient to do Thy Holy Will. Give us compassion for all who are living without Thee in the world. Send forth, we beseech Thee, labourers into Thy harvest. Pro-tect and guide them wherever they go. Give them patience, love, and a right judgment in all things. Gather in Thine elect from all nations and hasten Thy kingdom; through Jesus Christ our Lord. Amen. (*Rev. A. F. Thornhill, Nineteenth Century.*)

For Grace to Walk in Holiness.

O GOD of strength, passing all understanding, Who merci-fully givest to Thy people mercy and judgment; grant to us, we beseech Thee, faithfully to love Thee, and to walk this day in the way of righteousness; through Jesus Christ our Lord. Amen.   (*Sarum Breviary.*)

For Unity with the Divine Purpose.

ETERNAL God, Who committest to us the swift and solemn trust of life; since we know not what a day may bring forth, but only that the hour for serving Thee is always present, may we wake to the instant claims of Thy holy will, not waiting for to-morrow, but yielding to-day. Consecrate with Thy presence the way our feet may go, and the humblest work will shine, and the roughest place be made plain. Lift us above unrighteous anger and mistrust, into faith, and hope, and charity, by a simple and steadfast reliance on Thy sure will. In all things draw us to the mind of Christ, that Thy lost image may be traced again, and Thou mayest own us as at one with Him and Thee, to the glory of Thy great Name. Amen.

(James Martineau, Published A.D. 1891.)

For Meekness.

GIVE unto us, Lord Jesus, grace to be meek and patient as Thou wast, that we may gently bear with the faults of others, and strive always to root out our own. For Thy sake. Amen.

(The Narrow Way, A.D. 1869.)

For the Spread of Christianity.

O GOD of unchangeable power and eternal light, look favourably on Thy whole Church, that wonderful and sacred mystery; and by the tranquil operation of Thy perpetual providence, carry out the work of man's salvation; let the whole world feel and see that things which were cast down are being raised up, that those which had grown old are being made new, and that all things are returning to perfection; through Him from Whom they took their origin, even Jesus Christ Thy Son our Lord. Amen.   *(Gelasian Sacramentary.)*

For our Countrymen Abroad, and Others.

O JESUS, Saviour of the world, have pity on those who know Thee not, on those who have forgotten Thee, and on those who are far from the Church of their fathers, in a strange land. Visit them with Thy salvation. Hasten, we pray Thee, Thy kingdom, that the earth may be filled with the knowledge of Thy glory as the waters cover the sea. May these our prayers be acceptable in Thy sight, O Lord our Strength and our Redeemer. Amen.   *(Wells Office Book, Nineteenth Century.)*

For Protection.

O LORD, give ear unto our prayers and dispose the way of Thy servants in safety under Thy protection, that amid all the changes of this our pilgrimage, we may ever be guarded by Thine Almighty aid; through Jesus Christ our Lord. Amen.

(Gelasian Sacramentary.)

Thanksgiving and Prayer for Grace.

..ER, with thankful and humble hearts we appear before
Thee. We would thank Thee for all the benefits that we
have received from Thy goodness. It is to Thy blessing we
owe what success we have found. Every opportunity for doing
good, every impulse in the right way, each victory we have
gained over ourselves, every thought of Thy presence, O Father,
every silent but loving glance on the example of our Pattern,
Thy Son our Lord,—all are alike Thy gifts to us. Give us
strength and wisdom to walk faithfully and joyfully in the way
of willing obedience to Thy laws, and cheerful trust in Thy love.
The best thanksgiving we can offer to Thee is to live according
to Thy holy will; grant us every day to offer it more perfectly,
and to grow in the knowledge of Thy will and the love thereof
evermore; for the sake of Jesus Christ our Lord and Saviour.
Amen.   (*Rev. Michael Sailer*, A.D.B. 1751.)

For Preparedness.

O LORD Jesus Christ, Who hast promised to come again
in like manner as Thou hast ascended into heaven, keep
us, we beseech Thee, ever watchful for Thy glorious appearing.
Help us to set our affections upon things above, not on things
on the earth. May we live as those who wait for their Lord,
that when Thou shalt appear we may be made like unto Thee,
and see Thee as Thou art; Who livest and reignest with the
Father and the Holy Ghost, ever one God, world without end.
Amen.   (*Rev. A. F. Thornhill, Nineteenth Century.*)

For Missionary Societies and Converts.

WE humbly beseech Thee, O most merciful God and Father,
to bless abundantly those Societies which are labouring
for the extension of Thy kingdom in foreign lands. Build up
the native churches, enable all converts to walk worthy of the
vocation wherewith they have been called, and give light to
those now beginning to seek after Thy truth, so that they may
pass out of darkness and become children of the day; through
Jesus Christ our Lord. Amen. (*Rev. Sir J. E. Phillips*, A.D. 1793.)

For the Sorrowful.

COMFORT, we beseech Thee, most gracious God, all that
are cast down and faint of heart amidst the sorrows and
difficulties of the world, and grant that by the energy of
Thy Holy Spirit they may be enabled to go upon their way
rejoicing, and give Thee continual thanks for Thy sustaining
Providence, through Jesus Christ our Saviour. Amen.
                    (*Rev. R. M. Benson*, A.D. 1824.)

For Ready Obedience.

MAKE us of quick and tender conscience, O Lord; that understanding, we may obey every word of Thine this day, and discerning, may follow every suggestion of Thine indwelling Spirit. Speak, Lord, for Thy servant heareth; through Jesus Christ our Lord. Amen.

(Christina G. Rossetti, A.D. 1830.)

For the Jews.

O GOD, Who dost build up the heavenly Jerusalem, Who tellest the number of the stars, and callest them all by their names, heal, we beseech Thee, those that are broken in heart, gather together the outcasts of Thy people, and enrich us all with Thine inestimable wisdom; through Jesus Christ our Lord. Amen. *(Psalterium cxlvii.)*

For the King.

O GOD, in Whose hands are the hearts of Kings, incline Thy merciful ears to our humble entreaty, and govern with Thy wisdom our King, Thy servant, that his counsels may be drawn from Thy fountain and he may be well pleasing in Thy sight; through Jesus Christ our Lord. Amen.

(Gelasian Sacramentary.)

For Bishops and Pastors.

O GOD, Who rulest over Thy people with Fatherly love, give the Spirit of wisdom to all who have received from Thee authority of government, that the welfare of Thy people may turn to the everlasting joy of their pastors, through Jesus Christ our Lord. Amen. *(Gregorian Sacramentary.)*

For Love of God.

O LORD, grant us to love Thee; grant that we may love those that love Thee; grant that we may do the deeds that win Thy love. Make the love of Thee to be dearer to us than ourselves, our families, than wealth, and even than cool water. Amen. *(Mohammed, A.D. 570.)*

(A prayer related by Mohammed as heard on the lips of David in Paradise. Quoted by Dean Stanley.)

For Faithfulness.

O LORD, our Saviour, Who hast warned us that Thou wilt require much of those to whom much is given; grant that we whose lot is cast in so goodly a heritage may strive together the more abundantly by prayer, by almsgiving, by fasting, and by every other appointed means, to extend to others what we so richly enjoy; and as we have entered into the labours of other men, so to labour that in their turn other men may enter into ours, to the fulfilment of Thy holy will, and our own everlasting salvation; through Jesus Christ our Lord. Amen.

(St. Augustine, A.D. 354.)

For Conformity to God's Will.

O ALMIGHTY God, help us now to worship Thee with reverence and humility. Grant us Thy presence this day; in all our trials and disappointments sustain our courage, and make us patient. If Thou sendest trouble, comfort us with thoughts of Thy love; if our plans and hopes are not realized, supply our need in Thine own way. In prosperity teach us to say, "The Lord gave," and in adversity, "The Lord hath taken away, blessed be the Name of the Lord." Draw us nearer and nearer to Thyself. May we each cast our burden upon Thee, never trusting to our own strength, but in Thy mercies, which are infinite; for the sake of Jesus Christ our Saviour. Amen.   (*O. H. C.*, A.D. 1880.)

For Faithfulness.

O ALMIGHTY God and Heavenly Father, Who by Thy Divine Providence hast appointed for each one of us our work in life, and hast commanded that we should not be slothful in business, but fervent in spirit, serving Thee, help us always to remember that our work is Thy appointment, and to do it heartily as unto Thee. Preserve us from slothfulness, and make us to live with loins girded and lamps burning, that whensoever our Lord may come, we may be found striving earnestly to finish the work that Thou hast given us to do; through the same Jesus Christ our Saviour. Amen. (*Dean Goulburn*, A.D. 1818.)

For the Ministry.

O CHRIST, the true Priest, Whose Priesthood continueth for ever, help, we beseech Thee, Thy servants our ministers, that they, carefully discharging the holy offices of their ministry, may through the guidance of Thy Holy Spirit use their talents to Thy service and our need. May they go on, O Lord, from strength to strength; lift them up while they worship Thee, perfect Thy gifts in them, crown them with Thy glory, and fill their hearts with Thy grace, that they may gather into Thy kingdom in heaven a rich harvest of many souls. Prepare, we beseech Thee, all Thy servants for Thy worship on the morrow. Who with the Father and the Holy Ghost livest and reignest ever one God, world without end. Amen.

(*Treasury of Devotion*, A.D. 1869.)

For a Clearer Vision.

GRANT unto us, O Lord, the heavenly vision, that we may behold not only the things of sense in their turmoil and transience, but the things which remain in their rest and ever-lastingness. Grant us the sweet peace of the eternal years, and may we ever rejoice in the duties which bring with them a quiet heart; through Jesus Christ our Lord. Amen.

(*Ladies' College, Cheltenham, Nineteenth Century.*)

For Newness of Life.

O LORD Jesus Christ, Who on this day didst rise again, raise up our souls unto newness of life, granting us repentance from dead works, and planting us in the likeness of Thy resurrection. O Thou Who didst also on this day of the week send down on Thy Apostles Thy most Holy Spirit, take not the same Spirit away from us, but grant to all Thy servants who ask of Thee, that they may be daily renewed and more plentifully enriched in the same, for Thine own mercies' sake; Who livest and reignest with the Father and the Holy Spirit, ever one God, world without end. Amen.   (*Bishop Andrewes*, A.D. 1555.)

For Divine Control.

O THOU, Who art the author of all good things in Thy holy Church, work mightily in all Thy servants, that they may be profitable to all men, and vessels of Thy mercy and grace. Control us all, and so govern our thoughts and deeds, that we may serve Thee in righteousness and true holiness; and sanctify us all unto that eternal life, which we, with all Thy creatures, groaning and travailing together, wait for and expect; through Jesus Christ our Lord. Amen.

(*Philip Melanchthon*, A.D. 1497.)

A Prayer for Daily Spiritual Needs.

O LORD God Almighty, of Thy great charity, pour down upon us a spirit of tender love to Thee, and a pitiful compassion towards all sufferers. Be Thou in every difficulty our Guide, in temptation our Defence, in weakness our Strength, in weariness our Rest; that, transformed by Thy Spirit into the image of Thy holiness, we may finally attain to that blessed home of everlasting rest and joy, where Thou, O Father, with the Son, and the Holy Spirit, livest and reignest, one God, for ever and ever. Amen.

(*Manual of the Guild of St. Barnabas, Nineteenth Century.*)

For the Ministry.

O LORD God Almighty, Who didst endue Thine Apostles with singular gifts of the Holy Ghost, grant to all Thy servants who minister and teach in Thy Holy Name, the spirit of wisdom and love, that in all their words and deeds they may seek Thy glory and the increase of Thy kingdom; through Jesus Christ our Lord. Amen.   (*An old Collect adapted.*)

For Heavenly Joys.

GRANT, O Lord, unto those who fear Thy Name, a happiness that shall endure for ever, that by their deeds and by their life, they may lay up in store for themselves in heaven a harvest of good fruits; through Jesus Christ our Lord. Amen.

(*Psalterium* xxvii.)

For a Clearer Knowledge of God's Will.

GOD Almighty, Eternal, Righteous, and Merciful, give to us poor sinners to do for Thy sake all that we know of Thy will, and to will always what pleases Thee, so that inwardly purified, enlightened, and kindled by the fire of the Holy Spirit, we may follow in the footprints of Thy Well-Beloved Son, our Lord Jesus Christ. Amen. (*St. Francis of Assisi*, A.D. 1182.)

For Loyalty to the Lord's Control.

GIVE us grace, O Lord, to work while it is day, fulfilling diligently and patiently whatever duty Thou appointest us; doing small things in the day of small things, and great labours if Thou summon us to any; rising and working, sitting still and suffering, according to Thy word. Go with us, and we will go, but if Thou go not with us, send us not; go before us, if Thou put us forth; let us hear Thy voice when we follow. Hear us, we beseech Thee, for the glory of Thy great Name. Amen.
(Christina G. Rossetti, A.D. 1830.)

For the Blind, the Deaf and Dumb.

ALMIGHTY Father, Who in the afflictions of Thy people art Thyself afflicted; Whose blessed Son, Jesus Christ, went about doing good, healing all manner of sickness, opening the eyes of the blind and unstopping the ears of the deaf, we bring to Thee all those to whom is denied the gift of hearing. Amid the silence of their lives do Thou make music in their souls; speak as of old in the Voice Whose tender compassion all may hear, and may Thy new Ephphatha mean to them new joys and interests as we Thy servants minister to their needs ; We ask it for Thy Son's Name sake. Amen.
(C.E.Z.M.S., A.D. 1880.)

For Those in Poverty and the Wayward.

O LORD Jesus, Who didst choose to be poor rather than rich, have mercy on all who are in need and want. Comfort them in all sorrows, supply their needs, raise up friends for them, and give them grace to learn of Thee, and always to put their trust in Thy help. Have mercy, O blessed Saviour, on all who are living in sin, all who pray not for themselves, and who care not for their own souls. Turn them to Thyself, and teach them to look to the things which belong to their peace before they are hidden from their eyes; for Thy sake, Who died to save us all. Amen.   (*The Narrow Way*, A.D. 1869.)

Commendation.

LET Thy Fatherly hand, we beseech Thee, ever be over us; let Thy Holy Spirit ever be with us, and so lead us in the knowledge and obedience of Thy Word, that in the end we may obtain everlasting life; through Jesus Christ our Lord. Amen.
(Archbishop Hermann, A.D. 1477.)

For Blessing on the Opening Day.

ALMIGHTY God, we kneel before Thee to ask Thy blessing upon us this morning. We thank Thee for the care which has watched over us in the hours of darkness, and we now beseech Thee to go forth with us to our daily work. Keep us pure and holy by the indwelling of Thy Holy Spirit. Make us strong and of good courage; let us remember that Thou wilt never fail nor forsake us. Let neither the cares nor the business of the day disturb our trust in Thee. May we never murmur under any trial, nor be discontented with our lot, but raise our affections to things above, that we may even now behold Thy presence in righteousness. We ask every blessing in the name and for the sake of Jesus Christ, our Lord and Saviour. Amen.

(O. H. C., A.D. 1880.)

For our Merchant Sailors.

O ETERNAL Lord God, Whose voice, mighty in operation, the raging seas and the stormy winds obey; Who, in Thy mercy, guidest the mariner in safety through the trackless deep; receive, we beseech Thee, into Thy gracious and Almighty protection, the fleets of Thy servant our Soveriegn, the vessels of our merchants, and the persons of all those that serve in them. Preserve them from the perils of the seas, from the efforts of the enemy, and from the danger of disease in foreign climates; that they may return in safety, and crowned, if it be Thy good pleasure, with success in their enterprises, to enjoy the blessings of their native land, and with thankful remembrance of Thy mercies, to unite with us in rendering praise and glory to Thy Holy Name; through Jesus Christ our Lord. Amen.

(By Authority, March 20, A.D. 1811.)

For the Love of our Neighbour.

O ALMIGHTY God, inspire us with this divine Principle; kill in us, all the Seeds of Envy and Ill-will; and help us, by cultivating within ourselves the Love of our Neighbour, to improve in the love of Thee. Thou hast placed us in various Kindreds, Friendships, and Relations, as the School of Disciple for our Affections: Help us, by the due exercise of them, to improve to Perfection; till all partial Affection be lost in that entire universal one, and Thou, O God, shalt be all in all. Amen.

(Bishop Joseph Butler, A.D. 1692.)

Prayer for Acceptance.

ALMIGHTY Father, mercifully accept these our unworthy prayers, which we have offered unto Thy Divine Majesty; look not, we pray Thee, on our faltering lips, but heal our infirmities, and receive our prayers for Thine own mercies' sake, in Christ Jesus our Lord, Who liveth and reigneth with Thee and the Holy Ghost, one God, world without end. Amen.

(Treasury of Devotion, A.D. 1872.)

For Christian Graces.

GRANT Thy servants, O God, to be set on fire with Thy Spirit, strengthened by Thy power, illuminated by Thy splendour, filled with Thy grace, and to go forward by Thine aid. Give them, O Lord, a right faith, perfect love, true humility. Grant, O Lord, that there may be in us simple affection, brave patience, persevering obedience, perpetual peace, a pure mind, a right and honest heart, a good will, a holy conscience, spiritual strength, a life unspotted and unblamable; and after having manfully finished our course, may we be enabled happily to enter into Thy kingdom; through Jesus Christ our Lord.   Amen.
(Gallican Sacramentary.)

For Spiritual Development.

GRANT unto us, Almighty God, that by increase of love of that which is true, by increase of vision of that which is fair, we may know Thee more, and rising by Thy Spirit's gifts into spiritual pureness, may behold Thee, the Spirit, in spirit and in truth; and so passing on from strength to strength of human endeavour and human reaching, come to the beatific vision of God, which shall give us perfect peace.   Comfort us in the hour of death, and bring us safe to the land of eternal rest.   Of Thy mercy hear us; through Jesus Christ our Lord.   Amen.
(Rev. George Dawson, A.D. 1821.)

For the Spread of Christ's Kingdom.

O MERCIFUL Father, Whose blessed Son was lifted up, that He might draw all men unto Him, take away, we beseech Thee, from all who profess to be His disciples, whatever hinders the spread of His kingdom. Arouse the indifferent, lift up the fallen, strengthen the weak-hearted, bring back the wanderers, enlighten the ignorant, convert the wicked, and make the Gospel of Thy Son known throughout the world. We pray Thee, O Lord, look down and bless all those that are over us in Thee, preserve our Sovereign the King, guide and strengthen all those in authority, both in Church and State.   Unite all Christians, and prepare us all for the coming of our Lord Jesus Christ, to Thy honour and glory.   Amen.   *(Rev. L. Tuttiett, A.D. 1825.)*

Intercession.

BLESS, O Lord, all our relations, friends, and all who have been kind to us, all who love us, and care for our good. Turn the hearts of those who love us not, and think evil of us. Comfort and relieve the sick, and all who are in trouble.   Teach the ignorant.   Look, we pray Thee, upon all who are out of work.   Have mercy, O Lord, upon all who are starving, and relieve them in Thine own good time; for the sake of Jesus Christ our Lord.   Amen.   *(Rev. H. W. Turner, Nineteenth Century.)*

For Protection.

ALMIGHTY God, Who seest that we have no power of ourselves to help ourselves; keep us both outwardly in our
bodies, and inwardly in our souls; that we may be defended
from all adversities which may happen to the body, and from all
evil thoughts which may assault and hurt the soul; through Jesus
Christ our Lord. Amen.   (*Gregorian Sacramentary.*)

Intercession for Relations and Friends.

KEEP, O Lord, we beseech Thee, under the shadow of Thy
wings, ourselves, our relations and friends, that we may
obey Thy will, and enjoy Thy presence always. Compass us
about with Thy holy angels. Shield us with the armour of Thy
righteousness upon the right hand and upon the left. Deliver
us from the snares of the evil one, and grant us to pass this day,
and all the days of our life, without stumbling and without
offence; for Thine it is, O Lord, to pity and to save; through
Jesus Christ our Lord. Amen. (*Dean Goulburn*, A.D. 1818.)

For the King and All Rulers.

REMEMBER, O Lord, according to the multitude of Thy
mercies, all those whom Thou hast appointed to rule over
the several nations of the earth, especially Thy servant, our
King; and grant to Thy Church faithful and wise pastors, who
may enlighten it, both by their life and doctrine, and having
turned many to righteousness, may shine in glory, as stars, for
ever and ever; through Jesus Christ our Lord. Amen.
(*Adapted*) (*Rev. H. Stobart, Nineteenth Century.*)

For Pastors and their Work.

WE beseech Thee, O Lord, for special blessing this day on all
Thy servants who to-morrow shall minister in Thy word
and ordinances. Bless all who, anywhere, are called to any
pastoral work for Christ. Prepare them to-day for their preaching and teaching of Thy holy word on the morrow, by sending
to them the fulness of Thy light and truth and peace; through our
Lord Jesus Christ. Amen. (*Bishop H. C. G. Moule*, A.D. 1841.)

For the Care of "The Least of His Brethren."

O LORD, Who, though Thou wast rich, yet for our sakes didst
become poor, and hast promised in Thy Gospel that whatsoever is done unto the least of Thy brethren, Thou wilt receive
as done unto Thee; give us grace, we humbly beseech Thee, to
be ever willing and ready to minister, as Thou enablest us,
to the necessities of our fellow-creatures, and to extend the
blessings of Thy kingdom over all the world, to Thy praise
and glory, Who art God over all, blessed for ever. Amen.
(*St. Augustine*, A.D. 354.)

Blessing on Sunday.

O LORD God, our most blessed Saviour, Who on this day didst rise from the grave, lift up our hearts to follow Thee. Make us rise to a better life. Be with each one of us, O Lord, throughout this day, wherever we may be, especially in Thy house, and grant that we may remain Thine for ever. Amen.

(Rev. H. W. Turner, Nineteenth Century.)

Confession and Intercession.

O GOD the Father Almighty, Creator and Governor of all things; O God the Son Eternal, our Redeemer, Intercessor and Judge; O God the Holy Ghost, the Sanctifier, Who with the Father and the Son together art worshipped and glorified, have mercy upon us. Pardon, O Lord, the sins and offences of our past lives, for Thy mercy's sake; from pride and vanity, from selfishness and envy, from love of the world and forgetfulness of Thee, good Lord, deliver us. O Lord, we beseech Thee mercifully to hear our prayers and supplications for all mankind, and especially for Thy Holy Church throughout the land. For the King and all who are in authority, that they may rule in righteousness and minister true judgment unto the people. For all bishops and ministers, that they may be guided by Thy Holy Spirit to a knowledge of the Truth, and may be both teachers and patterns to their flocks. We beseech Thee to hear us, O Lord, for all who are in trouble, suffering, or distress; for the needy and them that have no helper; for the sick, the dying, and the mourners. For our relations, friends and benefactors; for our enemies, persecutors and slanderers; for all with whom we live or have to do. Hear us, O Lord, we humbly beseech Thee, for the sake of Jesus Christ the Son of God. Amen.

(An Ancient Litany, adapted, A.D. 1489.)

For Love to Christ.

O MOST gracious Lord Jesus Christ, pour into our souls the most precious gift of Thy Love, that our hearts may ever long for Thee, and desire to be in Thy courts and to live with Thee. Grant that our souls may hunger after Thee, Who art full of all pleasure and delight. May we ever thirst for Thee, the fountain of life and light. Let us seek Thee and find Thee, think of Thee and speak of Thee, and do all things to the praise and glory of Thy Holy Name. Be Thou our hope and joy, our rest and peace, our refuge and help, our wisdom and treasure, both now and evermore. Amen. *(The Narrow Way, A.D. 1869.)*

Prayer for God's Keeping.

INTO Thy hands we commend ourselves, for Thou hast redeemed us. Thou, Lord, Who hast redeemed us all for Thine own sake, sanctify and save us this day. Amen.

(Christina G. Rossetti, A.D. 1830.)

A Morning Supplication.

O GREAT King of Heaven and Earth, the Lord and Giver of life, receive us Thy servants, drawing near to the throne of grace in the name of Jesus Christ; give unto every one of us what is best for us, cast out all evil from within us, work in us a fulness of holiness, of wisdom and spiritual understanding, that we, increasing in the knowledge of God, may be fruitful in every good work; through Jesus Christ our Lord.   Amen.

(Bishop Jeremy Taylor, A.D. 1613.)

Dedication to God's Service.

O LORD, give Thy blessing, we pray Thee, to our daily work, that we may do it in faith and heartily, as to the Lord and not unto men.   All our powers of body and mind are Thine, and we would fain devote them to Thy service.   Sanctify them, and the work in which they are engaged; let us not be slothful, but fervent in spirit, and do Thou, O Lord, so bless our efforts that they may bring forth in us the fruits of true wisdom.   Teach us to seek after truth and enable us to gain it; but grant that we may ever speak the truth in love; that, while we know earthly things, we may know Thee, and be known by Thee, through and in Thy Son Jesus Christ.   Give us this day Thy Holy Spirit that we may be Thine in body and spirit in all our work and all our refreshments; through Jesus Christ, Thy Son, our Lord. Amen.   *(Rev. Dr. Thomas Arnold, A.D. 1795.)*

For the Manifestations of God's Kingdom on Earth.

O LORD, make bare Thy Holy Arm in the eyes of all the nations, that all the ends of the world may see Thy salvation; show forth Thy righteousness openly in the sight of the heathen, that the Kingdom of Thy Christ may be established over all mankind; hasten the coming of the end when He shall deliver up the Kingdom unto Thee, and having put down all rule, and authority, and power, and put all things under His feet, He Himself shall be subject unto Thee, and with Thee in the Unity of the Holy Ghost, Three Persons in one God, shall be our All in All for ever and ever.   Amen.   *(Isa. lii. 10; Ps. xcviii.; 1 Cor. xv.; Adapted, Eighth Century, B.C.—First Century A.D.)*

For Perseverance.

L OOK upon us and hear us, O Lord our God; and assist those endeavours to please Thee which Thou Thyself hast granted to us; as Thou hast given the first act of will, so give the completion of the work; grant that we may be able to finish what Thou hast granted us to wish to begin; through Jesus Christ our Lord.   Amen.   *(Mozarabic Liturgy.)*

For the Love of God.

O GOD, Who through the grace of Thy Holy Spirit, dost pour the gift of love into the hearts of Thy faithful people, grant unto us health, both of mind and body, that we may love Thee with our whole strength, and with entire satisfaction may perform those things which are pleasing unto Thee this day; through Christ our Lord.   Amen.   *(Sarum Breviary.)*

For Light.

WE give Thee thanks, Almighty God, for that inward light by which in the midst of outward darkness we may behold, as far as may be, Thy purposes and Thy doings, and see under all things Thy judgments, and being upheld by perfect trust in Thee, in times of evil we may rejoice, and in days of darkness be fearless, and pass on through life in safety, guided by Thy light.   Forgive us when we fall away from Thee.   Restore us by Thy free Spirit, and lead us all through the varying changes of life, in lowly obedience to Thy will, safe into the land of the eternal peace.   Hear us of Thy mercy; through Jesus Christ our Lord.   Amen.   *(Rev. George Dawson, A.D. 1821.)*

For the Church.

O LORD, we beseech Thee to visit with Thy grace and heavenly benediction Thy Church in this land.   Give to the bishops, pastors, and ministers, wisdom, and holiness, and unwearied zeal for souls.   Forgive the sins of Thy people, and bestow upon us the increase of faith, hope, and love.   Grant us to be all of one mind, and one heart, that we may diligently do Thy will, and show forth Thy glory before the world; through Jesus Christ our Lord and Saviour.   Amen.
(Rev. W. Bellars, "Before the Throne," Nineteenth Century.)

For Labourers in the Mission Field.

O GREAT Lord of the harvest, send forth, we beseech Thee, labourers into the harvest of the world, that the grain which is even now ripe may not fall and perish through our neglect. Pour forth Thy sanctifying Spirit on our fellow-Christians abroad, and Thy converting grace on those who are living in darkness.   Raise up, we beseech Thee, a devout ministry among the native believers, that, all Thy people being knit together in one body, in love, Thy Church may grow up into the measure of the stature of the fulness of Christ; through Him Who died and rose again for us all, the same Jesus Christ our Lord.   Amen.
(Bishop Milman, A.D. 1816.)

For Grace.

O LORD, give us all grace, by constant obedience, to offer up our wills and hearts an acceptable sacrifice unto Thee; through Jesus Christ. Amen. *(Christina G. Rossetti, A.D. 1830.)*

Confession of Sin.

ALMIGHTY Father, Lord of heaven and earth, we confess that we have often sinned against Thee in thought, word, and deed. Have mercy upon us, O Lord; have mercy upon us, after Thy great goodness; according to the multitude of Thy mercies, put away our offences and cleanse us from our sins; through Jesus Christ Thy Son, our Lord. Amen.   (*Ps.* li., *adapted.*)

For Knowledge of the Divine Will.

O HEAVENLY Father, subdue in us whatever is contrary to Thy Holy Will. Grant that we may ever study to know Thy will, that we may know how to please Thee. Grant, O God, that we may never run into those temptations which in our prayers we desire to avoid. Lord, never permit our trials to be above our strength; through Jesus Christ our Lord. Amen.

          (*Bishop Thomas Wilson*, A.D. 1663.)

A Prayer for All Conditions of Men.

O GOD, the Creator and Preserver of all mankind, we humbly beseech Thee for all sorts and conditions of men; that Thou wouldest be pleased to make Thy ways known unto them, Thy saving health unto all nations. More especially we pray for the good estate of the Catholick Church; that it may be so guided and governed by Thy good Spirit, that all who profess and call themselves Christians may be led into the way of truth, and hold the faith in unity of spirit, in the bond of peace, and in righteousness of life. Finally, we commend to Thy fatherly goodness all those who are any ways afflicted or distressed in mind, body, or estate; [*especially those for whom our prayers are desired*], that it may please Thee to comfort and relieve them, according to their several necessities, giving them patience under their sufferings, and a happy issue out of all their afflictions. And this we beg for Jesus Christ His sake. Amen.

          (*Bishop Gunning*, A.D. 1614; *B. of C.P.*, A.D. 1662.)

For Unity and Comfort.

O THOU God of peace, unite our hearts by Thy bond of peace, that we may live with one another continually in gentleness and humility, in peace and unity. O Thou God of patience, give us patience in the time of trial, and steadfastness to endure to the end. O Thou Spirit of prayer, awaken our hearts, that we may lift up holy hands to God, and cry unto Him in all our distresses. Be our Defence and Shade in the time of need, our Help in trial, our Consolation when all things are against us. Come, O Thou eternal Light, Salvation, and Comfort, be our Light in darkness, our Salvation in life, our Comfort in death, and lead us in the strait way to everlasting life, that we may praise Thee for ever; through Jesus Christ our Lord. Amen.

          (*Rev. Bernhard Albrecht*, A.D. 1569.)

FOR TRUST AND CONFIDENCE.

O LORD God, in Whom we live, and move, and have our being, open our eyes that we may behold Thy Fatherly presence ever about us. Draw our hearts to Thee with the power of Thy love. Teach us to be anxious for nothing, and when we have done what Thou hast given us to do, help us, O God our Saviour, to leave the issue to Thy wisdom. Take from us all doubt and mistrust. Lift our thoughts up to Thee in heaven, and make us to know that all things are possible to us through Thy Son our Redeemer. Amen. (*Bishop Westcott*, A.D. 1825.)

A MISSIONARY PRAYER.

O LORD our God, Who in the days of Thine Apostles didst pour out Thy Spirit upon Thine handmaidens, and didst enable them to labour much in the Lord, be with all who are labouring in Thy service among the women and children of the East. Keep them under Thy continual protection. Guide, strengthen, and comfort them. Help them to feel and know that Thou art with them. Raise up more such labourers, for the harvest truly is plenteous, but the labourers are few. Gather in more from the heathen and the Mohammedans; give a more abundant increase. Bless all converts from among the women and children of the East. Endue them with constancy. Keep them faithful. Enable them to endure hardness in Thy service. Sustain them in persecution. Cause them to adorn the doctrine, and to grow in grace, and to be faithful in heart and life to Thy glory. Thou knowest all who are in trouble, have compassion upon them, and help them, binding up the broken-hearted, proclaiming liberty to the captives, and the opening of the prison to them that are bound, giving them beauty for ashes, the oil of joy for mourning, the garment of praise for the spirit of heaviness.

Grant us all, whether at home or abroad, to be faithful in Thy service, without spot and without reproach, until the appearing of our Lord Jesus Christ, to Whom with Thee and the Holy Ghost, be honour and glory, world without end. Amen.
(*Church of England Zenana Missionary Society*, A.D. 1880.)

FOR THE SUFFERING AND PERPLEXED.

O THOU, Who art Love, and Who seest all the suffering, injustice and misery which reign in this world, have pity, we implore Thee, on the work of Thy hands. Look mercifully upon the poor, the oppressed, and all who are heavy laden with error, labour, and sorrow. Fill our hearts with deep compassion for those who suffer, and hasten the coming of Thy kingdom of justice and truth; for the sake of Jesus Christ our Lord. Amen.
(*Rev. Eugène Bersier*, A.D. 1831.)

For Love of God's Law.

WE beseech Thee, O Lord, be gracious to Thy people, that we, leaving day by day the things which displease Thee, may be more and more filled with the love of Thy commandments, and being supported by Thy comfort in this present life, may advance to the full enjoyment of life immortal; through Jesus Christ our Lord. Amen.

(Leonine Sacramentary.)

A Memorial of Christ's Passion.

O GOD the Father, Who didst not spare Thy only begotten Son, but didst deliver Him up for us all; O God the Son, Who didst die upon the cross that Thou mightest put away sin by the sacrifice of Thyself; O God the Eternal Spirit, through Whom that sacrifice was offered—three Persons and one God—we adore the unspeakable greatness of redeeming love. Inasmuch as we are partakers of His death, we are called upon to take up our cross daily. Lord, enable us to deny ourselves, to spend and be spent in Thy service. Grant us grace to glorify Thy Name; through Jesus Christ our Lord. Amen.

(Rev. G. Calthrop, Nineteenth Century.)

Intercession.

WE most earnestly beseech Thee, O Thou lover of mankind, to bless all Thy people, the flocks of Thy fold. Send down into our hearts the peace of heaven, and grant us also the peace of this life. Give life to the souls of all of us, and let no deadly sin prevail against us, or any of Thy people. Deliver all who are in trouble, for Thou art our God, Who settest the captives free; Who givest hope to the hopeless, and help to the helpless; Who liftest up the fallen; and Who art the Haven of the shipwrecked. Give Thy pity, pardon, and refreshment to every Christian soul, whether in affliction or error. Preserve us, in our pilgrimage through this life from hurt and danger, and grant that we may end our lives as Christians, well-pleasing to Thee, and free from sin, and that we may have our portion and lot with all Thy saints; for the sake of Jesus Christ our Lord and Saviour. Amen.

(Liturgy of St. Mark.)

For Faithful Work.

GRACIOUS God, remember us, we beseech Thee, in our work this day. If it be Thy will, give unto us a prosperous day. May all our work be well done. May we turn nothing out half done. May we glorify Thee by honest good work; for the sake of Him Who completed His work for us, even Jesus Christ our Lord. Amen.

(Rev. J. H. Jowett, A.D. 1864.)

41

For Light, Truth, and Sanctification.

LIGHT of the world, shine upon our minds and hearts. Spirit of truth, guide us into all truth. Holy Father, sanctify us through Thy truth, and make us wise unto salvation; through Jesus Christ our Lord. Amen. *(Rev. L. Tuttiett, A.D. 1825.)*

For Brotherly Kindness.

POUR upon us, O Lord, the spirit of brotherly kindness and peace; so that, sprinkled with the dew of Thy benediction, we may be made glad by Thy glory and grace; through Jesus Christ our Lord. Amen.   .   *(Sarum Breviary.)*

For Steadfast Faith.

ALMIGHTY and everlasting God, Who hast revealed Thy glory by Christ among all nations, preserve the works of Thy mercy; that Thy Church, which is spread throughout the world, may persevere with steadfast faith in confession of Thy Name; through Jesus Christ our Lord. Amen.
(Gelasian Sacramentary: Intercessions for Good Friday.)

For Ministers and Congregations.

ALMIGHTY and Eternal Father, we Thy children entreat Thee, for the sake of Jesus Christ our Saviour, to bless all ministers of religion in every land, and of every creed. Enlighten them with Thy Holy Spirit—the Spirit of truth—and endue them with innocency of life. Take from them all prejudice, all love of priestly power, all fear of men. Fill them with a hunger and thirst after righteousness and truth, and a spirit of longing after Thyself. Teach them that they may teach others, and lead them to the fount and source of all that is beautiful and true. May Thy blessing descend to-morrow on all congregations, to enable them to worship Thee in spirit and in truth, and to honour Thee by holy and generous lives. We ask Thy Fatherly blessing, O Lord, especially on our work in this place. Do Thou in mercy prosper all that is really good in it, and show us how to amend our mistakes. Make our work a blessing to ourselves, and to all others among whom, by Thy Providence, we have been placed. And in all we say, and in all we do, may we ever and only seek to please Thee, and to magnify Thy glorious Name; through Jesus Christ our Lord. Amen. *(Original source not found.)*

For Those in Sorrow.

COMFORT, O merciful Father, by Thy Word and Holy Spirit all who are afflicted or distressed, and so turn their hearts unto Thee, that they may serve Thee in truth, and bring forth fruit to Thy glory. Be Thou, O Lord, their succour and defence through Jesus Christ our Lord. Amen.
(Philip Melanchthon, A.D. 1497.)

For Heavenly Mindedness.

THOU, O Lord, art the Father of mercies, and the Author of all blessings we have now or at any time received. Let us never have cause to repent that Thou hast bestowed them upon us. Give unto us such a right notion and esteem of all the earthly privileges and enjoyments, that we may never be brought under the power of any of them, but may constantly use all of them to Thy glory. Help us ever to have a care to lay up for ourselves a treasure in heaven, by a great improvement of whatever we enjoy here below. Grant that we may never be high-minded, nor trust in uncertain riches, but in Thee, the living God, Who givest us all things richly to enjoy. May we ever be rich in good works, ready to distribute, willing to communicate, and so may lay up for ourselves a good foundation against the time to come, that we may lay hold on eternal life. Make us truly sensible how impossible it is to serve both God and mammon. Be Thou our God, and our Guide, in all our concerns, and grant us to pass through things temporal, that we finally lose not the things eternal. This we beg for Thy mercy's sake, Who liveth and reigneth with Thee and the Holy Ghost, ever one God, world without end. Amen.

(Rev. Nathaniel Spinckes, A.D. 1653.)

For Missionaries.

MOST Merciful Father, we beseech Thee to send upon Thy servants who preach the Gospel to those in darkness, Thy heavenly blessing. Give them courage, and faith, and health, and strength in their difficult work. May Thy light shine through them into dark and ignorant lives, and may the knowledge of Thy dear Son be brought to many who know Him not; and this we ask for Jesus Christ's sake. Amen.

(Church Missionary Society, A.D. 1799.)

For the Church of Christ throughout the World.

LET us pray for the Churches throughout the world, for their truth, unity, and stability; that in all, charity may flourish, and truth may live. For our own Church, that what is lacking in it may be supplied, and what is unsound corrected; for the sake of Jesus Christ, our only Lord and Saviour. Amen.

(Bishop Andrewes, A.D. 1555.)

Ascription.

ALL praise and glory be to Thee, O God, Who hast exalted Thy Son Jesus Christ to Thy right hand in Heaven. We thank Thee that He has raised our human nature to the glory of Thy Presence, and that He has gone to prepare a place for us. Grant that where He is, thither we may also ascend and reign with Him in glory; through His merits, Who ever liveth to make intercession for us, Jesus Christ our Lord. Amen.

(Rev. A. F. Thornhill, Nineteenth Century.)

For Divine Control.

TEACH us, O Father, how to ask Thee each moment silently for Thy help. If we fail, teach us at once to ask Thee to forgive us. If we are disquieted, enable us, by Thy grace, quickly to turn to Thee. May nothing come between us and Thee. May we will, do, and say, just what Thou, our loving and tender Father, willest us to will, do, and say. Work Thy holy will in us, and through us, this day. Protect us, guide us, bless us within and without, that we may do something this day for love of Thee; something which shall please Thee; and that we may this evening be nearer to Thee, though we see it not nor know it. Lead us, O Lord, in a straight way unto Thyself, and keep us in Thy grace unto the end; through Jesus Christ our Lord. Amen. *(Canon E. B. Pusey, A.D. 1800.)*

For Protection and Peace.

O LORD, our Hiding-place, grant us wisdom, we pray Thee, to seek no hiding-place out of Thee in life or in death. Now hide us in Thine own presence from the provoking of all men, and keep us from the strife of tongues. Make us meek, humble, patient, and teach us to seek peace and ensue it; for Thy Name's sake we ask it. Amen. *(Christina G. Rossetti, A.D. 1830.)*

A Daily Prayer.

O LORD, Thou lover of souls, we beseech Thee to give courage to Thy soldiers, wisdom to the perplexed, endurance to sufferers, fresh vigour and interest in life to those who have lost heart, a sense of Thy Presence to the lonely, comfort to the dying, and a clear vision of Thy truth to those who are seeking Thee; for the sake of Jesus Christ our Lord. Amen.
(L. H. M. Soulsby, Twentieth Century.)

A Prayer for All Men.

LET Thy mercy, O God, extend to the whole race of man-kind. Bring all nations to the knowledge and belief of Thy true religion; and to those who profess it already, give Thy heavenly grace, that they may strive to adorn their holy pro-fession, by a suitable life and conversation. Be merciful and gracious to this, our beloved land, endue all orders and degrees of men amongst us, and especially our governors, in Church and State, with those graces and virtues which may enable them to discharge their several trusts, in such a manner as will be most for Thine honour and glory, and for the peace and prosperity of this land and nation ; through Jesus Christ our Lord, Who liveth with Thee, and the Holy Spirit, ever one God, world with-out end. Amen. *(Rev. Fitz-Henry Hele, Nineteenth Century.)*

A Morning Prayer.

O LORD, lift up the light of Thy countenance upon us; let Thy peace rule in our hearts, and may it be our strength and our song, in the house of our pilgrimage. We commit ourselves to Thy care and keeping this day; let Thy grace be mighty in us, and sufficient for us, and let it work in us both to will and to do of Thine own good pleasure, and grant us strength for all the duties of the day. Keep us from sin. Give us the rule over our own spirits, and keep us from speaking unadvisedly with our lips. May we live together in peace and holy love, and do Thou command Thy blessing upon us, even life for evermore. Prepare us for all the events of the day, for we know not what a day may bring forth. Give us grace to deny ourselves; to take up our cross daily, and to follow in the steps of our Lord and Master, Jesus Christ our Lord. Amen.

(Rev. Matthew Henry, A.D. 1662.)

For All Ministering Servants.

LET Thy blessing, O Lord Jesus, be upon Thy holy Church in all the world. Grant to Thy faithful people grace to live in the fear and love of Thy holy Name, in perfect unity with each other in Thyself, Who art their Head. Bless, O Lord, the work of all who are teaching Thy faith among the people who know Thee not. Give strength to those who preach, and pardon and peace to all who believe through their preaching.

Have mercy, O God, on our King and all who rule over us in Thy Name. Grant them prudence and wisdom, and to Thy people give the spirit of obedience and love, that we may live all our days in peace and plenty, and in Thy holy religion. Let Thy Holy Spirit, O most gracious God, rest upon all Thy ministering servants everywhere. Grant them, by the special help of Thy grace, to be holy in their lives, to be zealous in their work, and to minister for Thy people according to Thy will. These, and all other blessings for all men, we ask in the Name and for the sake of Jesus Christ, our Intercessor and Redeemer. Amen. *(The Narrow Way, A.D. 1869.)*

For Judges and Magistrates.

O JUDGE of all, let Thine eternal justice be meted out in every court of law; cause quarrelling to cease, and make all men reverence law, and live in harmony and obedience, as those who shall one day stand before Thy judgment-seat. May we find mercy then of Thee, O righteous Judge; for the sake and honour of Thy great Name. Amen.

(Sursum Corda, A.D. 1898.)

For Light and Peace.

ALMIGHTY God, Maker of heaven and earth, Giver of light and life, so teach us those things which belong to the heavenly kingdom, and those duties which are of the earth, that we, stirred by the light and life of the peace of God, may be enabled faithfully to do the things committed to us, looking ever unto Thee for light and life, that, being lifted above ourselves, the life of God in the soul of man may be ours, and the peace of God which passeth all understanding, may then keep our hearts and minds; through Jesus Christ our Lord. Amen.

(Rev. George Dawson, A.D. 1821.)

For Children.

ALMIGHTY and everlasting God, we make our humble supplications unto Thee for the children (of this home) of our nation. Let Thy Fatherly Hand, we beseech Thee, ever be over them. Let Thy Holy Spirit ever be with them, and so lead them in the knowledge and obedience of Thy word, that in the end they may obtain everlasting life; through our Lord Jesus Christ. Amen.   *(Rev. A. F. Thornhill, Nineteenth Century.)*

For the Misjudged.

O LORD, strengthen and support, we entreat Thee, all persons unjustly accused or underrated. Comfort them by the ever-present thought that Thou knowest the whole truth, and wilt, in Thine own good time, make their righteousness as clear as the light. Give them grace to pray for such as do them wrong, and hear and bless them when they pray; for the sake of Jesus Christ our Lord and Saviour. Amen.

(Christina G. Rossetti, A.D. 1830.)

General Intercession.

ALMIGHTY God, the Father of mankind, Who hast commanded us to make intercession for all men, hear us while we pray, we beseech Thee. Bless the whole family of mankind from one end of the earth to the other, and give light to those who sit in darkness and in the shadow of death. Bless our King and all the members of the Royal Family, and rule their hearts in Thy faith, fear, and love. Bless all classes of our people that the brotherhood of men which Thy Son came to establish, may exist among us. Purify and exalt the domestic life of our people and deepen their sense of the worth and sacredness of home. We beseech Thee, O Lord our God, to hear us on behalf of all men everywhere; for we ask all in the Name of Jesus Christ our Lord. Amen. *(Rev. Dr. John Hunter, A.D. 1849.)*

For Light.

WE beseech Thee, O Lord, in Thy loving-kindness, to pour Thy holy light into our souls; that we may ever be devoted to Thee, by Whose wisdom we were created, and by Whose providence we are governed; through Jesus Christ our Lord. Amen. *(Gelasian Sacramentary.)*

Memorial of the Ascension.

O LORD Jesu Christ, Who on this day didst ascend into the heavens, grant that we may rise with Thee above all wicked thoughts and evil desires. Lift up our hearts to the throne of Thy holiness, and make us dwell with Thee, now and hereafter. Who livest and reignest, with the Father and the Holy Ghost, one God, world without end. Amen.

(Rev. H. W. Turner, Nineteenth Century.)

Intercession for All Men.

O LORD, to Thy merciful providence we commend the wants of all mankind. Cause the light of Thy glorious Gospel to shine throughout the world. Bless Thy whole Church, heal the divisions of it, and grant to it the blessings of truth, unity, and peace. Bless our country, defend our King and all in authority; give faith and diligence to the clergy; hear the cry of the poor and needy; bless the members, absent and present, of this household, be gracious to all our relations and friends, and grant, O Lord, that we may all, at length, find rest and peace with Thy saints in Thine eternal kingdom; through Jesus Christ our Lord. Amen. *(Rev. W. E. Scudamore, A.D. 1813.)*

For Honesty in Commerce.

O ALMIGHTY God, enlighten all merchants and tradesmen with the gift of Thy Holy Spirit, that they may consider, not what the world would sanction, but what Thy law commands. Prosper with Thy blessing all who are thus striving to regulate their dealings by the rule of truth and love; and if difficulty compass them in the world, quicken Thou within them such a desire of laying up treasure in heaven, as may cause them to accept Thy perfect will, teaching them so to use earthly things that they may become partakers of the true riches which cannot fail; through Jesus Christ our Lord. Amen.

(Rev. R. M. Benson, A.D. 1824.)

For the Divine Presence in the Home.

A LMIGHTY and everlasting God, be Thou present with us in all our duties, and grant the protection of Thy presence to all that dwell in this house, that Thou mayest be known to be the Defender of this household and the Inhabitant of this dwelling; through Jesus Christ our Lord. Amen.

(Gelasian Sacramentary.)

MEMORIAL OF CHRIST'S PASSION.

O LORD Jesus Christ, Who as on this day didst suffer death upon the cross for us, forgive us all our sins, cleanse and make us pure. O Thou, Who didst die that we might live, let us not grieve Thee by our sins, but soften our hard hearts, and bend our wills, that we may hear Thy voice and live. O Thou, Who for us didst bear bitter sufferings, and dost not send us more than we are able to bear, give us help and strength to bear meekly and patiently all our troubles, and to forgive as we hope to be forgiven. Give us grace and strength so to live in this world, that at last we may dwell in that home which Thou by Thy death didst win for us; for Thine own Name's sake. Amen. *(Rev. H. W. Turner, Nineteenth Century.)*

FOR CHARITY.

O GOD of love, Who hast given a new commandment through Thine only begotten Son, that we should love one another, even as Thou didst love us, the unworthy and the wandering, and gavest Thy beloved Son for our life and salvation; we pray Thee, Lord, give to us, Thy servants, in all time of our life on the earth, a mind forgetful of past ill-will, a pure conscience and sincere thoughts, and a heart to love our brethren; for the sake of Jesus Christ, Thy Son, our Lord and only Saviour. Amen. *(Coptic Liturgy of St. Cyril.)*

A PRAYER FOR MISSIONARY STUDENTS.

WE pray Thee, O heavenly Father and Lord of the harvest that Thou wilt send forth additional labourers into Thy harvest. Prosper, we beseech Thee, all efforts that are made to train and prepare those whom Thou dost call to devote their lives to the service of Thy Church abroad. We pray especially for all missionary colleges at home and abroad. Bless those who teach therein, and grant that their labours may abound to Thy honour and glory. Purify and enlighten the students. Put far from them all selfish ambitions and aims; fill them with wisdom and understanding, that they may become fit to act as Thy messengers, and to accomplish the work to which Thou hast called them. We ask all in the name of Jesus Christ, Thy Son and our Saviour. Amen.

(Society for the Propagation of the Gospel, A.D. 1701.)

BENEDICTION.

MAY Thy Holy Spirit continually descend and rest upon all in this house and upon all who are in any way connected with it. Send down Thy blessing upon our handiwork, and keep each of us this day in body and soul, for the sake of Jesus Christ our Lord. Amen. *(Rev. H. W. Turner, Nineteenth Century.)*

A Morning Prayer.

HEAVENLY King, Holy Ghost, Spirit of Truth, Who art
everywhere present, and fillest all things; the Treasury of
good things, and the Bestower of life; come and dwell in us, and
purify us from every stain, and save our souls in Thy goodness;
through Jesus Christ our Lord.   Amen.
(Eastern Church Liturgy, Midnight Office.)

A General Intercession.

REMEMBER, O Lord, for good, the Church which Thou hast
purchased with Thy precious Blood.   Heal the divisions
of it, grant it Thy peace, and so plentifully furnish it with the
gifts of Thy Holy Spirit, that it may witness for Thy truth,
even unto the ends of the earth.   Shed the light of Thy truth
on the people who are still walking in darkness, and bring home
to Thy flock the lost sheep of the house of Israel.   Have mercy
on all who are in error or in sin.   Bless our King, and endue his
counsellors with wisdom.   Protect with Thy power, this Church
and nation.   Visit with Thy love all those whom Thou hast
given to be near and dear to us; and hear us, O Almighty God,
for the sake of Thy dear Son, Jesus Christ our Lord.   Amen.
(Rev. E. Bickersteth, A.D. 1786.)

"Have Mercy, O Lord, on All Men."

LOOK in mercy and loving-kindness upon all our families and
friends, and all who have been kind to us, all who have
asked for our prayers, and all for whom we ought to pray.   Let
Thy Holy Spirit ever be with them to keep them from all evil,
and to guide them to all that is good for their souls and bodies.
Look down, most merciful Lord, on all or any who may have
done us wrong or spoken evil against us.   Turn their hearts,
and have mercy upon them and us.

Have mercy, O Lord God, upon all who are in trouble or
misery, either of mind or body.   Let Thy grace and mercy be
upon them to keep them from falling from Thee.   Look with
pity, O Lord, upon all who are sick and in pain.   Teach them to
feel Thy hand upon them and to turn to Thee.   Restore them to
health, when it shall please Thee and be best for them; for the
sake of Jesus Christ, Who suffered for all.   Amen.
(The Narrow Way, A.D. 1869.)

For the Saturday Half-Holiday.

O GOD, bless and keep all those who are seeking rest or recreation this afternoon.   Grant to them increase of strength and
health.   Preserve them from all harm and accident.   Defend
them in temptation, and deliver them from all evil.   Grant that
they may be more ready in body and soul to serve and worship
Thee on Thy Holy Day; through Jesus Christ our Lord.   Amen.
(Rev. A. F. Thornhill, Nineteenth Century.)

For Divine Worship.

O GOD the Holy Ghost, Lord and Giver of life, Who on this day didst come down from Heaven to sanctify, to guide, to teach, and to comfort Thy people; shed abroad Thy life-giving Spirit in our hearts, to purify and cleanse them from all sinful and wandering thoughts. Give us grace to receive Thy Word meekly and to bring forth fruit with patience. Be Thou, we pray Thee, this day with all who minister in Thy Word and Sacraments, especially with our congregation in this parish, and may we together with them inherit everlasting life. Who with the Father, and Jesus Christ the Son, be all glory and honour, world without end. Amen. (*Rev. H. W. Turner, Nineteenth Century.*)

For the Presence of the Holy Spirit.

O THOU Whose eye is over all the children of men, and Who hast called them by Thy Prince of Peace into a kingdom not of this world, send forth Thy Spirit into all the dark places of life. Let Him still the noise of our strife, and the tumult of the people, carry faith to the doubting, hope to the fearful, strength to the weak, light to the mourners, and more and more increase the pure in heart who see their God. Commit Thy Word, O Lord, to the lips of faithful servants, that soon the knowledge of Thee may cover the earth, as the waters cover the channels of the deep, and so let Thy Kingdom come, and Thy will be done on earth as it is in heaven; through Jesus Christ our Lord. Amen

(*J. Martineau, Published* A.D. 1891.)

General Intercession.

O MERCIFUL God, bless Thy holy Church throughout all the world; bless especially the portion of it in which we live, make all the members of it sound in faith, and holy in life, that they may truly and heartily serve Thee. We commend to Thy Fatherly goodness our relations, friends, and neighbours, and all who desire or ought to be specially remembered in our prayers. Succour the poor, comfort all in trouble, have mercy on the sick and dying, and help us by Thy grace to prepare ourselves daily for the life to come; through Jesus Christ our Lord. Amen.

(*Dean Goulburn,* A.D. 1818.)

For Our Absent Ones.

O GOD, merciful and gracious, Who art everywhere present, we beseech Thee to have in Thy keeping the absent members of our family and household, and all who desire our prayers. Let the hand of Thy blessing be upon them day and night, sanctify them throughout, in their bodies, souls, and spirits, keep them unblamable to the coming of the Lord Jesus, and make them and us to dwell for ever in Thy favour, in the light of Thy countenance, and in Thy glory; for Jesus Christ's sake, Amen. (*Canon E. Hawkins,* 1802.)

A Prayer for To-day's Grace.

WE thank Thee that we have again laid us down in peace and slept, because Thou, O Lord, hast made us to dwell in safety. Into Thy hands we commit our bodies and spirits, for our going out and coming in this day. We are more exposed by day than by night, more surrounded with evil, and more liable to the seductions of sin. May we ever regard sin as our greatest enemy, and holiness as our noblest attainment. And whether we are in solitude or society, may we derive comfort from the fact that Thou God seest us. Hear us, we beseech Thee, for Jesus Christ's sake. Amen.

(Rev. Fielding Ould, A.D. 1864.)

A Prayer for Usefulness.

O GOD, our everlasting hope, as disciples of One Who had not where to lay His head, may we freely welcome the toils and sufferings of our humanity, and seek only strength to glorify the cross Thou layest on us. Every work of our hand may we do unto Thee; in every trouble trace some lights of Thine; and let no blessing fall on dry and thankless hearts. Redeeming the time, may we fill every waking hour with faithful duty and well-ordered affections, as the sacrifice which Thou hast provided. Fill us with patient tenderness for others, seeing that we also are in the same case before Thee; and make us ready to help, and quick to forgive. And then, fix every grace, compose every fear, by a steady trust in Thine eternal realities. Grant this O Heavenly Father, for the sake of Jesus Christ, our Lord and Saviour. Amen. *(James Martineau, Published A.D. 1891.)*

A Prayer for the Nation.

LET Thy mercy and blessing, O Lord of Lords, rest upon our land and nation; upon all the powers which Thou hast ordained over us; our King, and all in authority under him; the Ministers of State, the great Councils of the Nation; all Judges and Magistrates; that we may lead a quiet and peaceable life in all godliness and honesty. Rule the hearts of men in all classes of our people; and in these days of restlessness and self-will, draw all together in true brotherhood and sympathy. Rebuke the power of unbelief and of superstition, and preserve to us Thy pure Word in its liberty and glory even to the end of days; through Jesus Christ our Lord. Amen.

(Bishop H. C. G. Moule, A.D. 1841.)

For Growth in Grace.

O LORD, do Thou create in our hearts a sincere desire to become better, and a steadfast resolution to endeavour to grow in grace and in the knowledge of Jesus Christ our Lord. Amen. *(Bishop Patrick, A.D. 1626.)*

For Preservation from Doubt and Affliction.

LORD, Who knowest all things, and lovest all men better than we know; Thine is might, and wisdom, and love to save us. As our fathers called unto Thee, and were holpen, and were led along the ways Thou sawest good, so, in all time of need, from all evil, the evil of our time and of our hearts, deliver us, good Lord.

From all perplexity of mind; from loneliness of thought, and discontented brooding; from wondering what Thou wouldst have us do, deliver us, Lord. Especially from whatever sin besets us, save and deliver us with might, O Lord.

From all bereavement, sorrow, and desertion; from all things that separate us from each other and from our God; from all evils we have prayed against, and from all evils we have not thought of, deliver, O Lord, Thy servants, whose hope is in Thy goodness for ever; through Jesus Christ our Lord. Amen.

(Rev. Rowland Williams, A.D. 1818.)

For Guidance in Study.

O GOD, Who hast ordained that whatever is to be desired, should be sought by labour; and Who, by Thy blessing, bringest honest labour to good effect, look with mercy upon all our work (studies) and endeavours. Grant us, O Lord, to design only what is lawful and right; afford us calmness of mind, and steadiness of purpose, that we may so do Thy will in this short life, as to obtain happiness in the world to come; for the sake of Jesus Christ our Lord. Amen. *(Dr. Samuel Johnson, A.D. 1709.)*

For Charity between Class and Class.

WE pray Thee, O Lord, for all states and orders of men in our country; for those who bear rule and office, for all who have voice in elections, for all whom Thou hast entrusted with wealth, for the middle classes, and for the multitudes of the poor. Let Thy good Spirit stir up men in ever greater numbers, to seek their neighbours' good, and to do the will of God in truth and love, to Thy glory and the blessing of our land; through Jesus Christ our Lord. Amen.

(Bishop H. C. G. Moule, A.D. 1841.)

For Unity among Christians.

O LORD God, the one God, make Thy people one. Whatever be our differences, even in matters essential, may we ever realize that we are one in Christ Jesus. Let not Satan break the blessed bond of union between believers, but may it be increasingly strengthened in our own experience, and in all Thy people everywhere; for the sake of Jesus Christ our Redeemer. Amen. *(Rev. Benjamin Jenks, A.D. 1646.)*

Thanksgiving and Prayer.

WE give Thee thanks—yea, more than thanks, O Lord our God, for all Thy goodness at all times, and in all places. because Thou hast shielded, rescued, helped, and guided us all the days of our lives, and brought us unto this hour. We pray and beseech Thee, merciful God, to grant in Thy goodness that we may spend this day, and all the time of our lives, without sin, in fulness of joy, holiness, and reverence of Thee. But drive away from us, O Lord, all envy, all fear, and all temptations. Bestow upon us what is good and meet. Whatever sin we commit in thought, word, or deed, do Thou in Thy goodness and mercy be pleased to pardon. And lead us not into temptation, but deliver us from evil; through the grace, mercy, and love of Thine only begotten Son. Amen.   (*Liturgy of S. Mark.*)

Thanksgiving.

O GOD, I thank Thee for all the joy I have had in life. Amen.
(*Earl Brihtnoth*, A.D. 991.)

For Harmony with God's Will.

O GOD, Who hast commanded us to be perfect, as Thou our Father in heaven art perfect; put into our hearts, we pray Thee, a continual desire to obey Thy holy will. Teach us day by day, what Thou wouldest have us do, and give us grace and power to fulfil the same. May we never from love of ease, decline the path which Thou pointest out, nor, for fear of shame, turn away from it; for the sake of Christ Jesus our Lord. Amen.
(*Dean Henry Alford*, A.D. 1810.)

A General Intercession.

O ALMIGHTY God, we pray Thee to have mercy upon all conditions of men. Especially we pray for our Church in this land. Bless all Thy ministering servants. Bless the King, and all who are in authority under him. Bless our relations, friends, and benefactors. Bless the children of our schools and neighbourhood. Bless the poor, the sick, and the distressed; and Thy children the deaf and dumb who live in silence, and those who see no light of the sun; to each, Lord, grant that which Thou knowest to be best; through Jesus Christ our Lord. Amen.   (*Rev. W. E. Scudamore*, A.D. 1813.)

For Illumination.

O THOU that art the Light eternal, the Sun of righteousness, evermore arising and never going down, giving light, food, and gladness unto all; mercifully vouchsafe to shine upon us, and cast Thy blessed beams upon the dulness of our understanding, and upon the dark mists of our sins and errors; for Thine only merits, Who art alone our Saviour, Jesus Christ our Lord. Amen.   (*Desiderius Erasmus*, A.D. 1467.)

For Divine Control.

WHEN we awake, we are still with Thee, O God most merciful, and Thy hand is over us for good. Be Thou the Desire of our hearts, and the Ruler of our thoughts. O heavenly Father, we need Thy love, and Thy calm breath shed abroad in our souls, to be a fountain of strength; we know not, without Thee, what may befall us this day, either of peril, or of temptation, or of sorrow. But Thou canst put a guard about our path, and canst fence all our senses from temptation, by sobering them with Thy holy fear. Give us, then, we pray Thee, a right sense of duty, to shield us in all conflict, and guard us against sin and death. Lead us not into temptation; or, when we are tempted, deliver us by humble watchfulness from all power of evil, through Jesus Christ our Lord and Saviour. Amen.

(Rev. Rowland Williams, A.D. 1818.)

For the King and Nation.

ALMIGHTY Lord, of Whose righteous Will all things are, and were created; Thou hast gathered our people into a great nation, and sent them to sow beside all waters, and multiply sure dwellings on the earth. Deepen the root of our life in everlasting righteousness. Make us equal to our high trusts, reverent in the use of freedom, just in the exercise of power, generous in the protection of weakness. With all Thy blessings, bless Thy servant George our King, with all the members of the Royal House. Fill his heart and theirs with such loyalty to Thee, that his people may be exalted by their loyalty to him. To our legislators and counsellors give insight and faithfulness, that our laws may clearly speak the right, and our judges purely interpret them. May wisdom and knowledge be the stability of our times, and our deepest trust be in Thee, the Lord of Nations, and the King of Kings, even Jesus Christ our Lord. Amen. *(J. Martineau, Published A.D. 1891.)*

For a Realization of our Blessings.

O GOD our Father, we would thank Thee for all the bright things of life. Help us to see them, and to count them, and to remember them, that our lives may flow in ceaseless praise; for the sake of Christ Jesus our Lord. Amen.

(Rev. J. H. Jowett, A.D. 1864.)

Universal Dependence upon God.

ALL things wait upon Thee, O Lord. Thou openest Thy hand, and they are filled with good. Hear us, O Lord God, and be merciful unto us, for Thy Name's sake. Thou knowest our needs, teach us to feel them. Thou knowest our ignorance, teach us how to pray. Thou knowest our weakness, teach us how to look to Thee for strength; for Jesus Christ's sake. Amen.

(Bishop Westcott, A.D. 1825.)

For Mercy and Forgiveness.

ALMIGHTY and everlasting God, Who art always more ready to hear than we to pray, and art wont to give more than either we desire or deserve, pour down upon us the abundance of Thy mercy, forgiving us those things whereof our conscience is afraid, and giving us those good things which we are not worthy to ask, but through the merits and mediation of Jesus Christ, Thy Son, our Lord. Amen. (*Gelasian Sacramentary, B.C.P.* 1549.)

For Missionaries.

ALMIGHTY God, Who by Thy Son Jesus Christ has granted unto us a knowledge of Thy love, and hast bidden us to share, with others, that which we have ourselves received, we thank Thee for Thy servants that have gone forth from our midst, to spread the knowledge of Thy love amongst those nations and peoples, who are all living in ignorance of Thy love. Grant that we, who remain at home, may continually support and aid them by our sympathy, that we may rejoice with them in the success of their work, and sorrow with them in their difficulties and disappointments, that so we may at length share with them in the joy of their reward. We ask this in the Name of our Saviour Jesus Christ. Amen.
(*Society for the Propagation of the Gospel*, A.D. 1701.)

For Grace to follow God's Laws.

O GOD, Who declarest Thy almighty power most chiefly in showing mercy and pity, mercifully grant unto us such a measure of Thy grace, that we, running the way of Thy commandments, may obtain Thy gracious promises, and be made partakers of Thy heavenly treasure; through Jesus Christ our Lord. Amen.   (*Gelasian Sacramentary, B.C.P.* 1549.)

For Sufferers in Mind and Body.

O ALMIGHTY and merciful Father, Who art the help of the helpless, and the lifter up of the fallen, look down with Thy mercy on all who are oppressed in mind, body, or estate; comfort and relieve them, according to their several necessities; give them patience under their sufferings, and a happy issue out of all their afflictions; and this we beg for Jesus Christ His sake. Amen.   (*Dean Goulburn*, A.D. 1818, *adapted*.)

For Faith in God's Mercies.

WHAT may happen to us this day, O our God, we know not. We give ourselves up to Thee, to love and obey Thee this day, willing in all things to do Thy holy will. We offer unto Thee our body, soul, and spirit, asking Thee to accept them for the sake of Thy Son, our Lord and Saviour. Amen.
(*The Narrow Way*, A.D. 1869.)

For Zeal and Obedience.

ALMIGHTY God, Holy Spirit, Who proceedeth from the Father and the Son, and by the Eternal Son, our Redeemer, hast promised unto us, to kindle in us the true knowledge and love of God; stir up in our hearts, we beseech Thee, true fear, true faith, and acknowledgment of the mercy which the Father of our Lord Jesus Christ hast promised unto us for His sake. Be Thou our Comforter in all difficulties and dangers, and so kindle the Divine love in our hearts, that by true obedience, we may offer perpetual praise to Thyself, and to the Father of our Lord Jesus Christ, and to His blessed Son, our Saviour and Redeemer. Amen.   *(Philip Melanchthon, A.D. 1497.)*

For Steadfastness of Purpose.

O THOU, Who hast taught us that all things work together for good to them that love Thee, help us to trust in that Eternal will which works within our changeful life, to guide it everlastingly. Help, O Lord, the upward strivings of Thy servants, that we be not henceforward betrayed, to the right hand or to the left by those things which in past times have led us astray, and destroyed our peace. This we ask through Jesus Christ our Lord. Amen.

(Professor Knight, Nineteenth Century.)

A Prayer for the Homeland.

O THOU, upon Whom the isles do wait, and in Whom is their trust, save this island and all the country in which we sojourn, from all affliction, peril, and necessity; for the sake of Jesus Christ. Amen.   *(Bishop Andrewes, A.D. 1555.)*

For All Men.

O THOU Who art the confidence of all the ends of the earth, grant Thy blessing upon all mankind, and visit the whole world with Thy mercy. Let Thy way be known upon earth, and Thy saving health among all nations; through Jesus Christ our Lord, Who, with the Father and the Holy Ghost, liveth and reigneth, world without end. Amen.   *(Adapted.)*

For Comfort for the Suffering and Sorrowful.

O GOD, to Whom alone is known the meaning of the mystery of suffering, we beseech Thee in behalf of the many who are afflicted in mind or body. May they have faith to resist the assaults of the Evil One, and to claim the healing of the Great Physician. May those around them continue instant in prayer, even in the prayer of faith, which shall save the sick, and cause them to be raised by the Lord, in Whose Name alone we ask these blessings: even Jesus Christ our Lord and Saviour. Amen.

(Original source not found.)

For the Love of God's House.

O MOST holy and most merciful Father, Who of Thy goodness
hast provided for us in this place a House set apart for
Thy worship and service; dispose our hearts to reverence Thy
Sanctuary. Vouchsafe, we beseech Thee, to be there in the
midst of us this day. Pardon all our unworthiness, and enable
us to present ourselves, our souls, and bodies, a living sacrifice
holy and acceptable unto Thee. Grant to us the most precious
gift of Thy Holy Spirit, that we may be holy in heart and life,
and may at last be counted worthy to enter Thy Temple above,
to live in Thy Presence, and to praise Thee evermore; through
Jesus Christ our Lord. Amen.

(Rev. H. Stobart, Nineteenth Century.)

A Memorial of the Resurrection.

O LORD Jesus Christ, Who on the first day of the week didst
rise from the dead, that Thou mightest be our Resurrection
and Life; raise us up now from the death of sin, that we may walk
in newness of life, and hereafter rise to a happy eternity with
Thee. Give us grace to spend this day as a day holy unto Thee,
to Thy honour and glory, for the good of others, and our own
salvation; for Thy Name's sake. Amen.

(The Narrow Way, A.D. 1869.)

For Reverence of God's Word.

BLESSED Lord, by Whose Providence all Holy Scriptures
were written and preserved for our instruction, give us
grace to study them this and every day, with patience and love.
Strengthen our souls with the fulness of their Divine teaching.
Keep from us all pride and irreverence. Guide us in the deep
things of Thy heavenly wisdom, and of Thy great mercy lead
us by Thy word unto everlasting life; through Jesus Christ our
Lord and Saviour. Amen. *(Bishop Westcott, A.D. 1825.)*

For a Sense of God's Presence Everywhere.

WE are forced, O Father, to seek Thee daily, and Thou offerest
Thyself daily to be found; wheresoever we seek we find
Thee, in the house, in the fields, in the temple, and in the high-
way. Whatsoever we do, Thou art with us, whether we eat or
drink, whether we write or work, read, meditate or pray, Thou
art ever with us; wheresoever we are or whatsoever we do, we
feel some measure of Thy mercies and love. If we be oppressed,
Thou defendest us; if we hunger, Thou feedest us. Whatsoever
we need, Thou givest us. O continue this Thy loving-kindness
towards us for ever, that all the world may see Thy power, Thy
mercy, and Thy love, wherein Thou hast not failed us, that all
shall see that Thy mercies endure for ever; through Jesus Christ
Thy Son our Lord. Amen. *(J. Norden, A.D. 1548.)*

A Morning Prayer.

O LORD God, our heavenly Father, help us to praise Thee for the new mercies of another day; for Thy kind and loving care over us; for Thy patience with our infirmities; for Thy merciful forgiveness of all our sins, through Jesus Christ our Lord. Be with us in all the changes and chances of this mortal life, so that trouble may never overtake us unprepared, nor temptation assail us undefended by Thy grace. May we so live, rejoicing in Thee, that our several duties may be cheerfully and faithfully done, that we may be a real help and comfort to one another, bearing each other's burdens, and making the path of life less difficult and sad. Heavenly Father, we pray Thee to make our lives happy, notwithstanding all our trials and our little or great difficulties. Grant us Thy peace which passeth all understanding, and which will keep us wise and steadfast in prosperity, and will bear us up in times of adversity. Graciously receive, O Lord, these, our prayers and praises, and let the blessings we have asked for ourselves, fall bountifully over all mankind, to the honour and glory of Thy Name; through Jesus Christ our Lord. Amen. *(Rev. C. J. N. Child, Twentieth Century.)*

For Ministers and Pastors.

BE pleased, O Lord Jesus Christ, to bless the labours of Thy ministers, both at home and abroad. Strengthen them for their work. Grant that they may bring many souls to Thee. Bless them and make them a blessing; for the glory of Thy Name. Amen. *(Rev. H. W. Turner, Nineteenth Century.)*

An Intercession.

GRANT us peace, and establish Thy truth in us, as Thou fillest all things living with plenteousness. Remember every faithful soul in trial, and comfort, if it be possible, everyone in sorrow and distress. O Helper of the helpless, bring the wanderer home, and give health to the sick, and deliverance to the captive. Sustain the aged, comfort the weak-hearted, set free those whose souls are bound in misery and iron; remember all those who are in affliction, necessity, and emergency everywhere. Let us dwell with Thee in peace, as children of light, and in Thy light, Lord, let us see the light.

Direct, O Lord, in peace, the close of our life, trustfully, fearlessly, and, if it be Thy will, painlessly. Gather us when Thou wilt, into the abode of Thy chosen, without shame, or stain, or sin: for the sake of Jesus Christ Thy Son our Lord. Amen.

(Rev. Rowland Williams, A.D. 1818.)

For Trust in God.

IN submission to Thy will may our purposes be formed, our labour carried on and ended, and when we are weary of our work, may we continue to put our trust in Thee; through Jesus Christ our Lord. Amen. *(Original source not found.)*

For Divine Assistance.

ALMIGHTY God, Who alone gavest us the breath of life, and alone canst keep alive in us the breathing of holy desires, we beseech Thee, for Thy compassion's sake, to sanctify all our thoughts and endeavours, that we may neither begin any action without a pure intention, nor continue it without Thy blessing; and grant that, having the eyes of our understanding purged to behold things visible and unseen, we may in heart be inspired by Thy wisdom, and in work be upheld by Thy strength, and in the end be accepted of Thee, as Thy faithful servants, having done all things to Thy glory, and thereby to our endless peace. Grant this prayer, O heavenly Father, for the sake of Jesus Christ our Lord and Saviour. Amen. (*Rev. Rowland Williams*, A.D. 1818.)

For Humility and Unselfishness.

O LORD, give us more charity, more self-denial, more likeness to Thee. Teach us to sacrifice our comforts to others, and our likings for the sake of doing good. Make us kindly in thought, gentle in word, generous in deed. Teach us that it is better to give than to receive, better to forget ourselves than to put ourselves forward; better to minister than to be ministered unto. And unto Thee, the God of Love, be all glory and praise, both now and for evermore. Amen. (*Dean Henry Alford*, A.D. 1810.)

An Intercession.

WE earnestly pray that Thou wilt let Thy blessing rest upon us, and upon this household. May it be meet for Thy Sacred Presence. Bless, we beseech Thee, every member of it; let not one heart be estranged from Thee by doubt or fear, by pride or selfishness. Thou art our Father; teach us to be trustful as children. We would also remember before Thee those who are bound to us by ties of kinship and friendship, those who have become dear to us in our religious life, those who serve us in any way, great or small, our benefactors; knowing, too, Thy tender compassion, we ask that Thy blessed comfort and hope may be bestowed upon the suffering in mind and body, especially the mourners, the troubled, the sick, the weary, the poor, the lonely. And may those who are sorely tempted to sin, or who have fallen into sin which separates their hearts from Thee, be often reminded of Thy merciful kindness towards them, and so be strengthened to resist the evil, and turn from it to Thee, their Father and Friend; through Jesus Christ our Lord. Amen.
(*Rev. L. Tuttiett*, A.D. 1825.)

Preparation for Christ's Appearing.

HELP us, O Lord, always to wait for Thee, to wish for Thee, and to watch for Thee, that at Thy coming again Thou mayest find us ready; for Thy sake we ask it. Amen.
(*An Ancient Collect.*)

For the Holy Spirit.

O HOLY spirit, the Comforter, Who with the Father and the Son abidest one God, descend this day into our hearts, that while Thou makest intercession for us, we may with full confidence call upon our Father; through Jesus Christ our Lord. Amen.   (*Mozarabic Liturgy.*)

For the Children.

O GOD, since Thou hast laid the little children into our arms in utter helplessness, with no protection save our love, we pray that the sweet appeal of their baby hands may not be in vain. Let no innocent life in our cities be quenched again in useless pain through our ignorance and sin. May we who are mothers and fathers seek eagerly to join wisdom to our love, lest love itself be deadly when unguided by knowledge. Bless the doctors and nurses, and all the friends of men who are giving of their skill and devotion to the care of our children. If there are any who were kissed by love in their own infancy, but who have no child to whom they may give as they have received, grant them such largeness of sympathy that they may rejoice to pay their debt in full to all children who have need of them. Forgive us, our Father, for the heartlessness of the past. Grant us great tenderness for all babes who suffer, and a growing sense of the Divine mystery that is brooding in the soul of every child; for the sake of Jesus Christ our Saviour. Amen.

(*W. Rauschenbusch, Twentieth Century.*)

For our Countrymen Abroad.

K EEP, we beseech Thee, O Lord, our brethren who are dwelling in foreign lands; protect them from the dangers which surround them, and supply them with the means of grace. Make them steadfast in Thy ways, pure and holy in their lives. Preserve them from the sin of offending Thy little ones which believe in Thee, and from causing Thy word to be dishonoured among the heathen. Grant that they may shine as lights in the world, and adorn the doctrine of God our Saviour in all things; through Jesus Christ our Lord. Amen.

(*Mission Manual, Nineteenth Century.*)

For the King.

O GOD of all Kingdoms, Who art Guardian especially of every Christian realm, grant to Thy servant George our King to triumph over every foe, that as he has been consecrated to rule by Thy Divine Providence, so by Thy Protection he may long reign in supremacy and peace; through Jesus Christ our Lord. Amen.   (*Gelasian Sacramentary.*)

For Trust in God.

O LORD, Whose way is perfect, help us, we pray Thee, always to trust in Thy goodness; that, walking with Thee and following Thee in all simplicity, we may possess quiet and contented minds, and may cast all our care on Thee, for Thou carest for us; for the sake of Jesus Christ our Lord. Amen.

(Christina G. Rossetti, A.D. 1830.)

For Spiritual Desires.

O HEAVENLY Father, we humbly beseech Thee to give unto this household, and unto each member of it in particular, a desire and taste for the things that are high and spiritual, the love of holiness, and the longing for the life of heaven. Grant that whatsoever things are true, whatsoever things are honourable, whatsoever things are just, whatsoever things are pure, whatsoever things are lovely and of good report, if there be anything which is unselfish and generous, if there be anything which Thou wilt accept and reward, we may think on these things, and by the help of Thy Holy Spirit may order our lives and form our characters according to them; through Jesus Christ our Lord. Amen.

(St. Paul, First Century ; adapted from Phil. iv. 8.)

For Consistency of Life.

A LMIGHTY God, Who showest to them that be in error the light of Thy truth, to the intent that they may return into the way of righteousness; grant unto all them that are admitted into the fellowship of Christ's religion, that they may eschew those things that are contrary to their profession, and follow all such things as are agreeable to the same; through our Lord Jesus Christ. Amen. *(Leonine Sacramentary, B.C.P., 1549.)*

For Worthy Citizenship.

O GOD, Who hast given unto us an Empire upon which the sun never sets, may we as a nation have grace so to live, both at home and abroad, that we may glorify Thy holy Name, and may be worthy members of this great earthly kingdom, for Thine honour and glory; through Jesus Christ our Lord. Amen.

(Source not found.)

For Christ's Servants Everywhere.

O GOD of infinite mercy and boundless majesty, Whom no distance can part from those for whom Thou carest, be present to Thy servants who everywhere confide in Thee, and through all the way in which they are to go be pleased to be their Guide and Companion. May no adversity harm them, no difficulty oppose them; may all things turn out happily and prosperously for them; that by the aid of Thy right hand, whatsoever they have asked for with reasonable desire they may speedily find brought to good effect; through Jesus Christ our Lord. Amen.   *(Gelasian Sacramentary.)*

A Morning Prayer.

VOUCHSAFE to bestow upon us some portion of Thy heavenly Bread, day by day, that the hunger and thirst for earthly things may diminish in us continually. And although, as long as we dwell in the flesh, we sin daily through our natural infirmity, still, let us not fall from Thy grace and favour, but strengthen us, that we may continue in that peace, which Thy Son Jesus Christ has made for us by the Blood of His Cross. Grant also, that we, remembering how Thou hast mercifully pardoned our misdeeds, may frankly forgive all those who trespass against us, and may maintain constant peace and charity among ourselves. Finally, knowing how our adversary, the devil, ceaseth not in his efforts to draw us back again into his bondage, we cry unto Thee to keep us from his assaults, and so to preserve us in the fellowship of Thy dear Son, that we may come at last to that blessed life, where neither sin nor temptation shall any longer trouble us. Grant this, heavenly Father, for Thy dear Son's sake, Jesus Christ our Lord. Amen.

(Desiderius Erasmus, A.D. 1467)

Grace to serve God Faithfully.

ALMIGHTY and everlasting God, Thou lover of peace and concord, Who hast called us in Christ to love and unity, we pray Thee so rule our hearts by Thy Holy Spirit, that we, being delivered by the true fear of God from all fear of man, may evermore serve Thee in righteousness, mercy, humility, and gentleness towards each other; through Thy dear Son Jesus Christ our Lord. Amen. *(Baron Christian C. J. Bunsen, A.D. 1791.)*

For Missionaries and their Work.

O GOD of all the ends of the earth, and of all its families, we ask Thee for the missionary work of Thy Church in foreign and distant lands. We commit to Thee Thy missionary servants in every land. Strengthen them continually with the Holy Ghost the Comforter, and if it please Thee, keep them in outward health and safety. Prosper the work of their hands, to Thy glory, and the salvation of all men, and the hastening of the coming of our Lord Jesus Christ; for His Name's sake we ask it. Amen. *(Bishop H. C. G. Moule, A.D. 1841.)*

For Grace and Love for Daily Life.

LORD Jesus, grant us daily grace for daily need; daily patience for a daily cross; daily, hourly, incessant love of Thee to take up our cross daily and bear it after Thee. We ask this for Thine own Name's sake. Amen.

(Christina G. Rossetti, A.D. 1830.)

For a Sense of God's Presence.

ALMIGHTY God, Who fillest all things with Thy presence, we meekly beseech Thee, of Thy great love, to keep us near unto Thee this day; grant that in all our ways and doings we may remember that Thou seest us, and may always have grace to know and perceive what things Thou wouldst have us to do, and strength to fulfil the same; through Jesus Christ our Lord. Amen.   (*Ancient Collect, adapted.*)

For Divine Control.

O LORD, we acknowledge Thy dominion over us; our life, our death, our soul and body, all belong to Thee. Oh, grant that we may willingly consecrate them all to Thee, and use them in Thy service. Let us walk before Thee in childlike simplicity, steadfast in prayer; looking ever unto Thee, that whatsoever we do or abstain from, we may in all things follow the least indications of Thy will. Become Lord of our hearts and spirits; that the whole inner man may be brought under Thy rule, and that Thy life of love and righteousness may pervade all our thoughts and energies, and the very ground of our souls; that we may be wholly filled with it. Come, O Lord and King, enter into our hearts, and live and reign there for ever and ever. O faithful Lord, teach us to trust Thee for life and death, and to take Thee for our All in All, Thou Who art the Son of God, our Lord and Saviour. Amen.

(*Gerhard Tersteegen*, A.D. 1697.)

For Class Unity.

O LORD God, Who by Thy Providence hast ordered various ranks among men, draw them ever closer together by Thy Holy Spirit. Teach us to know that all differences of class are done away in Christ. Take from us and from our countrymen all jealousy and discontent. Unite us one to another by a common zeal for Thy cause, and enable us by Thy grace to offer unto Thee the manifold fruits of our service; through Jesus Christ our Lord. Amen.   (*Bishop Westcott*, A.D. 1825.)

For Missionary Workers.

O GOD, our Heavenly Father, Who didst manifest Thy love by sending Thine only begotten Son into the world that all might live through Him, pour Thy Spirit upon Thy Church that it may fulfil His commands to preach the Gospel to every creature; send forth, we beseech Thee, labourers into Thy harvest. Defend them in all dangers and temptations, and hasten the time when the fulness of the Gentiles shall be gathered in, and all Israel shall be saved; through Jesus Christ our Lord. Amen.   (*Source not found.*)

For a Sunday Blessing.

O GOD, our heavenly Father, let this holy day be indeed holy. Make it a time of unbroken peace, unwavering desire to walk and please Thee. To-day let no iniquity have dominion over us, to-day let us not give way to any kind of sin; so, Lord, we humbly set out on the path of this new week, walking in Thy name with the watchful and even steps of faith and surrender. We thank Thee that we belong to Thee, and that we believe in Thee; through Him Who died for us and rose again, and by Whom and in Whom we live, Jesus Christ our Lord. Amen.

(Bishop H. C. G. Moule, A.D. 1841.)

For the Ministry.

O ALMIGHTY God, be pleased to remember with Thy mercy and love all those who minister before Thee in holy things. Prosper the great work in which they are engaged, enable them faithfully to preach Thy Word, and rightly and duly administer Thy Holy Sacraments. May they uphold Christ, both by their words and in their lives. Raise up, we pray Thee, faithful and true men for the work of Thy Church. O Thou Lord of the harvest, prepare Thy own labourers and send them forth into Thy harvest. Grant this, O heavenly Father, for Jesus Christ's sake. Amen. *(Bishop Ashton Oxenden, A.D. 1808.)*

For those who forget thy Holy Day.

O GOD, grant that they who, neglecting Thy worship on Thy holy day, give themselves rather to the business or pleasures of the world, may turn to Thee while it is yet time, so that they perish not when the world and its lust shall have passed away, but being found in Him Who died for us and rose again, may be saved by grace; through the same Jesus Christ our Lord. Amen. *(Adapted, Rev. R. M. Benson, A.D. 1824.)*

For Quietness of Soul.

G RANT us grace to rest from all sinful deeds and thoughts, to surrender ourselves wholly unto Thee, and to keep our souls still before Thee like a still lake; that so the beams of Thy grace may be mirrored therein, and may kindle in our hearts the glow of faith, and love, and prayer. May we, through such stillness and hope, find strength and gladness in Thee, O God, now and for evermore. Amen.

(Rev. Joachim Embden, A.D. 1595.)

For the Holy Spirit.

G IVE us Thy Holy Spirit, O God, that, forsaking our sins, we may love Thee more, and serve Thee better every hour; through Jesus Christ our Lord. Amen.

(The Narrow Way, A.D. 1869.)

FOR CONFORMITY TO GOD'S WILL.

O GOD, our Everliving Refuge, with grateful hearts we lay at Thy feet the folded hours when Thou knowest us, but we know not Thee; and with joy receive from Thy hand once more our open task and conscious communion with Thy life and thought. Day by day liken us more to the spirits of the wise and good who have entered into Thy Presence, and fit us in our generation to carry on their work below, till we are ready for more perfect union with them above. And if ever we faint under any appointed cross and say, "It is too hard to bear," may we look to the steps of the Man of Sorrows toiling on to Calvary, and pass freely into Thy hand and become one with Him and Thee. Dedicate us to the joyful service of Thy will, and own us as Thy children in time and in eternity; for the sake of Jesus Christ. Amen. (*James Martineau, Published* A.D. 1891.)

FOR THE HOME.

O BLESSED Jesus, Who for thirty years didst dwell in Thy humble home at Nazareth, be with Thy servants in this our home, keep from it all pride and selfishness and impurity, that it may be a dwelling-place meet for Thy sacred Presence. Grant us to grow in grace and in the knowledge and love of Thee; guide us throughout our life on earth, comfort us in all troubles, strengthen us in all weakness, and bring us at last to Thy Home in heaven, where, with the Father and the Holy Spirit, Thou livest and reignest, one God, world without end. Amen.

(*Rev. Fielding Ould*, A.D. 1864.)

FOR THE POOR AND NEEDY.

O GOD, our heavenly Father, in Whom we live and move and have our being, have mercy upon all who are in poverty and distress. Be Thou their succour and defence, provide them with food and clothing sufficient for their bodily needs, and grant them day by day to cast all their care upon Thee. Help us in some way to help them; through Jesus Christ our Lord. Amen.

(*Rev. Dr. John Hunter*, A.D. 1849.)

FOR GOD'S SAFE KEEPING.

M AY the strength of God pilot us. May the power of God preserve us. May the wisdom of God instruct us. May the hand of God protect us. May the way of God direct us. May the shield of God defend us.

May the host of God guard us against the snares of the Evil One and the temptations of the world.

May Christ be with us. Christ before us. Christ in us. Christ over us. May Thy salvation, O Lord, be always ours this day and for evermore. Amen.

(*Prayer of St. Patrick*, A.D. 373.)

For Charity and Divine Guidance.

GRANT unto us, O Lord, the spirit of mutual love and duty, and, above all, of grateful obedience to Thee; give us comfort and support under all circumstances of our life, and Thy merciful guidance unto the end, that living in all holy and godly conversation, we may be afflicted by no adversity, and may finally attain to the perpetual enjoyment of Thy loving mercy; through Jesus Christ our Lord. Amen. (*Rev. James Skinner*, A.D. 1818.)

The King, Country, and Nation.

O THOU Who art the Prince of the Kings and peoples of the earth, receive our prayer, we beseech Thee, for our own Country. We pray Thee for our King, for the Royal Family; for all the Ministers of State, and all Members of Parliament; that Thy power and mercy may rule those who guide, and order those who legislate. If it please Thee, bring all their wills into true accord with Thy will. Let all seek the good not of parties, but of the whole people. Let them govern in the fear of God, and not in too much fear of man, or for any private advantage of their own. O Lord, we deserve chastisement at Thy hands and not prosperity. To us belongeth confusion of face, because we have sinned against Thee; yet for Thy Name's sake bless us, cleanse us, and defend us, and make use of us in the world for Thee; to the praise and honour of Jesus Christ our Lord. Amen.   (*Bishop H. C. G. Moule*, A.D. 1841.)

For our Sailors and Soldiers.

O LORD of Hosts, bless our sailors and soldiers, keep them pure and loyal amid all their temptations, and grant that all their operations may tend to peace on earth; that war being done away, they may fight only in their Christian conflict against sin, the world, and the devil, and triumph therein by Thy victorious might, O Lord, Thou God of Hosts; through Jesus Christ our Lord. Amen.   (*Sursum Corda*, A.D. 1898.)

For the Indwelling of the Holy Spirit.

O THOU Who didst say to Thy disciples regarding the Holy Spirit, "He dwelleth with you, and shall be in you," grant that we may claim the Divine Comforter as our constant Indweller, and may be filled with the Holy Ghost; for Thy mercy's sake. Amen.   (*Source not found.*)

Commendation.

INTO Thy hands, O Lord, we commit ourselves this day. Give to each one of us a watchful, a humble, and a diligent spirit that we may seek in all things to know Thy will, and when we know it may perform it perfectly and gladly, to the honour and glory of Thy Name; through Jesus Christ our Lord. Amen.
(*Gelasian Sacramentary*.)

For Consistency and Perseverance.

O GOD, Who hast commanded that no man should be idle, look graciously upon us, Thy servants, now going forth to do our duty in that state of life unto which Thou hast been pleased to call us. May Thy blessing be upon our persons, upon our labours, upon our substance, and upon all that belongs to us. Enable us to resist the temptations of the world, the flesh, and the devil; to follow the motions of Thy good Spirit; to be serious and holy in our lives, true and just in our dealings, watchful over our thoughts, words, and actions, diligent in our business, and temperate in all things. Give us grace that we may honestly improve all the talents Thou hast committed to our trust, and that no worldly business, no worldly pleasures, may ever divert us from our preparation for the life to come; through Jesus Christ our Lord. Amen.

(Rev. Thomas Dee, Nineteenth Century.)

Acknowledgment of God's Sovereignty.

WE worship Thee, O Lord God, and give thanks to Thee for Thy great glory and power, which Thou showest to Thy servants in Thy wonderful works. All the things which we enjoy are from Thy mighty hand, and Thou alone art to be praised for all the blessings of the life that now is. Make us thankful to Thee for all Thy mercies, and more ready to serve Thee with all our heart; for the sake of Jesus Christ. Amen.

(The Narrow Way, A.D. 1869.)

For a Daily Blessing.

AS Thou makest the outgoings of the morning and evening to rejoice, so lift up the light of Thy countenance upon us, and make us glad with the tokens of Thy love. Be Thou with us, O Lord, and let Thy grace follow us this day, and all the days of our life. Be Thou our Guide unto death, in death our Comfort, and after death our Portion and Happiness everlasting; for the sake of Jesus Christ Thy Son, our Lord and Saviour. Amen.

(Rev. Benjamin Jenks, A.D. 1646.)

For the King and those in Authority.

O ALMIGHTY and Everlasting God, we pray Thee to bless and preserve Thy Servant, King George who in Thy good Providence rules these realms. Grant to him and all his councillors, that out of godly hearts they may devise godly measures. May they seek first Thy kingdom and righteousness. May we yield obedience to our King and rulers as Thy appointed ministers. Thus may our lives be quiet and peaceable in all godliness and honesty. Thou Who hearest prayer, hear us, for the sake of Him Thou hearest always, Jesus Christ our Lord. Amen.

(Rev. Robert Collyer, A.D. 1823.)

A Morning Prayer.

FROM the night our spirit awaketh unto Thee, O God, for Thy precepts are light unto us. Teach us, O God, Thy righteousness, Thy commandments, and Thy judgments. Enlighten the eyes of our mind, that we sleep not in sins unto death. Drive away all darkness from our hearts. Vouchsafe us the Sun of righteousness. Guard our life from all reproach by the seal of Thy Holy Spirit. Guide our steps into the way of peace. Grant us to behold the dawn and the day with joyfulness, that we may send up to Thee our prayers at eventide; through Jesus Christ our Lord. Amen.   *(Eastern Church, Daybreak Office.)*

For a Realization of the Presence of God.

O ALMIGHTY God, Who hast made us in Thine image, and given unto us the enjoyment of many excellent gifts, enable us by Thy Holy Spirit to use these blessings to Thy glory. Grant unto us a devout reverence of all Thy works. Pour into our hearts a true love for all who are called by Thy Name. Quicken our souls that we may at all times be sensible of Thy Presence, and make us day by day more fit to see Thee hereafter as Thou art in heaven; through Jesus Christ our Lord. Amen.

(Bishop Westcott, A.D. 1825.)

For Assurance of God's Compassion.

LET Thy tender mercy, O Lord, enfold the sick, the suffering and the mourning. O God, Who seest that our cheerfulness is the companion of our strength, but in time of weakness, quick to take wings and fly away, lay no more upon Thy suffering children than they are able to bear, but temper every trial to the measure of their endurance. And since the fretfulness of our spirits is more hurtful than the heaviness of our burden, let those who are afflicted know that in quietness and confidence lieth their strength. Give them a calm trust that Thou doest all things well. In Thy good time and way grant them to regain health and gladness, through the love and power of our Saviour, Jesus Christ. Amen.   *(Rev. Rowland Williams, A.D. 1818.)*

For God's Guidance in Thought and Act.

O LORD, from Whom all good things do come; grant to us, Thy humble servants, that by Thy holy inspiration we may think those things that be good, and by Thy merciful guiding may perform the same, through Jesus Christ our Lord. Amen.

(Gelasian Sacramentary.)

Commendation.

INTO Thy hands, O Lord, we commit ourselves this day. Grant to each one of us so to pass the waves of this troublous world, that finally we lose not the world eternal; through Jesus Christ our Lord Amen.   *(From an Ancient Collect.)*

Praise and Adoration.

O GOD, the Father of our Lord God and Saviour Jesus Christ,
Lord, Whose Name is great, Whose goodness is inexhaustible,
Thou God and Master of all things, Who art blessed for ever,
Who sittest on the Cherubim and art glorified by the Seraphim,
before Whom stand thousands of thousands, and ten thousand
times ten thousand, the hosts of holy angels and archangels.
Sanctify, O Lord, our souls, bodies and spirits, and touch our
apprehensions and search out our consciences, and cast out of
us every evil thought, every base desire, all envy and pride and
hypocrisy, all falsehood, all deceit, all worldly anxiety, all
covetousness, vainglory and sloth, all malice, all wroth, all
anger, all remembrance of injuries, every motion of the flesh and
spirit that is contrary to Thy holy will; and grant us, O Lord,
the Lover of men, with freedom, with a pure heart and a contrite
soul, without confusion of face, and with sanctified lips, boldly
to call upon Thee, our holy God and Father, Who art in heaven.
Amen.   (*Liturgy of St. James.*)

For Missionary Societies.

O GOD, we pray Thee at this time to bless all Missionary
Societies. Prosper the work of their committees. Give
to the members the spirit of faith, patience, and perseverance.
May offerings of money and of service abound as an encourage-
ment to unceasing prayer, and hasten the time when the knowledge of the Lord shall cover the earth, as the waters cover the
sea; for the sake of Jesus Christ. Amen. (*Source not found.*)

For our Country and Nation.

WE humbly thank Thee, Almighty God, for the many blessings
which Thou hast given to our Country, and add this, O
Lord, to Thy other mercies, that we may be enabled to use them
better to Thy service. O take from among us all contempt of
Thy Word and Commandments. Break down all the barriers
of selfishness and ignorance which keep men from Thee. Convince the impenitent of the misery of sin, and comfort the broken-
hearted with the assurance of Thy love. Teach us all to be
evangelists, not in word only, but in everything which we do.
This we ask in the Name and for the sake of Jesus Christ our
Lord.   Amen.   (*Bishop Westcott*, A.D. 1825.)

Intercession.

MAY God the Father, and the Eternal High Priest Jesus
Christ, build us up in faith and truth and love, and grant
to us our portion among the saints with all those who believe on
our Lord Jesus Christ. We pray for all saints, for kings and
rulers, for the enemies of the Cross of Christ, and for ourselves
we pray that our fruit may abound and we may be made perfect
in Christ Jesus our Lord. Amen. (*Bishop Polycarp*, A.D. 69.)

"For a Knowledge of His Will."

O LORD, keep Thyself present to us always, and teach us to come to Thee by the One and Living Way, Thy Son Jesus Christ. Keep us humble and gentle, self-denying, firm and patient, active, wise to know Thy will and to discern the truth; loving, that we may learn to resemble Thee and our Saviour. O Lord, forgive us all our sins and save us, and guide us, and strengthen us; through Jesus Christ our Lord. Amen.

(Dr. Arnold, A.D. 1795.)

For the King's Protection.

O LORD, Who of Thy favour towards us hast set George our King, to reign over us, keep him, we beseech Thee, under Thy almighty protection, save and defend him from all his enemies, both ghostly and bodily; give him grace to rule Thy people according to Thy will, that he may here govern to Thy honour and glory, and after this life receive and enjoy the inheritance of Thy heavenly kingdom, in the life and bliss that never shall have an end; through Jesus Christ our Lord. Amen.

(Treasury of Devotion, A.D. 1869.)

For those in Doubt.

A LMIGHTY and everliving God, Who hast given us the Faith of Christ for a light to our feet amid the darkness of this world, have pity upon all who, by doubting or denying it, are gone astray from the path of safety, bring home the truth to their hearts, and grant them to receive it as little children; through the same Jesus Christ, our Lord and Saviour. Amen.

(William Bright, A.D. 1824.)

For Trust and Fuller Knowledge.

M ERCIFUL Lord, the Comforter and Teacher of Thy faithful people, increase in Thy Church the desires which Thou hast given, and confirm the hearts of those who hope in Thee by enabling them to understand the depth of Thy promises, that all Thine adopted sons may even now behold, with the eyes of faith, and patiently wait for, the light which as yet Thou dost not openly manifest; through Jesus Christ our Lord. Amen.

(St. Ambrose, A.D. 340.)

Commendation.

I NTO Thy hands, O God, we commend ourselves and all who are dear to us this day. Let the gift of Thy special Presence be with us even to its close. Grant us never to lose sight of Thee all the day long, but to worship and pray to Thee, that at eventide we may again give thanks unto Thee; through Jesus Christ our Lord. Amen.   *(Gelasian Sacramentary.)*

For a Knowledge of God's Will.

MOST gracious God, to know and love Whose will is righteousness, enlighten our souls with the brightness of Thy presence, that we may both know Thy will and be enabled to perform it; through Jesus Christ our Lord. Amen.

(Roman Breviary.)

For Communicants.

HEAR us, O merciful Father, we most humbly beseech Thee, and grant to all communicants of Thy Church this day, true repentance and living faith. And we pray that all those who shall from time to time receive Thy creatures of bread and wine, according to Thy Son our Saviour Jesus Christ's Holy Institution, in remembrance of His Death and Passion, may be partakers of His most blessed Body and Blood; to Whom with Thee and the Holy Ghost, be all honour and glory, world without end. Amen. *(Ancient Liturgy.)*

For the Peace of Christ's Flock.

O SOVEREIGN and Almighty Lord, bless all Thy people and all Thy flock. Give peace, Thy help, Thy love unto us, Thy servants the sheep of Thy fold, that we may be united in the bond of peace and love, one body and one spirit, in one hope of our calling, in Thy Divine and boundless love; for the sake of Jesus Christ, the great Shepherd of the sheep. Amen.

(Liturgy of St. Mark.)

An Intercession.

WE beseech Thee, O Lord, remember all for good; have mercy upon all, O God. Remember every soul who, being in any affliction, trouble, or agony, stands in need of Thy mercy and help, all who are in necessity or distress, all who love or hate us.

Thou, O Lord, art the Helper of the helpless, the Hope of the hopeless, the Saviour of them who are tossed with tempests, the Haven of them who sail; be Thou All to all. The glorious majesty of the Lord our God be upon us; prosper Thou the work of our hands upon us, oh! prosper Thou our handiwork. Lord, be Thou within us, to strengthen us; without us, to keep us; above us, to protect us; beneath us, to uphold us; before us, to direct us; behind us, to keep us from straying; round about us, to defend us. Blessed be Thou, O Lord our Father, for ever and ever. Amen. *(Bishop Lancelot Andrewes, A.D. 1555.)*

For Peace.

WE beseech Thee, O Lord, to keep us in perpetual peace, as Thou hast vouchsafed us confidence in Thee; through Jesus Christ our Lord. Amen. *(Gelasian Sacramentary.)*

For Light and Love.

LOOK upon us, O Lord, and let all the darkness of our souls vanish before the beams of Thy brightness. Fill us with holy love, and open to us the treasures of Thy wisdom. All our desire is known unto Thee, therefore perfect what Thou hast begun, and what Thy Spirit has awakened us to ask in prayer. We seek Thy face; turn Thy face unto us and show us Thy glory, then shall our longing be satisfied, and our peace shall be perfect; through Jesus Christ our Lord. Amen.

(St. Augustine, A.D. 354.)

Confession and Prayer for Pardon.

O LORD, we draw near unto Thee, acknowledging our unworthiness, and we beseech Thee that all the sins and defects of our past services may be freely pardoned and entirely done away, through the precious Blood of Thy dear Son Jesus Christ our Lord. Amen.   *(From an Ancient Collect.)*

For Daily Trust in God.

O FATHER, this day may bring some hard task to our life, or some hard trial to our love. We may grow weary, or sad, or hopeless in our lot. But, Father, our whole life until now has been one great proof of Thy care. Bread has come for our bodies, thoughts to our mind, love to our heart, and all from Thee. So help us, we implore Thee, while we stand still on this side of all that the day may bring, to resolve that we will trust Thee this day to shine into any gloom of the mind, to stand by us in any trial of our love, and to give us rest in Thy good time as we need. May this day be full of a power that shall bring us near to Thee, and make us more like Thee; and, O God, may we so trust Thee this day, that when the day is done our trust shall be firmer than ever. Then, when our last day comes and our work is done, may we trust Thee in death and for ever, in the spirit of Jesus Christ our Lord. Amen.

(Rev. Robert Collyer, A.D. 1823.)

For Missionaries.

ALMIGHTY and eternal God, from Whose Presence the angels go forth to do Thy will; grant to all Thy missionary servants that in obedience to Thy commands they may serve to the glory of Thy Name and, overshadowed by Thy protection, receive at last the crown of life; through Jesus Christ our Lord. Amen.   *(Sursum Corda, A.D. 1898.)*

For Christian Graces.

O LORD, fill us, we beseech Thee, with adoring gratitude to Thee, for all Thou art for us, to us, and in us; fill us with love, joy, peace, and all the fruits of the Spirit; through Jesus Christ our Lord. Amen.   *(Christina G. Rossetti, A.D. 1830.)*

A Morning Prayer.

O MOST merciful Saviour, we come to offer Thee the incense of worshipping hearts. We come as those who by faith behold Him that is invisible, we speak to Thee as simply as if our bodily eyes saw Thee, as if Thou wert openly seated in the midst of us, and Thy hand were visibly outstretched to give the gift we ask. We thank Thee for Thy mercies, for the safety and rest of the night, for the hopes and the duties of the day. We cannot know what the day will bring, but we know that it will bring most surely Thy love and grace for Thy people, and continual opportunities of doing Thy will and giving ourselves up to Thy use. Knowing Thee, we know all we need to know of the unknown future, near or far away. May this day, then, be a day of holy peace and happiness in our home and in each heart. If it pleases Thee, keep us from all accident and illness and evil tidings. But, above all, fill us from within with that holy calm which circumstances can neither give nor take away, for it is Thyself dwelling and ruling in us. May we recollect and realize Thy presence, not at another time only, but to-day, and in the secret power of it may we meet in peace the common things of life as they come, all calls to act and think for others, all crossings of our wills, all pains and joys. Let nothing take us unawares, inasmuch as we are found in Thee; for Thine own Name's sake. Amen. (*Bishop H. C. G. Moule*, A.D. 1841.)

For those in Sorrow.

HAVE compassion, we pray Thee, upon all those whose hearts are touched with sorrow, whose spirits are troubled or cast down within them. O Lord, remember those to whom the burdens of this life bring dimness and darkness of soul, and have mercy upon all who suffer in body or mind from whatever cause. Let Thy mercy rest upon them according as they hope in Thee; for the sake of Jesus Christ, Who is the Burden-Bearer and the Redeemer. Amen. (*Source not found.*)

For Sympathy for Others' Burdens.

O GOD Who art Love, grant to Thy children to bear one another's burdens in perfect goodwill, that Thy peace which passeth understanding may keep our hearts and minds in Christ Jesus our Lord. Amen. (*Book of Hours*, A.D. 1865.)

For Protection.

BE gracious to our prayers, O merciful God, and guard Thy people with loving protection; that they who confess Thine only begotten Son as God, born in our bodily flesh, may never be corrupted by the deceits of the devil; through the same Jesus Christ our Lord. Amen. (*St. Ambrose*, A.D. 340.)

Praise and Thanksgiving.

O LORD our God, Who hast bidden the light to shine out of darkness, Who hast again wakened us to praise Thy goodness and ask for Thy grace; accept now, in Thy endless mercy, the sacrifice of our worship and thanksgiving, and grant unto us all such requests as may be wholesome for us. Make us to be children of the light and of the day, and heirs of Thy everlasting inheritance. Remember, O Lord, according to the multitude of Thy mercies, Thy whole Church; all who join with us in prayer, all our brethren by land or sea, or wherever they may be in Thy vast kingdom who stand in need of Thy grace and succour. Pour out upon them the riches of Thy mercy, so that we, redeemed in soul and body, and steadfast in faith, may ever praise Thy wonderful and Holy Name; through Jesus Christ our Lord. Amen.   (*Greek Church Liturgy.*)

For Heavenly-Mindedness.

O THOU Spirit of Life, breathe upon Thy graces in us, take us by the hand and lift us from earth, that we may see what glory Thou hast prepared for them that love Thee; through Jesus Christ our Lord. Amen. (*Rev. Richard Baxter*, A.D. 1615.)

For Labourers in Christ's Vineyard.

A LMIGHTY God, Who by Thy Son Jesus Christ didst give commandment to the holy Apostles that they should go into all the world and preach the Gospel to every creature, grant to us, whom Thou hast called to follow Thee, a ready will to obey Thy Word, and fill us with a hearty desire to make Thy way known upon earth, Thy saving health among all nations. Look with compassion upon all who are living without Thee, and on the multitudes who even in this land are scattered abroad as sheep having no shepherd, or who in strange lands are far from the Church of their fathers. Visit them with Thy salvation. O heavenly Father, Lord of the harvest, have respect, we beseech Thee, to these our prayers, and send forth labourers into Thy harvest. Fit and prepare them by Thy grace for the work of their ministry. Give them the spirit of power, and of love, and of a sound mind. Strengthen them to endure hardness, and grant that both by their life and doctrine they may set forth Thy glory and set forward the salvation of all men; through Jesus Christ our Lord. Amen.

(*Prayer-Book of the Church of Ireland*, A.D. 1877.)

For the Power of the Holy Spirit.

W E beseech Thee, O Lord, let the power of the Holy Spirit be present with us, that He may both mercifully cleanse our hearts, and protect us from all adversities; through Jesus Christ our Lord. Amen.   (*Leonine Sacramentary.*)

Morning Worship and Thanksgiving.

MAY we lift our hearts to Thee this day in great thankfulness, humbly acknowledging Thy mercy and Thy truth,
Thy large and tender providence, Thy nearness to us at all times,
Thy Spirit of Wisdom and Might and Peace, the works and the
joys and the discipline of earth, which Thou dost appoint, the
promises that lay hold of the things to come. O Spirit of all
grace and benediction, Father of our dear Lord and Saviour,
coming to us in Him and in His, Creator of these dying bodies,
Life and Light of these undying souls, Thy gifts are new upon
us every morning. May Thy great love redeem us, and from
the light of a true life below, may we pass at length into that
Presence where there is fulness of joy and abundance of peace
for ever; through the merits of Jesus Christ our Lord. Amen.

(Rev. Rufus Ellis, A.D. 1819.)

For Love of God.

GRANT, most gracious God, that we may love and seek Thee
always and everywhere, above all things and for Thy sake,
in the life present, and may at length find Thee and for ever
hold Thee fast in the life to come. Grant this for the sake of
Jesus Christ our Lord. Amen.

(Archbishop Thomas Bradwardine, A.D. 1290.)

For All Nations.

O LORD, be merciful to us and bless us. As Thou hast made
our Nation mighty in this world, and a ruler over other
Nations, so make it a source of wisdom and truth, of order and
sanctity, to all who come under its influence. Let Thy Light
pass from clime to clime and enlighten us all. Let Thy Truth
be our truth. Let Thy Truth be known widely upon earth, and
distant Nations glorify Thy Name. Unite us all, as Thy children,
in Thy common blessing, while we celebrate Thee, the Divine
Creator and sole Governor, revering Thy Name and obeying Thy
laws. Let the knowledge of Thy Righteousness redound to
general goodwill, and charity unfeigned reign in all our hearts.
The Lord bless us and keep us, the Lord cause His face to shine
upon us and give us His peace; through Jesus Christ our Lord
Amen.   *(Prof. Francis W. Newman, A.D. 1805.)*

For Dependence upon God.

GRANT, O Lord, that when we are tempted, we may resist
the devil; that when we are worried, we may cast all our
care upon Thee; that when we are weary, we may seek Thy rest;
and that in all things we may live this day to Thy glory; through
Jesus Christ our Lord. Amen.   *(Source not found.)*

For Heavenly-Mindedness.

O MERCIFUL God, grant that all worldly affections may die in us, and that all things belonging to the Spirit may live and grow in us. Grant that we may have power and strength to have victory, and to triumph against the devil, the world, and the flesh. Grant that we who are dedicated to Thee, may also be endued with heavenly virtues, and everlastingly rewarded through Thy mercy. O Saviour of the world, Who by Thy Cross and precious Blood hast redeemed us, save us and help us, we humbly beseech Thee, O Lord. Amen.

(From "The Vision of Righteousness.")

For Faithful Stewardship.

O ALMIGHTY and most gracious God, we heartily thank Thee for the sleep and rest which Thou hast given us this night past, and forasmuch as Thou hast commanded by Thy Holy Word that no man should be idle, but all given continually to every good work, every man according to his calling, we most humbly beseech Thee that Thine eyes may attend upon us, daily defend us, nourish, comfort, and govern us and all our counsels, studies, and labours, in such wise that we may spend and bestow this day according to Thy most holy will, setting Thee always before our eyes, living in Thy fear, working that which may be found acceptable before Thy Divine Majesty; through Jesus Christ our Lord. Amen.

(Christian Prayers, A.D. 1566.)

For the Heathen World.

O GOD of all the nations of the earth, remember the multitudes of the heathen, who, though created in Thine Image, are perishing in their ignorance; and grant that, by the prayers and labours of Thy holy Church, they may be delivered from all superstition and unbelief, and brought to worship Thee; through Him Whom Thou hast sent to be our Salvation, the Resurrection and the Life of all the Faithful, Thy Son Jesus Christ our Lord. Amen.   *(Rev. R. M. Benson, A.D. 1824.)*

For the Guidance and Control of the Holy Spirit.

A LMIGHTY and eternal God, there is no number of Thy days or of Thy mercies; Thou hast sent us into this world to serve Thee, and to live according to Thy laws. O Lord, look upon us in mercy and pity. Let Thy Holy Spirit lead us through this world with safety and peace, with holiness and religion, with spiritual comforts and joy in the Holy Ghost; that when we have served Thee in our generation, we may be gathered into our eternal home; that neither death, nor life, nor angels, nor principalities, nor powers, nor things present, nor things to come, nor height, nor depth, nor any other creature, may be able to separate us from the love of God, which is in Christ Jesus our Lord. Amen.

(Bishop Jeremy Taylor, A.D. 1613.)

76

For a Clearer Vision of God.

O GOD, in Whom we have our being, Who in Thy light hast revealed Thyself unto us, but Whom in our darkness we cannot comprehend, grant that we may think worthily of Thee, as we ought to think, and may renew Thine Image in us according to the pattern of Thy Son, the Man Christ Jesus, and by the grace of Thy Holy Spirit. Amen.

(Professor Knight, Nineteenth Century.)

Strength for Daily Needs.

O GOD, from Whom we have received life and all earthly blessings, vouchsafe to give unto us each day what we need. Give unto all of us strength to perform faithfully our appointed tasks; bless the work of our hands and of our minds. Grant that we may ever serve Thee, in sickness and in health, in necessity and in abundance; sanctify our joys and our trials, and give us grace to seek first Thy Kingdom and its righteousness, in the sure and certain faith that all else shall be added unto us; through Jesus Christ, Thy Son, our Lord and Saviour. Amen.

(Rev. Eugène Bersier, A.D. 1831.)

"That it may please Thee to have Mercy upon All Men."

O CHRIST, our God, remember Thy strong and Thy weak ones, great and small, men and women, for good. Remember the righteous who worship Thee by faith, and bestow on them the blessing of those who not having seen, believed. Remember and bless all who worship Thee by prayer, and reveal Thy gracious Presence unto them. Remember any overthrown through frailty, raise them up and perfect Thy strength in their weakness. Remember the bereaved in their anguish, and make their latter end better than their beginning. Furnish the fallen with love, and accept their love. Grant to sufferers faith, and reward their faith. Remember the despised, the overlooked, the misunderstood, reserving mercy for them in the day of Thy justice. Remember munificent hands to refill them, and generous hearts to spiritualize them. Remember us all, O God, for good; for the sake of Thy holy Name. Amen.

(Christina G. Rossetti, A.D. 1830.)

Surrender of Ourselves to God.

O UR God, we heartily thank Thee for all Thy goodness to us, body and soul. We want Thy guidance and direction in all we do. Let Thy Wisdom counsel us, Thy Hand lead us, and Thine Arm support us. We put ourselves into Thy Hands. Breathe into our souls holy and heavenly desires. Conform us to Thine own image. Make us like our Saviour. Enable us in some measure to live here on earth as He lived, and to act in all things as He would have acted; for His sake we ask this. Amen. *(Bishop Ashton Oxenden, A.D. 1808.)*

For a Right Spending of God's Holy Day.

O GOD, let Thy Holy Spirit, Who on the first day of the week descended on the Apostles, descend also upon us, that we may be in the Spirit on the Lord's Day. Help us to worship Thee as we ought—in spirit and in truth. Let us join in the prayers and praises and services of Thy Church with heavenly affection. Let us hear Thy Word with earnest attention and hide it in our hearts. Let us devote this day of rest to praise and prayer, and let the words of our mouth and the meditation of our heart be always acceptable in Thy sight, O Lord, our Strength and our Redeemer; through Christ our Lord. Amen.

(Source not found.)

Thanksgiving for "the Liberty that is in Christ Jesus."

LET us this day, O Lord, learn somewhat concerning Thee, and concerning Thy Law which is unchangeable. Make us truly wise to salvation. Guide us to seek for that which alone is true salvation, deliverance from the dominion of sin. We thank Thee for the freedom of worship, of thought, and of speech here enjoyed. Let our religion not divide us from our fellowmen, but knit us together as children of one God, in earnest and universal kindness, even to those who disown Thee, or scorn reverence. Thus shall our hearts sincerely echo the heavenly song, "Glory be to Thee, O God, on high, on earth peace, goodwill to men." For the sake of Jesus Christ our Lord. Amen.

(Prof. Francis W. Newman, A.D. 1805.)

For Those in Special Temptation.

O MOST Holy Spirit, give Thy strength unto all who are tried by any special temptation. Help them to stand fast in Thee, and make for them a way to escape, that they may be able to bear it; for the sake of Jesus Christ, our Lord and Saviour. Amen.

(The Narrow Way, A.D. 1869.)

For Peace.

O GOD, the consolation of all such as be sorrowful, and the salvation of them that put their trust in Thee, grant unto us, in this dying life, that peace for which we humbly pray, and hereafter to attain unto everlasting joy in Thy presence; through our Lord Jesus Christ. Amen.

(Roman Breviary.)

For Grace and Protection.

INCLINE mercifully Thine ear, O Lord, to these our prayers, and fill our hearts with Thy grace, that loving Thee with an unfeigned love we may evermore be defended under Thy most gracious protection, and be accepted in all our prayers and services; through Jesus Christ our Lord. Amen.

(An Ancient Collect.)

For Faithfulness in Service.

GIVE us grace, O God, to discharge our respective duties this day with fidelity and cheerfulness. Make us diligent in business, fervent in spirit, serving the Lord. May we be zealously affected in every good cause, steadfast, immovable, always abounding in the work of the Lord; through Jesus Christ our Lord. Amen. *(Rev. Fielding Ould, A.D. 1864.)*

For All Kings and Rulers.

GRANT unto all Kings and Rulers, O Lord, health, peace, concord, and stability, that they may administer the government which Thou hast given them without failure. For Thou, O heavenly Master, King of the Ages, givest to the sons of men glory and honour, and power over all things that are upon the earth. Do Thou, Lord, direct their counsel according to that which is good and well pleasing in Thy sight, that administering in peace and gentleness, with godliness, the power which Thou hast given them, they may obtain Thy favour. O Thou Who alone art able to do these things, and things far more exceeding good than these, for us, we praise Thee, through the High Priest and Guardian of our souls, Jesus Christ; through Whom be the glory and the majesty, unto Thee, both now and for all generations, and for ever and ever. Amen. *(St. Clement of Rome, A.D. 95.)*

For Medical Missions.

MERCIFUL Saviour, Who of old time didst have compassion on the multitudes, give to us and to all Thy people the same spirit of love. Teach us to pity and care for all who in heathen and Moslem lands are living without Thee. There are many who are sick and suffering, but have none to heal them. Send forth more of Thy servants to help them. Give skill of hand and eye, strength of patience and heart, and, above all things, Thine own love to every doctor, nurse, and assistant engaged in medical missions. Bless all the means taken to cure or relieve the sufferers. May the heavenly medicine of Thy Gospel bring life and health to many souls. These and all other mercies, we beseech Thee to bestow on them and those who minister to them, according to Thy promises and for Thy holy Name's sake. Amen. *(Church Missionary Society, A.D. 1799.)*

For Joy in God's Service.

O LORD, renew our spirits and draw our hearts unto Thyself, that our work may not be to us a burden, but a delight; and give us such a mighty love to Thee as may sweeten all our obedience. Oh, let us not serve Thee with the spirit of bondage as slaves, but with cheerfulness and gladness of children, delighting ourselves in Thee, and rejoicing in Thy work for the sake of Jesus Christ. Amen. *(Rev. Benjamin Jenks, A.D. 1646.)*

Our Weakness made Perfect in His Strength.

O LORD God Almighty, Who givest power to the faint, and increasest strength to them that have no might; without Thee we can do nothing, but by Thy gracious assistance we are enabled for the performance of every duty laid upon us. Lord of power and love, we come, trusting in Thine Almighty strength, and Thine infinite goodness, to ask from Thee what is wanting in ourselves; even that grace which shall help us such to be, and such to do, as Thou wouldst have us. O our God, let Thy grace be sufficient for us, and ever present with us, that we may do all things as we ought. We will trust in Thee, in Whom is everlasting strength. Be Thou our Helper, to carry us on beyond our own strength, and to make all that we think, and speak, and do, acceptable in Thy sight; through Jesus Christ. Amen.

(Rev. Benjamin Jenks, A.D. 1646.)

For the Fruit of the Spirit.

WE beseech Thee, O Lord, for the gifts and for the grace of the Holy Spirit; give us more love to Thee and to our neighbours; more joy in worship, more peace at all times, more long-suffering, gentleness, and kindness of heart and manner. May we know something of what it means, to be filled with the Holy Ghost. For the sake of Jesus Christ our Lord. Amen.

(Anon., Twentieth Century.)

For the Nation.

O GOD, Who makest men to be of one mind in a house, we pray Thee for this great house of our Nation. Have mercy upon our Country in these days of division and unrest. Be pleased to abate all selfish ambition, all envy in the various classes of men, and strengthen all desires for mutual benefit. Thou art the Maker of the rich and of the poor, remember them both for blessing, and draw them together in a true community of goodwill in Thy faith and fear. Stir up all who have wealth and personal power, to labour wisely for those who need and suffer. And grant to the masses of the people whom Thou hast now permitted to have rule in our State, the blessing of wise guidance and enlightenment of aims, and the spirit of patience, justice, and self-control; and revive Thy work in this Nation that we may indeed be a people fearing Thee and doing righteousness; through Jesus Christ our Lord. Amen.

(Bishop H. C. G. Moule, A.D. 1841.)

General Intercession.

A LMIGHTY God, our heavenly Father, Who lovest all and forgettest none, we bring to Thee our supplications for all Thy creatures and all Thy children everywhere. May Thy blessing be upon them, for the sake of Jesus Christ our Lord. Amen. *Devotional Services, by Rev. Dr. John Hunter, A.D. 1849.)*

A Morning Prayer.

O GOD, our heavenly Father, we Thy children come now to Thy feet with our supplications. We cannot live without Thy blessing. Life is too hard for us, duty is too large. We get discouraged, and our feeble hands hang down. We come to Thee with our weakness, asking Thee for strength. Help us always to be of good cheer. Let us not be disheartened by difficulties. Let us never doubt Thy love or any of Thy promises. Give us grace to be encouragers of others, never discouragers. Let us not go about with sadness or fear among men, but may we be a benediction to everyone we meet, always making life easier, never harder, for those who come within our influence. Help us to be as Christ to others, that they may see something of His love in our lives, and learn to love Him in us. We beseech Thee to hear us, to receive our prayer, and to forgive our sins; for the sake of Jesus Christ. **Amen.**

(Rev. J. R. Miller, B. 1840.)

For Purity of Heart.

O ETERNAL God, Who hast taught us by Thy Holy Word that our bodies are temples of Thy Spirit, keep us, we most humbly beseech Thee, temperate and holy in thought, word, and deed, that we with all the pure in heart may see Thee, and be made like unto Thee in Thy heavenly Kingdom; through Jesus Christ our Lord. Amen. *(Bishop Westcott, A.D. 1825.)*

For All Christian Kings and Governors.

WE pray unto Thee, O great King of heaven and earth, for all Christian Kings, Princes, Governors, and States. Crown them with justice and peace, and with the love of God, and the love of their people. Let holiness unto the Lord be on their foreheads, invest them with the armour of righteousness, and let the anointing from above make them sacred and venerable, wise and holy; that, being servants of the King of kings, friends of religion, ministers of justice, patrons of the poor, they may at last inherit a portion in the Kingdom of our Lord and Saviour Jesus Christ. Grant this for the sake of Christ Jesus, Who is the King of kings and Lord of lords. Amen.

(Bishop Jeremy Taylor, A.D. 1613.)

An Intercession.

BLESS, O Lord, Thy holy Church throughout the world; all Bishops, Clergy, and Ministers. Convert all those in unbelief and misbelief. Have mercy on our Country. Pour down Thy blessing on our friends and relations, and on those who may wish us harm. Bless this parish; give aid to the poor, comfort to the sorrowful, health to the sick, support to the dying, and to all men grant Thy peace; for the sake of Jesus Christ. **Amen.** *(Adapted) (Archbishop Laud, A.D. 1573.)*

For the Bright Shining of the Sun of Righteousness.

O THOU Who art the true Sun of the world, evermore rising and never going down, Who by Thy most wholesome appearing and sight dost nourish and make joyful all things, as well that are in heaven as also that are on earth, we beseech Thee mercifully and favourably to shine into our hearts, that the night and darkness of sin, and the mists of error on every side being driven away, Thou brightly shining within our hearts, we may all our life long, go without any stumbling or offence, and may walk as in the daytime, being pure and clean from the works of darkness, and abounding in all good works which Thou hast prepared for us to walk in; through Jesus Christ our Lord. Amen.   *(Desiderius Erasmus, A.D. 1467.)*

For Perfect Truthfulness.

A LMIGHTY God, Who hast sent the Spirit of truth unto us to guide us into all truth, so rule our lives by Thy power, that we may be truthful in word, deed, and thought. O keep us, most merciful Saviour, with Thy gracious protection, that no fear or hope may ever make us false in act or speech. Cast out from us whatsoever loveth or maketh a lie, and bring us all to the perfect freedom of Thy truth; through Jesus Christ Thy Son our Lord. Amen.   *(Bishop Westcott, A.D. 1825.)*

For this Kingdom.

L ORD, bless this Kingdom, we beseech Thee, that religion and virtue may increase amongst us, that there may be peace within the gates, and plenty within the palaces of it. In peace, we beseech Thee, so preserve it, that it corrupt not; in war, so defend it, that it suffer not; in plenty, so order it, that it riot not; in want, so pacify and moderate it, that it may patiently and peaceably seek Thee, the only full supply both of men and state; that so it may continue a place and a people to do Thee service to the end of time; through Jesus Christ our only Saviour and Redeemer. Amen.   *(Archbishop Laud, A.D. 1573.)*

For the Imitation of Christ.

O GOD, Who hast given unto us Thy Son to be an example and a help to our weakness in following the path that leadeth unto life, grant us so to be His disciples that we may tread in His footsteps; for His Name's sake. Amen.

(Roman Breviary.)

Sanctification of Life's Small Duties.

O FATHER, light up the small duties of this day's life. May they shine with the beauty of Thy countenance. May we believe that glory may dwell in the commonest task. For the sake of Jesus Christ our Lord we ask it. Amen.

(Rev. J. H. Jowett, A.D. 1864.)

A Morning Thanksgiving.

ALMIGHTY God, we thank Thee for rest and health; for work to do, and strength to do it; and for all the surroundings of our life that make it desirable and enjoyable. Do Thou raise our thoughts and purify our aspirations. Strengthen our wills, we beseech Thee, on the side of what is right and good, and against what is wrong and evil; through Jesus Christ our Lord. Amen. *(Source not found.)*

An Intercession.

VOUCHSAFE, O Lord, we beseech Thee, to receive our prayers and intercessions for all mankind, for Thy universal Church, for the Church and people of this country, and for our brethren and sisters in all lands. Look graciously upon all who desire our prayers, and visit them with Thy salvation. Bless our relations and friends, and grant unto them all things which are necessary both for the soul and body. Enlighten those who are in darkness, convert those who are in sin, and of Thy great goodness comfort and succour all them who in this transitory life are in trouble, sorrow, need, sickness, or any other adversity. O Lord, we pray Thee, send Thy Holy Spirit into our hearts, and grant us that peace which the world cannot give. Keep us this day without sin, and be in all things our Protection and Defence now and evermore; for the sake of Thy only Son our Saviour Jesus Christ. Amen. *(Canon E. Hawkins, A.D. 1802.)*

For Spiritual Work in Prisons.

O LORD Jesus Christ, the Great Shepherd of the sheep, Who seekest those that are gone astray, bindest up those that are broken, and healest those that are sick; bless, we beseech Thee, the efforts made in prisons to convert souls unto Thee. Open the deaf ears of the wanderers, that they may hear the words which belong unto their salvation; and grant that those whom Thou dost raise into newness of life may, through Thy grace, persevere unto the end, for Thy honour and glory. Amen. *(Guild of SS. Paul and Silas, A.D. 1881.)*

A Prayer for the Sorrowing.

ALMIGHTY and everlasting God, the Comfort of the sad, the Strength of sufferers, let the prayers of those that cry out of any tribulation come unto Thee, that all may rejoice to find that Thy mercy is present with them in their afflictions; through Jesus Christ our Lord. Amen. *(Gelasian Sacramentary.)*

O LORD of Hosts, God of Israel, that dwellest between the Cherubim, Thou art the God, even Thou alone, of all the kingdoms of the earth; Thou hast made heaven and earth. Incline Thine ear, O Lord, and hear; open Thine eyes, O Lord, and see; and save us from the hand of our enemies, that all the kingdoms of the earth may know that Thou art the Lord, even Thou only. Amen.

(Hezekiah, Eighth Century, B.C.; Isa. xxxvii. 15-20.)

For a Fuller Realization of our Dependence upon God.

ETERNAL Ruler of our lives, to Thee, O God, we look up for daily guidance, daily blessing, daily supplies of strength and love; strength to serve in duty, love to make all duty cheerful, willing, and happy. O Lord, give us more of Thy justice, and more of Thy pity for the distressed. Grant us also Thy peace, Thy tranquillity. Thou sittest above all our storms. Thou art our Divine Shepherd, and we are the sheep of Thy pasture. Thou leadest us by ways which we know not, and often turnest pain into profit, evil into good. Thy power works around us in all the world. O make us conscious of Thy inward Presence, and full of that holy gratitude which causes content and peace. Thou, Lord, art the Rewarder of those that seek Thee, Source of strength, Creator of life and joy, in Whom we live and move and have our being. In Thee let us rejoice, and let Thy joy establish us; through Jesus Christ our Lord. Amen.   (*Prof. Francis W. Newman*, A.D. 1805.)

For the Heavy-Laden.

O LORD, we beseech Thee to have compassion on those who in this life are burdened with perplexity, or troubled by manifold cares and distractions. Help them to commit their cares to Thee, and to possess their souls in patience, and may Thy peace console them; through Jesus Christ our Lord. Amen.

For Friends and Those in Need.

O GOD of all mercy, we call to mind before Thy throne of grace all our relations and friends, all for whom we are in duty bound to pray, and all for whom Thou wilt be pleased to hear us. Fill all minds, we beseech Thee, with the knowledge and power of Thy truth, and knit all hearts more closely to Thee and to one another. Arise, O God, and show Thyself the Helper of the helpless, the Light of the blind, the Strength of the weak, the Deliverer of the captive, the Comforter of the mourner, and the Saviour of all that trust in Thee; through Jesus Christ our Lord. Amen.   (*Rev. L. Tuttiett*, A.D. 1825.)

A Prayer for the Heathen.

ALMIGHTY and everlasting God, Who desirest not the death, but always the life of sinners, mercifully receive our prayer, and deliver the heathen from idolatry, and gather them into Thy holy Church, to the praise and glory of Thy Name; through Jesus Christ our Lord. Amen.   (*Gelasian Sacramentary.*)

For a Knowledge of God's Will.

OUR Father, teach us not only Thy will, but how to do it. Teach us the best way of doing the best thing, lest we spoil the end by unworthy means; for the sake of Christ Jesus our Lord. Amen.   (*Rev. J. H. Jowett*, A.D. 1864.)

For a Fuller Knowledge of God.

ALMIGHTY God, Who wast, and art, and art to come, Eternal Home of man, Refuge of the weary, Strength of the weak, of Thy loving-kindness and tender mercy grant unto us that we, being guided by Thy good Spirit, and coming with lowly hearts unto Thee, may know Thy Truth, feel Thy Light, drink of the Living Water, and eat of the Bread of Heaven, and that passing through the gate of death, we may enter at last into the life everlasting; through Jesus Christ our Lord.   Amen.

(Rev. George Dawson, A.D. 1821.)

For a Blessing of Divine Worship.

AS for us, we will go into Thy house in the multitude of Thy mercies: and in Thy fear will we worship towards Thy holy temple (Ps. v. 7).   Hear the voice of our supplications when we cry unto Thee (Ps. xxviii. 2).   We have thought of Thy loving-kindness, O God, in the midst of Thy temple (Ps. xlviii. 9).   Be mindful, O Lord, of those who will be present with us, and pray with us this day; be mindful of those also who upon good cause are absent; and have mercy upon them and us according to the multitudes of Thy mercies, O Lord.   Let, O Lord, we beseech Thee, Thine eyes be open, and let Thine ears be attentive unto the prayer which Thy servant prayeth toward Thy holy place, which is called by Thy Name; for the sake of Jesus Christ, Thy Son, our Lord. Amen. *(From 2 Chron. vi. 20, 33; Psalms, B.C.; arranged by Bishop Andrewes, A.D. 1555.)*

For the Ministry.

WE beseech Thee to hear us, O God, and grant that all ministers and teachers of religion may be so endued with the healthful spirit of Thy grace, that they may be men of honest mind and simple heart, and set forth Thy truth, both by their word and life; through Jesus Christ our Lord.   Amen.

(Rev. Dr. John Hunter, A.D. 1849.)

Praise and Thanksgiving.

WE give Thee humble and hearty thanks, O most merciful Father, for all Thy goodness and loving-kindness to us and to all men, for the blessings of this life, and for the promise of everlasting happiness.   And, as we are bound, we specially praise Thee for the mercies which we have ourselves received from Thee in the past.   We thank Thee, O God, for every blessing of soul and body, and do Thou add this, O Lord, to Thy other mercies, that we may praise Thee not with our lips only, but with our lives, always looking to Thee as the Author and Giver of all good things.   We ask all for Jesus Christ's sake. Amen.   *(Bishop Westcott, A.D. 1825.)*

For God's Rule in our Hearts.

O MERCIFUL Lord God, heavenly Father, we render praise and thanks unto Thee, that Thou hast preserved us both this night, and all the times and days of our lives hitherto, under Thy protection, and hast suffered us to live until this present hour. And we beseech Thee heartily that Thou wilt vouchsafe to receive us this day, and the residue of our whole lives, from henceforth into Thy good keeping; ruling and governing us with Thy Holy Spirit, that all manner of darkness and evil may be utterly chased and driven out of our hearts, and that we may walk in the light of Thy Truth, to Thy glory and praise, and to the help and furtherance of our neighbours; through Jesus Christ our Lord and Saviour. Amen.

(Henry VIII.'s Primer, A.D. 1545.)

For Increased Godly Knowledge.

GRANT us, even us, O Lord, to know Thee, and love Thee, and rejoice in Thee. And if we cannot do these perfectly in this life, let us, at least, advance to higher degrees every day, till we can come to do them in perfection. Let the knowledge of Thee increase in us here, that it may be full hereafter. Let the love of Thee grow every day more and more here, that it may be perfect hereafter; that our joy may be great in itself and full in Thee. We know, O God, that Thou art a God of truth, O make good Thy gracious promises to us, that our joy may be full. To Thine honour and glory, Who with the Father and the Holy Ghost liveth and reigneth one God, world without end. Amen.

(St. Augustine, A.D. 354.)

An Intercession.

WE beseech Thee, Lord and Master, to be our help and succour. Save those who are in tribulation; have mercy on the lonely; lift up the fallen; show Thyself unto the needy; heal the ungodly; convert the wanderers of Thy people; feed the hungry; raise up the weak; comfort the faint-hearted. Let all the peoples know that Thou art God alone, and Jesus Christ is Thy Son, and we are Thy people and the sheep of Thy pasture; for the sake of Christ Jesus. Amen. *(St. Clement of Rome, A.D. 95.)*

For Divine Direction.

O LORD our God, teach us, we beseech Thee, to ask Thee aright for the right blessings. Steer Thou the vessel of our life towards Thyself, Thou tranquil Haven of all storm-tossed souls. Show us the course wherein we should go. Renew a willing spirit within us. Let Thy Spirit curb our wayward senses, and guide and enable us unto that which is our true good, to keep Thy laws, and in all our works evermore to rejoice in Thy glorious and gladdening Presence. For Thine is the glory and praise from all Thy saints, for ever and ever. Amen.

(St. Basil, A.D. 379.)

A Morning Thanksgiving.

O THOU most holy and ever-loving God, we thank Thee once more for the quiet rest of the night that has gone by, for the new promise that has come with this fresh morning, and for the hope of this day. While we have slept, the world in which we live has swept on, and we have rested under the shadow of Thy love. May we trust Thee this day for all the needs of the body, the soul, and the spirit. Give us this day our daily bread. Amen.   (*Rev. Robert Collyer*, A.D. 1823.)

For Support in Times of Temptation.

O LORD, our Defender, have pity upon us; behold the armies of the flesh, the world, and the devil fight against our souls, and multiply against us every day temptations and disadvantages. We are not able of ourselves, as of ourselves, to think a good thought, much less put to flight the armies of them that have set themselves against us round about. But Thou, O Lord, art our Defender, Thou art our Worship and the Lifter-up of our heads. Up, Lord, and help us; arm us with the shield of faith and the sword of the spirit, and in all times of temptation and battle, cover our heads with the helmet of salvation, so shall we not be afraid of ten thousands of our enemies, for salvation belongeth unto Thee; through Jesus Christ our Lord. Amen.   (*Bishop Jeremy Taylor*, A.D. 1613.)

An Intercession.

O LORD, we pray for the universal Church, for all sections of Thy Church throughout the world, for their truth, unity, and stability, that love may abound, and truth flourish in them all. We pray for all Thy ministering servants that they may rightly divide the Word of Truth, that they may walk circumspectly; that teaching others they may themselves learn both the way and the truth. We pray for the people, that they make not themselves over-wise, but be persuaded by reason, and yield to the authority of their superiors. We pray for the Kingdoms of the World, their stability and peace; for our own Nation, Kingdom, and Empire, that they may abide in prosperity and happiness, and be delivered from all peril and disaster. For the King, O Lord, save him; O Lord, give him prosperity, compass him with the shield of truth and glory, speak good things unto him, in behalf of Thy Church and people. Unto all men everywhere give Thy grace and Thy blessing; through Jesus Christ. Amen.   (*Bishop Andrewes*, A.D. 1555.)

For Perception of God's Goodness.

O LORD, keep us sensitive to the grace that is around us. May the familiar not become neglected. May we see Thy goodness in our daily bread, and may the comforts of our home take our thoughts to the mercy-seat of God; through Jesus Christ. Amen.   (*Rev. J. H. Jowett*, A.D. 1864.)

Praise and Intercession for the Coming Day.

HEAVENLY Father, Who watchest over Thy faithful people and mightily defendest them, we thank Thee that it has pleased Thee to take care of us Thy servants during the night past, and to give us needful sleep to refresh our bodies. We beseech Thee to show the same goodness to us this day, so preserving and ruling over us that we may neither think, nor speak, nor do anything displeasing to Thee, or hurtful to our neighbour, but that all our doings may be agreeable to Thy most holy will, and may advance Thy glory, so that, when Thou shalt call us hence, we may be found the children, not of darkness, but of light; for the sake of Jesus Christ our Lord. Amen.

(Rev. T. Becon, A.D. 1511.)

For Growth in Grace.

O HOLY Spirit, make to arise in our hearts a true fear of God and a true faith and knowledge of the mercy which the eternal Father of our Lord Jesus Christ has promised unto us for His Son's sake. Be our Comforter in all counsels and dangers; illuminate our understanding, and fill our hearts with new affections and spiritual motions, and renew us both in soul and body, that we may die to sin and live to righteousness, and so in true obedience may praise the Father of our Lord Jesus Christ and His Son, our Redeemer, and Thee also, our Comforter everlastingly. Amen.   *(Christian Prayers, A.D. 1566.)*

For the King.

WE beseech Thee, Almighty God, that Thy servant George who by Thy mercy hath undertaken the government of the Realm, may also receive the increase of all virtues, and, being beautified therewith, may be able to avoid all sin, and attain to Thee, Who art the Way, the Truth, and the Life, and be acceptable in Thy sight; through Jesus Christ our Lord. Amen.

(Gregorian Sacramentary.)

For the Spirit of Christ in our Lives.

O THOU Who art the Life of all that lives, the Strength of the weak, and the Hope of those that be cast down, inform our minds with Thy Truth, we beseech Thee, and our hearts with righteousness; strengthen our wills to choose the good and to refuse the evil; help us to bear each other's burdens, to forgive one another's faults, and to forbear with every defect of judgment and of temper in those with whom we live and who daily help us. Grant this through Jesus Christ our Lord. Amen.

(Professor Knight, Nineteenth Century.)

A Worker's Prayer.

O LORD, let us not live to be useless; for Christ's sake. Amen.

(Rev. John Wesley, A.D. 1703.)

For Fuller Knowledge.

O FATHER Almighty, we give Thee thanks that Thou hast
called us unto godliness and to the remission of sins, that we
have been named after the name of Christ; unite us with those
who are hallowed to Thee. Establish us in Thy Truth by the
inspiration of Thy Holy Spirit; that which we know not, do Thou
reveal; that which is wanting in us, do Thou fill up; in that
which we know, do Thou strengthen us; for the sake of Jesus
Christ our Lord and Master. Amen.

(Liturgy of the Greek Church.)

An Intercession.

O LORD, graciously accept our prayers for all our kindred
and friends. O God, do good unto them all. To those that
err, show Thy truth; and to those that seek it, keep from error.
To those that do amiss, give grace to do better ; and those
that do well, continue in well doing. To those that are afflicted
give comfort and deliverance. To those that prosper, humility
and temperance. Bless the sick with health, and keep the
healthy from sickness. Supply those that are in want, and
let those that want not, give supply. To all grant Thy grace,
O God, and show Thy mercy. Let love bind us one to another,
and may religion knit us all to Thee. Grant that we may live
and be in joy together in the bliss of heaven by the union of the
Holy Spirit, and through the sacrifice of Christ Jesus our Saviour.
Amen.   *(Bishop Ken, A.D. 1637.)*

For Mutual Help in the Household.

O HEAVENLY Father, shed forth Thy blessed Spirit richly
on all the members of this household. Make each one of us
an instrument in Thy hands for good. Purify our hearts,
strengthen our minds and bodies, fill us with mutual love. Let
no pride, no self-conceit, no rivalry, no dispute, ever spring up
among us. ˙ Make us earnest and true, wise and prudent, giving
no just cause for offence; and may Thy holy peace rest upon us
this day and every day, sweetening our trials, cheering us in our
work, and keeping us faithful to the end; through Jesus Christ
our Lord. Amen.   *(Church Guild, Nineteenth Century.)*

For a True Understanding of God's Word.

G IVE us a pure judgment and a true understanding of Thy
Word, O Lord, that we be not deceived and carried away by
any error; but grant that we may grow in grace and in the knowledge of our Lord and Saviour Jesus Christ. Amen.

(Christian Prayers, A.D. 1566.)

For Pardon.

GRACIOUS Father, give us perfect pardon for what is past, and a perfect repentance for all our evils, that for the time to come we may, with pure spirits, with broken and contrite hearts, with sanctified lips and holy desires, serve Thee religiously, walk humbly with Thee our God, converse justly and charitably with men, and possess our souls in patience and holiness, and our bodies in sanctification and honour; through Jesus Christ our Lord. Amen. *(Bishop Jeremy Taylor, A.D. 1613.)*

For the Jews.

ALMIGHTY and everlasting God, Who repellest not even the faithless Jews from Thy mercy, hear our prayers which we offer unto Thee for that blinded people; that by acknowledging the Light of Thy Truth, which is Christ, they may be rescued from their own darkness; through the same Jesus Christ our Lord. Amen. *(Gelasian Sacramentary.)*

For Missionaries and their Needs.

O HOLY GHOST, Who in diversities of gifts art the same Spirit, and dividest to every man severally as Thou wilt, we thank Thee for the many members in the one Body of Christ in which Thou art working. We pray for the Societies and Missions of our own Country and Colonies, as well as of other lands and other Churches, which are making known the salvation of God throughout the world. Grant that as the Lord appointed disciples and sent them before His face, so these also may go forth whither He Himself will come. May all their need be supplied according to the riches in glory by Christ Jesus. May they consider one another to provoke unto love and good works, and when the harvest shall come may sowers and reapers rejoice together in the Kingdom of God; through the mercy and might of Jesus Christ our Lord. Amen.

(Church Missionary Society, A.D. 1799.)

For the Afflicted and Distressed.

WE bring before Thee, O Lord, the troubles and perils of people and nations, the sighing of prisoners and captives, the sorrows of the bereaved, the necessities of strangers, the helplessness of the weak, the despondency of the weary, the failing powers of the aged. O Lord, draw near to each; for the sake of Jesus Christ our Lord. Amen. *(St. Anselm, A.D. 1033.)*

A Memorial of our Lord's Passion.

LORD, let the view of the Cross of Christ ever fill our souls with happy peace, with holy love, and with heavenly joy; through Jesus Christ. Amen.

(Bishop Bickersteth, A.D. 1825.)

For Well-Ordered Lives.

GRANT us grace, O Lord, to order our lives according to Thy will, and enable us to live in charity with all men. Uphold us by Thy free Spirit, that we may be inspired with inward might, and endued with true humility; and grant that both when we labour and while we rest, both when we sleep and when we wake, Thy light may be around us and Thy Presence overshadowing us; through Jesus Christ our Lord. Amen.

(Baron Christian C. J. Bunsen, A.D. 1791.)

For Pardon, Grace, and Guidance.

O THOU plenteous Source of every good and perfect gift, shed abroad the cheering light of Thy sevenfold grace over our hearts. Yea, Spirit of love and gentleness, we most humbly implore Thy assistance. Thou knowest our faults, our failings, our necessities, the dulness of our understanding, the wayward-ness of our affections, the perverseness of our will. When, there-fore, we neglect to practise what we know, visit us, we beseech Thee, with Thy grace, enlighten our minds, rectify our desires, correct our wanderings, and pardon our omissions, so that by Thy guidance we may be preserved from making shipwreck of faith, and keep a good conscience, and may at length be landed safe in the haven of eternal rest; through Jesus Christ our Lord. Amen. *(St. Anselm, A.D. 1033.)*

For Faith in God's Providence.

WHAT will befall us to-day, O God, we know not; we only know that nothing will happen which Thou hast not foreseen, determined, desired, and ordered—that is enough for us. Thee do we worship and adore. We ask in the Name of Jesus Christ our Saviour, and through His infinite merits, patience in all our sufferings, perfect submission to Thee for all that Thou desirest or permittest, guidance in all that we undertake; for Thine honour and glory we ask it. Amen.

(Prayer of Princess Eliazbeth, A.D. 1770.)

An Intercession.

OUR Father, we commend to Thee all those whom we love, and all for whom we specially wish to pray. There is no space or time for special prayer for each, but Thou, O God, knowest what they all need. Have mercy upon their infirmities, upon their weaknesses, and in the hour of special trial, be it sickness or temptation, give them Thy help to rise stronger and better for the proving. Human nature is weak, but Thou, O God, art strong. Thou canst support the wavering; be near, then, to all for whom we ask for help, our relations, our friends, dependents, and all in whom we are interested. Help all, O Lord, for Christ's sake. Amen. *(Source not found.)*

For Christ's Presence.

BE present, O Lord, to our supplications; that as we trust that the Saviour of mankind is seated with Thee in Thy Majesty, so we may feel that, according to His promise, He abideth with us unto the end of the world; through the same Jesus Christ our Lord. Amen.   (*Leonine Sacramentary.*)

For Blessing on Public Worship.

O HEAVENLY Father, forasmuch as none can come to receive Thy Holy Word, except Thou draw them by Thy gracious inspiration, we beseech Thee to pour out Thy Holy Spirit upon those who worship to-day in Thy holy house of prayer, that their hearts may be inclined favourably to receive, steadfastly to retain, and obediently to perform, whatsoever shall be taught them in Thy Name; and that they may manifest, in the dedication to Thee of their lives and substance, that thankfulness which they owe to Thee for Thy redeeming love; through Jesus Christ our Lord. Amen.   (*Rev. R. M. Benson*, A.D. 1824.)

A Morning Prayer and Thanksgiving.

LORD, our God, heavenly Father, we give Thee heartfelt praise and thanks for all Thy grace, and love, and goodness which Thou hast bestowed upon us for body and soul unto this present hour. Furthermore, we thank Thee that Thou hast graciously sheltered us during the past night from all evil and danger, and hast in Thy Fatherly love preserved to us our life and all Thy daily blessing. O Lord our God, how great is Thy goodness, that the children of men can trust themselves under the shadow of Thy wings. In childlike trust, we beseech Thee, our heavenly Father, that Thou wouldst this day gladden us with Thy goodness and safeguard us and all Thy people with Thy defence. Lead us by Thy Holy Spirit in all goodness, and teach us to do the things well-pleasing in Thy sight. Protect us, O God, that we sin not against Thee, and keep our conscience free from stain. Strengthen us in all our doings and undertakings. Give us strength and comfort in all unexpected troubles, and be Thou with us in all our ways. Be gracious, Lord, to us Thy children. Fill us with Thy grace, so will we be glad and rejoice all the days of our life; through Jesus Christ our Lord. Amen.   (*Weimarischer Gesangbuch*, A.D. 1873.)

For Faith, Love, Hope and Stability.

INCREASE our faith, O Lord our God, in Thee, and in Thy Christ; increase our love, O our Redeemer, to Thee, and to Thy righteous people; increase a sure hope in us of our salvation; increase strength in us to overcome sin, and to stand against all temptation; for Thy Name's sake. Amen.
                                (*Christian Prayers*, A.D. 1566.)

Thanksgiving.

WE give Thee thanks, Lord God of our salvation, because Thou doest all things for the good of our life, that we may always look steadfastly unto Thee, the Saviour and Benefactor of our souls, for Thou hast refreshed us in the night past, and raised us up, and brought us to worship Thy glorious Name. Wherefore, we beseech Thee, O Lord, give us grace and power, that we may be accounted worthy to sing praise to Thee with understanding, and to pray to Thee without ceasing, in fear and trembling working out our own salvation; through Jesus Christ our Lord. Amen. (*Eastern Church Liturgy, Daybreak Office.*)

For Grace.

O LORD Jesus, grant us Thy grace and give unto us time for repentance. We would keep Thy commandments and do Thy bidding, choose the better part and no longer follow after evil; grant us Thy strength that this may so be, O loving Saviour for Thine own Name's sake. Amen.

(*Archdeacon Dan Jeremy, A.D. 1170.*)

For a Blessing on the Home.

BLESS, O Lord, this house and all who dwell in it, as Thou wast pleased to bless the house of Abraham, Isaac, and Jacob; that within these walls may dwell an angel of light, and that we who dwell together in it, may receive the abundant dew of heavenly blessing, and through Thy tenderness rejoice in peace and quiet; through Jesus Christ our Lord. Amen.

(*Gelasian Sacramentary.*)

For Missions.

O ALMIGHTY and most merciful Father, Who didst send Thy beloved Son to die for the sins of the whole world, look down, we beseech Thee, upon all nations who have not known His Name, and in Thine own good time lead them to His Cross. Strengthen with the comfort of Thy Spirit all who bear abroad the message of the Gospel. Raise up among us a lively sympathy with their labours. Take away from those who hear all hardness of heart, and pride, and impenitence; and so move them, blessed Lord, with Thine infinite love, that the day may speedily come when all the ends of the world shall be turned unto Thee, and there shall be one flock and one Shepherd; we ask all for the sake of Jesus Christ our Lord. Amen.

(*Bishop Westcott, A D. 1825.*)

For Controlled Lives.

KEEP us from all hastiness of speech or of temper, from slothfulness, and from repining; and in us let patience have her perfect work; through Jesus Christ our Lord. Amen.

(*Professor Knight, Nineteenth Century.*)

For Forgiveness and Strength.

O LORD, we humbly beseech Thee, blot out our past transgressions, heal the evils of our past negligences and ignorances, make us amend our past mistakes and misunderstandings; uplift our hearts to new love, new energy, and devotion, that we may be unburthened from the grief and shame of past faithlessness, to go forth in Thy strength to persevere through success and failure, through good report and evil report, even to the end; and in all time of our tribulation, in all time of our wealth, save us and help us, we humbly beseech Thee, O Lord.

(Bishop George Ridding, A.D. 1828.)

For Deliverance from Sin.

O LORD, vouchsafe to look mercifully upon us, and grant that we may choose the way of peace; so that, rescued from the captivity of the sins which have oppressed us, we may attain the dwellings of the heavenly Jerusalem; through Jesus Christ. Amen.   *(Sarum Breviary.)*

For Confidence in God.

A LMIGHTY God, Lord of the storm and of the calm, the vexed sea and the quiet haven, of day and night, of life and of death; grant unto us so to have our hearts stayed upon Thy faithfulness, Thine unchangingness and love, that, whatsoever betide us, however black the cloud or dark the night, with quiet faith trusting in Thee, we may look upon Thee with untroubled eye, and walking in lowliness towards Thee, and in lovingness towards one another, abide all storms and troubles of this mortal life, beseeching Thee that they may turn to the soul's true good; we ask it for Thy mercy's sake, shown in Jesus Christ our Lord. Amen.   *(Rev. George Dawson, A.D. 1821.)*

For a Fuller Knowledge of God.

O GOD of our life, Whom we dimly apprehend and never can comprehend, to Whom nevertheless we justly ascribe all goodness as well as all greatness; as a father teaches his children, so teach us, Lord, truer thoughts of Thee. Teach us to aspire, so far as man may lawfully aspire, to a knowledge of Thee. Thou art not only a God to be honoured in times of rest and ease, Thou art also the Refuge of the distressed, the Comforter of the afflicted, the Healer of the contrite, and the Support of the unstable. As we sympathize with those who are sore smitten by calamity, wounded by sudden accident, wrecked in the midst of security, so must we believe that Thy mighty all-embracing heart sympathizes. Pitier of the orphan, God of the widow, cause us to share Thy pity and become Thy messengers of tenderness in our small measure. Be Thou the Stay of all in life and death. Teach all to know and trust Thee, give us a portion here and everywhere with Thy saints; through Jesus Christ our Lord. Amen.   *(Prof. Francis W. Newman, A.D. 1805.)*

Thanksgiving for Pardon of Sins.

ALMIGHTY and most merciful God, in Whom we live and move and have our being; Lord of all life, Source of all light, guiding and governing all things of Thy loving-kindness and power. Hear our thanksgiving unto Thee for all the joy that Thou puttest into mortal life; but chiefly for the joy that comes of sin forgiven, weakness strengthened, victory promised, life eternal looked for. To everyone of us grant that, being fully conscious of having erred and strayed from Thy ways, we may be equally conscious of our need to go back again to the Good Shepherd. Let there be no doubt with any one of us that Thou dost forgive, even to the uttermost, all those who draw nigh in penitence to Thee: that so, those of us who are sinful, and sad because sinful, and sorrowful in sinning, may have this day the joy of the Lord: through Jesus Christ. Amen. (*Rev. George Dawson*, A.D. 1821.)

A Morning Petition.

OUR Father, may we walk as Thy children to-day. May the sense of our relationship to Thee fill us with a saving self-respect. May our lives be as glorious as our relationship. May we walk as children of God; through Jesus Christ our Lord. Amen. (*Rev. J. H. Jowett*, A.D. 1864.)

For Love to God.

O GOD, the God of all goodness and of all grace, Who art worthy of a greater love than we can either give or understand, fill our hearts, we beseech Thee, with such love toward Thee, that nothing may seem too hard for us to do or to suffer in obedience to Thy will; and grant that thus loving Thee, we may become daily more like unto Thee, and finally obtain the crown of life which Thou hast promised to those that love Thee; through Jesus Christ our Lord. Amen.

(*Farnham Hostel Manual, Nineteenth Century.*)

For Unity in Christ's Church.

WE commend to Thee, Almighty God, the whole Christian Church in the world. Bless all in every place who call on the Name of our Lord Jesus Christ. May the grace and power of the Holy Ghost fill every member, so that the whole company of Thy faithful people may bear witness for Thee on the earth. Look in mercy on the errors and confusions of our time, and be pleased amidst them to speak Thine own peace, and to draw the hearts of Christians everywhere nearer to the Lord Jesus Christ. If it be good in Thy sight, heal the outward divisions of Thy people, disposing all Christian hearts to a true union of order in the truth, for the work of the one Lord. But above all things we ask Thee for the unity of the Holy Spirit, that we may all be one in the Father and in the Son; to the glory of Thy Name. through Jesus Christ our Lord. Amen.

(*Bishop H. C. G. Moule*, A.D. 1841.)

For Pardon.

O LORD, we acknowledge our failures and defects; we humbly confess our errors and our sins; but forasmuch as Thou delightest to show mercy, we beseech Thee to pardon and absolve us, to deliver us from the burden of transgression, and to release us from the power of sin; through Jesus Christ our Lord. Amen.   (*Gelasian Sacramentary.*)

For Perfect Surrender to God's Will.

O OUR God, bestow upon us such confidence, such peace, such happiness in Thee, that Thy will may always be dearer to us than our own will, and Thy pleasure than our own pleasure. All that Thou givest is Thy free gift to us, all that Thou takest away is Thy grace to us. Be Thou thanked for all, praised for all, loved for all; through Jesus Christ our Lord. Amen.
(*Christina G. Rossetti*, A.D. 1830.)

For the Lonely.

O LORD, grant, we beseech Thee, the gladness of home to those who are far away, to captives liberty, and the opening of the prison to them that are in bondage; that Thy people may rejoice in the freedom which Thy mercy vouchsafes both in this world and in that which is to come; through Jesus Christ our Lord. Amen.   (*Gothic Missal.*)

For Trust in God.

O GOD, our Lord, the stay of all them that put their trust in Thee, wherever Thou leadest we would go, for Thy ways are perfect wisdom and love. Even when we walk through the dark valley, Thy light can shine into our hearts and guide us safely through the night of sorrow. Be Thou our Friend, and we need ask no more in heaven or earth, for Thou art the Comfort of all who trust in Thee, the Help and Defence of all who hope in Thee. O Lord, we would be Thine; let us never fall away from Thee. We would accept all things without murmuring from Thy hand, for whatever Thou dost is right. Blend our wills with Thine, and then we need fear no evil nor death itself, for all things must work together for our good. Lord, keep us in Thy love and truth, comfort us with Thy light, and guide us by Thy Holy Spirit; through Jesus Christ our Lord. Amen.
(*Rev. S. Weiss*, A.D. 1738.)

For Unity.

VOUCHSAFE, we beseech Thee, Almighty God, to grant unto the whole Christian people unity, peace, and true concord both visible and invisible; through Jesus Christ our Lord Amen. (*Intercessory Manual, Rev. R. M. Benson*, A.D. 1824.)

A Morning Petition.

O THOU Almighty Helper and ever-present God, we bring to Thee all our needs. O Thou Author of all good, from Whom cometh every good and perfect gift, may Thy mercies be our daily song, and may the light of Thy countenance in this world of power and beauty, move our hearts to great thankfulness and a sweet trust. Day by day dost Thou appoint our portion, especially revealing Thy glory in the dear Son of Thy love, and calling us into His kingdom of service and blessedness. May this be our love of Thee in Him, that we love one another and keep all His commandments; through Jesus Christ. Amen.

(Rev. Rufus Ellis, A.D. 1819.)

For Shelter in Temptation.

O LORD, Shield of our help, Who wilt not suffer us to be tempted above that we are able, help us, we entreat Thee, in all our straits and wrestlings, to lift up our eyes unto Thee, and stay our hearts on Thee; through Jesus Christ. Amen.

(Christina G. Rossetti, A.D. 1830.)

For the Spread of Christ's Kingdom.

A LMIGHTY God and heavenly Father, Who of Thine infinite love and goodness towards us, hast given to us Thy only and most dearly beloved Son, Jesus Christ, to be our Redeemer and the Author of everlasting life. Who, after He had made perfect our redemption by His death and was ascended into heaven, sent abroad into the world His Apostles, prophets, evangelists, doctors, and pastors; by whose labour and ministry He gathered together a great flock from all parts of the world, to set forth the eternal praise of Thy holy Name: for these so great benefits of Thy eternal goodness we render unto Thee most hearty thanks. We praise and worship Thee, and we humbly beseech Thee, by the same Thy blessed Son, to grant unto all which here or elsewhere, call upon Thy holy Name, that we may continue to show ourselves thankful unto Thee for these and all other Thy benefits, and that we may daily increase and go forward in the knowledge and faith of Thee and Thy Son by the Holy Spirit, so that Thy holy Name may be for ever glorified, and Thy blessed Kingdom enlarged; through the same Thy son Jesus Christ our Lord, Who liveth and reigneth with Thee in the unity of the same Holy Spirit, world without end. Amen.

(Sarum Breviary.)

Commendation.

I NTO Thy hands, O God, we commit ourselves this day. Be with us throughout this day until its close. May we remember that Thine eye is upon us, that Thou seest all we do, and knowest all we think, and carest for all our joys and our sorrows. Look in tender love upon each one of us, and keep us safe unto the end; for the sake of Jesus Christ our Lord. Amen. *(Source not found.)*

For Light.

O LORD, Thou greatest and most true Light, from whence this light of the day and sun doth spring; O Light, Which dost lighten every man that cometh into the world; O Light, Which knowest no night nor evening, but art always a midday most clear and fair, without Whom all is most dark darkness, by Whom all things are most splendent; O Thou Wisdom of the Eternal Father of mercies, lighten our minds, that we may only see those things that please Thee, and may be blinded to all other things. Grant that we may walk in Thy ways this day, and that nothing else may be light unto us. Lighten our eyes, O Lord, that we sleep not in death, lest our enemy say, "I have prevailed against him" (Ps. xiii. 3, 4); for the sake of Thyself, our Lord. Amen. *(Christian Prayers, A.D. 1566.)*

For Submission to God's Will.

O LORD, save us from idle words, and grant that our hearts may be truly cleansed and filled with Thy Holy Spirit, and that we may arise to serve Thee or lie down to sleep in entire confidence in Thee and submission to Thy will ready for life or for death. Let us live for the day, not overcharged with worldly cares, but feeling that our treasure is not here, and desiring truly to be joined to Thee in Thy heavenly Kingdom and to those who are already gone to Thee. O Lord, let us wait patiently; but do Thou save us from sin, and guide us with Thy Spirit, and keep us with Thee and in faithful obedience to Thee; through Jesus Christ Thy Son our Lord. Amen.

(Dr. Arnold, A.D. 1795.)

A Prayer for Missionaries.

O GOD our Saviour, Who willest that all men should be saved and come to the knowledge of the truth, prosper, we pray Thee, our brethren who labour in distant lands. Protect them in all perils by land and sea, support them in loneliness and in the hour of trial; give them grace to bear faithful witness unto Thee, and endue them with burning zeal and love, that they may turn many to righteousness and finally obtain a crown of glory; through Jesus Christ. Amen.

(Scottish Book of Common Prayer, A.D. 1912.)

For Rulers and the Nations.

O HEAVENLY Father, we bend the knee before Thee on behalf of all Kings, Princes, and Governors of this world, beseeching Thee to grant unto them by Thy inspiration, to rule in righteousness, to rejoice in peace, to shine in piety, and to labour for the well-being of the people committed unto them, so that, by the rectitude of the government, all faithful people may live without disturbance in the knowledge of Thee, and labour without hindrance for Thy glory. Amen.

(Mozarabic Liturgy.)

For a Blessing on Divine Worship.

O GOD, Who makest us glad with the weekly remembrance of the glorious resurrection of Thy Son our Lord, vouchsafe us this day such a blessing through Thy worship, that the days which follow it may be spent in Thy favour; through the same Jesus Christ our Lord. Amen.   (*William Bright,* A.D. 1824.)

For Entire Surrender to God's Service.

LET Thy love so warm our souls, O Lord, that we may gladly surrender ourselves with all we are and have unto Thee. Let Thy love fall as fire from heaven upon the altar of our hearts; teach us to guard it heedfully by continual devotion and quietness of mind, and to cherish with anxious care every spark of its holy flame, with which Thy good Spirit would quicken us, so that neither height, nor depth, things present, nor things to come, may ever separate us therefrom. Strengthen Thou our souls, animate our cold hearts with Thy warmth and tenderness, that we may no more live as in a dream, but walk before Thee as pilgrims in earnest to reach their home. And grant us all at last to meet with Thy holy saints before Thy throne, and there rejoice in Thy love. Amen. (*Gerhard Tersteegen,* A.D. 1697.)

A General Supplication.

BLESS, O Lord, those whom Thou hast set over us both in Church and State; govern their hearts in Thy fear, and guide their understandings to do those things which will be acceptable to Thee, and beneficial to Thy Church and this Kingdom. Give the King loving and loyal subjects, and confound and defeat his open and secret enemies. Comfort the comfortless and helpless; show the light of Thy Truth to those who wander out of the right way; give to all sinners true repentance; strengthen and assist with Thy grace those who have begun well, that they may persevere in goodness. To all our friends, kindred, and enemies, give all Thy good blessings. Keep us from all evil, and make us to continue in Thy service to our lives' end; and after the course of this life is ended, bring us to Thine everlasting Kingdom; through Jesus Christ our Lord. Amen.

(Bishop Hamilton, A.D. 1561.)

For Light.

O LORD our God, accept, we beseech Thee, the prayers which we Thy servants now make unto Thee; manifest Thyself unto us, feeling after Thee and seeking Thee in the shades of ignorance. Scatter our darkness, Thou source of light and wisdom. Stretch forth Thy hand to help us, who cannot without Thee come to Thee, and preserve us this and all our days from error, and from every evil; through Jesus Christ our Lord. Amen.   (*Professor Knight, Nineteenth Century.*)

For Light and Truth.

MAY the Spirit, O Lord, Who proceedeth from Thee, illuminate our minds, and, as Thy Son hath promised, lead us into all truth; through the same our Lord Jesus Christ. Amen.   (*Gelasian Sacramentary.*)

For Love of God and His Laws.

O MOST gracious God, from Whom every good and perfect gift cometh, we beseech Thee to work in us both to will and to do according to Thy good pleasure. Enlighten our minds that we may know Thee, and let us not be unfruitful in that knowledge. Lord, work in our hearts a true faith, a purifying hope, and an unfeigned love towards Thee. Give us a full trust in Thee, zeal for Thee, reverence of all things that relate to Thee. Make us fearful to offend Thee, thankful for Thy mercies, humble under Thy corrections, devout in Thy service, and sorrowful for our sins. Grant that in all things we may behave ourselves so as befits a creature to his Creator, a servant to his Lord. Make us diligent in all our duties, watchful against all temptations, pure and temperate and moderate in Thy most lawful enjoyments, that they may never become a snare to us. Help us, O Lord, to act towards our neighbour that we may never transgress the royal law of Thine, of loving him as ourselves. Finally, we beseech Thee, O Lord, to sanctify us throughout, that our whole spirit, soul, and body, may be preserved blameless unto the coming of our Lord Jesus Christ; to Whom with Thee and the Holy Ghost be all honour and glory for ever. Amen.   (*St. Thomas à Kempis,* A.D. 1379.)

The King and Court.

ALMIGHTY God, the Source of all rightful power amongst us Thy creatures, give Thy grace unto our Sovereign Lord King George and all the Royal Family, that, acknowledging their power to be dependent on Thy supreme Majesty, they may come to reign with Thee in Thine everlasting Kingdom. Grant also that the spirit of godliness ruling their hearts, may quicken all those who are round about them to a sense of the nothingness of earthly glory, and the necessity of striving after that which is eternal; so may all their counsels and actions be directed to Thine honour, and the nation at large be brought to participate in Thine acceptance of their faith; through Jesus Christ our Lord. Amen.   (*Rev. R. M. Benson,* A.D. 1824.)

For Protection of Body and Soul.

KEEP us this day in our bodies as well as in our souls, let no accident befall us or ours, and whatever temptation crosses our path, may we be enabled to look upward and take courage, proving under every trial of faith, that we are indeed faithful disciples and good soldiers of the Lord Jesus Christ. (*E. J. P.,* A.D. 1843.)

For Peace and the Presence of the Holy Spirit.

AH, Lord, unto Whom all hearts are open, Thou canst govern the vessel of our souls far better than we can. Arise, O Lord, and command the stormy wind and the troubled sea of our hearts to be still, and at peace in Thee, that we may look up to Thee undisturbed, and abide in union with Thee, our Lord. Let us not be carried hither and thither by wandering thoughts, but, forgetting all else, let us see and hear Thee. Renew our spirits; kindle in us Thy light, that it may shine within us, and our hearts may burn in love and adoration towards Thee. Let Thy Holy Spirit dwell in us continually, and make us Thy temples and sanctuary, and fill us with Divine love and light and life, with devout and heavenly thoughts, with comfort and strength, with joy and peace. Amen. *(Rev. Johann Arndt, A.D. 1555.)*

For the Guidance of the Holy Spirit.

ENLIGHTEN our understandings with knowledge of right, and govern our wills by Thy laws, that no deceit may mislead us, no temptation corrupt us; that we may always endeavour to do good and hinder evil. Amidst all the hopes and fears of this world, take not Thy Holy Spirit from us; for the sake of Jesus Christ our Lord. Amen. *(Dr. S. Johnson, A.D. 1709.)*

A General Intercession.

O GOD, almighty and merciful, let Thy Fatherly kindness be upon all whom Thou hast made. Hear the prayers of all that call upon Thee; open the eyes of them that never pray for themselves; pity the sighs of such as are in misery; deal mercifully with them that are in darkness; increase the number and graces of such as fear and serve Thee daily. Preserve this land from the misfortunes of war; this Church from all wild and dangerous errors; this people from forgetting Thee their Lord and Benefactor. Be gracious to all those countries that are made desolate by the sword, famine, pestilence, or persecution. Bless all persons and places to which Thy providence has made us debtors; all who have been instrumental to our good by their assistance, advice, example, or writings, and make us in our turn useful to others. Let none of those that desire our prayers want Thy mercy, but defend and comfort and conduct them through to their lives' end; for the sake of Jesus Christ our Lord. Amen. *(Bishop Thomas Wilson, A.D. 1663.)*

"Lord, Remember Me."

O LORD, Thou knowest how busy we must be this day; if we forget Thee, do not Thou forget us; for Christ's sake. Amen. *(General Lord Astley, A.D. 1579. Before the Battle of Edgehill, A.D. 1642.)*

For Perseverance in our Work.

GREAT God, Who seest all we do, come and bless all the work we have in hand. Let it be begun, continued, and ended in Thee. Let no weakness of ours hinder its usefulness, but let Thy blessing be with us in our going out and coming in. We wish to glorify Thee, O Lord, and in Thy strength to bear witness of Thy power to save and help all who call earnestly upon Thee. In all human work there must be some failures, let us not be downcast if this is so. By Thy grace may we rise up and try again and again, although success may be difficult, and effort appear but vain. So help us, Lord, in this and all work done for Thee; for the sake of Jesus Christ our Lord and Master. Amen. *(Source not found.)*

For Quiet Trust in God.

GRANT, O most merciful Father, that we, whom Thou hast by Thy mighty power set free, may serve Thee evermore with quiet minds, taking up the burdens laid upon us because they are Thy will; through Jesus Christ our Lord. Amen. *(Professor Knight, Nineteenth Century.)*

For Divine Help and Protection.

O THOU that art our Helper, the Mighty One, Thou that respecteth not the persons of men, be Thou the help of all Thy people, whom Thou hast purchased with the precious blood of Christ. Thou art our Fortress and Defender, and none can pluck us out of Thy hand. There is none other God like unto Thee; in Thee is our trust. Sanctify us through Thy Truth. Thy Word is truth. Preserve us and all Thy people from all injury and deceit, from the fear of the enemy, from the arrow that flieth by day, and the mischief that walketh in darkness, and vouchsafe unto us the eternal life which is in Christ Thy Son, our Lord and Saviour. Amen. *(Liturgy of the Greek Church.)*

A Prayer for Converts.

O LORD God, remember those who in many lands are preparing for Holy Baptism. Have mercy upon them, strengthen their faith, enlighten their minds, purify their hearts, fit them to be a habitation of the Holy Ghost; and grant that they may receive the washing of regeneration for the remission of their sins, to the glory of Thy Name; through Jesus Christ our Lord. Amen. *(Church Missionary Society, A.D. 1799.)*

For Daily Protection and Growth in Grace.

DEFEND us, O Lord, with Thy heavenly grace, that we may continue Thine for ever, and daily increase in Thy Holy Spirit more and more, until we come unto Thine everlasting Kingdom; through Jesus Christ our Lord. Amen. *(Adapted from Book of Common Prayer, A.D. 1552.)*

A Morning Supplication.

WE bless and praise and magnify Thee, O God of our fathers, Who hast led us out of the shadows of night once more into the light of day. Unto Thy loving-kindness we make our entreaty. Be merciful to our misdeeds; accept our prayers in the fulness of Thy compassions, for Thou art our Refuge from one generation to another, O merciful and Almighty God. Suffer the true Son of Thy righteousness to shine in our hearts, enlighten our reason, and purify our senses; that so we may walk honestly as in the day, in the way of Thy commandments, and reach at last the life eternal, where we shall rejoice in Thy inaccessible life. For Thou art the Fountain of Life, and in Thy light shall we see light; through Jesus Christ Thy Son our Lord. Amen.   (*Greek Church Liturgy.*)

A Supplication for All Men.

WE beseech Thee, O Lord, to bless our King, and to endue his counsellors with grace and wisdom. We pray Thee also to be gracious and favourable to our country. May it ever abound with that righteousness which exalteth a nation. Bless the ministers of Thy Gospel, and enable them rightly to divide the Word of Truth. Give them grace to warn the unruly, to comfort the feeble-minded, to support the weak, and to be patient towards all men. Bless, O Lord, all our relations and friends. Extend to them, we beseech Thee, Thy grace and favour. Have mercy upon all men; comfort the sick; succour the tempted; relieve the oppressed; be the Father of the fatherless, and the God of the widow. Into Thy hands we now commend ourselves, and all Thy people everywhere; through Jesus Christ our Lord. Amen.   (*Tent and Altar,* A.D. 1847.)

For Missionaries and their Work.

O GOD, cause, we beseech Thee, Thy blessing to rest upon the efforts of all Christian people for the spiritual welfare of men; accompany with Thy Holy Spirit the preaching of the Gospel and the religious instruction of the young; sustain and preserve all missionaries to the heathen, and prosper their efforts to reveal and establish the Kingdom of Christ among the nations of the earth; for the sake of Christ Jesus our Lord. Amen.
(*Rev. Dr. John Hunter,* A.D. 1849.)

For Grace to serve our Generation.

MAY we be kept humble and zealous, and may God give us grace to labour in our generation for the good of our brethren and for His glory. May He keep us His by night and day, and strengthen us to hear and to do His will; through Jesus Christ. Amen.   (*Dr. Arnold,* A.D. 1795.)

A Morning Sacrifice of Prayer.

LET our prayer, O Lord, come before Thee in the morning. Thou didst take upon Thee our feeble and suffering nature; grant us to pass this day in gladness and peace, without stumbling and without stain, that, reaching the eventide without any temptation, we may praise Thee, the eternal King; through Thy mercy, O our God, Who art blessed, and dost live and govern all things, world without end. Amen.

(Mozarabic Liturgy.)

"Thy Kingdom come, O Lord."

O LORD, our most gracious Redeemer and King, dwell and reign within us, take possession of us by Thy Spirit, and reign where Thou hast the right to reign, and spread Thy Kingdom throughout the world; through Jesus Christ our Lord. Amen.

(Father John of the Russian Church, Nineteenth Century.)

Intercession.

ALMIGHTY God, we beseech Thee to hear our prayers for all who sin against Thee, or neglect to serve Thee, all who forget Thee, all who leave Thee out of their lives. O Lord, have mercy upon them; bestow upon us all true repentance and an earnest longing for Thyself. Vouchsafe, we beseech Thee, O Lord, to strengthen and confirm all Thy faithful people, and to lift up the light of Thy face upon them, giving them continually heavenly desires; through Jesus Christ our Lord. Amen.

(From an Ancient Collect.)

For the Distressed in Mind.

O BLESSED Lord, the Father of mercies, and the God of all comfort, we commend to Thy Fatherly goodness all those who are any ways afflicted or distressed in mind. Cheer the melancholy; restore hope to the hopeless; protect the unconscious; calm the violent, suffer them not to do harm to themselves or others, and let no one do injury to them; dispel all vain delusions; confirm the health of the recovering; comfort the sick; receive the spirits of the dying, lay not to their charge whatever evil any of them may say or do in time of their affliction; bless the endeavours of all who labour and pray on behalf of the afflicted in mind, and bring us all to Thine everlasting Kingdom; through Jesus Christ our Lord. Amen.

(Canon E. Hawkins, A.D. 1802.)

For the Jews.

O GOD, the God of Abraham, look upon Thine everlasting covenant, and cause the captivity of Judah and Israel to return. They are Thy people. O! be Thou their Saviour, that all who love Jerusalem and mourn for her may rejoice with her; for Jesus Christ's sake, their Saviour and ours. Amen.

(Bishop Thomas Wilson, A.D. 1663.)

Thanksgiving and Prayer.

ALMIGHTY and most merciful God, we give thanks to Thee for the light of another day, for the work we have to do, and for the strength to do it. Guide us, we pray Thee, by Thy Truth, uphold us by Thy power, and purify us by the continual indwelling of Thy Spirit. Grant that by every opportunity we have we may grow in wisdom, and, knowing the things that belong to our peace, obtain strength to persevere unto the end; through Jesus Christ our Lord. Amen.

(Dean Goulburn, A.D. 1818.)

Against Reprisals.

O HOLY and ever-blessed Lord, teach us, we beseech Thee, to love one another, to exercise forbearance and forgiveness towards our enemies, to recompense no man evil for evil, but to be merciful even as Thou, our Father in heaven, art merciful; that so we may continually follow after Thee in all our doings, and be more and more conformed to Thine image and likeness; through Jesus Christ our Lord. Amen.

(New Book of Worship, A.D. 1876.)

For the Extension of God's Kingdom.

O GOD, Who hast knit together Thine elect in one communion and fellowship in the mystical body of Thy dear Son, unite us in true fellowship in the furtherance of the Gospel, both at home and abroad and in heathen lands. Use each of us as Thou wilt in preparing Thy way; make us to abound more and more in prayers and in freewill offerings for the extension of Thy Kingdom throughout the world. Bestow upon us the manifold gifts of Thy Holy Spirit, and grant us grace to stir up those gifts and use them always to Thy glory and the salvation of mankind; through Jesus Christ our Lord. Amen.

(Church Missionary Society, A.D. 1799.)

For Increased Love towards God.

O LORD, we beseech Thee that Thy people may grow ever in love toward Thee, their Father, Who art in Heaven, and may so be schooled by holy works, that ever, as Thou dost pour Thy gifts upon them, they may walk before Thee in all such things as be well-pleasing in the sight of Thy Divine Majesty; for the sake of Christ Jesus our Lord. Amen.

(Roman Breviary.)

For Trust in God's Providence.

LORD Jesus Christ, Who alone art wisdom, Thou knowest what is best for us; mercifully grant that it may happen to us only as it is pleasing to Thee and as seems good in Thy sight this day; for Thy Name's sake. Amen.

(Henry VI., A.D. 1421.)

For Growth in Grace.

GRANT unto us, Almighty God, that we, communing with one another and with Thee, may feel our hearts burn within us, until all pure, and just, and holy, and noble things of God and man may be to us lovely, and we may find nothing to fear but that which is hateful in Thine eyes, and nothing worth seeking but that which is lovely and fair therein. Let the divine brightness and peace possess our souls, so that, fearing neither life nor death, we may look to Thy loving-kindness and tender mercy to lift us above that which is low and mean within us, and at last to give the spirit within us the victory, and bring us safe through death into the life everlasting. Hear us of Thy mercy; through Jesus Christ our Lord. Amen.

(Rev. George Dawson, A.D. 1821.)

For Brotherly Love.

O GOD, the Enlightener of men, Who of all graces givest the most abundant blessing upon heavenly love; we beseech Thee to cleanse us from selfishness, and grant us, for Thy love, so to love our brethren that we may be Thy children upon earth; and thereby, walking in Thy Truth, attain to Thy unspeakable joy, Who art the Giver of life to all who truly love Thee. Grant this prayer, O Lord, for Jesus Christ's sake. Amen.

(Rev. Rowland Williams, A.D. 1818.)

For Missionaries.

O THOU Good Shepherd of the sheep, look mercifully upon those who have none to watch over them in Thy Name. Prepare them to receive Thy Truth, and send them pastors after Thine own heart. Replenish with Thine abundant grace those whom Thou dost send, and awaken the pity of Thy people for all who know Thee not, so that by their cheerful contributions, and the co-operation of Thy Holy Spirit, multitudes may daily be added to the Lord, and become partakers of the salvation which Thou hast promised, O Lord and Lover of souls; through Jesus Christ. Amen. *(Bishop Thomas Wilson, A.D. 1663.)*

Intercession for All Men.

MERCIFUL Lord, Who givest us more than we ask or think, do unto us and all who desire our prayers, and to all Thy Church and people, according to Thy mercy and goodness. Give health to the sick, rest to the weary and heavy-laden, comfort to the mourner; be a Father to the fatherless and a God of the widow; uphold them that are tempted; raise up them that fall; pardon and restore the penitent; strengthen us to run with patience our appointed race, and make us all such as Thou wouldst have us to be in all holy conversation and godliness; through Jesus Christ our Lord. Amen.

(Canon E. Hawkins, A.D. 1802.)

For Strength for the Duties of the Coming Week.

O GOD, most merciful Father, Thou speakest through Thine only begotten Son, our Lord Jesus Christ, saying: "Ask, and it shall be given unto you." Give us now Thy Holy Spirit, that our hearts may be strengthened for the work of this week; through Jesus Christ. Amen.

(Father John of the Russian Church, Nineteenth Century.)

For Defence in Temptation.

O THOU Who knowest our hearts, and Who seest our temptations and struggles, have pity upon us, and deliver us from the sins which make war upon our souls. Thou art all-powerful, and we are weak and erring. Our trust is in Thee, O Thou faithful God. Deliver us from the bondage of evil, and grant that we may hereafter be Thy devoted servants, serving Thee in the freedom of holy love; for Jesus Christ's sake. Amen.

(Rev. Eugène Bersier, A.D. 1831.)

A Prayer for Pardon.

GRANT us, O Lord, such true repentance as may, through the blood of Jesus Christ our Saviour, blot out the stains of our sins and iniquities. Forgive us our sins, O Lord; forgive us our sins for Thine infinite mercies' sake, and for the sake of Jesus Christ our Saviour. Amen. *(Archbishop Grindal, 1519.)*

For All Men.

O OUR Father, grant peace, happiness, and blessing; grace, favour, and mercy, unto all Thy people. Bless us, even all of us together, with the light of Thy countenance; for by the light of Thy face hast Thou given us, O Eternal God, the law of life, gracious love, righteousness, blessing, mercy, life, and peace. May it be pleasing in Thy sight to bless Thy people at all times, and at all seasons, with Thy peace; for Thy Name's sake. Amen. *(Daily Prayers of the Jews. Rabbi of Lissa.*
Jewish Calendar, 5671.)

For a Right Use of Wealth.

O LORD Jesus Christ, Who for our sakes didst become poor, we pray Thee to protect them that are rich in this world, that they may be not high-minded, nor trust in uncertain riches, but in Thee, the living God, Who givest us richly all things to enjoy. Grant them grace so to use their wealth that they may do good, and be rich in good works, ready to distribute and willing to communicate; laying up in store for themselves a good foundation against the time to come, that they may lay hold on eternal life; through Jesus Christ our Lord. Amen.

(Sursum Corda; 1 Tim. vi. 17; S. Paul, First Century A.D.)

For a Wise and Sympathetic Spirit.

GRACIOUS Lord, in Whom are laid up all the treasures of knowledge and wisdom, direct us in the ways of life, remove from us the ways of death. Give us a soft and meek spirit, that we may help the succourless, and comfort the comfortless. O our Lord, pardon us for the neglect of this duty, and make us to redeem the time with a cheerful constancy. Amen.

(The Penitent Pilgrim, A.D. 1641.)

For Harmony of Heart with God.

O MERCIFUL God, be Thou now unto us a strong tower of defence, we humbly entreat Thee. Give us grace to await Thy leisure, and patiently to bear what Thou doest unto us, nothing doubting, or mistrusting Thy goodness towards us; for Thou knowest what is good for us better than we do. Therefore do with us in all things what Thou wilt; only arm us, we beseech Thee, with Thine armour, that we may stand fast; above all things, taking to us the shield of faith, praying always that we may refer ourselves wholly to Thy will, abiding Thy pleasure, and comforting ourselves in those troubles which it shall please Thee to send us, seeing such troubles are profitable for us. We are assuredly persuaded that all Thou doest cannot but be well; and unto Thee be all honour and glory, both now and ever. Amen.   *(Lady Jane Grey, A.D. 1537.)*

An Intercession.

O LORD our heavenly Father, may our minds be kept throughout this day in a calm, peaceful, and collected state; may our hearts be freed from all unholy desires, and may our affections be regulated according to Thy righteous will. Though we be utterly unworthy of our high and holy calling as children of God, unworthy of any place in Thy Kingdom, yet, we beseech Thee, graciously to employ us for the honour of Thy Name, for the good of Thy people, for relief to those who are in want or misery, and for bringing souls to the knowledge of Thy Truth. Whatever openings Thy Providence may afford to any of us through the hours of this day, for the benefit of others, grant us grace and wisdom and courage to speak and to act for Thy glory, and for the welfare of those around us. May we be ready to give at all times and in all places a reason of the hope that is in us, with meekness and fear. May we be followers of God as dear children, giving no occasion of offence to any, but walking before all in honesty, sobriety, purity, godliness, and truth. Enable those in authority to rule with firmness, yet with all affection and tenderness, as becomes their calling. May those whose place it is to obey be diligent, and conscientious in all things as serving Thee, the living and true God; and give to all, the love which delights in helpfulness; for the sake of Jesus Christ our Lord. Amen.   *(E. J. P., A.D. 1843.)*

A Morning Supplication.

O LORD our God, as Thou hast in mercy preserved us to the beginning of another day, enable us by Thy grace to live to Thee, and to set our affections on things above, not on things upon the earth. Pour into our minds the light of Thy Truth and cause us to rejoice in Thy Word. Shed abroad Thy love in our hearts, and bestow upon us abundantly the peace and comfort of Thy Holy Spirit. Graciously increase in us that faith which works by love, which purifies the heart, and overcomes the world, that we may have the victory over every sin, and, according to Thy promise, do Thou bruise Satan under our feet shortly, and deliver us from all his soul-destroying power. Make us watchful against his devices, against all the evil of our hearts, and especially those sins which do most easily beset us; for the sake of Jesus Christ our Lord. Amen.

(Rev. Isaac Ashe, A.D. 1802.)

For Divine Blessing on Life's Callings.

O BLESSED Lord and loving Father, except Thou direct us we cannot stand, but shall fall into many sins; for no estate, no degree, no calling, office, function, or trade of life, can prosper or be rightly performed without Thy continual aid, direction, and providence. Therefore, Lord, guide us by Thy Spirit, increase our faith, give us wisdom and ableness in all things to execute our calling as we ought. Be present, good and gracious Father, with us, and grant that all things that we take in hand may begin in knowledge, proceed in fear of Thee, and end in love, that our whole course of life may be blessed by Thee; for the sake of Christ Jesus our Lord. Amen. *(J. Norden, A.D. 1548.)*

For the Household.

O ALMIGHTY God, look graciously upon this household as we are now gathered together in Thy Name. Give them whom Thou hast set over it, wisdom to direct those committed to their charge; give to all its members strength to fulfil Thy will in the daily work to which Thou hast appointed them. grant that love and peace with all other graces may live and grow among them, and that finally we may meet before Thy throne in heaven, and be united in Thy love for ever; through Jesus Christ our Lord. Amen.

(Edward Benson, Archbishop of Canterbury, A.D. 1829.)

For Surrender to God's Will.

L ORD, here we are, do with us as seemeth best in Thine own eyes, only give us, we humbly beseech Thee, a penitent and a patient spirit to expect Thee. Lord, make our service acceptable to Thee while we live, and our souls ready for Thee when we die; for the sake of Jesus Christ Thy Son our Saviour. Amen.

(Archbishop Laud, A.D. 1573.)

For Divine Assistance in Worship.

ALMIGHTY God, Whom the eye cannot behold, Whom we cannot hear with the hearing of the ear, still let us this day feel Thy Presence and know Thy love, and, being stirred and moved above ourselves, thus be lifted into the knowledge of God and the hearing of His holy way. Help us to worship Thee in spirit and in truth, and may this spiritual worship keep bright within us all the higher things of life; through Jesus Christ our Lord. Amen.   (*Rev. George Dawson,* A.D. 1821.)

For the Lonely.

LORD Jesus, we beseech Thee, by the loneliness of Thy suffering on the Cross, be nigh unto all them that are desolate, in pain or sorrow to-day; and let the beauty of Thy Presence transform their loneliness into comfort, consolation, and holy fellowship with Thee. Lord Jesus, Thou pitiful Saviour, hear us, we beseech Thee. Amen.   (*Sursum Corda,* A.D. 1898.)

A Prayer for Spiritual Blessings.

MOST high God, our loving Father, infinite in majesty, we humbly beseech Thee for all Thy servants everywhere, that Thou wouldst give us a pure mind, perfect love, sincerity in conduct, purity in heart, strength in action, courage in distress, self-command in character. May our prayers ascend to Thy gracious ears, and Thy loving benediction descend upon us all, that we may in all things be protected under the shadow of Thy wings. Grant us pardon of our sins; perfect our work; accept our prayers; protect us by Thine own Name, O God of Jacob; send us Thy saving help from Thy holy place, and strengthen us out of Zion. Remember all Thy people everywhere, give us all the grace of devotion to Thy will; fulfil our desires with good gifts, and crown us with Thy mercy. When we serve Thee with faithful devotion, pardon our sins and correct us with Fatherly tenderness. Grant that, being delivered from all adversity, and both here and eternally justified, we may praise Thee for ever and ever, saying, Holy, Holy, Holy; through Jesus Christ our Lord and Saviour, Who with Thee and the Holy Ghost, liveth and reigneth, ever one God, world without end. Amen.

(*Gallican Sacramentary.*)

For the Indian Princes.

WE make our prayer to Thee, O merciful God, for all Indian Princes and Rulers within the Empire, beseeching Thee so to guide and bless them, that under them Thy people may lead peaceable lives in all godliness and honesty; through Jesu Christ our Lord. Amen.

(*Adapted for use during the Royal Visit to India, November,* 1911.

Confession of Sin.

O THOU that beholdest all things, we have sinned against
Thee in thought, word, and deed; blot out our transgressions,
be merciful to us sinners, and grant that our names may be
found written in the book of life, for the sake of Christ Jesus our
Saviour. Amen.   (*St. Nerses of Clajes, Fourth Century.*)

For Loyal Service.

O ETERNAL God, Who hast made all things for man, and
man for Thy glory; sanctify our bodies and souls, our
thoughts and our intentions, our words and actions, that whatsoever we shall think, or speak, or do this day, may be by us,
designed to the glorification of Thy Name, and by Thy blessing
it may be effective and successful in the work of God, according
as it can be capable. Let our body be a servant of our mind,
and both body and spirit servants of Jesus Christ, that doing all
things for Thy glory here we may be partakers of Thy glory
hereafter; through Jesus Christ our Lord. Amen.
                        (*Bishop Jeremy Taylor, A.D. 1613.*)

For All Christian Institutions.

VOUCHSAFE, we beseech Thee, merciful Lord, to prosper with
Thy blessing all institutions designed for the promotion of
Thy glory and the spiritual good of Thy people. Grant that
those who serve Thee in religious homes, hospitals, and schools,
may set Thy holy will ever before them, and do that which is
well-pleasing in Thy sight, and persevere in Thy service unto
the end; through Jesus Christ our Lord. Amen.
                        (*Cuddesdon Manual, Nineteenth Century.*)

For the King.

MAY God of His goodness and love keep me/our King on
my/his throne in honour. Amen.
        (*Canute King of England, A.D. 994.   Reigned 1016–1035.*)

A Prayer for Divine Help.

STRETCH forth, O Lord, Thy mercy over all Thy servants
everywhere, even the right hand of heavenly help, that they
may seek Thee with their whole heart, and obtain what they
rightly ask for; through Jesus Christ our Lord. Amen.
                        (*Gelasian Sacramentary.*)

For the Spirit of Christ.

GRANT that the meek and humble spirit of the lowly Jesus
may dwell and reign within our hearts, and in following the
steps of His most holy life may we enjoy that peace which
passeth all understanding, and know the power of Thy Spirit,
bearing witness with our spirits, that we are indeed Thy children;
through Jesus Christ our Lord. Amen.
                        (*Rev. Isaac Ashe, A.D. 1802.*)

For Acceptable Worship.

O ALMIGHTY God, from Whom every good prayer cometh, and Who pourest out on all who desire it the spirit of grace and supplication, deliver us, when we draw nigh to Thee, from coldness of heart and wanderings of mind, that with steadfast thoughts and kindled affections we may worship Thee in spirit and in truth; through Jesus Christ our Lord.   Amen.

(William Bright, A.D. 1824.)

For the Operation of the Holy Spirit.

O BLESSED Spirit, Who dost teach us all things, and in Whom is the Spring of Divine Wisdom and Grace that issues forth from the Throne of God for the healing of the Nations; enlighten the conscience of this people, that we, relying only upon Thee, and not trusting in any human devices, may be led into the way of truth, and by Thy Divine power may bring about in God's own time the victorious reign of justice on the earth; Who with the Father and the Son livest and reignest one God, world without end.   Amen.   *(Social Prayers, Nineteenth Century.)*

For the Ministry.

O GOD, Who makest Thine angels spirits and Thy ministers a flame of fire, vouchsafe, we beseech Thee, to stir up and confirm the sacred grace in all stewards of Thy mysteries, that as ministering spirits they may gather out of Thy Kingdom all things that offend, and may kindle in the hearts of all, that fire which Thou camest to send upon the earth; Who with the Father and the Holy Ghost, livest and reignest, ever world without end. Amen.   *(Henry P. Liddon, Canon of St. Paul's, A.D. 1829.)*

For Right Intentions in Prayer.

G RANT, O Lord, that our petitions may always be for those things that may fit us to please Thee, and not for such as may be the fittest to please ourselves; and for an accumulation of blessings, so influence our souls with Thy Divine Spirit, that Thy will may ever be our pleasure; through Jesus Christ our Lord.   Amen.   *(Charles How, A.D. 1661.)*

For Union with God's Purposes.

A LMIGHTY God, of Thy fulness grant to us who need so much, who lack so much, who have so little, wisdom and strength.   Bring our wills unto Thine.   Lift our understandings into Thy heavenly light, that we thereby beholding those things which are right, and being drawn by Thy love, may bring our will and our understanding together to Thy service, until at last, body and soul and spirit may be all Thine, and Thou be our Father and our eternal Friend; through Jesus Christ our Lord.   Amen.   *(Rev. George Dawson, A.D. 1821.)*

CONFIDENCE IN GOD'S PROVIDENCE.

GRANT unto us, Almighty God, the peace of God that passeth understanding, that we, amid the storms and troubles of this our life, may rest in Thee, knowing that all things are in Thee; not beneath Thine eye only, but under Thy care, governed by Thy will, guarded by Thy love, so that with a quiet heart we may see the storms of life, the cloud and the thick darkness, ever rejoicing to know that the darkness and the light are both alike to Thee. Guide, guard, and govern us even to the end, that none of us may fail to lay hold upon the immortal life; through Jesus Christ our Lord. Amen. (*Rev. G. Dawson*, A.D. 1821.)

FOR THE GENTLENESS OF CHRIST.

O LORD and Saviour Christ, Who camest not to strive nor cry, but to let Thy words fall as the drops that water the earth, grant all who contend for the Faith once delivered, never to injure it by clamour and impatience; but speaking Thy precious Truth in love, so to present it, that it may be loved, and that men may see it in Thy goodness and Thy beauty; who livest and reignest with the Father and the Holy Ghost, ever one God, world without end. Amen. (*William Bright*, A.D. 1824.)

FOR THE SICK AND SUFFERING.

O CHRIST our Lord, Who art the Physician of salvation, grant unto all who are sick the aid of heavenly healing. Look upon all faithful people who are sick and who love to call upon Thy Name, and take their souls into Thy keeping, and vouchsafe to deliver them from all sickness and infirmity; through Jesus Christ. Amen. (*Mozarabic Liturgy*.)

PRAISE.

GREAT art Thou, O Lord, and greatly to be praised; great is Thy power, and Thy wisdom is infinite. Thee would we praise without ceasing. Thou callest us to delight in Thy praise, for Thou hast made us for Thyself, and our hearts find no rest until we rest in Thee; Who with the Father and the Holy Ghost all glory, praise, and honour be ascribed, both now and for evermore. Amen. (*St. Augustine*, A.D. 354.)

A PETITION.

AND now, we beseech Thee Lord Jesus, that to whom Thou dost vouchsafe sweet draughts of the words of Thy knowledge, Thou wilt also, of Thy goodness, grant that we may, in due time, come to Thee, the fountain of all wisdom, and ever stand before Thy face; for Thy sake. Amen.

(*Venerable Bede*, A.D. 673.)

For Cheerfulness.

O GOD, Who hast folded back the mantle of the night to clothe us in the golden glory of the day, chase from our hearts all gloomy thoughts, and make us glad with the brightness of hope, that we may effectively aspire to unwon virtues, through Jesus Christ our Lord. Amen.

(Bishop Brent (20th Century), American Church.)

For the Gift of the Holy Spirit.

O GOD, Whose blessed Son hast taught us to call Thee our Father, and hast told us that, as a father gives good things to his children, so Thou wilt give the Holy Spirit to those that ask Thee, we ask Thee for this great gift. We need to be mightily strengthened by Thy Holy Spirit in the inner man, that we may love the thing that Thou commandest, and desire that which Thou dost promise. We pray that He will enlighten our understandings and purify our hearts, that so we may be filled with the love of Christ our Saviour; and having learnt to love Him with all our hearts, may we walk in His footsteps, and serve Him in holiness and pureness of living, to Thy honour and glory; through the same Thy Son Jesus Christ our Lord. Amen.

(Rev. F. P. Wickham, A.D. 1871.)

For Mutual Sympathy.

A LMIGHTY God, our heavenly Father, of Thy loving kindness and tender mercy help us to help one another in the way of life; and, by due understanding of Thy Word, grant that we may know Thy mind concerning us, and conform ourselves thereto, and so at last lay hold upon eternal life; through Jesus Christ our Lord. Amen. *(Rev. George Dawson, A.D. 1821.)*

For our Friends.

O FOUNTAIN of love, love Thou our friends and teach them to love Thee with all their hearts, that they may think and speak and do only such things as are well-pleasing to Thee; through Jesus Christ our Lord. Amen. *(St. Anselm, A.D. 1033.)*

For Acceptance of God's Will.

O GOD, the Redeemer of our souls, and the Comforter of them that mourn, Whose will is our peace, and to Whom obedience is true freedom, grant us to be led by Thy Holy Spirit, that we may be free from vain hopes and repinings, and from all wrong desires; but may we through patience have experience, and through experience hope, and not be ashamed of hoping in Thee, our Father and our Friend, Whose holy will be done, now and for ever. Amen. *(Rev. Rowland Williams, A.D. 1818.)*

For Love to God.

O GOD, Who hast commanded all men to love Thee, and hast drawn them to Thyself by Thy mercy and goodness; fill our hearts with the love of Thee. We are weak and sinful, and cannot love Thee enough without Thy help. All our desire is to give Thee the service of loving hearts all the days of our life, and to love Thee throughout the ages of eternity; through Jesus Christ our Lord. Amen.   *(The Narrow Way, A.D. 1869.)*

For Light.

ALMIGHTY and everlasting God, at evening, and morning, and noonday, we humbly beseech Thee That Thou wouldst drive from our hearts the darkness of sin, and make us to come to the true Light, which is Christ; through the same Jesus Christ Thy Son. Amen.   *(Gelasian Sacramentary.)*

For Perfect Trust in God.

O LORD, our heavenly Father, Who orderest all things for our eternal good, mercifully enlighten our minds, and give us a firm and abiding trust in Thy love and care. Silence our murmurings, quiet our fears, and dispel our doubts, that, rising above our afflictions and our anxieties, we may rest on Thee, the Rock of everlasting Strength; through Jesus Christ our Lord. Amen.   *(New Book of Worship, A.D. 1876.)*

For Women's Work among Women and Children.

GRACIOUS Lord, Who wast born of a woman, Who didst accept the ministry of women, and Who didst take into Thine arms little children to bless them, be present, we pray Thee, with the women who now minister for Thee to their sisters in heathen and Moslem countries; and be with all those to whom Thou hast given the care of children to be brought up in Thy fear and love. By means of these Thy servants raise the women of these lands to know and enjoy the blessing and honour that Thou didst purpose for women, and so give Thy Word that great may be the company of the women who labour in the Lord, and carry into darkened homes the light of Thy Presence and the joy of Thy peace; hear us for Thy Name's sake. Amen.   *(Church Missionary Society, A.D. 1799.)*

For our Relations and Friends and All Men.

WE commend to Thy loving-kindness, O God, all our relations and friends, that they may be filled with Thy grace. Have mercy on all sick and dying persons, all who are suffering or in sorrow, and grant to all who are living in error, or ignorance, or sin, the grace of repentance; through Jesus Christ our Lord. Amen.   *(Rev. T. T. Carter, A.D. 1808.)*

Confession, and a Prayer for Usefulness.

O OUR God, we would not hide our daily shortcomings from Thee. Oh! forgive us in Christ. Our Father, never let us be without the indwelling of Thy Holy Spirit for an hour. Let our lives be every day more unconscious of our own presence and more conscious of Thine. Make us instruments in Thy hand for advancing Thy Kingdom, and for uniting all Christians in this land; for the sake of Him Who loved us, and died for us, ever Jesus Christ our Saviour. Amen.

(Dr. Norman Macleod, A.D. 1812.)

For Heavenly-Mindedness.

A LMIGHTY God, Who hast caused the light of eternal life to shine upon the world, we beseech Thee that our hearts may be so kindled with heavenly desires, and Thy love so shed abroad in us by Thy Holy Spirit, that we may continually seek the things which are above; and, abiding in purity of heart and mind, may at length attain unto Thine everlasting Kingdom, there to dwell in the glorious light of Thy Presence, world without end. Amen.   *(Book of Prayers, A.D. 1851.)*

A Prayer for All Men.

O LORD our God, Whose providence extends over all Thy creatures, we beseech Thee to hear us in behalf of Thy Holy Church, which Thou hast redeemed with the precious blood of Thy Son. Bless all bishops, pastors, and ministers who are separated for Thy ministry, that they may adorn it by purity of life, and diligently and faithfully feed Thy flock committed to their charge. Bless our Sovereign Lord the King, that he may abide in Thy fear, and govern Thy people in righteousness. Bless all the Royal Family. Have pity upon all widows and the fatherless, the sick and the needy, and abundantly sustain them by Thy heavenly grace. Accept also our intercessions, however unworthy, for our relations, friends, and benefactors; be gracious unto them, and enrich them by Thy heavenly gifts. Turn the hearts of any who may be enemies to us, and deliver both them and us from all envy, hatred, and malice, and keep us all in unity of spirit and in the bond of peace. Finally, grant to us and to Thy whole Church blameless lives, happy and prepared deaths, and hereafter an eternal possession and enjoyment of Thy heavenly kingdom; through the merits and mediation of Thy blessed Son, Jesus Christ our Lord. Amen.

(Canon E. Hawkins, A.D. 1802.)

For Peace.

S O teach us to number our days that we may apply our hearts unto wisdom. Lighten, if it be Thy will, the pressure of this world's cares, and, above all, reconcile us to Thy will, and give us a peace which the world cannot take away; through Jesus Christ our Lord. Amen. *(Dr. Chalmers, A.D. 1780.)*

THAT WE MAY "ASK ACCORDING TO HIS WILL."

WE beseech Thee, O Lord, to look upon Thy servants, Whom Thou hast enabled to put their trust in Thee, and grant us both to ask such things as shall please Thee, and also to obtain what we ask; through Jesus Christ our Lord.   Amen.

(Leonine Sacramentary.)

REMEMBRANCE OF OUR LORD'S PASSION.

O LORD, do Thou, in Thy great mercy, keep us from forgetting what Thou hast suffered for us in body and soul.   May we never be drawn by the cares of this life from Jesus our Friend and Saviour, but may we daily live closer to His Cross. Above all, would we ask Thee to fill us with the Holy Ghost; through Jesus Christ. Amen. *(Capt. Hedley Vicars, A.D. 1826.)*

FOR GROWTH IN GRACE.

GUIDE us, teach us, and strengthen us, O Lord, we beseech Thee, until we become such as Thou wouldst have us be; pure, gentle, truthful, high-minded, courteous, generous, able, dutiful and useful; for Thy honour and glory.   Amen.

(Rev. Charles Kingsley, A.D. 1819.)

FOR AN INCREASE OF CHRISTIAN WORKERS.

O GOD, Who on the Day of Pentecost didst send down tongues of fire on the heads of Thy holy Apostles, to teach them and lead them unto all truth, giving them boldness with fervent zeal to preach the Gospel to all nations; raise up, we pray Thee, Thy power and come among Thy people, and with great might succour us.   Bless, O Lord, all Thy servants everywhere; give the Holy Spirit to all who teach and all who learn; send forth men and women full of faith and of the Holy Ghost, mighty in the Scriptures, and able ministers of the New Testament.   Let Thy ministers be examples to their flock in word, in conversation, in charity, in spirit, in faith, in purity; workmen that need not be ashamed, rightly dividing the Word of Truth, prepared and willing to endure affliction, to do the work of evangelists, and to make full proof of their ministry; and upon the seed of Thy Word sown by them pour down, O Lord, we beseech Thee, the continual dew of Thy heavenly blessing, that it may take root downwards, and bear fruit upwards, to Thy honour and glory, and to a joyful ingathering of a spiritual harvest of souls at the great day of harvest, to glorify for ever Thy holy Name; through Jesus Christ our Lord.   Amen.

(Archbishop Benson, A.D. 1829.)

FOR CHRISTIAN PERFECTION.

O LORD, may Thy all-powerful grace make us as perfect as Thou hast commanded us to be; through Jesus Christ. Amen. *(Bishop Wilson, A.D. 1663.)*

For the Defence of Christ's Church.

O LORD, we beseech Thee to keep Thy Church and household continually in Thy true religion, that they who do lean only upon the hope of Thy heavenly grace may evermore be defended by Thy mighty power; through Jesus Christ our Lord.   Amen.

(Gregorian Sacramentary.)

For Reverence of Parents.

THOU hast given a commandment in Thy law, O heavenly Father, that children should honour their parents. We most humbly beseech Thee, therefore, to breathe Thy Holy Spirit in the hearts of the children of our nation, that they may reverence their parents not only with outward forms, but also obey them both in word and deed so far as lieth in their power; that Thou, seeing their hearty goodwill, may become their heavenly Father, and that they may be numbered amongst Thy children whom Thou hast appointed from everlasting, heirs of Thy glorious Kingdom; through Thy well-beloved Son Jesus Christ our Lord.   Amen.   *(Rev. Thomas Becon, A.D. 1512.)*

For a Christ-like Spirit.

O GRACIOUS Father, keep us through Thy Holy Spirit; keep our hearts soft and tender now in health and amidst the bustle of the world; keep the thought of Thyself present to us as our Father in Jesus Christ; and keep alive in us a spirit of love and meekness to all men, that we may be at once gentle and active and firm. O strengthen us to bear pain, or sickness, or danger, or whatever Thou shalt be pleased to lay upon us as Christ's soldiers and servants, and let our faith overcome the world daily. Perfect and bless the work of Thy Holy Spirit in the hearts of all Thy people, and may Thy Kingdom come, and Thy will be done in earth as it is in heaven. We pray for this, and for all that Thou seest us to need; for Jesus Christ's sake.   Amen.   *(Dr. Thomas Arnold, A.D. 1795.)*

A Prayer for the Moslem World.

O GOD, our Father in heaven, hear us as we pray to Thee for the millions of the Moslem world, who know Thee not as their Father, nor understand Thy love to us in Jesus Christ our Lord. Take from them all ignorance, hardness of heart, and contempt of Thy Word, and lead them to Him Who came to be the Way, the Truth, and the Life. We pray Thee for all Christians living in Moslem lands: wilt Thou give them a special measure of Thy grace, that they may show forth the love and gentleness and purity of Christ.

O Lord Jesus, wilt Thou be very near to all who are preaching Thy Name among those who in blindness deny Thee; give them courage and grace to endure, and may Thy love constrain us to give our lives to Thee for Thy glory; for Thy Name's sake.
Amen.   *(Church Missionary Society, A.D. 1799.)*

For a Right Understanding of Life's Responsibilities.

O SOURCE of life and strength, many of Thy mercies do we plainly see, and we believe in a boundless store behind. None can have deeper call than we for grateful joy. Thou hast given us a life of high vocation, and Thine own breathing in our hearts interprets for us its sacred opportunities. Thou hast cheered the way with many dear affections, and glimpses of solemn beauty and everlasting truth. Not a cloud of sorrow, but Thou hast touched with glory; not a dusty atmosphere of care, but Thy light shines through; and, lest our spirits should fail before Thine unattainable perfections, Thou hast set us in the train of Thy saints, who have learned to take up the cross of sacrifice. Let the time past suffice to have wrought our own will, and now make us consecrate all to Thine; through Jesus Christ our Lord. Amen.

(James Martineau, Published A.D. 1891.)

For the Lonely.

BE Thou, O God, we beseech Thee, with the lonely and the desolate; sanctify their solitude with a closer sense of Thy Presence and protection, and lead them by Thy Holy Spirit to satisfy the longings of their hearts by abiding in the Communion of Thy Saints; through Jesus Christ. Amen.

(Hon. Mrs. Lyttelton Gell, Nineteenth Century.)

For National Peace.

WE beseech Thee, O Lord, be gracious to our times; that both national quietness and Christian devotion may be duly maintained by Thy bounty; through Jesus Christ our Lord. Amen.   *(Leonine Sacramentary.)*

A Prayer for the Clergy and People.

ALMIGHTY and everlasting God, Who alone workest great marvels; send down upon our Bishops and Curates, and all congregations committed to their charge, the healthful spirit of Thy grace; and that they may truly please Thee, pour upon them the continual dew of Thy blessing. Grant this, O Lord, for the honour of our Advocate and Mediator Jesus Christ. Amen.   *(Gelasian Sacramentary: B. of C. P.,* A.D. 1662.)

For Happy and Loyal Service.

GIVE us, O Lord, a mind after Thine own heart, that we may delight to do Thy will, O our God; and let Thy Law be written on our hearts. Give us courage and resolution to do our duty, and a heart to be spent in Thy service, and in doing all the good that possibly we can the few remaining days of our pilgrimage here on earth. Grant this, we humbly beseech Thee for the sake of Jesus Christ Thy Son our Lord. Amen.

(Archbishop John Tillotson, A.D. 1630.)

For Acceptable Worship.

O OUR God, we humbly beseech Thee to purify our hearts from all vain and worldly and sinful thoughts, and so prepare our souls to worship Thee this day acceptably, with reverence and godly fear. O Lord, set our affection on things above all the day long, and give us grace to receive Thy Word which we shall hear this day, into honest and good hearts, and bring forth fruit with patience. Hear us, O God, for the sake of Jesus Christ our Saviour. Amen. *(Bishop Hamilton, A.D. 1561.)*

Self-Dedication.

O THOU in Whom we live and move and have our being, we offer and present unto Thee our souls and our bodies, our thoughts and our desires, our words and our deeds, to be a living and continual sacrifice. We are not our own, therefore would we glorify Thee in our bodies and in our spirits which are Thine; through Jesus Christ our Lord. Amen.

(Professor Knight, Nineteenth Century.)

Intercession.

B LESS, we pray Thee, good Lord, all who are set over us in Church and State; our friends and neighbours, and all belonging to us. Help those that are in trouble, bring back those who are gone astray, give strength to the weak, and light to the blind, and more grace to those who know and serve Thee; through Jesus Christ our Lord. Amen.

(Rev. Thomas Furlong, Nineteenth Century.)

For the Spread of Christ's Kingdom in the World.

E NLARGE Thy kingdom, O God, and deliver the world from the dominion and tyranny of Satan. Hasten the time, which Thy Spirit hath foretold, when all nations, Whom Thou hast made shall worship Thee, and glorify Thy Name. Bless the good endeavours of those who strive to propagate the Truth, and prepare the hearts of all men to receive it; to the honour of Thy holy Name. Amen. *(Bishop Wilson, A.D. 1663.)*

A New Song.

I NSTRUCT our mouth, O good Lord, with a new song, that our hearts being renewed, we may sing in the company of Thy saints, and rejoice in Thee our Creator and Redeemer. Let us possess such peace of conscience, that may strengthen work in Thee, and being girt with the two-edged sword of Thy Word and Holy Spirit, we may strive against all things that oppose themselves to the glory of Thy most holy Name; and that through Jesus Christ Thy dear Son, our only Lord and Redeemer. So be it. *(Scottish Psalter, A.D. 1595.)*

For an Answer to Prayer.

HEAR our voice, O Eternal God; pity and compassionate us, and receive our prayers with mercy and favour, for Thou art the God Who hearkeneth to prayers and supplications. Therefore from Thy Presence dismiss us not empty, O our King, for Thou dost in mercy hearken unto the prayer of Thy people; for the honour of Thy great Name. Amen.

(*Daily Prayers of the Jews, Jewish Calendar*, 5671.)

For Protection.

O GOD, Whose never-failing providence ordereth all things both in heaven and earth; we humbly beseech Thee to put away from us all hurtful things, and to give us those things which are profitable for us; through Jesus Christ our Lord. Amen.   (*Gelasian Sacramentary: B. of C. P.*, A.D. 1549.)

An Intercession for All Men.

O THOU, Who art the confidence of all the ends of the earth, remember every work of Thy hand for good, and visit the world in Thy mercy. O Thou the God of grace and truth, establish all who stand in Thy truth and grace, and restore all who labour under heresy or sin. O Thou the Lord of the harvest, send forth labourers into Thy harvest, and make them sufficient for their work. Grant unto Thy ministers that they may rightly divide the Word of Truth, and themselves walk uprightly in the same. O Lord of lords, and King of kings, be mindful of all Princes whom Thou hast deputed to rule on earth, and especially be mindful of our gracious King, Thy servant. Assist him more and more, and prosper him in all things; suggest good counsels unto his heart, for Thy Church and for Thy people's sake; grant and continue unto him profound peace, that we all, partaking of his peace, may lead a quiet life in all godliness and honesty; through Jesus Christ our Lord. Amen.

(*Bishop Hamilton*, A.D. 1561.)

"Teach us Thy Way."

GIVE ear, O Lord, unto our prayer, and attend unto the voice of our supplications. Teach us Thy way, O Lord. We will walk in Thy Truth. Unite our hearts to fear Thy Name. We will praise Thee, O Lord our God, with all our heart, and we will glorify Thy Name for evermore; for great is Thy mercy towards us. Amen. (*Ps.* lxxxvi. 6-13; *King David, Eleventh Century B.C.*)

Commendation.

O LORD, preserve us this day and strengthen us to bear whatever Thou shalt see fit to lay on us, whether pain, sickness, danger or distress; through Jesus Christ our Lord. Amen.

(*Dr. Arnold*, A.D. 1795.)

For Protection.

WE pray Thee, O Lord, be present to Thy suppliants, and amid the snares of a wicked world protect our weakness with Thy never-failing love; through Jesus Christ our Lord. Amen. *(Gelasian Sacramentary.)*

For Peace and a Quiet Mind.

O LORD, this is all our desire—to walk along the path of life that Thou hast appointed us, even as Jesus our Lord would walk along it, in steadfastness of faith, in meekness of spirit, in lowliness of heart, in gentleness of love. And because outward events have so much power in scattering our thoughts and disturbing the inward peace in which alone the voice of Thy Spirit is heard, do Thou, gracious Lord, calm and settle our souls, by that subduing power which alone can bring all thoughts and desires of the heart into captivity to Thyself. All we have is Thine; do Thou with all as seemeth best to Thy Divine will, for we know not what is best. Let not the cares or duties of this life press on us too heavily; but lighten our burdens, that we may follow Thy way in quietness, filled with thankfulness for Thy mercy, and rendering acceptable service unto Thee; through Jesus Christ our Lord. Amen. *(Maria Hare, A.D. 1798.)*

For Schools and Schoolchildren.

GRANT we beseech Thee, O Lord Jesus, that all those in our schools may seek to find out what Thou wouldest have them to do in life, and earnestly strive to follow Thee, Who in Thy boyhood didst choose to do Thy Father's business; for Thy Name's sake. Amen. *(Original source not found.)*

For Guidance and Discernment in All Undertakings.

ALMIGHTY and eternal God, Who fillest all space, Whom nevertheless no space can contain; from Thee, as the source of all things, we have our being; to Thee, as the end of all things, we draw near. We acknowledge that every good and perfect gift is from above. May Thy blessing, therefore, descend upon us Thy servants who apply ourselves to our work or studies; inspire us in our enterprises, help on our endeavours, promote our designs, purify our minds that yearn to know themselves and Thee. Be present with us and direct such works as we undertake in dependence on Thee and devote to Thy honour. O Father of lights, give us discernment to know the truth. O Father of spirits, give us courage to uphold what we know to be true. O Prince of Peace, grant us wisdom to labour for peace, to uproot evil, to worship Thee with one heart and one mouth, and to pay Thee due reverence, to the glory of Thy Name, the good of Thy Church, the increase of piety, and the salvation of our own souls; through Jesus Christ Thy Son our Lord. Amen. *(Bishop John Pearson, A.D. 1613.)*

A Morning Commendation.

WHAT shall befall us hereafter we know not; but to God, Who cares for all men, Who will one day reveal the secrets of all hearts, we commit ourselves wholly, with all who are near. and dear to us. And we beseech the same most merciful and Almighty God, that for the time to come we may so bear the reproach of Christ with unbroken courage, as ever to remember that here we have no continuing city, but may seek one to come, by the grace and mercy of our Lord Jesus Christ; to Whom with the Father, and the Holy Ghost, be all honour and dominion, world without end. Amen.

(Matthew Parker, Archbishop of Canterbury, A.D. 1504.)

For Cheerful Service.

WE would walk through this world cheerfully and hopefully, seeking evermore to serve Thee with faithful hearts. Inspire us with the pure love of righteousness. Help us to resist what is evil, and to cleave to that which is good. Give us a wise and understanding heart to do Thy holy will. Grant us the spirit of graciousness and true humility, that in lowliness of mind we may esteem others better than ourselves. Help us to bear each other's burdens, and to do good to all men as we have opportunity, remembering the words of the Lord Jesus, how He said: "It is more blessed to give than to receive." Grant this, we humbly beseech Thee, for the sake of Jesus Christ our Lord. Amen. *(Professor Knight, Nineteenth Century.)*

For Missionaries and Students for the Ministry.

O EVERLASTING God, Who art ever adored by the holy angels, yet dost choose men to be the stewards of Thy mysteries; bless, we beseech Thee, all Thy missionary servants, and all those who are preparing and training for Thy work, that they who cannot do any good without Thee, may by Thee be illuminated with a true knowledge of Thy Word and Sacraments, and so being made able ministers of the New Testament, may advance Thy glory and the salvation of those who know Thee not; through Jesus Christ our Lord. Amen.

(Canon Henry Parry Liddon, A.D. 1829.)

For Protection of Soul and Body.

MAY the power of the Father govern us. May the wisdom of the Son enlighten us. May the operation of the Holy Spirit quicken us. O God, we beseech Thee guard our souls; sustain our bodies; exalt our senses; direct our course; regulate our manners; bless our undertakings; fulfil our petitions; inspire us with holy thoughts; pardon what is past; rectify what is present; order what is to come; and all for the sake of Jesus Christ our Lord and Saviour, Who alone can make us perfect even as He is perfect. Amen. *(Bishop Andrewes, A.D. 1555.)*

For Light.

ARISE, O Sun of Righteousness, upon us, with healing in Thy wings; make us children of the light and of the day! Show us the way in which we should walk, for unto Thee, O Lord, do we lift up our souls. Dispel all mists of ignorance which cloud our understandings. Let no false suggestion either withdraw our hearts from the love of Thy truth, or from the practice of it in all the actions of our lives; for the sake of Jesus Christ our Lord. Amen.   (*Bishop Sherlock*, A.D. 1678.)

For a Sympathetic and Loyal Service.

O GOD, the Father of the forsaken, the Help of the weak, the Supplier of the needy, Who hast diffused and proportioned Thy gifts to body and soul, in such sort that all may acknowledge and perform the joyous duty of mutual service; Who teachest us that love towards the race of men is the bond of perfectness, and the imitation of Thy Blessed Self; open our eyes and touch our hearts, that we may see and do, both for this world and for that which is to come, the things which belong to our peace. Strengthen us in the work we have undertaken; give us counsel and wisdom, perseverance, faith and zeal, and in Thine own good time, and according to Thy pleasure, prosper the issue. Pour into us a spirit of humility; let nothing be done but in devout obedience to Thy will, thankfulness for Thine unspeakable mercies, and love to Thine adorable Son Christ Jesus, Who with Thee, O Father, and the Holy Ghost, ever liveth one God, world without end. Amen.

(*Anthony Ashley Cooper, Earl of Shaftesbury*, A.D. 1801.)

A General Intercession.

BLESSED Lord, Who commandest us to watch and pray, we draw near to Thee at this time; hear us and answer us, we humbly beseech Thee, O Lord. We pray for one another, that Thou wilt bless Thine inheritance; feed them, and lift them up for ever. We pray for the peace of the Church and all its members, that they may live in unity and concord. We pray for all Who are sick or afflicted, that Thou the God of all comfort, will comfort them and make all their bed in their sickness. We pray for the poor and needy that Thou wilt satisfy every longing soul, and fill the hungry soul with goodness. For those who love and pray for us, we pray that Thou, O Father, wilt bless them. We pray for all in authority, our King, our Queen, and all the Royal Family. We pray, O Lord, for all men, and finally for this household and all our different families, that Thine everlasting arms may be underneath, that Thou wilt supply all our need both this day and evermore; for the sake of Jesus Christ our Lord and Saviour. Amen.

(*An old Bidding Prayer*, A.D. 1706.)

For Peace and Trustfulness.

GRANT unto us, Almighty God, the knowledge of Thy way, and the spirit of obedience thereunto, that being conformed in thought and words unto Thy way, Thy peace may rule in our hearts. Help us to cast out all those things which are contrary to Thy peace, or that are not according to Thy will, that so ours may be the quiet life of trust, and faith, and obedience, living lowly, longing for Thy truth, and walking in the light thereof, that Thy blessing may be upon us, and the light of Thy countenance our perpetual delight. Hear us of Thy mercy; through Jesus Christ our Lord. Amen.

(Rev. George Dawson, A.D. 1821.)

For Divine Strength.

WE confess unto Thee, O God, how weak we are in ourselves, how powerless to do the work of life, how prone to selfishness and sin. We beseech Thee to grant us strength, the strength of Thy Spirit, the power of Thy Christ, wherein we can do all things. Enable us thus to repress every selfish propensity, every wilful purpose, every unkind feeling, every thought and word and deed of anger and impatience, and to cherish perfect love, constant kindness, to think pure thoughts, to speak gentle words, to do helpful and generous deeds. Raise our minds to the contemplation of Thy beloved Son, that, seeing His Divine beauty, we may be drawn near unto Him, and changed into His image, and empowered to bring every thought into obedience to Christ, into harmony to His Spirit and His immortal life; for His sake we ask it. Amen. *(Rev. Thomas T. Stone, A.D. 1801.)*

Confidence in God's Love and Mercy.

WE thank Thee, O God, the Father of our Lord Jesus Christ, that Thou hast revealed Thy Son to us, on Whom we have believed, Whom we have loved, and Whom we worship. O Lord Jesus Christ, we commend our souls to Thee. O heavenly Father, we know that although we shall in Thine own good time be taken away from this life, we shall live for ever with Thee. "God so loved the world, that He gave His only begotten Son, that whosoever believeth in Him should not perish, but have everlasting life." Father, into Thy hands we commend our spirits; through Jesus Christ our Lord. Amen.

(Martin Luther, A.D. 1483.)

For the Gift of Sympathy.

BLESSED be God, even the Father of our Lord Jesus Christ, the Father of mercies, and the God of all comfort, Who comforteth us in all our tribulation. Grant that we may be able to comfort them which are in any trouble by the comfort wherewith we ourselves are comforted of God; through Jesus Christ our Lord. Amen.

(St. Paul, First Century, A.D.; 2 Cor. i. 3, 4.)

"For the Peace of God, which passeth all Understanding."

O GOD Who art Peace everlasting, Whose chosen reward is the gift of peace, and Who hast taught us that the peace-makers are Thy children, pour Thy peace into our souls, that everything discordant may utterly vanish, and all that makes for peace be sweet to us for ever; through Jesus Christ our Lord. Amen.   (*Mozarabic Liturgy.*)

For Grace and Deliverance.

FEED Thy people, O Lord, with Thy grace, and deliver our souls from the death of sin; so that, being filled with Thy mercy, we may be united with the joys of the righteous; through Jesus Christ our Lord. Amen.   (*Sarum Breviary.*)

For the Ministry at Home and Abroad.

MOST blessed Saviour, Who hast appointed divers orders of men in Thy Church, look graciously at this time upon Thy ministering servants. Endue them with Thy Holy Spirit; make them apt to teach, gentle to persuade, and wise to win souls; cheer and comfort them in their labours; feed them with the Bread of Life; bless them in their labours, and make them willing to spend and be spent for Thee. Lord Jesus, let Thine especial favour rest upon those who are preaching Thy Gospel to the heathen, and those who know Thee not. Support them amidst all their trials, and grant that the word spoken by their mouths may have such success, that it may never be spoken in vain. Hasten, Lord, the time when they shall no more teach every man his neighbour and every man his brother, saying: "Know the Lord, for all shall know Thee, from the least to the greatest." Grant this for Thine own Name's sake. Amen.   (*Bishop Ashton Oxenden,* A.D. 1808.)

For those in Special Need.

WE beseech Thee to hear us, O God, for all who are worn by illness; all who are wronged and oppressed; all who are suffering for righteousness' sake; the weary and heavy-laden; the aged and the dying, that they may be strengthened by Thy might, consoled by Thy love, and cherished by Thy Fatherly pity; through Jesus Christ our Saviour. Amen.
                              (*Rev. Dr. John Hunter,* A.D. 1849.)

Commendation.

INTO Thy hands, O Lord, we solemnly commend our souls and bodies, and we beseech Thee to keep us this day in safety under Thy protection. Strengthen us for Thy service on the morrow; through Jesus Christ our Lord, to Whom with Thee and the Holy Ghost be all honour and glory, world without end. Amen.   (*Archbishop Laud,* A.D. 1573.)

For Blessing.

BLESS all who worship Thee, from the rising of the sun unto the going down of the same. Of Thy goodness, give us; with Thy love, inspire us; by Thy spirit, guide us; by Thy power protect us; in Thy mercy, receive us now and always. Amen.
(An Ancient Collect.)

Tranquillity and Renewal of Strength.

GOD of all grace, grant unto us Thy peace that passeth understanding, that the quietness that comes from friendliness with man, and true Divine friendship with Thee may possess our souls; that we, withdrawn awhile from the turmoil of the world, may gather the strength that we have lost, and established and strengthened by Thy grace, pass on through all the troubles of this our earthly life, safe into the haven of eternal rest; this we ask through Jesus Christ our Lord. Amen.
(Rev. George Dawson, A.D. 1821.)

For the Ministry.

REMEMBER all them that do the Lord's work in the ministry and conduct of souls. Give them, we beseech Thee, O Father, great gifts and great holiness, that wisely and charitably, diligently and zealously, prudently and acceptably. they may be guides to the blind, comforters to the sad and weary; that they may strengthen the weak and confirm the strong, separate the worthless from the precious, boldly rebuke sin, patiently suffer for the truth, and be exemplary in their lives; that in all their actions and sermons, in their discipline and ministrations, they may advance the good of souls, and the honour of our Lord Jesus Christ; grant this for the sake of Thy Son our Lord. Amen.   *(Bishop Jeremy Taylor, A.D. 1613.)*

For Family and Household.

BLESS, O God, all the members of this our family and household, especially those who are absent from us. Preserve them waking, guard them in their going out and their coming in, free from sin and safe from danger, and when they sleep may they rest in peace; through Jesus Christ our Lord. Amen.
(Family Prayer Book of the Church of Ireland, A.D. 1895.)

For Light and Guidance.

WE beseech Thee, O Lord, let our hearts be graciously enlightened by Thy holy radiance, that we may serve Thee without fear in holiness and righteousness all the days of our life; that so we may survive the storms of this world, and with Thee for our Pilot attain the haven of eternal brightness; through Thy mercy, O blessed Lord, Who dost live and govern all things, world without end. Amen.   *(Leonine Sacramentary.)*

For Pure Thoughts and Intentions.

ALMIGHTY God, unto Whom all hearts be open, all desires known, and from Whom no secrets are hid, cleanse the thoughts of our hearts by the inspiration of Thy Holy Spirit, that we may perfectly love Thee, and worthily magnify Thy holy Name; through Christ our Lord. Amen.

(*Bishop Leofric*, A.D., *d.* 1072; *Sarum Missal* and *B. of C.P.*)

For Sole Dependence upon God.

O LORD Jesus Christ, give us grace, we beseech Thee, this day to do all we have to do in Thy Name. May we live as those who bear Thy holy Name, and solely to the glory of Thy Name. May we refer all things solely to Thee, and receive all from Thee. Be Thou the beginning and the end of all, the Pattern Whom we are to copy, the Redeemer in Whom is our strength, the Master Whom we are to serve, the Friend to Whom we may look for comfort and sympathy. May we fix our eyes on Thee as our help, our aim, the centre of our being, our everlasting Friend. O Thou Who hast so looked on us that we may see Thee, set Thine eyes upon us, we beseech Thee; steady our unsteadfastness, unite us to Thyself, and guide us in whatever path Thou seest fit to lead us, till of Thine infinite mercy Thou wilt bring us to Thine eternal Presence; for Thine own Name's sake we ask it. Amen. (*Canon Edward Pusey*, A.D. 1800.)

General Intercession.

WE humbly beseech Thee, O Father, to have mercy upon all men. Bless the King whom Thou hast put in authority over us. Bless the nation to which we belong. Remember with Thy most gracious favour all who are near and dear to us. Cause them to know Thy love, to rejoice in Thy salvation, and to live after Thy commandments. Be with us, we beseech Thee, through this day; let Thine arm defend and strengthen us, let Thy Holy Spirit be our Guide and Comforter in all our ways. Favourably with mercy, O Lord, hear these our supplications and prayers, and vouchsafe to accept our praises; through Jesus Christ, our only Mediator and Redeemer, to Whom with Thee and the Holy Ghost be all honour and glory, world without end. Amen.   (*Tent and Altar*, A.D. 1847.)

Thanksgiving.

HELP us to pray always and not to faint, in everything giving thanks, offering up the sacrifice of praise continually, possessing our souls in patience, and learning in whatsoever state we are therewith to be content; for the sake of Jesus Christ our Lord and Master. Amen.

(*Rev. Fielding Ould*, A.D. 1864.)

The Lord's Prayer Paraphrased.

OUR FATHER, which art in heaven, In Whom we live, and move, and have our being, grant that we and all Christians may live worthy of this glorious relation, and that we may not sin, knowing that we are accounted Thine. We are Thine by adoption, O make us Thine by the choice of our will. *Hallowed be Thy Name:* O God, Whose name is great, wonderful, and holy, grant that we and all Thy children may glorify Thee, not only with our lips, but in our lives; that others, seeing our good works, may glorify our Father which is in heaven. *Thy Kingdom come:* May the kingdoms of the world become the kingdom of the Lord and of His Christ, and may all that own Thee for their King become Thy faithful subjects, and obey Thy laws. Dethrone, O God, and destroy Satan and his kingdom, and enlarge the Kingdom of grace. *Thy will be done in earth as it is in heaven:* We adore Thy goodness, O God, in making Thy will known to us in Thy Holy Word. May this Thy Word be the rule of our will, of our desires, of our lives and actions. May we ever sacrifice our will to Thine, be pleased with all Thy choices for ourselves and others, and adore Thy providence in the government of the world. *Give us this day our daily bread:* O heavenly Father, Who knowest what we have need of, give us the necessaries and comforts of this life with Thy blessing; but, above all, give us the Bread that nourisheth to eternal life. O God, Who givest to all life and breath and all things, give us grace to impart to such as are in want, of what Thou hast given more than our daily bread. *And forgive us our trespasses, as we forgive them that trespass against us:* Make us truly sensible of Thy goodness, and mercy, and patience towards us, that we may from our hearts forgive every one his brother their trespasses. *And lead us not into temptation:* Support us, O heavenly Father, under all our trials, and grant that they may yield us the peaceable fruits of righteousness. *But deliver us from evil.* From all sin and wickedness, from our ghostly enemy, and from everlasting death, good Lord, deliver us. Deliver us from the evil of sin and from the evil of punishment. Deliver us, O heavenly Father, from our evil and corrupt nature, from the temptations and snares of an evil world, and from falling again into the sins repented of. *For Thine is the Kingdom, and the power and the glory, for ever and ever. Amen.* By Thy almighty power, O King of heaven, for the glory of Thy Name, and for the love of the Father, grant us all these blessings for which Thy Son has taught us to pray. Unto Him that is able to do for us abundantly more than we can ask or think, unto Him be glory in the Church by Christ Jesus, throughout all ages, world without end. Amen. *(Bishop Thomas Wilson,* A.D. 1663.)

For the Manifold Gifts of the Holy Spirit.

O GOD the Holy Ghost, Sanctifier of the faithful, visit us, we pray Thee, with Thy love and favour; enlighten our minds more and more with the everlasting Gospel; graft in our hearts a love of the truth; increase in us true religion; nourish us with all goodness, and of Thy great mercy keep us in the same, O blessed Spirit, Whom with the Father and Son together we worship and glorify as one God, world without end. Amen.   (*American Prayer Book*, A.D. 1789.)

For Defence from Evil.

GRANT unto us, we beseech Thee, O Almighty God, that we, who seek the shelter of Thy protection, being defended from all evils, may serve Thee in peace and quietness of spirit; through Jesus Christ our Lord. Amen.

                                        (*Roman Breviary*.)

Prayer for Christian Workers.

ALMIGHTY God, pour out Thy Holy Spirit upon all who are working for Thee. O Lord, take their minds and think through them; take their lips and speak through them; take their hearts and set them on fire with love to Thee; through Jesus Christ our Lord. Amen.

                              (*Mothers' Union, Twentieth Century*.)

For the Spread of Christ's Kingdom.

ALMIGHTY God, our heavenly Father, Who in Thy goodness hast caused the light of the Gospel to shine in our land, extend Thy mercy, we beseech Thee, to the nations of the world that still walk in darkness. Enlighten the Moslems with the knowledge of Thy truth, and grant that the Gospel of salvation may be made known in all lands, that the heart of the peoples may be turned unto Thee; through Jesus Christ our Lord. Amen.   (*Scottish Book of Common Prayer*, A.D. 1912.)

In Times of Calamity and Disappointment.

ALMIGHTY and most merciful Father, Who hast taught us not to think of ourselves only, but also for the wants of others, we remember before Thee all who are burdened and oppressed, those whose hopes have been crushed and whose purposes are overthrown. We remember all who are afflicted by poverty, or worn down by disease and illness, the weary and the heavy-laden those also who are in darkness or despair, or who are suffering for righteousness' sake. Help them all to rest in Thee; through Jesus Christ our Lord. Amen.

                              (*Professor Knight, Nineteenth Century*.)

For Pardon of Sin.

O LORD, we beseech Thee, absolve Thy people from their offences, that through Thy bountiful goodness we may all be delivered from the bands of those sins which by our frailty we have committed; grant this, O heavenly Father, for Jesus Christ's sake, our blessed Lord and Saviour. Amen.

(Gregorian Sacramentary: B. of C. P.)

For Assistance in Temptation.

ALMIGHTY and merciful God, Who dost grant unto Thy faithful people the grace to make every path of life temporal, the strait and narrow way which leadeth unto life eternal, grant that we, who know that we have no strength as of ourselves to help ourselves, and therefore do put all our trust in Thine almighty power, may, by the assistance of Thy heavenly grace, always prevail in all things, against whatsoever shall arise to fight against us; through Jesus Christ our Lord. Amen.

(Roman Breviary.)

For Direction by the Holy Spirit. (A Missionary Prayer.)

ALMIGHTY God, Who by the power of Thy Holy Spirit didst inspire the first disciples with missionary zeal for the conversion of the world, grant that Thy Spirit may so inspire us, that we may be ready to spend and be spent in Thy service, and may willingly lose our lives in this world in order that we may gather fruit unto life eternal. Show to each of Thy children in what way Thou wouldst have them labour, whether at home or abroad, for the establishment of Thy Kingdom amongst the heathen, and enable us all with cheerful readiness to carry out Thy will; we ask in the Name of Jesus Christ our Saviour. Amen.

(Society for the Propagation of the Gospel, A.D. 1701.)

For God's Enabling Grace.

NOT only lay Thy commands on us, O Lord, but be pleased to enable us for the performance of every duty required of us this day; and so engage our hearts to Thyself, that we may make it our meat and drink to do Thy will, and with enlarged hearts run the way of Thy commands. Be merciful to us, and bless us, and keep us this day in all our ways. Let Thy love abound in our hearts, and sweetly and powerfully constrain us to all faithful and cheerful obedience; through Jesus Christ our Lord. Amen.   *(Rev. Benjamin Jenks, A.D. 1646.)*

For Union with God.

LORD, keep us ever near to Thee, let nothing separate us from Thee, let nothing keep us back from Thee. If we fall, bring us back quickly to Thee, and make us hope in Thee, trust in Thee, love Thee everlastingly; through Jesus Christ. Amen.

(Canon E. B. Pusey, A.D. 1800.)

For the Gift of the Holy Spirit.

O LORD Jesus Christ, Son of the ever-living God, crucified for us, and raised also from the dead, and now reigning at the right hand of Thy Father, that Thou mayest give gifts unto men, Who hast said, "Come unto Me, all ye that labour and are heavy-laden, and I will refresh you"; have mercy upon us, and pray for us unto Thy Eternal Father. Sanctify and govern us with Thy Holy Spirit; help and succour us in all our necessities, as Thou hast promised, saying: "I will not leave you comfortless"; for Thine own Name's sake we ask it. Amen.

(Christian Prayers, A.D. 1556.)

For Conformity to the Will of God.

O LORD, forasmuch as all our strength is in Thee, grant unto us this grace, that we may allow Thee to do whatsoever Thou wilt; and that our doing may be to lie still in Thy hand, that thou mayest do with us that thing only which is most pleasing to Thee. Do Thou adorn us with holy virtues, giving unto us humbleness of mind, purity of heart, and all those gifts and graces which Thou knowest to be needful for us, and whatsoever Thou wouldst have to be in us, whether in body or soul; that so we may be able the better to please Thee, the more worthily and faithfully to serve Thee, and the more perfectly to love Thee. We pray, moreover, that Thou wouldest give us grace to arrive at that degree of perfection which Thou willest us to reach, and grant unto us the aids and dispositions needful for its attainments; for the sake of Jesus Christ Thy Son our Lord. Amen. *(Ludovicus Palma, Sixteenth Century.)*

"That we may be doers of the Word and not hearers only."

O LORD Jesus Christ, Co-eternal Word of the Father, Who didst become like unto us in all things, sin only excepted, for the salvation of our race, and didst send forth Thy disciples and Apostles to preach and teach the Gospel of Thy Kingdom, and to cure all sickness and all infirmity among Thy people, do Thou Thyself, O Lord, send out Thy Light and Thy Truth, and enlighten the eyes of our minds to understand Thy Divine Word. Give us grace to be hearers of it, and not hearers only, but doers of the Word, that we may bring forth good fruit abundantly, and be counted worthy of the Kingdom of heaven. And to Thee, O Lord our God, we ascribe glory, and thanksgiving, now and for ever. Amen. *(Liturgy of the Greek Church.)*

For Grateful Lives.

L ORD, as Thy mercies do surround us, so grant that our returns of duty may abound; and let us this day manifest our gratitude by doing something well-pleasing unto Thee; through Jesus Christ our Lord. Amen. *(Archdeacon Edward Lake, A.D. 1641.)*

A Morning Thanksgiving.

WE thank Thee, O Father, for Thy readiness to hear and to forgive; for Thy great love to us, in spite of our unworthiness; for the many blessings we enjoy above our deserving, hoping, or asking. Thou hast been so good to us in our ingratitude, thoughtlessness, and forgetfulness of Thee. For Thy pity, long-suffering, gentleness, and tenderness, we bow our heads in humble thankfulness of heart. We worship Thee Who art infinite love, infinite compassion, infinite power. Accept our praise and gratitude; through Jesus Christ our Lord and Saviour. Amen.   (*Rev. C. J. N. Child, Twentieth Century.*)

For Strength and Guidance.

LORD God Almighty, Shaper and Ruler of all creatures, we pray Thee for Thy great mercy, that Thou guide us better than we have done, towards Thee. And guide us to Thy will, to the need of our soul, better than we can ourselves. And steadfast our mind towards Thy will and to our soul's need. And strengthen us against the temptations of the devil, and put far from us all lust, and every unrighteousness, and shield us against our foes, seen and unseen. And teach us to do Thy will, that we may inwardly love Thee before all things, with a pure mind. For Thou art our Maker and our Redeemer, our Help, our Comfort, our Trust, our Hope; praise and glory be to Thee now, ever and ever, world without end. Amen. (*King Alfred, A.D. 849.*)

Dedication of Ourselves to God's Service.

O ALMIGHTY God, Who by Thy holy Apostle hast taught us to present our bodies a living sacrifice, holy, acceptable unto Thee, which is our reasonable service; we come unto Thee in the Name of Jesus Christ, and we devote and dedicate ourselves wholly to Thy service, henceforth to live only to Thy glory. Do Thou, the very God of peace, sanctify us wholly, and preserve our whole spirit and soul and body blameless, unto the coming of our Lord Jesus Christ. Amen.

(*Charles How, A.D. 1661.*)

For the Spread of Christ's Kingdom in the World.

O HEAVENLY Father, Who didst give Thy blessed Son to be the Light of the World, send out the knowledge of Thy Word to all lands, and hasten Thy Kingdom. Shine, we beseech Thee, with the fulness of Thy truth and grace upon the whole Church; more especially upon the members thereof in this land and parish. Scatter the darkness of ignorance and error, of sin and sorrow; knit all hearts unto Thee and to one another, and finally bring us all to the light of everlasting life; for His sake, Who died and rose again for us, Jesus Christ our Lord. Amen.

(*Rev. L. Tuttiett, A.D. 1825.*)

FOR LOVE AND PERSEVERANCE.

HEAVENLY Father, may we this day be followers of Thee, walking in love, even as Christ also has loved us. Grant us grace to draw water with joy out of the wells of salvation. Thus refreshed may we run with patience the Christian race, and fight the good fight of faith. Make us to abound in every good word and work. Keep us humble, thankful, and watchful to the end. God the Father, God the Son, and God the Holy Ghost, hear us, bless us, and keep us this day, we humbly beseech Thee. Amen.   (*Dean Goulburn*, A.D. 1818.)

FOR A CLEAR VISION IN SCIENTIFIC RESEARCH.

TO God the Father, God the Son, God the Spirit, we pour forth most humble and hearty supplications, that He, remembering the calamities of mankind, and the pilgrimage of this our life in which we spend our days, would please to open to us new consolations out of the fountain of His goodness for the alleviating of our miseries. We humbly and earnestly ask that human things may not prejudice such as are Divine, so that from the opening of the gates of sense, and the kindling of a greater natural light, nothing of incredulity or intellectual might might arise in our minds towards Divine mysteries; but rather, O Lord, that our minds being thoroughly cleansed, and purged from fancy, and yet subject to the Divine will, there may be given unto faith the things that are faith's, that so we may continually attain to a deeper knowledge and love of Thee, Who art the Fountain of Light, and dwellest in the Light which no man can approach unto; through Jesus Christ our Lord. Amen.   (*Francis Bacon*, A.D. 1561.)

FOR OUR SOVEREIGN AND PRINCE.

O EVERLASTING God, Who art Ruler and Guide of all things, that hast commanded us to obey our superiors and magistrates, let it please Thee, for Thy mercies' sake, to extend Thy mercy and blessing upon our King and Prince, and all our superiors, that they, living in Thy fear and protection, may overthrow their enemies, and we living in quietness under them, may praise Thee all our life; through Jesus Christ our Lord. So be it.   (*Scottish Psalter*, A.D. 1595.)

FOR JOY AND PEACE IN THE DAILY WALK.

GRANT us, O Lord, to pass this day in gladness and peace, without stumbling and without stain; that reaching the eventide victorious over all temptation, we may praise Thee, the eternal God, Who art blessed, and dost govern all things, world without end. Amen.   (*Mozarabic Liturgy*.)

A Morning Petition.

O MOST merciful God and Father, we commend ourselves and all we have to Thine almighty hands, and pray Thee to preserve us by Thy good Spirit from all sin, misfortune, and grief of heart. Give us the spirit of grace and prayer, that we may have a consoling trust in Thy love, and that our petitions may be acceptable in Thy sight. Give us the spirit of faith to kindle a bright flame of true and blessed faith in our hearts, that we may have a living knowledge of salvation, and our whole life may be a thank-offering for the mercies we have received. Give us the spirit of love, that we may experience the sweetness of Thy love toward us, and also love Thee in return, and render our obedience, not from constraint like slaves, but with the willing and joyful hearts of children; through Jesus Christ our Lord. Amen.   (*Rev. Gottfried Arnold*, A.D. 1665.)

For Growth in Grace.

GIVE perfection to beginners, O Father; give intelligence to the little ones; give aid to those who are running their course. Give sorrow to the negligent; give fervour of spirit to the lukewarm. Give to the perfect a good consummation; for the sake of Christ Jesus our Lord. Amen.

       (*Bishop Irenæus*, A.D. 130; *Old Gallican Sacramentary*.)

For All Doctors and Nurses.

O LORD Jesus Christ, Who hast power of life and death, of health and of sickness, give power, wisdom, and gentleness to all Thy ministering servants, all physicians and surgeons, nurses and watchers by the sick, that, always bearing Thy presence with them, they may not only heal but bless, and shine as lamps of hope in the darkest hours of distress and fear; Who with the Father and the Holy Ghost livest and reignest ever one God, world without end. Amen.

       (*Church Missionary Society*, A.D. 1799.)

For Peace among the Nations.

ALMIGHTY God, from Whom all thoughts of truth and peace proceed, kindle, we pray Thee, in the hearts of all men, the true love of peace, and guide with Thy pure and peaceable wisdom those who take counsel for the nations of the earth; that in tranquillity Thy kingdom may go forward, till the earth be filled with the knowledge of Thy love; through Jesus Christ our Lord. Amen.   (*Francis Paget, Bishop of Oxford*, A.D. 1851.)

For Holy and Well-ordered Lives.

GRANT, O Lord, that all the time of our life may be so spent in Thy true fear and obedience, that altogether we may end the same in the sanctification and honouring of Thy blessed Name; through Jesus Christ our Lord. Amen.

       (*Liturgy of the Church of Scotland*, A.D. 1637.)

A Morning Prayer.

O OUR God and Father, we firmly believe that Thou art here present and perfectly seest us, that Thou observest our actions, and knowest all our thoughts and motives. Forgive us when we have forgotten Thee, or have done, said, thought what hath displeased Thee. Help us to go into the world and to set Thee and only Thee before us, to seek simply Thy approval, and neither to fear men's censure nor to crave their praise; may we keep an especial watch over our tempers, and over our tongues, that we offend not in hastiness, ill-nature, idleness or vanity. Help us to do this day some act of love and self-denial, to speak some words of godly counsel, to set an example of humility, patience, unworldliness and Christian courage. May we remember that we are Thy servants, Thy children, and thus learn to know Thee more truly and love Thee more entirely. Prepare us for whatever Thou shalt appoint—for a useful life, or for ill health and suffering, or for an early death, just as Thou shalt see fit; may we follow Thy blessed saints gone to rest; above all may we follow Thy dear Son, this day and all our days, for His Name's sake, O Father, Who hath died for us and ever liveth to make intercession for us, Jesus Christ our Lord. Amen.

(Bishop Blunt, A.D. 1833.)

For Contrition and Sympathy for Others.

G IVE us all contrition and meekness of heart, O Father, grace to amend our sinful life, and the holy comfort of Thy Spirit to overcome and heal all our evils. Speak peace to all who are praying with us or for us, far away or near; and we beseech Thee give us the heart to consider the multitude of miserable souls and lives amongst us, to take effectual pity on them, and ever to render unto Thee the things that are Thine, according to the commandment and in the Name of our Master and only Saviour, Jesus Christ Thy Son our Lord, Who with Thee and the Holy Ghost livest and reignest one God, world without end. Amen.

(Archbishop Benson, A.D. 1829.)

For Light.

B ESTOW Thy Light upon us, O Lord, so that, being rid of the darkness of our hearts, we may attain unto the true Light; through Jesus Christ, Who is the Light of the World. Amen.   *(Sarum Breviary.)*

A Petition.

O THOU our Lord and our God, our merciful Father in heaven, we entreat Thee with childlike hearts, give us in this world whatever is really good and happy for us in soul and body, according to Thy holy will and pleasure. May we live as Christians, endure with patience, and at last die in peace and hope; for Jesus Christ's sake. Amen.

(Archdeacon Johann Quirsfeld, A.D. 1642.)

For Guidance and Protection.

WE humbly pray Thee, O Father in heaven, to guide us through the darkness of this world, to guard us from its perils, to hold us up and strengthen us when we grow weary in our mortal way, and to lead us by Thy chosen paths, through time and through death, to our eternal home in Thy heavenly Kingdom; which we ask in the Name of Jesus Christ our Lord. Amen.   (*King's Chapel Liturgy*, 1831.)

For the Protection of Christ's Little Ones.

GRANT, O Father of all, that Thy holy angels, as they do always behold Thy face in heaven, may evermore protect Thy little ones on earth from every danger, both of body and soul; through Jesus Christ our Lord.   Amen.
                    (*Rev. S. Gladstone*, A.D. 1844.)

For work among the Blind, the Deaf and Dumb.

O LORD, Jesus Christ, Who art both perfect God and perfect man, bless, we beseech Thee, all work that is being carried on in Thy Name, in this and in other lands on behalf of those who are blind, or deaf and dumb.   Strengthen and inspire with Thy Holy Spirit all chaplains, lay-workers, teachers, missionaries, and others called to any special office in this work. Endue them with patience, cheerfulness and courage, and make them zealous in their labours for the extension of Thy kingdom in the world—to Thine own honour and glory.   Amen.
                    (*Selwyn Oxley, Nineteenth Century, adapted.*)

For Missionary Schools and Colleges.

BLESSED Lord, Who didst condescend to be a learner, even through suffering, that Thou mightest become our Saviour and Teacher, grant unto all those who labour in mission schools and colleges, that, being taught by the Holy Spirit, they may be apt to teach and wise to win the souls committed to their care. May the seed of Thy Word sown by them in many young hearts spring up unto eternal life.   May the scholars and students seek Thee early and find Thee, their only Saviour and Lord.   More especially we pray for all who are being prepared for any ministry in Thy Church, that, as good soldiers of Jesus Christ, as husbandmen that labour, and as workmen that need not to be ashamed, they may learn rightly to divide the Word of Truth among Thy people; and so may there grow up in all lands a generation of holy men and women to bear witness unto Thee, Who art God over all, blessed for ever.   Amen.
                    (*Church Missionary Society*, A.D. 1799.)

Have Mercy upon us.

PITIFUL Father, Who art full of mercy, that never rejects the prayers of them that call upon Thee, in Truth and verity, have mercy upon us, and destroy the multitude of our iniquities. according to the truth of Thy promises which Thou hast promised unto us, and wherein we repose our whole confidence according as we are taught by the word of Thy Son our only Saviour.   So be it.   *(Scottish Psalter, A.D. 1595.)*

A Morning Prayer.

O GOD, Who art the unsearchable abyss of peace, the ineffable sea of love, the fountain of blessings, and the bestower of affection, Who sendest peace to those that receive it; open to us this day the sea of Thy love, and water us with the plenteous streams from the riches of Thy grace.   Make us children of quietness, and heirs of peace.   Enkindle in us the fire of Thy love; sow in us Thy fear; strengthen our weakness by Thy power; bind us closely to Thee and to each other in one firm bond of unity; for the sake of Jesus Christ.   Amen.

(Syrian Clementine Liturgy.)

A Prayer against Harsh Judgment.

LORD Jesus, everywhere and always inspire us to refuse the evil and to choose the good; and, we beseech Thee, give us grace never to judge our neighbour rashly, whilst one by one we ourselves endeavour to learn and perform Thy will; for Thine own Name's sake.   Amen.   *(Christina G. Rossetti, A.D. 1830.)*

For Protection in Times of Temptation.

WE know, O Lord, the weakness of ourselves, and how ready we are to fall from Thee, suffer not therefore Satan, to show his power and malice upon us; for we are not able to withstand his assaults.   Arm us, O Lord, always with Thy grace, and assist us with Thy Holy Spirit in all kinds of temptations; through Jesus Christ our Lord.   Amen.

(Archbishop Grindal, A.D. 1519.)

For the Loving Care of the Good Shepherd.

O LORD Jesus Christ, Thou Good Shepherd of the sheep, Who camest to seek the lost, and to gather them to Thy fold, have compassion upon those who have wandered from Thee; feed those who hunger, cause the weary to lie down in Thy pastures, bind up those who are broken in heart, and strengthen those who are weak, that we, relying on Thy care and being comforted by Thy love, may abide in Thy guidance to our lives' end; for Thy Name's sake.   Amen.

(From an Ancient Collect.)

For Divine Love.

ALMIGHTY and Eternal God, Who hast revealed Thy Nature in Christ Jesus Thy Son as Love, we humbly pray Thee give us Thy Holy Spirit to glorify Thee also in our hearts as pure Love, and thus constrain us by Thy Divine power to love Thee with our whole souls, and our brethren as ourselves; that so by Thy grace we may be fulfilled with love, and evermore abide in Thee, and Thou in us, with all joyfulness, and free from fear or distrust; through Jesus Christ our Lord.   Amen.

(Baron Christian C. J. Bunsen, A.D. 1791.)

For Heavenly-Mindedness.

O MERCIFUL God, fill our hearts, we pray Thee, with the graces of Thy Holy Spirit, with love, joy, peace, longsuffering, gentleness, goodness, faith, meekness, temperance.   Teach us to love those who hate us, to pray for those who despitefully use us, that we may be the children of Thee our Father, Who makest Thy sun to shine on the evil and on the good, and sendest rain on the just and on the unjust.   In adversity grant us grace to be patient; in prosperity keep us humble; may we guard the door of our lips; may we lightly esteem the pleasures of this world, and thirst after heavenly things; through Jesus Christ our Lord. Amen.   *(St. Anselm, A.D. 1033.)*

For Additional Labourers.

O ALMIGHTY God, look mercifully upon the world, redeemed by the blood of Thy dear Son, and send forth many more to do the work of the ministry, that perishing souls may be rescued, and Thy glorious triumph may be hastened by the perfecting of Thine elect; through the same Thy Son Jesus Christ our Lord.   Amen.   *(Rev. R. M. Benson, A.D. 1824.)*

For Forgiveness and Deliverance.

O CHRIST, our Creator and Redeemer, Almighty Lord God, forgive the sins of all who are joined to us by friendship and relationship, all for whom we are desired to pray, or have resolved to pray, and all Thy faithful people.   Deliver us all from evil, preserve us in all good, and bring us at last to everlasting joy; for Thine honour and glory.   Amen.

(MS. of Corbey on " Notes of the Gregorian Sacramentary," A.D. 590.)

For Christ's Companionship.

JESUS, our Master, do Thou meet us while we walk in the way, and long to reach the Country; so that, following Thy light, we may keep the way of righteousness, and never wander away into the darkness of this world's night, while Thou, Who art the Way, the Truth, and the Life, art shining within us; for Thine own Name's sake.   Amen.   *(Mozarabic Liturgy.)*

An Offering of Praise.

O GOD of hope, the true Light of faithful souls and perfect Brightness of the Blessed, Who art verily the Light of the world, grant that our hearts may both render Thee a worthy prayer, and always glorify Thee with the offering of praises; through Jesus Christ our Lord. Amen. (*Gelasian Sacramentary.*)

For the Church of Christ.

L ORD God, we pray for the Holy Catholic (Universal) Church, Thy new work, "Thy workmanship," "Thy Building," Thou "the Chief Corner-stone," Thou "the Living Rock" whence it was hewn. We pray for the Universal Church, for all the branches and all the members thereof wheresoever scattered throughout the world. Thou hast called it Thine own "Body," Thy "Bride," Thy "Household," Thy "Fold," Thy "Vineyard." We pray, Holy Father, for this Thy Son's work, the fruit of His Blood, this new-born world living through His death. We pray for its increase, that all nations may be gathered into it, the utmost ends of this earth; that all the heathen may be brought to a knowledge of the truth; that the Church may do her work of evangelizing the world; that her borders may be enlarged, the fold widened. We pray for its unity, that all who are called by Thy Name, Lord Jesus, may be one, even as Thou and the Father and the Holy Ghost are One: even as there is but "one Faith, one Lord, one Baptism, one God and Father of all." We pray for its purity, that it may be "the salt of the earth," purifying the world, destroying the power of Satan, manifesting holiness, preparing a holy people for the Lord. We pray for its order, that it may approve itself the work of Thy hand, for Thou art not the Author of confusion, but of peace. We pray for its peace that it may be the peacemaker of the world, and accomplish Thy work of peace, for Thou hast spoken peace to them that are afar off and to them that are near; Thy peace hast Thou left with us. We pray for its doctrine, that it may be sound, that it may keep the spirit of truth. We pray for all the branches of this Tree, all the members of this Body, all the sheep of this Fold, all the brethren of this Household of Faith; for the whole company of faithful people, friends and strangers, our own countrymen and foreigners; for all that are called by Thy Name. We pray for the healing of wounds, the mending of nets, the destruction of heresies, the reformation of manners, the salvation of all men; through the merits of Thy most precious Blood. Amen.

(*Bishop Armstrong*, A.D. 1813.)

Ascription.

N OW unto Him that loved us, and washed us from our sins in His own blood, and hath made us kings and priests unto God and His Father, to Him be glory and dominion; for ever and ever. Amen. (*Rev.* i. 6; *St. John, First Century* A.D.)

A Morning Supplication.

O GREAT and lofty God, Thou Father in the Highest, Who hast promised to dwell with them that are of a lowly spirit and fear Thy Word; create now in us such lowly hearts, and give us a reverential awe of Thy commandments. O come, Thou Holy Spirit, and kindle our hearts with holy love; come, Thou Spirit of Strength, and arouse our souls to hunger and thirst after Thee, their true Guide, that they may be sustained by Thy all-powerful influence. Arise, O Spirit of Life, that through Thee we may begin to live; descend upon us and transform us into such human beings as the heart of God longs to see, renewed into the image of Christ, and going on from glory to glory. O God, Thou Supreme Good, make Thyself known to us; through Jesus Christ our Lord. Amen. (*Gerhard Tersteegen*, A.D. 1697.)

"O Lord, hear."

L ORD God of Israel, there is no God like Thee in heaven above or on earth beneath, Who keepest covenant and mercy with Thy servants that walk before Thee with all their heart. Have Thou respect unto the prayers of Thy servants and to their supplications, O Lord our God, and hearken unto the cry and to the prayer which Thy servants pray before Thee this day. Forgive all that have sinned against Thee and all that have transgressed against Thee. Hear Thou our prayer and our supplications in heaven Thy dwelling-place, and when Thou hearest, forgive. Amen. (*King Solomon, Eleventh Century B.C.*)

A Prayer for Bishops.

L ORD Jesus Christ, Thou didst choose Thine Apostles that they might preside over us as teachers; so also may it please Thee to teach doctrine to our Bishops in the place of Thine Apostles, and to bless and instruct them, that they may preserve their lives unharmed and undefiled for ever and ever. Amen.
(*Archbishop Egbert*, A.D. 734.)

For Quiet Trust.

O LORD God, our Governor, we beseech Thee, of Thy mercy, that we may have the heavenly vision, and behold things as they seem unto Thee, that the turmoil of this world may be seen by us, to be bringing forth the sweet peace of the eternal years, and that in all the troubles and sorrows of our own hearts we may behold good; and so, with quiet mind and inward peace, careless of outward storm, we may do the duty of life which brings to us a quiet heart, ever trusting in Thee. We give Thee thanks for all Thy mercy. We beseech Thy forgiveness of all our sins. We pray for Thy guidance in all things. Thy Presence in the hour of death, Thy glory in the life to come. Of Thy mercy hear us. Amen. (*Rev. George Dawson*, A.D. 1821.)

For Single-hearted Love to God.

ALMIGHTY God, the Fountain of Holiness, Who by Thy Word and Thy Spirit dost conduct all Thy servants in the ways of peace and sanctity, grant unto us so truly to repent of our sins, so carefully to reform our errors, so diligently to watch over all our actions, that we may never willingly transgress Thy holy laws, but that it may be the work of our life to obey Thee; the joy of our soul to please Thee; the satisfaction of all our hopes, and the perfection of our desires to be with Thee in Thy Kingdom of grace and glory; through Jesus Christ our Lord. Amen.

(Hon. Mrs. Lyttelton Gell, Nineteenth Century.)

For Trust in God's Providence.

HOLD us fast, O Lord of Hosts, that we fall not from Thee; grant us thankful and obedient hearts, that we may increase daily in the love, knowledge, and fear of Thee; increase our faith and help our unbelief, that we, being provided for and relieved in all our needs by Thy Fatherly care and providence, as Thou shalt think good, may live a godly life, to the praise and good example of Thy people, and after this life may reign with Thee for ever, through Christ our Saviour. Amen.

(Bishop James Pilkington, A.D. 1520.)

For an Increase of Christ's Labourers.

O BLESSED Jesus, Lord of the harvest, we pray Thee send forth labourers into Thy harvest, and by Thy Holy Spirit stir the hearts of many that they may be ready to spend and be spent in Thy service, and if it please Thee, so to lose their life in this world, that they may gather fruit unto life eternal. O Lord, Thou lover of souls, hear us, we humbly beseech Thee. Amen.   *(Bishop Milman, A.D. 1816.)*

A Prayer for Ourselves.

GIVE us, O Lord, purity of lips, clean and innocent hearts, and rectitude of action; give us humility, patience, self-control, prudence, justice, and courage; give us the spirit of wisdom and understanding, the spirit of counsel and strength, the spirit of knowledge and godliness, and of Thy fear; make us ever to seek Thy face with all our heart, all our soul, all our mind; grant us to have a contrite and humbled heart in Thy Presence, to prefer nothing to Thy love. Have mercy upon us, we humbly beseech Thee; through Jesus our Lord. Amen.

(Gallican Sacramentary.)

For a Holy Influence.

OUR Father, may the world not mould us to-day, but may we be so strong as to help to mould the world; through Jesu Christ our Lord. Amen.

(Rev. J. H. Jowett, A.D. 1864.)

For Harmony of Heart with God.

O SEND Thy Light and Thy Truth, that we may live alway near to Thee, our God. Let us feel Thy love, that we may be as it were already in heaven, that we may do all our work as the angels do theirs. Let us be ready for every work, be ready to go out or come in, to stay or to depart, just as Thou shalt appoint. Lord, let us have no will of our own, or consider our true happiness as depending in the slightest degree on anything that can befall us outwardly, but as consisting altogether in conformity to Thy will; through Jesus Christ our Lord. Amen.

(Rev. Henry Martyn, A.D. 1781.)

For Submission to, and Confidence in, God's Will.

O GOD, Who seest all our weaknesses and the troubles that we labour under, have regard, we beseech Thee, unto the prayers of Thy servants, who stand in need of Thy comfort, Thy direction, and Thy help. Thou alone knowest what is best for them; let them never dispute Thy wisdom or Thy goodness. Lord, so prepare our hearts, that no affliction may ever so surprise as to overbear us. Dispose us at all times to a readiness to suffer what Thy Providence shall order or permit. Grant that we may never murmur at Thy appointments, nor be exasperated at the ministers of Thy Providence; for the sake of Jesus Christ our Lord. Amen.   *(Bishop Thomas Wilson, A.D. 1663.)*

A Prayer for Missionaries.

O GOD, Who by Thy Son Jesus Christ didst charge Thine Apostles to preach the Gospel to every creature, prosper, we pray Thee, all missions of Thy Church. Send forth labourers into Thy vineyard, and bestow upon them all things needful for their work. Grant them wisdom in all difficulties, help in trouble, the sense of Thy Presence in loneliness, and, if it be Thy will, visible success after labour. that Thy holy Name may be glorified; through Jesus Christ our Lord and Saviour. Amen.

(Guild of St. Paul, Nineteenth Century.)

For Protection.

O GOD, the Shepherd of all Thy people, deliver the same from all sins which do assail them, that so they may ever be pleasing in Thy sight, and safe under Thy shelter; for Christ's sake. Amen.   *(Roman Breviary.)*

For the Perfecting of our Imperfections.

LORD, hear; Lord, forgive; Lord, do; hear what we speak not; forgive what we speak amiss; do what we leave undone; that not according to our words, or our deeds, but according to Thy mercy and truth, all may issue to Thy glory, and the good of Thy Kingdom; through Jesus Christ. Amen.

(Maria Hare, A.D. 1798.)

For Acceptable Petitions.

LET the prayers of Thy children, O Lord, come up to the ears of Thy mercy; and that we may obtain what we ask, make us ever to ask what pleaseth Thee; through Jesus Christ our Lord. Amen. *(Leonine Sacramentary.)*

A Prayer for Increased Heavenly-Mindedness.

MOST merciful Father, Giver of every good gift, Who hast given us, Thy servants, so many and great blessings, forgive us, we beseech Thee, our sins; sanctify us with Thy Truth, O Thou Who art the most merciful Sanctifier of all. Kindle our hearts with the fire of Thy love; grant us ever to walk in the light of Thy Divine Presence; and that, seeking Thee alone, we may attain unto Thee, and taught by Thee, we may teach others Thy paths, so that we may together hasten unto Thee, the true Shepherd of our souls. And do Thou, Lord Jesus, vouchsafe to bear us on Thy shoulders, us whom Thou hast redeemed with Thy most precious blood, and to place us in Thy green pastures; Who livest and reignest, ever one God, world without end. Amen. *(Canon E. B. Pusey, A.D. 1800.)*

For the Church of Christ.

WE beseech Thee, O Lord, to guide Thy Church with Thy perpetual governance, that it may walk warily in times of quiet and boldly in times of trouble; through our Lord Jesus Christ. Amen. *(Franciscan Breviary.)*

For Christ's Compassion on Sorrowing Mankind.

GRACIOUS Lord Jesus, regard Thy creation for good: men to befriend them; women, to protect them; babes, to nurture them; sufferers, to ease them; tremblers, to reassure them wanderers, to reclaim them; the sick, to heal them; sinners, to convert them; saints to perfect them; the dying, to receive them; the dead, to keep them. Yea, our compassionate and loving Saviour, Thou Who of Thine own free will and for our sakes didst become an Infant of days, wast born of a woman didst grow up to perfect manhood, wert pleased to share human sufferings, to face fear, to seek the lost, to heal the sick, to forgive sinners, to lead saints, to open Paradise to the dying, and then Thyself to receive the dead; hear this our prayer, we beseech Thee, for Thine own Name's sake. Amen.

(Christina G. Rossetti, A.D. 1830.)

For "A Perfect Heart."

GIVE unto us, O Lord, we humbly beseech Thee, a wise, a sober, a patient, an understanding, a devout, a religious, a courageous heart; a soul full of devotion to do Thee service strength against all temptations; through Jesus Christ our Lord. Amen. *(Archbishop Laud, A.D. 1573.)*

For a Rightful Approach to God.

WE beseech Thee, O Lord, make Thy servants always to join together in seeking Thee with their whole heart, to serve Thee with submissive mind, humbly to implore Thy mercy, and perpetually to rejoice in Thy blessings; through Jesus Christ our Lord. Amen. *(Gelasian Sacramentary.)*

For Unity amongst Christians.

O LORD God Almighty, look down upon Thy Church and people throughout the whole world; enable them everywhere to witness by their lives to the worthiness of Thy Name, and the greatness of Thy power. Knit them together in love, peace, and in wise and mutual sympathy. Send upon all the enlightening gift of Thy most Holy Spirit, that as there is one body and one spirit, they may attain the one hope of their calling; through Jesus Christ our Lord. Amen.

(Bishop Boyd Carpenter, A.D. 1841.)

Fellow Workers with God.

O ETERNAL Father, we believe that in Thy Son Thou art satisfied with our race. We believe that Thou has created us in Him, and that Thou lookest upon us as we really are, not as we are made by the unbelief which separates us from Thee and from our brethren. Only thus, do we find that peace which Thy Son left His disciples. We believe that in Christ Thou wilt restore all things. Use us, each one of us, we humbly beseech Thee, to work with Thee in Thy purpose of restoration, blotting out our sins, that we may serve Thee day by day with free hearts. Thy free Spirit dwelling and working within us to Thy honour and glory. *(Rev. Frederick D. Maurice, A.D. 1805.)*

"Be ye therefore Ready."

O HEAVENLY Father, Whose most dearly beloved Son has come once to save the world, and will come again to judge the world; help us, we pray Thee, to watch, like servants who wait for the coming of their Lord. May we endure unto the end, and be found with our lamps burning. May we abound in hope through the power of the Holy Ghost; and, having this hope, may we purify ourselves by Thy grace, even as Christ is pure. Grant this our prayer, most merciful Father, for the sake of Him Who once visited us in great humility, and will come again in glorious majesty at the last day; Thy blessed Son, our Saviour Jesus Christ. Amen. *(Bishop Walsham How, A.D. 1823.)*

For Loyal Service.

ALMIGHTY and everlasting God, grant that our wills be ever meekly subject to Thy will, and our hearts be ever honestly ready to serve Thee; for the sake of Jesus Christ our Lord. Amen. *(Roman Breviary.)*

Morning Praise and Prayer.

O LORD our God, Who hast chased the slumber from our eyes, and once more assembled us to lift up our hands unto Thee and to praise Thy just judgments, accept our prayers and supplications, and give us faith and love. Bless our coming in and our going out, our thoughts, words, and works, and let us begin this day with the praise of the unspeakable sweetness of Thy mercy. Hallowed be Thy name. Thy kingdom come; through Jesus Christ our Lord. Amen.

(Greek Church Liturgy.)

Thanksgiving for our Redemption through Christ.

GLORY be to God in the highest, the Creator, and Lord of heaven and earth, the Preserver of all things, the Father of mercies, Who so loved mankind as to send His only begotten Son into the world, to redeem us from sin and misery, and to obtain for us everlasting life. Accept, O gracious God, our praises and our thanksgivings for Thine infinite mercies towards us. And teach us, O Lord, to love Thee more and serve Thee better; through Jesus Christ our Lord. Amen.

(Bishop Hamilton, A.D. 1561.)

Faith in God's Unchangeableness.

O GOD, Who art, and wast, and art to come, before Whose face the generations rise and pass away, age after age the living seek Thee and find that of Thy faithfulness there is no end. Our fathers in their pilgrimage walked by Thy guidance, and rested on Thy compassion, still to their children be Thou the cloud by day, and the fire by night. Where but in Thee have we a covert from the storm, or shadow from the heat of life; In our manifold temptations, Thou alone knowest and art ever nigh; in sorrow, Thy pity revives the fainting soul; in our prosperity and ease, it is Thy Spirit only that can keep us from pride and keep us humble. O Thou sole Source of peace and righteousness, take now the veil from every heart, and join us in one communion with Thy prophets and saints who have trusted in Thee and were not ashamed. Not of our worthiness, but of Thy tender mercy hear our prayer; for the sake of Jesus Christ Thy Son our Lord. Amen.

(James Martineau, Published A.D. 1891.)

For the Family and Household.

VISIT, we beseech Thee, most gracious Father, this family and household with Thy protection. Let Thy blessing descend and rest on all that belong to it, as well absent as present. Grant us and them whatever may be expedient or profitable for our bodies or our souls. Guide us by Thy good Providence here and hereafter bring us all to Thy glory; through Jesus Christ our Lord. Amen.

(Rev. Dr. Digby.)

For a Constant Sense of God's Presence.

O GOD our heavenly Father, renew in us the sense of Thy gracious Presence, and let it be a constant impulse within us to peace, trustfulness, and courage on our pilgrimage. Let us hold Thee fast with a loving and adoring heart, and let our affections be fixed on Thee, that so the unbroken communion of our hearts with Thee may accompany us whatsoever we do, through life and in death. Teach us to pray heartily; to listen for Thy voice within, and never to stifle its warnings. Behold, we bring our poor hearts as a sacrifice unto Thee; come and fill Thy sanctuary, and suffer nought impure to enter there. O Thou who art Love, let Thy Divine Spirit flow like a river through our whole souls, and lead us in the right way till we pass into the Land of Promise; through Jesus Christ. Amen.

(G. Tersteegen, A.D. 1697.)

Dedication of Ourselves to God's Service.

O MAKE Thy way plain before our face; support us this day under all the difficulties we shall meet with. We offer ourselves to Thee, O God, this day to do in us, and with us, as to Thee seems most meet; through Jesus Christ our Lord. Amen.

(Bishop Wilson, A.D. 1663.)

For the Empire and Nation.

O LORD, All Sovereign and Merciful, look down in Thy mercy upon our Church and Realm, especially upon those to whom Thou hast given the trust of high office, that they may do their duty as unto Thee and not unto men. Bless the great Council of the Nation (and those who are called upon to elect its members). Direct the course of this world in peace. Watch over our Church and Empire throughout the world. Preserve us from civil strife, and knit the hearts of our brethren in the Dominions over seas and in India to the hearts of those who remain at home. Give honesty, truthfulness, strength, and wisdom to those who govern; and grant us grace willingly to do our part in supporting them in their great work for Thee; through Jesus Christ our King. Amen.

(Recommended by Archbishop Randall Davidson, A.D. 1848.)

For Unity.

O GOD the Father, Origin of Divinity, Good beyond all that is good, Fair beyond all that is fair, in Whom is calmness, peace, and concord; do Thou make up the dissensions which divide us from each other, and bring us back into a unity of love, which may bear some likeness to Thy Divine Nature. And as Thou art above all things, make us one by the unanimity of a good mind, that through the embrace of charity and the bonds of affection, we may be spiritually one, as well in ourselves as in each other ; through that peace of Thine which maketh all things peaceful, and through the grace, mercy, and tenderness of Thy Son, Jesus Christ. Amen. *(St. Dionysius, A.D. 818.)*

A Prayer for the Whole World.

O LORD, unto Whom all glory and honour do appertain, replenish us with spiritual joy. Grant that all idolatry and superstition being put away, the whole world may be so enlightened with the light of Thy Holy Word, that every man may give up himself to a perpetual praising of Thy holy Name, and may give unto Thee most hearty thanks for all the benefits which we continually receive at Thy Fatherly hand; through Jesus Christ Thy Son. So be it. (*Scottish Psalter*, A.D. 1595.)

For Boldness in Christ's Servants.

O HEAVENLY Father, the Father of all wisdom, understanding, and true strength, we beseech Thee look mercifully upon Thy servants, and send Thy Holy Spirit into their hearts, that when they must join to fight in the field for the glory of Thy holy Name, then they, being strengthened with the defence of Thy right hand, may manfully stand in the confession of Thy faith and of Thy truth, and continue in the same unto the end of their lives; through Jesus Christ our Lord. Amen.

(*Bishop Nicholas Ridley*, A.D. 1500.)

"O Lord, Hearken."

ALMIGHTY God, we will come into Thy house, even upon the multitude of Thy mercies, and in Thy fear will we worship toward Thy holy Temple. Hear the voice of our humble petitions, when we cry unto Thee, when we hold up our hands towards Thy mercy-seat. Let Thine eyes be open, and let Thine ears be attentive to hearken unto the prayer which Thy servants pray toward the place, whereof Thou hast said, that Thou wouldest put Thy Name there; for the sake of Jesus Christ. Amen. (*Bishop Andrewes*, A.D. 1555.)

A Memorial of the Resurrection.

O LORD Jesus Christ, by Thy glorious Resurrection, in which Thou didst appear alive and immortal to Thy disciples and faithful followers, by Thy forty days' abiding and sweet converse, in which by many infallible proofs, speaking of things pertaining to the Kingdom of God, Thou didst comfort them and assure them of Thine actual Resurrection, removing all doubt from their hearts. We beseech Thee, O Lord, grant that we may be numbered among those who were foreordained by God to be witnesses of Thy Resurrection, not only by word of mouth, but in reality of good works; for Thine honour and glory, Who with the Father and the Holy Ghost livest and reignest ever one God, world without end. Amen.

(*Ludolphus of Saxony (Monk)*, A.D. d. 1370.)

For Knowledge and the Fruit of the Spirit.

O LORD, Who hast breathed into us the breath of life and endued us with an immortal spirit, which looks up unto Thee, and remembers it is made after Thine own image, behold with grace and favour the desires which are in our hearts to recover a perfect likeness to Thee. Fill us, O Lord, with the knowledge of Thy will in all wisdom and spiritual understanding. Fill us with goodness and the fruits of righteousness, and fill us with all joy and peace in believing that Thou wilt never leave us nor forsake us, but make us perfect, stablish, strengthen, settle us, and be our God for ever and ever, our Guide even over death. Amen.   (*Bishop Simon Patrick*, A.D. 1626.)

A Prayer for the Nation.

WE thank Thee, O heavenly Father, for Thine abundant mercies poured upon this Church and Nation, and most of all for the increase of the open knowledge of Thee, the only true God, and Jesus Christ, Whom Thou hast sent. But Thou, O Lord, dost mark what is amiss, and canst correct with judgment, not in anger; we therefore pray Thee forgive us those things whereof our conscience is afraid, and of Thy tender mercy deliver us from trials above what we can bear, and from dangers seen and unseen round about us. Have compassion, good Lord, on suffering men and sorrowful homes, on the wounded, sick, bereaved, and desolate. Be to the Army and the Fleet their health and confidence and safety, according to Thy perfect will; through Jesus Christ our Lord. Amen. (*Archbishop E. W. Benson*, A.D. 1829.)

For Absent Loved Ones.

O GOD, our Keeper and Helper, we humbly pray Thee to watch over those who have gone forth from us to enter upon their several callings in this world. May Thy Fatherly care shield them, the love of Thy dear Son preserve them from all evil, and the guidance of Thy Holy Spirit keep them in the way that leadeth to Eternal Life; through Jesus Christ. Amen.
(*Rev. C. J. N. Child, Twentieth Century.*)

For Mercy and Guidance.

O GOD and merciful Father, Thou knowest and hast taught us also to know that the weakness of man is such, that without Thy grace, he can neither do, nor think any good thing. Have mercy upon us, we humbly beseech Thee; O Father, be gracious unto us. Lighten us, that we may with pleasure look upon good things only; inflame our hearts with the love thereof, that we may covet them carefully; lead us and guide us, that we may follow and at the last attain them. We, distrusting ourselves, commend and offer ourselves wholly—soul, body, life—into Thy hands. Let Thy loving Spirit lead us forth into the land of righteousness; for the sake of Jesus Christ our Lord. Amen.   (*Christian Prayers*, A.D. 1566.)

Praise and Thanksgiving.

MERCIFUL God, kind and loving Father, for that Thou hast created us, giving us reason; for that through Jesus Christ Thou hast redeemed us; and for that Thou hast through the Holy Spirit called us to eternal life, for these things we give Thee praise and thanks now and always. We thank Thee further with all our hearts for the grace and kindness that Thou, O heavenly Father, hast bestowed upon us during the past days. From danger to body and soul hast Thou protected us; with kindnesses beyond our ken hast Thou overwhelmed us; and with much patience hast Thou borne with our faults. We are not worthy of all the mercy and truth which Thou hast shown us, and we pray with hearty repentance for pardon of any evil we have done, or for anything wherein we have misused Thy grace. Enter not into judgment with Thy servants, let Thy goodness and truth protect us this day and always. Thou Who art the Keeper of Israel, Thou Who neither slumberest nor sleepest, be Thou the Guardian of our souls. We commend to Thy gracious protection our bodies and souls, our property and our powers, our waking and sleeping, our life and death; cover us with Thy hand, and shelter us from all evil, from fear, and from all danger. And now, Lord, we hope in Thee. Let Thy gracious Name shield us, and help us unto everlasting life; through Jesus Christ. Amen.   *(Weimarischer Gesangbuch, A.D. 1873.)*

For Grace to Walk Worthily.

O LORD, give us grace to walk before Thee all the days of this our pilgrimage with a good conscience and pure mind, that when Thou shalt appear to reward every man according to his deeds, we may rejoice and not be ashamed before Thee at Thy coming. Grant this for the sake of Jesus Christ our Lord and Saviour. Amen.   *(Christian Prayers, A.D. 1566.)*

For Rulers, Ministers, and People of our Nation.

GIVE us new hearts, and renew Thy Holy Spirit within, O Lord, that both the rulers of our land may faithfully minister justice, punish sin, defend and maintain the preaching of Thy Word, and that all ministers may diligently teach Thy dearly beloved flock, purchased by the blood and death of Thine own, and only dear Son our Lord, and that all people may obediently learn and follow Thy law, to the glory of Thy holy Name; for Christ's sake, our only Lord and Saviour. Amen.
(Bishop James Pilkington, A.D. 1520.)

For Guidance.

GUIDE us, O Christ, in all the perplexities of our modern social life, and in Thine own good time bring us together in love and unity, making the kingdoms of this world Thy kingdom as Thou willest. Amen. *(Rev. The Hon. James Adderley, A.D. 1861.)*

For Consistent Christian Lives.

LORD, Thou hast made Thyself to be ours, therefore now show Thyself to us in Thy wisdom, goodness and power. To walk faithfully in our Christian course we need much grace. Supply us out of Thy rich store. We need wisdom to go in and out inoffensively before others, furnish us with Thy Spirit. We need patience and comfort, Thou that art the God of consolations bestow it upon us; for Christ's sake. Amen.

(Rev. Richard Sibbes, A.D. 1577.)

For Brotherly Love.

WE would further entreat Thee to plant in our hearts gentleness and patience, a meek and long-suffering spirit. Endow us, we beseech Thee, with such charity, that we may be enabled to return blessing for cursing, good for evil, kind words for harsh reproaches. Thus living all our days with meekness and loving-kindness, keeping peace with all men, and loving our neighbours as ourselves, and Thee, Lord Jesus, more than ourselves, we may at last enter with them into the regions of everlasting love, where Thou livest, who lovest all men, and wouldest not that any should perish, but that all men should turn to Thee and be saved; for Thy Name's sake. Amen.

(Rev. Fielding Ould, A.D. 1864.)

For Unity and Righteousness.

O BLESSED Jesu, Who art the confidence of all the ends of the earth, may Thy truth and peace be spread among all people; more especially we pray for the Catholic (Universal) Church, that it may be purged from all error, and be reunited as at the beginning, in one faith and love. We humbly beseech Thee so to dispose the hearts of all kings, princes, and governors of this world, that by Thy inspiration they may rule in righteousness, and labour for the well-being of the people committed to them. Prosper and bless all who are striving to do Thy will, that, having faithfully ministered before Thee, they may receive the recompense of Thy reward; Who, with the Father and Holy Ghost, livest and reignest, One God, world without end. Amen.

(Rev. T. T. Carter, A.D. 1808.)

For Grace to Look upon the Bright Side of Life.

O GOD, animate us to cheerfulness. May we have a joyful sense of our blessings, learn to look on the bright circumstances of our lot, and maintain a perpetual contentedness under Thy allotments. Fortify our minds against disappointment and calamity. Preserve us from despondency, from yielding to dejection. Teach us that no evil is intolerable but a guilty conscience, and that nothing can hurt us, if, with true loyalty of affection, we keep Thy commandments and take refuge in Thee; through Jesus Christ our Lord. Amen.

(Rev. William Ellery Channing, A.D. 1780.)

PRAISE, AND PRAYER FOR CONFIDENCE AND GRACE.

O ETERNAL and glorious Lord God, since Thy glory and honour is the great end of all Thy works, we desire that it may be the beginning and end of all our prayers and services. Let Thy great Name be glorious, and glorified, and sanctified throughout the World. Let the knowledge of Thee fill all the earth as the waters cover the sea. Let that be done in the world that may most advance Thy glory. Let all Thy works praise Thee. Let Thy wisdom, power, justice, goodness, mercy, and truth be evident unto all mankind, that they may observe, acknowledge, and admire it, and magnify the Name of Thee, the Eternal God. In all the dispensations of Thy Providence, enable us to see Thee, and to sanctify Thy Name in our hearts with thankfulness, in our lips with thanksgiving, in our lives with dutifulness and obedience. Enable us to live to the honour of that great Name of Thine by which we are called, and that, as we profess ourselves to be Thy children, so we may study and sincerely endeavour to be like Thee in all goodness and righteousness, that we may thereby bring glory to Thee our Father which art in heaven; that we and all mankind may have high and honourable thoughts concerning Thee, in some measure suitable to Thy glory, majesty, goodness, wisdom, bounty, and purity, and may in all our words and actions manifest these inward thoughts touching Thee with suitable and becoming words and actions; through Jesus Christ our Lord. Amen.

(Lord Chief Justice Sir Matthew Hale, A.D. 1609.)

A PRAYER FOR THE GREAT COUNCIL OF OUR NATION.

A LMIGHTY God, by Whom alone kings reign, and princes decree justice; and from Whom alone cometh all counsel, wisdom, and understanding. We, Thine unworthy servants, here gathered together in Thy Name, do most humbly beseech Thee to send down Thy heavenly wisdom from above, to direct and guide Thy servants who sit as representatives of the people in Parliament. Grant, we beseech Thee, that they, having Thy grace always before their eyes, and laying aside all private interests, prejudices and partial affections, the result of that which they do may be to the glory of Thy blessed Name, the maintenance of true Religion and Justice, the safety, honour and happiness of the King, the public wealth, peace and tranquillity of the Realm, and the uniting and knitting together of the hearts of all persons and estates within the same, in true Christian love and charity one towards another; through Jesus Christ our Saviour. Amen. *(A prayer based upon the form used daily in both Houses of Parliament during the Session, A.D. 1661.)*

COMMENDATION.

I NTO the faithful hands of our God we commit ourselves now and always. O Lord, let us be Thine and remain Thine for ever; through Jesus Christ Thy Son our Lord. Amen.

(Weimarischer Gesangbuch, A.D. 1873.)

For Protection.

WE pray Thee to compassionate our weakness, O Lord, to guard us in peril, to direct us in doubt, to save us from falling into sin. From the evil that is around and within us, graciously deliver us. Make the path of duty plain before us, and keep us in it even unto the end; through Jesus Christ our Lord. Amen. *(King's Chapel Liturgy, A.D. 1831.)*

For Pardon, Purity, and Grace.

O HOLY God, in Whom is all goodness, Whose pity and mercy made Thee to descend from the high throne down into this world, the valley of woe and weeping, and here to take our nature, and in that nature to suffer pain and death, to bring our souls to Thy Kingdom. Merciful Lord, forgive us all our sins that we have done, thought, and said. O glorious Trinity, send us cleanness of heart and purity of soul; restore us with Thy Holy Spirit, and strengthen us with Thy might, that we may always withstand evil temptations. Comfort us with Thy Holy Ghost, and fulfil us with grace and charity, that we may henceforth live virtuously and love Thee with all our heart, with all our might, and with all our soul, so that we may never offend Thee, but ever follow Thy pleasure in will, word, thought, and deed. Now grant us this, good Lord, that art infinite, which eternally shall endure; through Jesus Christ Thy Son. Amen.

(Hermit Richard Rolle, A.D. 1290.)

A Prayer for All Nations.

ALMIGHTY and everlasting God, that hast wrought the Redemption of man after a miraculous manner, in sending Thy only Son to fulfil the promises made unto our fathers. Open up more and more the knowledge of that salvation, that in all places of the earth, Thy Truth and power may be made known, to the intent that all nations may praise, honour, and glorify Thee; through the selfsame Son, Jesus Christ. So be it.

(The Scottish Psalter, A.D. 1595.)

A Prayer for our Friends and Ourselves.

MAY every thought be brought into obedience to the Gospel of our Saviour Jesus Christ, and let our heart's desire for our friends and adversaries be, that they may be saved. May peace and righteousness, unity and Christian charity, alone rule in our hearts; through Christ Jesus our Lord. Amen.

(Rev. Samuel Green, Nineteenth Century.)

Thanksgiving.

FOR those who have passed into the marvellous light of Thy Presence, we give Thee thanks, O Lord. Amen. (A.D. 1940.)

Invocation.

O SAVIOUR of the World, who by Thy Cross and precious Blood hast redeemed us, save us and help us, we humbly beseech Thee, O Lord. Amen.

(Sarum Manual; B. of C.P., A.D. 1549.)

FAITH IN GOD'S UNCHANGEABLENESS.

BE present, O Lord, to our prayers, and protect us by day as well as by night, that in all successive changes of time we may ever be strengthened by Thine unchangeableness; through Jesus Christ our Lord. Amen.

(Leonine Sacramentary.)

A PRAYER FOR HEAVENLY-MINDEDNESS.

TAKE from us, O God, the care of worldly vanities; make us content with necessaries. Keep our hearts from delighting in honours, treasures, and pleasures of this life, and engender in us a desire to be with Thee in Thy eternal Kingdom. Give us, O Lord, such taste and feeling for Thy unspeakable joys in heaven, that we may always long therefor, and saying, with all Thy people, "Hasten Thy Kingdom, O Lord, take us to Thee"; for the sake of Jesus Christ, Who liveth and reigneth, ever one God, world without end. Amen.

(Archbishop Grindal, A.D. 1519.)

FOR POWER TO DO GOD'S WILL.

LORD, Who didst bid Thy seraph purge the prophet's lips with fire from off the altar, that so he might be free to preach Thy Word unto the people, whether they would hear or whether they would forbear; give Thy ministers and people pure and wise hearts, that so they may desire to go whither Thou dost send them, and to do that which Thou dost will, in the power of Him through Whom we do all things, even Thy Son Jesus Christ our Lord. Amen. *(Bishop Hornby, Nineteenth Century.)*

A MORNING PETITION.

WARM our cold hearts, Lord, we beseech Thee. Take away all that hinders us from giving ourselves to Thee. Mould us according to Thine own image. Give us grace to obey Thee in all things, and ever to follow Thy gracious leading. Make us this day to be kind to our fellow-men, to be gentle and unselfish, careful to hurt no one by word or deed, but anxious to do good to all, and to make others happy. O Lord, forgive the sins of our tempers. Pardon all our hasty words and unchristian thoughts. Make us watchful, that we offend not with our tongue. Give us a meek and a loving spirit, which is in Thy sight of great price. We would not live unto ourselves, but unto Thee. Keep us from sin this day, and all that may offend Thee; for Jesus Christ's sake. Amen. *(Bishop Ashton Oxenden, A.D. 1808.)*

FOR THE DIRECTION OF THE HOLY SPIRIT.

O GOD, forasmuch as our strength is in Thee, mercifully grant that Thy Holy Spirit may in all things direct and rule our hearts; through Jesus Christ our Lord. Amen.

(Gelasian Sacramentary; B. of C.P., A.D. 1549.)

"WHERE TWO OR THREE ARE GATHERED TOGETHER IN MY
NAME, THERE AM I IN THE MIDST."

O LORD God, Who hast taught us to pray all together, and
hast promised to hear the united voices of two or three
invoking Thy Name; hear now, O Lord, the prayers of Thy
servants unto their salvation, and give us in this world knowledge of Thy Truth, and in the world to come life everlasting;
for the sake of Jesus Christ our Lord.   Amen.

(Armenian Liturgy.)

"WHOSO OFFERETH PRAISE GLORIFIETH ME" (Ps. l. 23.)

O GOD, Who art holy, and restest in the holy places, Who art
hymned by the Seraphim, glorified by the Cherubim, and
adored by all the heavenly powers, Who hast vouchsafed that
we, Thy humble and unworthy servants, should now pay to Thee
worship and praise.   Receive, O Lord, we beseech Thee, our
fervent thanksgiving, and grant that we may serve Thee in holiness and peace all the days of our life.   Blessed art Thou, O Lord
God of our fathers, and art to be praised and exalted above all
for ever, and blessed be Thy glorious and holy Name.   Thine,
O Lord, is the greatness and the power, and the glory, and the
victory, and the majesty, for all that is in the heaven and in the
earth is Thine.   Thine is the kingdom, O Lord, and Thou art
exalted as Head above all.   We will sing unto the Lord a new
song.   O Lord, Thou art great and glorious, wonderful in strength
and invincible.   Let all creatures serve Thee, for Thou spakest
and they were made.   Thou didst send forth Thy Spirit and
they were created.   O God, Thou art worthy to be praised with
all pure and holy praise, therefore let Thy saints praise Thee
with all Thy creatures, and let all thine angels and Thy elect praise
Thee for ever.   Let our soul bless God, the great King, for worthy
is the Lamb that was slain to receive power and riches, and
wisdom, and strength, and honour, and glory, and blessing,
both now and evermore.   Amen.   *(St. Chrysostom,* A.D. 347.)

FOR ALL IN SPECIAL NEED OF PROTECTION.

O GOD, Who willest not the death of a sinner, protect with
Thy heavenly aid those persons who may now be exposed to
special temptations; and grant that in the fulfilment of Thy
commandments they may be strengthened by the assistance of
Thy grace; through Jesus Christ our Lord.   Amen.

(Gregorian Sacramentary.)

FOR LIGHT.

SHED forth, O Lord, we pray Thee, Thy light into our hearts,
that we may perceive the light of Thy commandments, and
walking in Thy way may fall into no error; through Jesus Christ
our Lord.   Amen.   *(Gelasian Sacramentary.)*

For God's Presence.

O GOD of peace, the true Light of faithful souls, the Helper of the needy, and the Saviour of the sinful, be present unto our prayers, and give unto us the spirit of wisdom, that we may hear and understand Thy Word, and strength that we may keep it unto life eternal; for Christ's sake.   Amen.

(Rev. Dr. John Hunter, A.D. 1849.)

For our Sovereign.

B LESSED Lord, Who has called Christian Princes to the defence of Thy faith, and hast made it their duty to promote the spiritual welfare, together with the temporal interest of their people; we acknowledge with humble and thankful hearts Thy great goodness to us, in setting Thy Servant, our most gracious King, over this Church and Nation; give him, we beseech Thee, all those heavenly graces that are requisite for so high a trust. Let the work of Thee his God prosper in his hands; let his eyes behold the success of his designs for the service of Thy true Religion established amongst us, and make him a blessed instrument of protecting and advancing Thy Truth, whenever it is persecuted and oppressed; let hypocrisy and profaneness, superstitions and idolatry, fly before his face; let not heresies and false doctrines disturb the peace of the Church, nor schisms and causeless divisions weaken it; but grant us to be of one heart and one mind in serving Thee our God, and obeying him according to Thy will.   And that these blessings may be continued to after-ages, let there never be one wanting in his house to succeed him in the government of this United Kingdom, that our posterity may see his children's children, and peace upon Israel; so we that are Thy people, and sheep of Thy pasture, shall give Thee thanks for ever, and will always be showing forth Thy praise from generation to generation; through Jesus Christ Thy Son our Lord.   Amen.   *(Book of Common Prayer,* A.D. 1704.)

For the Family and Household.

A LMIGHTY God, Who art the Author of all goodness, look down in mercy upon this family and household, and bless all who belong to it, present or absent.   Save and defend us in all dangers and adversities, give us all things that be needful for our souls and bodies, and bring us safely to Thy heavenly Kingdom; through Jesus Christ our Lord.   Amen.

(Family Prayer Book of the Church of Ireland, A.D. 1895.)

For Strength in Difficulties.

O ALMIGHTY God, grant, we beseech Thee, that we whose trust is under the shadow of Thy wings, may, through the help of Thy power, overcome all evils that rise up against us; through Jesus Christ our Lord.   Amen.   *(Roman Breviary.)*

PRAISE AND THANKSGIVING.

WE gratefully acknowledge unto Thee, that Thou art the Eternal One, our God, and the God of our fathers for evermore; the Rock of our life, and the Shield of our salvation. Thou art He Who existeth to all ages. We will therefore render thanks unto Thee, and declare Thy praise, for our lives which are delivered into Thine hand, and for our souls, which are confided to Thy care; for Thy goodness which is displayed to us daily; for Thy wonders, and Thy bounty which are at all times given unto us. Thou art the most gracious, for Thy mercies never fail; and Thou art the most compassionate, for Thy kindnesses never cease. Evermore do we hope in Thee, O Lord our God. Amen.

(*Daily Prayers, Jewish Book of Service, Jewish Calendar,* 5671.)

FOR THE GIFT OF GOD'S LOVE.

O GOD, fountain of love, pour Thy love into our souls, that we may love those whom Thou lovest with the love Thou givest us, and think and speak of them tenderly, meekly, lovingly; and so loving our brethren and sisters for Thy sake, may grow in Thy love, and dwelling in love may dwell in Thee; for Jesus Christ's sake. Amen.   (*Canon E. B. Pusey,* A.D. 1800.)

GENERAL INTERCESSION.

O FATHER of all, we humbly beseech Thee to show Thy mercy to the whole world. Let the Gospel of Thy Son run and be glorified throughout the earth. Let it be known by those who as yet know it not, let it be obeyed by all who profess and call themselves Christians. Continue Thy loving kindness, O Lord, to this Nation to which we belong, and increase in us true religion. Multiply Thy blessings upon our King, Queen Elizabeth, and all the Royal Family, giving them grace in all things to set forward Thy glory and the public good. Endue with Thy best gifts all who minister, that they may earnestly feed Thy flock. Visit in compassion all the children of affliction, relieve their necessities, and lighten their burdens, giving them patience and submission to Thy holy will, and in due time deliver them from all their troubles. Into Thy hand we commend all Thy people everywhere. Hear us, O Lord, we humbly beseech Thee, for the sake of Christ Jesus our Lord. Amen. (*Rev. L. Tuttiett,* A.D. 1825.)

FOR CHRISTIAN PERFECTION.

O LORD, our Guide even unto death, grant us, we beseech Thee, grace to follow Thee whithersoever Thou goest. In little daily duties to which Thou callest us, bow down our wills to simple obedience, patience under pain or provocation, strict truthfulness of word and manner, humility, kindness. In great acts of duty or perfection, if Thou shouldst call us to them, uplift us to self-sacrifice, heroic courage, laying down of life for Thy truth's sake or for a brother; through Christ our Lord. Amen.

(*Christina G. Rossetti,* A.D. 1830.)

For Purity of Heart.

O MOST merciful and gracious God, we beseech Thee to hear our prayers, and to deliver our hearts from the temptation of evil thoughts, that, by Thy goodness, we may become a fitting habitation for Thy Holy Spirit; through Jesus Christ our Lord. Amen.   (*Priest's Prayer Book*, A.D. 1870.)

For Harmony with the Divine Purposes.

GRANT, O Lord, that all whom Thou dost choose to work for Thee may this day labour in union with Thy holy purposes and in living unity with Thy dear Son Jesus Christ, that by the power of Thy Holy Spirit they may accomplish far more than they ever know, and work not for results, but for the single love of Thee. Amen.   (*From Sursum Corda*, A.D. 1898.)

A General Intercession.

O GOD, Who art loving unto every man, and whose mercy is over all Thy works, we beseech Thee to extend Thy mercy and compassion to the whole race of mankind, that their souls may be saved in the great day of the Lord Jesus Christ. Bless our native land, turn from us those national judgments which we have deserved, put an end to profaneness, intemperance, impiety, indifference of Thee. Bless our gracious King, and grant him a long, peaceful, and prosperous reign in Thy faith and fear. Bless our Queen Elizabeth and all members of the Royal Family. Bless Thy holy Church throughout the world, pour Thy Divine grace on every Bishop and minister, and grant to them all zeal, wisdom, and piety in their ministry. Bless all Thy missionary servants, and grant them grace to lead to the Cross of Christ those who know Thee not, and who are lying in darkness and in the shadow of death. Bless, O Lord, the work of Christian education, that the young may be trained up in the way they should go, and that every child may be imbued with early piety. Bless the widow and the orphan, the sick and the afflicted, the injured and the dying. Comfort them, O Lord, in their grief and sorrow, for Thou only, O Saviour, canst wipe away all tears from their eyes, and be an ever-present help in trouble. Bless all those who are in any way connected with us, our relations and friends. Wherever this day we can send a loving thought, there send, we humbly beseech Thee, a Father's blessing. Hear us, O God, for the sake of Jesus Christ Thy Son our Saviour. Amen.   (*Source not found.*)

For Sanctification.

LORD, sanctify us wholly, that our whole spirit, soul, and body may become Thy temple. Oh, do Thou dwell in us and be Thou our God, and we will be Thy servants, through Jesus Christ. Amen.   (*Bishop Ken*, A.D. 1637.)

For Renewed Consecration.

O ALMIGHTY God, Thou Who sittest on the throne, make all things within us new this day. Renew our faith, and hope, and love. Renew our wills, that we may serve Thee more gladly and watchfully than ever; renew our delight in Thy Word and Thy worship; renew our joy in Thee; renew our longing that all may know Thee; renew our desires and labours to serve others; and so take care of us Thy people, who embrace the Cross of Thy Son, and desire to walk in the light and power of Thy Spirit now and evermore; through Jesus Christ our Lord and Saviour. Amen.

(Source not found.)

For Consistent Lives.

O GOD, grant unto us that we be not unwise, but understanding Thy will; not slothful, but diligent in Thy work; that we run not as uncertainly, nor fight Thy battles as those that beat the air. Whatsoever our hand findeth to do, may we do it with our might; that when Thou shalt call Thy labourers to give them their reward, we may so have run that we may obtain; so have fought the good fight, as to receive the crown of eternal life; through Jesus Christ our Lord. Amen.

(Dean Henry Alford, A.D. 1810.)

For Missionaries and Teachers.

MOST merciful Father, we beseech Thee to send Thy heavenly blessing upon Thy servants, the missionary clergy and teachers of Thy Church; that they may be clothed with righteousness, and that Thy words spoken by their mouth may have such success that it may never be spoken in vain. Grant also to Thy children scattered abroad, grace to hear and receive what they shall deliver out of Thy Holy Word, as the means of salvation, that all may receive the crown of everlasting glory; through Jesus Christ our Lord. Amen.

(Book of Common Prayer, A.D. 1552, adapted.)

For the Sorrowful.

HAVE mercy, O Lord, on all who are homeless, bereaved, and sorrowful and give them comfort. Have mercy on all who have none to pray for them, and none to succour them. Have mercy on those who have brought punishment and trouble on themselves, and on those who have injured others. Have mercy on all, and give them this day some token of grace, and some sign of hope; through Jesus Christ our Saviour. Amen.   *(Anon.)*

Dedication.

TEACH us, good Lord, to serve Thee as Thou deservest; to give and not to count the cost; to fight and not to heed the wounds; to toil and not to seek for rest; to labour and not to ask for any reward, save that of knowing that we do Thy will: through Jesus Christ our Lord. Amen.

(Ignatius Loyola, A.D. 1491.)

An Acknowledgment of God's Supremacy.

O THOU Who art the Father of that Son which hast awakened us, and yet urgest us out of the sleep of our sins, and exhortest us that we become Thine, to Thee, Lord, we pray, Who art the supreme Truth, for all truth that is, is from Thee. Thee we implore, O Lord, Who art the highest Wisdom, through Thee are wise, all those that are so. Thou art the supreme Joy, and from Thee all have become happy that are so. Thou art the highest Good, and from Thee all beauty springs. Thou art the intellectual Light, and from Thee man derives his understanding. To Thee, O God, we call and speak. Hear us, O Lord, for Thou art our God and our Lord, our Father and our Creator, our Ruler and our Hope, our Wealth and our Honour, our Home, our Country, our Salvation, and our Life; hear, hear us, O Lord. Few of Thy servants comprehend Thee, but at least we love Thee—yea, love Thee above all other things. We seek Thee, we follow Thee, we are ready to serve Thee; under Thy power we desire to abide, for Thou art the Sovereign of all. We pray Thee to command us as Thou wilt; through Jesus Christ Thy Son our Lord. Amen.   (*King Alfred*, A.D. 849.)

For Christ-like Lives.

O LORD, our God, we beseech Thee to give us patience in troubles, humility in comforts, constancy in temptations, and victory against all our ghostly enemies. Grant us sorrow for our sins, thankfulness for Thy benefits, fear of Thy judgments, love of Thy mercies, and mindfulness of Thy Presence for evermore. Make us humble to our superiors, and friendly to our equals, ready to please all, loath to offend any; loving to our friends, and charitable to our enemies. Give us holiness in our thoughts, and righteousness in all our actions; let Thy mercy cleanse us from our sins, and Thy grace bring forth in us the fruits of everlasting life; through Jesus Christ our Lord. Amen.   (*Bishop Cosin*, A.D. 1595.)

For the Spread of Christ's Kingdom.

O ALMIGHTY Father, Who didst give Thine only begotten Son Jesus Christ to die for our sins, and for the sins of the whole world, help us to carry to others the goodness of Thy love. Send forth more labourers into Thy harvest, we pray Thee, and grant that the Gospel may be preached in all lands and among all nations; for Thy dear Son's sake, Jesus Christ our Lord. Amen.
(*S.P.G.*, A.D. 1701.)

For Union with Christ.

O LORD our God, Whose compassion is the cause of our fearing and loving Thy Name, mercifully pour Thy grace into our hearts, that we, casting away what displeases Thee, may be united to Thee with an honest will; through Jesus Christ our Lord. Amen.   (*Leonine Sacramentary*.)

For Protection from Evil.

O BLESSED Jesus, keep us this day and ever from evil and danger of soul and body, and from all that would offend Thee. Come, O Holy Spirit, and help us in all our temptations, and in all our desires to advance in holiness, that, living holy lives, we may die happy deaths. Never leave us to ourselves, lest we fall. Guide us to the strait gate, lead us in the narrow path, so that, saved at last, we may have no more to fear, but may rejoice before Thee for ever and ever. Amen.

(The Narrow Way, A.D. 1869.)

For an Increase of Love to God and Sympathy with Others.

E NLARGE our souls with a Divine charity, that we may hope all things, endure all things, and become messengers of Thy healing mercy to the grievances and infirmities of men. In all things attune our hearts to the holiness and harmony of Thy Kingdom; and hasten the time when Thy Kingdom shall come, and Thy will be done on earth as it is in heaven; through Jesus Christ our Lord. Amen. *(James Martineau, Published A.D. 1891.)*

For the Rich and Influential.

W E beseech Thee, O Lord, that all those to whom Thou hast given positions of influence may praise Thee in their lives, honour Thee with their wealth, and induce others by their example to seek for that incorruptible inheritance which Thy beloved Son will give to all who have followed Him in meekness, and purity, and faith; through the same Jesus Christ our Lord. Amen. *(Rev. R. M. Benson, A.D. 1824.)*

For the Fruit of the Spirit.

O LORD God, Whose strength is sufficient for all who lay hold on it, grant us in Thee to comfort our hearts and be strong. Humility, meekness, temperance, purity, large-heartedness, sympathy, zeal—grant us these evidences of faith, handmaids of hope, fruits of love; for the sake of Jesus Christ, our Strength, our Righteousness, and our Hope of glory. Amen.

(Christina G. Rossetti, A.D. 1830.)

For a Right Use of God's Gifts.

O LORD our God, without Whose will and pleasure not a sparrow can fall to the ground, grant to us in times of trouble to be patient without murmuring or despair, and in prosperity to acknowledge Thy gifts, and to confess that all our endowments come from Thee, O Father of lights, Who givest liberally and upbraidest not. Give us, by Thy Holy Spirit, a willing heart and a ready hand to use all Thy gifts to Thy praise and glory; through Jesus Christ our Lord. Amen.

(Archbishop Cranmer, A.D. 1489.)

Praise and Thanksgiving.

WE praise Thee, Father, Lord Almighty, for all the blessings of this life, for Thy wondrous mercies vouchsafed to us hitherto. Manifold are Thy gifts, Lord God of Hosts. Teach us to magnify Thy Name, even as the angels around Thy throne pour forth unceasing hallelujahs, so would we join with them in all humility. The more we know ourselves the more we recognize our great unworthiness. Everything in creation testifies to Thy greatness, therefore we pray Thee to accept our song of praise, as we lift up our hearts and voices to Thee, saying, Holy, Holy, Holy, Lord God of Hosts, glory to Thee, O Lord most High, both now and evermore. Amen. *(Source not found.)*

For More Love to God.

O LORD God, accept our humble thanks for Thy great mercy bestowed upon us. We confess that we are not worthy of the least of all Thy mercies, yet grant, we beseech Thee, that every fresh proof of Thy goodness may cause us to love Thee more, and make us to use our strength and all Thy gifts in doing Thy holy will more perfectly for the time to come; through Jesus Christ our Lord. Amen. *(Canon E. Hawkins, A.D. 1802.)*

For Heavenly Light.

O GOD, with Whom is the well of life, and in Whose light we see light, increase in us, we beseech Thee, the brightness of Divine knowledge, whereby we may be able to reach Thy plenteous fountain; impart to our thirsting souls the draught of life, and restore to our darkened minds the light from Heaven; through Jesus Christ our Lord. Amen. *(Mozarabic Liturgy.)*

For a Blessing on the Services of the Day.

MERCIFUL Father, we commend to Thee the worship and ordinances of this day. Bless all our souls, keep our hearts and thoughts in Thy House of Prayer. Speak to us through Thy Holy Word, which liveth and abideth for ever. Pour the continual dew of Thy blessing on all Thy ministers; for the sake of Jesus Christ our Lord. Amen.

(Bishop H. C. G. Moule, A.D. 1841.)

Supplication.

O GOD, Thou art my God; early will I seek Thee. My soul thirsteth for Thee, my flesh longeth for Thee in a dry and thirsty land where no water is; to see Thy power and glory, so as I have seen Thee in the sanctuary. Now therefore, O God, hear the prayers of Thy servants, and our supplications which we make before Thee; and when Thou hearest in heaven, Thy dwelling-place, answer and forgive, and cause Thy face to shine upon us. Amen. *(Ps. lxiii.; 1 Kings viii. 30, adapted, King David and King Solomon, Eleventh Century B.C.)*

A Morning Prayer.

O LORD, Who hast given us sleep to recruit our weakness, vouchsafe us this day, a holy peaceful and sinless course. Grant to our souls Thy Holy Spirit, to our bodies Thy blessed protection. Deliver us from all our enemies, and teach us to do the things that please Thee; through Jesus Christ our Lord. Amen.   (*Bishop Reynolds*, A.D. 1674.)

For Faithful Service.

O LORD, our heavenly Father, by Whose Providence the duties of men are variously ordered, grant to us all such a spirit that we may labour heartily to do our work in our several stations, as serving one Master and looking for one reward. Teach us to put to good account whatever talents Thou hast lent to us, and enable us to redeem our time by patience and zeal; through Jesus Christ Thy Son. Amen.

(*Bishop Westcott*, A.D. 1825.)

For Courage.

BLESSED Lord, Who wast tempted in all things like as we are, have mercy upon our frailty. Out of weakness give us strength. Grant to us Thy fear, that we may fear Thee only. Support us in time of temptation. Embolden us in the time of danger. Help us to do Thy work with good courage, and to continue Thy faithful soldiers and servants unto our life's end; through Jesus Christ our Lord. Amen.

(*Bishop Westcott*, A.D. 1825.)

For Unity.

O GOD, Who biddest us dwell with one mind in Thine house, of Thy mercy put away from us all that causeth us to differ, that through Thy bountiful goodness we may keep the Unity of the Spirit in the bond of peace; through Jesus Christ our Lord. Amen.   (*Canon E. B. Pusey*, A.D. 1800.)

For Grace to seek God's Kingdom and Righteousness.

WE ask not of Thee, O Father, silver and gold, honour and glory, nor the pleasures of the world, but do Thou grant us grace to seek Thy Kingdom and Thy righteousness, and do Thou add unto us things necessary for the body and for this life. Behold, O Lord, our desire; may it be pleasing in Thy sight. We present our petition unto Thee through our Lord Jesus Christ, Who is at Thy right hand, our Mediator and Advocate, through Whom Thou soughtest us that we might seek Thee; Thy Word, through Whom Thou madest us and all things; Thy only begotten Son, through Whom Thou callest us to adoption, Who intercedeth with Thee for us, and in Whom are hid all the treasures of wisdom and knowledge; to Him, with Thyself and the Holy Spirit, be all honour, praise, and glory, now and for ever. Amen.

(*St. Augustine*, A.D. 354.)

Thanksgiving.

O LORD God, our heavenly Father, we thank Thee that Thou hast called us to the knowledge of Thy grace, and faith in Thee. Increase this knowledge, and confirm this faith in us evermore. We thank Thee for all those who are called by Thy name in all parts of the world, praying Thee that they may steadfastly walk in the way that leadeth to eternal life. We thank Thee for all Thy servants departed this life in Thy faith and fear, beseeching Thee to give us grace so to follow their good examples, that with them we may be made partakers of Thy heavenly kingdom. Grant this, O Father, for Jesus Christ's sake, our only Mediator and Advocate. Amen. *(Adapted.)*

For Grace to live Consistent Lives.

GIVE us grace, most Blessed Lord, to live pure and holy lives, loving and serving Thee more and more, and loving our neighbours and serving them for Thy sake. Make us, we beseech Thee, one with Thyself, and let nothing ever separate us from Thee. Preserve us waking, defend us sleeping, that we may watch with Thee, and rest in peace; for Thy Name's sake. Amen.   *(The Narrow Way, A.D. 1869.)*

For Confidence in God.

O THOU Who pervadest and animatest all that lives, Who art the Source from which we come, the End to which we travel, and the Centre on which we rest, help us to put our trust in Thee for ever. Enable us to surrender our wills to Thine, and to sacrifice each desire that is contrary to Thy law; for the sake of Jesus Christ Thy Son our Lord. Amen.

(Professor Knight, Nineteenth Century.)

For Missionary Societies and Workers.

LORD, we pray Thee to bless the work of all Missionary Societies. Teach us to realize that the command to go into all the world and preach the Gospel to every creature is binding in measure to each individual. Show us what we ought to do. Increase our zeal, our interest, our service, our supplications. May we help in sending others, if we cannot go ourselves, by our prayers and offering; for the sake of Jesus Christ our Lord. Amen.   *(Church Missionary Society, A.D. 1799.)*

For Knowledge and Love.

O THOU, Who art the Light of the minds that know Thee, the Life of the souls that love Thee, and the Strength of the thoughts that seek Thee; help us so to know Thee, that we may truly love Thee, so to love Thee that we may fully serve Thee, Whose service is perfect freedom; through Jesus Christ our Lord. Amen. *(Gelasian Sacramentary, Source doubtful.)*

Thanksgiving.

WE give Thee thanks, O heavenly Father, Who hast preserved us through the night. We pray Thee to keep us through this day, and to bring us in safety to the evening hours, that Thou mayest receive our praise at all times; through Jesus Christ our Lord. Amen.   (*Gelasian Sacramentary.*)

For Light.

O THOU Who art the Sun of Righteousness and the Light eternal, giving gladness unto all things; shine upon us both now and for ever, that we may walk always in the light of Thy countenance; through Jesus Christ our Lord. Amen.
                              (*An Ancient Collect.*)

For Faith and Love.

O FAITHFUL Lord, grant to us, we pray Thee, faithful hearts devoted to Thee, and to the service of all men for Thy sake. Fill us with pure love of Thee, keep us steadfast in this love, give us faith that worketh by love, and preserve us faithful unto death; through Jesus Christ our Lord. Amen.
                         (*Christina G. Rossetti*, A.D. 1830.)

For the Household.

O ALMIGHTY God, we thank Thee for all Thy blessings and all Thy mercies which Thou in Thy love hast bestowed upon us. Do Thou continue Thy care for us. Do Thou, Who always hast loved us, make us also to love Thee. Help us to live as Thy obedient and dutiful children. Let us never forget Who Thou art, and Whose we are, and grant to every member of this house strength and courage for the battle of life; for the sake of Jesus Christ our Lord. Amen.
      (*Rev. H. W. Turner's Collection, Nineteenth Century.*)

A Prayer for Christ's Presence.

O HEAVENLY King, Thou Comforter and Spirit of Truth, Who art in every place, and fillest the whole world with the treasures of Thy goodness; O Life-giver, come into our hearts and dwell there, and save our souls alive; and unto Thee be glory now and evermore. Amen. (*Book of Hours*, A.D. 1865.)

For an Increase in Godliness.

O LORD, increase in us faith and devotion, replenish our hearts with all goodness, and by Thy great mercy keep us in the same. Give us godly zeal in prayer, true humility in prosperity, perfect patience in adversity, and continual joy in the Holy Ghost; even for the sake of Jesus Christ, our only Lord and Saviour. Amen. (*Archbishop Laud*, A.D. 1573.)

A Morning Intercession.

O LORD, we beseech Thee, listen now to the prayer of Thy servants, who desire to fear Thy Name. Prosper us, we pray Thee, this day in our work. Help us ever to remember that Thou art a God at hand, that no secret place is hidden from Thee, but that all our thoughts, and words, and actions, are seen and known by Thee. Make us truthful in all our words, holy in all our thoughts, and honest in every act. Make Thy presence a happiness to us. Let us often think of Thee as our Father, and Friend, and our Helper in every hour of need. Bless all who are dear to us, and teach them the paths of goodness and truth; for the sake of Jesus Christ our Saviour. Amen.

(O. H. C., Twentieth Century.)

For Heavenly Wisdom.

WE ask of Thee the wisdom that cometh from above, which is pure and peaceable, without partiality and without hypocrisy. Teach us to think soberly of ourselves, as we ought to think, and to bear each other's burdens always. Make us fruitful in every good work, to do Thy will; through Jesus Christ our Lord. Amen.

(Jas. iii. 17; Titus ii. 12; Col. i. 10, adapted, First Century A.D.)

A Prayer for Native Christians.

O LORD, we beseech Thee, pour out Thy Holy Spirit upon all the Native Converts whom Thou hast gathered to Thyself, through Thy labouring servants throughout the world, that as Thou hast begotten them again unto a lively hope, so they may ever be followers of Thee as dear children. Make them to be ready to do every good work, and more especially to exert themselves for the salvation of those around them; that, so by their zeal and faithful testimony, by their holy and consistent lives, they may glorify Thy Name before their countrymen, and bring in unto Thee from the midst of them those whom Thou dost save; through Jesus Christ our Lord. Amen.

(Church Missionary Society, A.D. 1799.)

A Prayer for Victory.

O GOD, the Might of all them that put their trust in Thee, grant that we may be more than conquerors over all that make war upon our souls, and in the end may enter into perfect peace in Thy Presence; through Jesus Christ our Lord. Amen.

(Roman Breviary.)

For Light and Love.

LET Thy mercy, O Lord, be upon us, and the brightness of Thy Spirit illumine our inward souls, that He may kindle our cold hearts, and light up our dark minds; Who abideth evermore with Thee in Thy glory. Amen. *(Mozarabic Liturgy.)*

For Grace to carry our Daily Cross.

O LORD Jesus Christ, Who hast bidden us take up our cross daily and follow Thee, make, we beseech Thee, the way of Thy commandments pleasant unto us, and the burden of Thy cross light unto our souls, that we may so faithfully follow Thee in this life, that finally we may share Thy home above; for Thine own Name's sake. Amen. (*Rev. G. H. Sharpe, Nineteenth Century.*)

Intercession for Missions.

MOST gracious God, Who through Thine infinite goodness hast been pleased to offer salvation to all mankind, and to receive all humble supplications as objects of Thy mercy, Thou didst communicate the glad tidings of our Saviour's appearing in the world to the people of Israel by the ministration of angels, and Thou didst vouchsafe to reveal the joyful news to Gentiles by ordering a bright star to point at the rising of the Sun of Righteousness with healing in His wings. Blessed be Thy holy Name for that glorious light, which dispersed itself through the dark regions of the world; which dispelled the thick clouds of ignorance and idolatry, of folly and vanity; which directed mankind to the true and most worthy object of their worship, and raised their nature to its utmost improvement. Adored be Thy infinite mercy, which brought the joyful sound to this land, and has permitted it to partake of the gracious and benign influences of Thy distinguishing providence. May we always value such an inestimable benefit by walking as Children of the Light, and by compassionating the miseries of those that still sit in darkness. To this end we humbly beseech Thee to prosper the undertakings of those Societies which are established among us for propagating the Gospel in foreign parts; make the members thereof zealous and diligent in that good work. Give them wisdom to discern the best and most proper means of promoting it, courage and resolution to pursue it, and by unity and affection in their consultations, and by Thy blessings upon their endeavours, the happiness to effect it; through Jesus Christ our Lord and Saviour. Amen. (*Robert Nelson, A.D. 1656.*)

For Faithful and Prepared Lives.

WHO can tell what a day may bring forth? Cause us, therefore, gracious God, to live every day as if it were to be our last, for that we know not but it may be such. Cause us to live so at present as we shall wish we had done when we come to die. O grant that we may not die with any guilt upon our consciences, or any known sin unrepented of, but that we may be found in Christ, Who is our only Saviour and Redeemer. Amen.
(*St. Thomas à Kempis, A.D. 1379.*)

For the Spread of Christ's Kingdom.

O LORD God, arise, may Thy kingdom come on earth, through Jesus Christ our Lord. Amen.
(*Bishop Vernon Herford, Twentieth Century.*)

For Christ's Companionship.

LORD, be with our spirit, and dwell in our hearts by faith
Oh! make us such as we should be towards Thee, and such
as Thou mayest take pleasure in us. Be with us everywhere,
and at all times, in all events and circumstances of our life,
to sanctify and sweeten to us whatever befalls us; and never
leave nor forsake us in our present pilgrimage here, till Thou
hast brought us safe through all trials and dangers to be ever
with Thee, there to live in Thy sight and love, world without
end. Amen.   (*Rev. Benjamin Jenks*, A.D. 1646.)

For Sympathy.

POUR into our hearts the spirit of unselfishness, so that, when
our cup overflows, we may seek to share our happiness with
our brethren. O Thou God of Love, Who makest Thy sun to rise
on the evil and on the good, and sendest rain on the just and on
the unjust, grant that we may become more and more Thy
true children, by receiving into our souls more of Thine own
spirit of ungrudging and unwearying kindness; which we ask in
the name of Jesus Christ. Amen.

(*Rev. Dr. John Hunter*, A.D. 1849.)

For Missions.

ALMIGHTY God, Lord of the Nations, Who didst send the
only begotten of the Father to become the Son of man, that
through His Cross and Passion the peoples might be redeemed
to Thy glory, send forth Thy Church, we beseech Thee, in the
spirit of the Incarnation to proclaim the message of the Cross.
Enable us in humility and lowliness, in poverty of spirit and
simplicity of life, in love and hope and patience to follow in the
steps of our Master, taking forth the precious from the vile, loving
even as He loved. Remove from us undue pride of Church
or Nation, all dominance and desire to rule, all faulty ideals,
all imposition on others of merely Western forms; so purify
us by Thy love shed abroad in our hearts, and Thy Truth still
proceeding from Thee, that we may reveal the Saviour of mankind to the men of the East, as He revealed Thee to the world.
For their sake enable us to sanctify ourselves, that through our
decrease in pre-eminence they may increase in knowledge of
Thee. Hear and answer us as we present these petitions to Thee,
in the Name of Him Who emptied Himself and for our sakes
became poor, Jesus Christ our Lord. Amen.

(*Georgina A. Gollock, Nineteenth Century*.)

For Joy, Peace, and Hope.

O GOD of hope, fill Thy children with all joy and peace in believing, that we and they may abound in hope in the power
of the Holy Ghost; through Jesus Christ our Lord. Amen.

(*St. Paul, First Century* A.D.; *Rom.* xv. 13.)

For the Presence of the Holy Spirit.

O HOLY Paraclete, sweetest Consolation of the sorrowful, gracious Spirit come down at this time with Thy mighty power into the depths of our hearts. Gladden there with Thy brightness every dark retreat, and enrich all with the dew of Thine abundant comfort. Kindle our inward parts with holy favour, that the incense of our prayers and praises may ever go up to Thee, O our God; through Jesus Christ Thy Son our Lord. Amen.   (*St. Anselm*, A.D. 1033.)

For Missionaries.

O GOD, Who (at this time) didst send the Holy Ghost upon the Apostles, to teach them and lead them into all truth, that they might go into all the world and preach the Gospel to every creature, pour out, we beseech Thee, the same Holy Spirit upon Thy Church, that it may send forth the good tidings of great joy unto all people. Hasten Thy work, O God; raise up labourers, and strengthen their hands, that they may tell of salvation unto the ends of the world. Bless with the mighty aid of Thy Holy Spirit those who now work to the glory of Thy Name in distant lands. Give them faithfulness and courage, and take out of their way all hindrances. Forward the time, O God, for the coming of Thy kingdom, and for the gathering in of all Nations unto Thee. And while we pray for the outward growth of Thy Kingdom in the world, we pray also for its inward growth in the hearts of men. And especially, O Lord, for our own Church and country, we pray that true religion may abound unto all righteousness and peace; through Thy only Son our Saviour Jesus Christ. Amen.   (*Source not found.*)

For the King.

O LORD, save the King, who putteth his trust in Thee. Send him help from Thy holy place, and evermore mightily defend him. Let his enemies have no advantage of him, nor the wicked approach to hurt him; O Lord, hear our prayer, and let our cry come unto Thee.   (*Accession Service*, A.D. 1626.)

For Friends and Relations.

O GOD, the Father of our Lord Jesus Christ, of Whom every family in heaven and earth is named, grant unto our friends, to all members of this household, and to all the members of our different families, that, according to the riches of Thy glory, we may be strengthened with might by Thy Spirit in the inner man; that Christ may dwell in our hearts by faith; that we, being rooted and grounded in love, may be able to comprehend with all saints what is the breadth, and length, and depth, and height; and to know the love of Christ which passeth knowledge, that we may be filled with all the fulness of God; through the same Jesus Christ our Lord. Amen.

(*From Eph.* iii. 14–19; *St. Paul, First Century* A.D.)

For Consecration.

A LMIGHTY God, Who hast made all things for man, and man
for Thy glory, sanctify our body and soul, our thoughts and
our intentions, our words and actions, that whatsoever we shall
think, or speak or do, may by us be designed to the glorification
of Thy Name, and by Thy blessing, it may be effectual and successful in the work of God, according as it can be capable.   Lord,
turn necessities into virtues, the works of Nature into the works
of grace, by making them orderly, regular and temperate, sub-
ordinate and profitable to ends beyond their own proper efficacy;
and let no pride or self-seeking, no impure motive, or unworthy
purpose, no little ends, and low imagination stain our spirit,
and unhallow any of our words and actions.   But let our body
be a servant to our spirit, and both body and spirit servants of
Jesus Christ, that doing all things for Thy glory here, we may be
partakers of Thy glory hereafter; through Jesus Christ.   Amen.
                            (*St. Thomas à Kempis*, A.D. 1379.)

For Acceptable Service.

O GLORIOUS and Almighty God, in Whom all the spirits of
the blessed place the confidence of their hope; grant to us
that, by Thy help, we may be able ever to serve Thee with a
pure mind; through Jesus Christ our Lord.   Amen.
                                    (*Sarum Breviary*.)

For Missionaries.

O HEAVENLY Father, we pray Thee to bless and protect
Thy servants who have gone forth to preach the Gospel
in distant lands; give them such success in their labours that
Thy way may be known upon earth, Thy saving health among
all Nations.   Hear and grant this our prayer, O God, for the
sake of Jesus Christ, our blessed Lord and Saviour.   Amen.
(*Family Prayer Book of the Church of Ireland*, A.D. 1895.)

For Watchfulness.

O THOU Who hast foretold that Thou wilt return again, to
judgment, in an hour that we are not aware of; grant us
grace to watch and pray always; that whether Thou shalt come
at even, or at midnight, or at the cock-crowing, or in the morning,
Thou mayest find us in the number of those servants who shall
be blessed for watching for their Lord; for Thy Name's sake.
Amen.   (*Non-Jurors' Prayer Book*, A.D. 1734.)

For Peace.

M ERCIFULLY receive, O Lord, the prayers of Thy people,
that all adversities and errors may be destroyed, and they
may serve Thee in quiet freedom, and give Thy peace in our
times; through Jesus Christ our Lord.   Amen.
                                (*Leonine Sacramentary*.)

For Zeal.

O ALMIGHTY and merciful Father, Who pourest Thy benefits upon us, forgive the unthankfulness with which we have requited Thy goodness. We have remained before Thee with dead and senseless hearts, unkindled with love of Thy gentle and enduring goodness. Turn Thou us, O merciful Father, and so shall we be turned. Make us with our whole heart to hunger and thirst after Thee, and with all our longing to desire Thee. Make us with our whole heart to serve Thee alone, and with all our zeal to seek those things which are well-pleasing in Thy sight; for the sake of Thine only begotten Son, to whom with Thee and the Holy Ghost be all honour and glory, for ever and ever. Amen.   (*St. Anselm*, A.D. 1033.)

For Christ's Comfort and Peace.

L ORD Jesus, so long as seemeth Thee good, give us faith rather than knowledge, and hope than assurance. Feed us when we need feeding; heal us when we need healing. Grant us to find peace by comforting ourselves lovingly to Thy goodwill and pleasure—peace here and peace hereafter; through Jesus Christ our Lord. Amen.

(*Christina G. Rossetti*, A.D. 1830.)

For Missions.

O LORD God, Who wilt have all men to be saved and come to the knowledge of the Truth, grant that Thy whole Church may readily obey the command of Thy Son, Jesus Christ, to go and teach all nations, so that the Gospel of Thy Grace may be known to the uttermost part of the earth, and the way be made ready for the coming of our King. Speedily fulfil Thy purposes concerning Jew and Gentile. Take away blindness from Thine ancient people, and cause them to see Jesus Christ, their Saviour, Hasten the day when all Israel shall be saved. These things we ask in the Name of Him Who was given to be a Light to lighten the Gentiles and the glory of Thy people Israel, Jesus Christ our Lord. Amen.   (*Church Missionary Society*, A.D. 1799.)

For Contented Hearts.

O GOD, the sure Defence of all who trust in Thee, we beseech Thee, give us contented and trustful hearts, that, casting all our care on Thee, and bearing all our trials cheerfully, we may be united to Thee in Thy love in this world, and finally, by Thy mercy, obtain that eternal reward which Thou hast prepared for all who trust in Thee; through Jesus Christ our Lord. Amen.

(*Rev. G. H. Sharpe, Nineteenth Century.*)

For Sanctification.

T HE very God of peace sanctify us wholly, and may our whole spirit and soul and body be preserved blameless unto the coming of our Lord Jesus Christ. Amen.

(*St. Paul, First Century* A.D.; 1 *Thess.* v. 23.)

For Repentance.

O GOD, Who, to such as seek first Thy Kingdom and righteousness, dost promise a sufficiency of all things needful in this our mortal state; let Thy blessing, we beseech Thee, be on the increase of the earth and on the labour of our hands, that we may eat bread without scarceness, and have to give to him that needeth. Preserve this land from the sore judgments which by our sins we have deserved, and grant that being led to repentance by Thy long-suffering and goodness, we may become a wise and understanding people, loving Thee, the Lord our God; through the merits and mediation of Jesus Christ, our only Advocate and Redeemer. Amen.

(Rev. W. E. Scudamore, A.D. 1813.)

For the Christian's Armour.

GIVE unto us, O God, the girdle, the helmet, the breastplate, the shield, the sandals, the sword—above all things, prayer. Grant unto us the power and opportunity of well-doing, that before the day of our departure may come, we may have wrought at least somewhat, whose good fruit may remain; that we may behold Thy Presence in righteousness, and be satisfied with Thy glory; for Christ's sake. Amen.

(Bishop Andrewes, A.D. 1555.)

For those who are Persecuted for Righteousness' Sake.

GRANT, O Lord, to Thy servants and followers who are persecuted for righteousness' sake, that their conversation may be as becometh the Gospel of Christ; that they may stand fast in one spirit, with one mind striving together for the faith of the Gospel; that in nothing terrified by their adversaries they may be bold in the behalf of Christ, not only to believe on Him, but also to suffer for His sake, Who liveth and reigneth, ever one God, world without end. Amen.

(St. Paul, First Century A.D.; Phil. i. 27–29.)

For the King and the Royal Family.

O LORD our God, Who upholdest and governest all things by the word of Thy power, receive our humble prayers for our Sovereign Lord, George, set over us by Thy grace and providence to be our King; and, together with him, bless, we beseech Thee, our gracious Queen Elizabeth, Mary the Queen Mother, Princess Elizabeth, and all the Royal Family; that they, ever trusting in Thy goodness, protected by Thy power, and crowned with Thy gracious and endless favour, may long continue before Thee in peace and safety, joy and honour, and after death may obtain everlasting life and glory; by the merits and mediation of Christ Jesus our Saviour, Who with Thee and the Holy Ghost liveth and reigneth, ever one God, world without end. Amen.

(Accession Service, A.D. 1640; Book of Common Prayer.)

For Knowledge of God's Will.

ALMIGHTY and everlasting God, Who maketh us both to
will and to do those things that be good and acceptable,
we offer unto Thee our humble supplications, beseeching Thee,
so to lead us in the knowledge of Thy truth, and obedience to
Thy will, that out of weakness we may be made strong, and
that finally we may obtain everlasting life; through Jesus Christ
our Lord. Amen.

(The Order of Confirmation in the B.C.P., 1661, adapted.)

For Divine Love.

SET our hearts on fire with the love of Thee, most loving
Father, and then to do Thy will, and to obey Thy commandments, will not be grevious to us. For to him that loveth,
nothing is difficult, nothing is impossible, because love is stronger
than death. Oh! may love fill and rule our hearts; for then
there will spring up and be cherished between Thee and us a
likeness of character and union of will, so that we may choose
and refuse what Thou dost. May Thy will be done in us, and by
us for ever; through Jesus Christ Thy Son our Lord. Amen.

(" Paradise for the Christian Soul," Nineteenth Century.)

For the Church.

HEAR us, O God of our salvation, Thou hope of all the ends
of the earth, and in Thy strength, set fast as the mountains,
the outposts of Thy power, and strongholds of lofty virtues. On
Thee we rely for gifts of aspiration, whereby to ascend to the
summit of all blessedness; that Thy Church, as it extends to
all corners of the world, may soar in faith, may rest in hope,
and rise to the full height of charity; through Jesus Christ our
Lord. Amen.   *(Mozarabic Liturgy.)*

For a Constant Recollection of Christ's Intercession for us.

GRANT, O Lord, that Christ Himself may be formed in us,
that we may be made conformable to His image, that when
we are lukewarm in prayer and stand in need of any grace or
of heavenly consolation, we may remember His appearance in
the Presence of God, and His intercession for us; for His Name's
sake. Amen.   *(Bishop Andrewes, A.D. 1555.)*

Ascription.

TO God the Father, Who first loved us and made us accepted
in the Beloved; to God the Son, Who loved us, and washed
us from our sins in His own Blood; to God the Holy Ghost, Who
sheds the love of God abroad in our hearts, be all love and all
glory, for time and for eternity. Amen.

(Bishop Ken, A.D. 1637.)

Confession of Sin.

ALMIGHTY and most merciful Father, look down upon us, Thy unworthy servants, who here prostrate ourselves at the footstool of Thy throne of grace. Look upon us, O Father, through the mediation and in the merits of Jesus Christ, in Whom only Thou art well pleased, for of ourselves we are not worthy to stand before Thee. As in sin we were born, so we have broken Thy commandments, by thought, words, and works. We confess, O Lord, that it is Thy mercy which endureth for ever. Thy compassion which never fails, which is the cause that we have not been consumed. With Thee there is mercy and plenteous redemption; in the multitude of Thy mercies and by the merits of Jesus Christ, enter not into judgment with Thy servants, but be Thou merciful unto us, and wash away all our sins with that precious blood which our Saviour shed for us. Purify our hearts by Thy Holy Spirit, and as Thou dost add days to our lives, so good Lord, we beseech Thee, to add repentance to our days, that when we have passed this mortal life we may be partakers of Thine everlasting Kingdom; through the merits of Jesus Christ our Lord. Amen.

(King Charles I., A.D. 1600.)

For Growth in Grace.

WE beseech Thee, most tender Father, that Thy most living fire may purify us, that Thy most clear light may illumine us, and that Thy most pure love may so avail us, that without let or hindrance of mortal things, we may return to Thee in happiness and security; through Jesus Christ Thy Son our Saviour. Amen.   *(Vittoria Colonna,* A.D. 1490.)

For Christ's Flock.

O GOD of all power, Who hast called from death the great Pastor of the sheep, our Lord Jesus, comfort and defend the flock which He hath redeemed by the blood of the eternal testament; increase the number of true preachers; mitigate and lighten the hearts of the ignorant; relieve the pains of such as be afflicted, but especially of those that suffer for the testimony of the Truth, by the power of our Lord Jesus Christ. Amen.

(John Knox, A.D. 1505 ?)

For Heavenly-Mindedness.

EXALT us with Thee, O Lord, to know the mystery of life, that we may use the earthly as the appointed expression and type of the heavenly, and by using to Thy glory the natural body may befit it to be exalted to the use of the spiritual body through Jesus Christ our Lord. Amen.

(Rev. Charles Kingsley, A.D. 1819.)

For Daily Help.

ABBA, Father, fulfil the office of Thy Name towards Thy servants; do Thou govern, protect, preserve, sanctify, guide, and console us. Let us be so enkindled with love for Thee, that we may not be despised by Thee, O most merciful Lord, most tender Father, for Jesus Christ's sake. Amen.

(Gallican Sacramentary.)

For Zeal in God's Service.

O GOD, the Sovereign Good of the soul, Who requirest the hearts of all Thy children, deliver us from all sloth in Thy work, all coldness in Thy cause; and grant us by looking unto Thee to rekindle our love, and by waiting upon Thee to renew our strength; through Jesus Christ our Lord. Amen.

(William Bright, A.D. 1824.)

For Love of God and His Laws.

O GOD, Who hast taught us to keep all Thy heavenly commandments by loving Thee and our neighbour; grant us the spirit of peace and grace, that we may be both devoted to Thee with our whole heart, and united to each other with a pure will; through Jesus Christ our Lord. Amen.

(Leonine Sacramentary.)

For the Distressed.

O MERCIFUL God, Who givest to us all more than we either think or ask, give health to the sick, to the weary ones rest, to the mourners comfort. Raise the fallen, and give life to the dead in heart. Defend and provide for the fatherless and the widow. Succour the tempted and keep them from falling, and make us all good and pure, such as Thou wouldst have us to be; for the sake of Jesus Christ our Lord. Amen.

(Rev. H. W. Turner, Nineteenth Century.)

For the Government.

ALMIGHTY God, the Father of lights, from Whom cometh every good and perfect gift, send down, we beseech Thee, upon Thy servant, our Prime Minister and all Members of the Cabinet, prudence, fortitude, temperance, and justice, that alike in framing policy and in debate they may be guided by eternal Truth and Right; this we ask in the Name of Thy Son Jesus Christ our Lord. Amen.   *(Original source not found.)*

For Blessing on Public Worship.

O LORD, grant unto Thy servants to speak Thy word with all boldness on the morrow, and may the good Lord pardon every one that setteth his heart to seek the Lord God of his fathers; through Jesus Christ our Lord. Amen.

(Acts iv. 29; First Century: and King Hezekiah. Eighth Century B.C.)

For Forgiveness.

WHEREINSOEVER we have erred and strayed from Thy ways, whereinsoever we have come short, or done that which we ought not to have done, graciously forgive us, we beseech Thee. Help us to turn from all evil, to that which is holy and good. Teach us to love what is right, and to do it for ever; through Jesus Christ our Lord. Amen.

(Professor Knight, Nineteenth Century.)

For Love of God and Man.

O GOD, we have known and believed the love that Thou hast for us, may we be by dwelling in love dwell in Thee, and Thou in us. May we learn to love Thee Whom we have not seen by loving our brethren whom we have seen. Teach us, O heavenly Father, the love wherewith Thou hast loved us. Fashion us, O blessed Lord, after Thine own example of love. Shed abroad, O Holy Spirit of love, the love of God and man in our hearts; for Thy Name's sake. Amen. *(Dean Henry Alford, A.D. 1810.)*

For those who Minister.

O GOD, Whose ways are all mercy and truth, carry on Thy gracious work, and bestow, by Thy benefits, what human frailty cannot attain; that they who attend upon the heavenly mysteries may be grounded in perfect faith, and shine forth conspicuous by the purity of their souls; through Jesus Christ our Lord. Amen. *(Leonine Sacramentary.)*

"My peace I give unto you."

LORD God Almighty, Who art our true Peace and Love eternal, enlighten our souls with the brightness of Thy peace, and purify our consciences with the sweetness of Thy love, that we may with peaceful hearts wait for the Author of peace, and in the adversities of this world may ever have Thee for our Guardian and Protector; and so being fenced about by Thy care, may heartily give ourselves to the love of Thy peace. To Thy honour and glory. Amen. *(Mozarabic Liturgy.)*

For the Holy Spirit.

WE beseech Thee, Almighty God, let our souls enjoy this their desire, to be enkindled by Thy Spirit, that being filled, as lamps, by the Divine gift, we may shine like blazing lights before the Presence of Thy Son Christ at His coming; through the same Jesus Christ our Lord. Amen.

(Gelasian Sacramentary.)

For Protection.

MERCIFULLY regard, O Lord, the prayers of Thy family, and while we submit ourselves to Thee with our whole heart, do Thou prosper, support, and encompass us; that, relying on Thee as our Guide, we may be entangled in no evils, and replenished with all good; through Jesus Christ our Lord. Amen.   (*Leonine Sacramentary.*)

For Love.

O GOD, Who by the grace of the Holy Ghost hast poured the gifts of love into the hearts of Thy faithful people, grant unto all Thy servants in Thy mercy health of body and soul, that they may love Thee with all their strength, and with perfect affection fulfil Thy pleasure; through Jesus Christ our Lord. Amen.   (*Gregorian Sacramentary.*)

For Unity.

O LORD Christ, Who camest that we might have life, and have it more abundantly, come and break down all that hinders life. Come and give us wisdom and patience, courage and resolution to discover how Thy goodwill may verify itself to all. Give us life that we may give out life. Give unity, give brotherhood, give peace for Thine own sake. Amen.

                  (*Canon H. Scott Holland,* A.D. 1847.)

For our Country.

BLESS, O Lord, Thy Holy Catholic Church, and all her bishops and clergy. Convert all those in unbelief and misbelief. Have mercy on our country. Pour down Thy blessing on our friends and relations. Bless this parish, give aid to the poor, comfort to the sorrowful, health to the sick, support to the dying, for the sake of Jesus Christ our Lord. Amen.

                  (*Archbishop Laud,* A.D. 1573.)

For our Nation and Leaders.

THOU all-wise Counsellor, the care of the many must ever rest upon the shoulders of the few, strengthen Thou the leaders of our Land. Conscious of their privilege and trust, help them to wield this power. Keen in mind and strong of heart, point out to them the way. Help them to work for the common good; and broaden Thou our minds, that we may understand the meaning of a Nation's life in Thine, through Jesus Christ. Amen.

                  (*Source not found.*)

For Holiness.

WE can do little, dear Lord, for Thee, but do Thou great things for us. Empty us of ourselves, fill us with Thyself, exterminate in us all evil desires and longings. Purify all our motives. Humble us that our wills may be broken. Wrap us around with Thy holy fear, and bless us with a deepening and abiding contrition for our unnumbered sins, for Thine own sake. Amen.

                  (*Bishop Grafton, Twentieth Century.*)

For Peace and Grace.

O GOD, Who by the power of Thy Majesty dispensest the number of our days and the measure of our time, favourably regard the service which we humbly render, and grant that our times may be filled with the abundance of Thy peace, and the grace of Thy bounty; through Jesus Christ our Lord.   Amen.

(Gelasian Sacramentary.)

For a Fuller Comprehension of God's Word.

ALMIGHTY and most merciful Father, Whose Word is a lantern unto our feet and a light unto our steps, we most humbly beseech Thee to illuminate our minds, that we may understand the mysteries contained in Thy Holy Law, and be virtuously transformed, so that of no part we offend Thy Divine Majesty; through Jesus Christ our Saviour.   Amen.

(Christian Prayers, A.D. 1566.)

For the Nation and Empire.

WE pray for our own Nation and Empire, and all whom we have in authority, and for all true Social Reformers therein, that the evils under which both Britons and other native races are crushed down may be abolished, and that peace and happiness, truth and justice, true religion and piety, may be established in the land and Empire for all generations; through Jesus Christ.   Amen.   *(Rev. William Graham, A.D. 1810.)*

For Protection.

LORD Jesus Christ, Keeper and Preserver of all things, let Thy right hand guard us by day and by night, when we sit at home, and when we walk abroad, when we lie down and when we rise up, that we may be kept from all evil, and have mercy upon us sinners.   Amen.

(St. Nerses of Clajes, Fourth Century.)

For Sympathy.

O GOD, Who knittest us all together in mutual love and responsibility one for another, stir up the stronger to help the weaker, the shielded to protect the unprotected; encourage the faithful to rescue the waverers, the earnest to recover the careless, the wayward and the abandoned, that we may draw closer in bonds of prayer and service and in joint consecration to Thy love and obedience; through the power of Thy Holy Spirit and in the Name of Jesus Christ our Lord.   Amen.

(Federation of Working Girls Clubs, Twentieth Century.)

For Holiness.

COME in, O Christ, and judge us; come and cast out for us every sin that hinders Thee; come purge our souls by Thy Presence. Come, be our King for ever. Amen.

(Bishop Phillips Brooks, A.D. 1835.)

For Mercy and Deliverance.

LOOK down, O Lord our God, from the throne of Thy glorious Kingdom; look down upon us and destroy us not, yea, rather deliver us from evil. From all evil and misfortune, deliver us. As of old time Thou didst deliver our fathers, deliver us. In all our straits, deliver us. From the evils of the world to come, from Thine anger, from being placed on the left hand, deliver us. Spare us, O Lord. Have mercy upon us. Deliver us and let us never be confounded; for the sake of Jesus Christ, our Saviour and Redeemer. Amen.

(Bishop Andrewes, A.D. 1555.)

For Purified Lives.

O GOD, mercifully grant unto us that the fire of Thy love may burn up in us all things that displease Thee, and make us meet for Thy heavenly Kingdom; for the sake of Jesus Christ our Saviour. Amen.   *(Roman Breviary.)*

For Christ's Church.

O LORD, we beseech Thee to maintain Thy Church in truth and patience; that her pastors may be faithful, her watchmen vigilant, her flock loyal, her camp united, her war spiritual, her weapons heavenly, her lamps burning and shining; and as Thy Son Jesus Christ hath given so great a price for us, let us not count it a hard thing to give up all for Him, and to spend and be spent for the souls He hath redeemed; through Jesus Christ our Lord. Amen.   *(Original source not found.)*

For the Nation.

O GOD, the God of all righteousness, mercy and love, give us all grace and strength to conceive and execute whatever may be for Thine honour and the welfare of the Nation, that we may become at last, through the merits and intercession of our common Redeemer, a great and a happy, because a wise and understanding people; to Thy honour and glory. Amen.

(Lord Salisbury, A.D. 1830.)

For Usefulness.

LORD of the depths and heights, Who abidest in all forms which Thou hast made, abide Thou in Thy mercy with the souls sunken in darkness. Sustain them by Thy life, comfort them with Thy love. Grant that we may be humble instruments and channels of Thy Power to them, to cheer and guide them to the heights of their glorious resurrection; through Jesus Christ our Saviour. Amen.   *(Michael Wood, Twentieth Century.)*

Thanksgiving.

WE give Thee hearty thanks for the rest of the past night and for the gift of a new day, with its opportunities of pleasing Thee. Grant that we may so pass its hours in the perfect freedom of Thy service, that at eventide we may again give thanks unto Thee; through Jesus Christ our Lord. Amen.

(Eastern Church Liturgy Daybreak Office.)

For Heavenly-Mindedness.

WHATSOEVER things are pure and lovely, whatsoever things are gentle and generous, whatsoever things are noble and self-forgetful, honourable and of good report, these things, O Lord, grant that we may with one accord pursue; through Jesus Christ our Lord. Amen.

(Professor Knight, Nineteenth Century.)

A General Intercession.

REMEMBER, O Lord, with Thy mercy all those who do the work of the world by land or sea, at home or abroad, that they may lead honest, sober, diligent, and Christian lives. Remember those who are journeying or in peril, especially our miners, seamen, and airmen. Remember our sailors and soldiers in peace and in war. Remember those who are in trouble and distress, the outcast, helpless and homeless, the widow and the orphan. Remember those who are handicapped in the race of life, the blind, the deaf and dumb, the anxious and the heart-broken, and those in debt and poverty. Remember the inmates of our workhouses, refuges, orphanages, and prisons. Give rest to the weary, the weak, and the aged. Give courage and strength to those who have power to work, that they may labour for themselves and their families, and may give thanks unto Thee; through Jesus Christ our Lord. Amen.

(Bishop of Salisbury, Nineteenth Century.)

For the Sick.

WE pray for the sick; grant them health, and raise them up from their sickness and make them to have perfect health of body and soul, for Thou art the Saviour and Benefactor, Thou art Lord and King of all. Amen.

(Bishop Serapion, Bishop of Thmuis, A.D. 350.)

For Christ's Companionship.

NOW, O Lord, we come before Thee through Christ, and beg of Thee to fill our souls with Thyself, to be near us day by day and hour by hour, strengthening us by Thy strength, and guiding us by Thy Hand, till Thou lead us home to Thine eternal peace and joy; through the same Jesus Christ. Amen.

(Anonymous, A.D. 1890.)

Confession and Prayer for Forgiveness.

O LORD, O King, resplendent on the citadel of heaven, all
hail continually; and of Thy clemency upon Thy people
still do Thou *have mercy*.

Lord, Whom the hosts of cherubim in songs and hymns with
praise continually proclaim, do Thou *upon us* eternally *have
mercy*.

The armies aloft, O *Lord*, do sing high praise to Thee, even
they to Whom the Seraphim reply, "do Thou *have mercy*."

O *Christ*, enthroned as King above, Whom the nine orders of
angels in their beauty praise without ceasing, deign Thou *upon
us*, Thy servants, ever to *have mercy*.

O *Christ*, Whom Thy one only Church throughout the world
doth hymn, O Thou to Whom the sun, and moon, and stars,
the land and sea, do service ever, do Thou *have mercy*.

O *Christ*, those holy ones, the heirs of the eternal country, one
and all with utter joy proclaim Thee in a most worthy strain:
do Thou *have mercy upon us*.

O *Lord*, O gentle Son of Mary free, O King of kings, Blessed
Redeemer, upon those who have been ransomed from the power
of death, by Thine own blood, ever *have mercy*.

O noblest unbegotten, yet Begotten Son, having no beginning
of age, yet without effort (in the weakness of God) excelling all
things, upon this Thy congregation in Thy pity, *Lord have
mercy*.

O Sun of Righteousness, in all unclouded glory, supreme Dis-
penser of Justice, in that great day when Thou shalt strictly
judge all nations, we earnestly beseech Thee, upon This Thy
people, who here stand before Thy presence, in Thy pity, *Lord,
then have mercy upon us*.

(*St. Dunstan, Archbishop of Canterbury*, A.D. 924.)

For Heavenly-Mindedness.

A BIDE in us, O Christ, that we may abide in Thee. Let Thy
Word dwell in us richly in all wisdom, that we may be full
of the thoughts of Thee, that we may keep our ideals bright in
the midst of the work-a-day world. From all the deceptive
attractions of the world, the flesh and the devil, save us, O Saviour
of the world, lest having received the Word with joy and for a
while believing, in time of temptation we fall away, lest being
choked with cares and riches and pleasures of this world we bring
no fruit to perfection, lest by not renewing our minds to know
Thy perfect will, we become conformed to this world. Keep us
O God of grace, ever in Thy Presence. Amen. (*Adapted.*)

For Knowledge.

L ORD, let us learn from the experiences of to-day the lessons
which Thou meanest to-day to teach.

(*Judge Sir Clement Bailhache*, A.D. 1856.)

A Morning Thanksgiving.

O GOD, by Whom the world is governed and preserved, we Thine unworthy creatures, under a thankful sense of Thy providential care, draw nigh unto Thee to offer our morning sacrifice of prayer and praise. We thank Thee that Thou hast protected us from all the dangers of the night. Continue Thy goodness to us through this day, and preserve us from all dangers both of body and soul. May we remember that every day is Thy gift, and to be used both in Thy service and in doing the work of our salvation. Enable us to resist all evil, and dispose us to follow the guidance of Thy good Spirit, not trusting to our own strength or wisdom, but looking to Thee for grace to establish us in every good work and word; through Jesus Christ Thy Son our Lord. Amen.   (*Bishop Blomfield*, A.D. 1786.)

For our Hospitals.

A LMIGHTY God, Whose blessed Son Jesus Christ went about doing good and healing all manner of sickness and disease among the people; continue, we beseech Thee, His gracious work among us in the hospitals and infirmaries of our land; console and heal the sufferers, grant to the physicians and surgeons wisdom and skill, and to the nurses diligence and patience. Prosper their work, O Lord, and vouchsafe Thy blessing to all who give of their substance for its maintenance; through Jesus Christ our Lord. Amen.
          (*Prayer-Book of the Scottish Church*, A.D. 1912.)

For our Absent Ones.

W E commend into Thy safe keeping all who are near and dear to us, all who are sick and sorrowing, and dying, all who are tempted and sinning and striving; through Jesus Christ our Lord. Amen.   (*Bishop C. J. Ridgeway*, A.D. 1841.)

For Forgiveness.

O LORD Almighty, Who endurest for ever, hear now our prayers; remember not the iniquities of our fathers, but think upon Thy power and Thy Name now at this time, for Thou art the Lord our God, and Thee, O Lord, will we praise.
          (*Baruch* iii. 5, 6. B.C.)

Benediction.

B LESS us, O God the Father, Who hast created us,
Bless us, O God the Son, Who hast redeemed us,
  Bless us, O God the Holy Ghost, Who sanctifieth us.
  O Blessed Trinity, keep us in body, soul, and spirit unto everlasting life. Amen.   (*Weimarischer Gesangbuch*, A.D. 1873.)

EVENING PRAYERS.

A Prayer for Sunday Evening.

O ALMIGHTY Father, we Thine unworthy children, present ourselves before the footstool of Thy mercy, beseeching Thee to forgive us the manifold sins, negligences, and ignorances of which we have been guilty on this day. Pardon our want of zeal in Thy service, the coldness of our hearts, and the wandering of our thoughts. We bless Thee, O Father, for the opportunities Thou hast given us of serving Thee, and pray Thee to give us and all hearers of Thy Word grace to understand, diligence and attention to consider, and watchfulness to carry into practice the holy lessons which we, this day, have heard. Let Thy Holy Spirit dwell in our hearts, sanctifying our thoughts, guiding our affections, directing our wills, that we may in all the work of the week glorify Thee, through Jesus Christ our Lord. Amen.

(Bishop Jeremy Taylor, A.D. 1613.)

Thanksgiving.

WE bless Thy holy Name for all the undeserved favours which we have received at Thy gracious hand this day; for life and health, for food and raiment, and for deliverance from dangers and difficulties of mind, body, and estate; but especially we thank Thee, O God of our salvation, for any measure of spiritual strength vouchsafed in the hour of trial, for every deliverance from the power of temptation, and for every victory which we have gained over the enemies of our souls, or over our own besetting sins. If we have fainted in the race it is because we have not been watchful against all evil, nor set Thee, O Lord, continually before us; and if we have come off more than conquerors, it is through Him alone Who loved us and gave Himself for us. We praise Thee, O Thou God of truth, for every measure of Thy Holy Spirit which Thou hast bestowed upon us during the past Day of Rest, in His enlightening, refreshing, and sanctifying influences; for the comfort of Thy Holy Word, and the rich treasures of spiritual knowledge which are revealed therein. O make us willing and humble learners of Thy Truth, and lead us in the way everlasting; for the sake of Jesus Christ our Lord and Saviour. Amen. *(Rev. Isaac Ashe, A.D. 1802.)*

For Consistent Lives.

GRANT, O Lord, that what we have said with our lips, we may believe in our hearts and practise in our lives; and of Thy mercy keep us faithful unto the end; for Christ's sake. Amen.

(From Rev. John Hunter's Devotional Services, A.D. 1892.)

For Peace.

O LORD God, grant Thy peace to us, for Thou hast supplied us with all things—the peace of rest, the peace of the Sabbath, which hath no evening; through Jesus Christ our Lord. Amen. *(St. Augustine, A.D. 354.)*

An Evening Prayer.

IN the evening and morning and noonday we praise Thee, we thank Thee, and pray Thee, Master of all, to direct our prayers as incense before Thee. Let not our hearts turn away to words or thoughts of wickedness, but keep us from all things that might hurt us; for to Thee, O Lord, our eyes look up, and our hope is in Thee: confound us not, O our God; for the sake of Jesus Christ our Lord. Amen. (*Eastern Church Liturgy*.)

For Rightful Recognition of God, "the Giver of All Good Things."

O GOD, Who, by making the evening to succeed the day, hast bestowed the gift of repose on human weakness, grant, we beseech Thee, that while we enjoy those timely blessings we may acknowledge Him from Whom they come, even Jesus Christ our Lord. Amen. (*Mozarabic Liturgy*.)

For those in Special Need.

RELIEVE and comfort, O Lord, all the persecuted and afflicted; speak peace to troubled consciences; strengthen the weak; confirm the strong; instruct the ignorant; deliver the oppressed from him that spoileth him; and relieve the needy that hath no helper; and bring us all, by the waters of comfort and in the ways of righteousness, to the kingdom of rest and glory; through Jesus Christ our Lord. Amen.

(*Bishop Jeremy Taylor*, A.D. 1613.)

For Peace Here and Hereafter.

O GOD, in Thee alone can our wearied spirits find full satisfaction and rest, and in Thy love is the highest joy. Lord, if we have Thee, we have enough, and we are happy if Thou wilt but give peace to our consciences, and make us know how gracious and merciful Thou art. Preserve in our hearts that peace which passeth all understanding, and make us better and holier in time to come. Strengthen those of us, and Thy people who are in any sorrow or perplexity, by the inward comfort of Thy Holy Spirit, and bid us all know that our light affliction, which is but for a moment, worketh for us a far more exceeding and eternal weight of glory; for there will come a time when Thou wilt bring us to the place of perfect rest, where we shall behold Thy face in righteousness, and be satisfied from Thy eternal fulness; through Jesus Christ our Lord. Amen.

(*Melchior Ritter*, A.D. 1689.)

Thanksgiving.

THANKS be to Thee, O Lord Jesus Christ, for all the benefits which Thou hast given us; for all the pains and insults which Thou hast borne for us. O most merciful Redeemer, Friend and Brother, may we know Thee more clearly, love Thee more dearly, and follow Thee more nearly; for Thine own sake. Amen.   (*St. Richard, Bishop of Chichester*, A.D. 1197.)

For Forgiveness and Mercy.

O FATHER of heaven, O Son of God, Redeemer of the world, O Holy Ghost proceeding from Them both, Three Persons and one God, have mercy upon us who have offended against Thee. Whither may we go, or whither should we fly for succour? O God, Thou art merciful, and refuseth none that come to Thee for help. To Thee therefore do we come. To Thee do we humble ourselves. O Lord God, our sins are great, but yet have mercy upon us for Thy great mercy. We ask nothing, O Lord, for our own merits, but for Thy Name's sake, that it may be glorified thereby, and Jesus Christ Thy Son our Saviour. Amen.   (*Archbishop Cranmer*, A.D. 1489.)

For Christ-likeness.

O LORD Jesus, acknowledge what is Thine in us, and take away from us all that is not Thine; for Thy honour and glory. Amen.   (*St. Bernardine*, A.D. 1380.)

For True Sympathy and Gentleness.

O THOU loving and tender Father in heaven, we confess before Thee, in sorrow, how hard and unsympathetic are our hearts; how often we have sinned against our neighbours by want of compassion and tenderness; how often we have felt no true pity for their trials and sorrows, and have neglected to comfort, help, and visit them. O Father, forgive this our sin, and lay it not to our charge. Give us grace ever to alleviate the crosses and difficulties of those around us, and never to add to them; teach us to be consolers in sorrow, to take thought for the stranger, the widow, and the orphan; let our charity show itself not in words only, but in deed and truth. Teach us to judge as Thou dost, with forbearance, with much pity and indulgence; and help us to avoid all unloving judgment of others; for the sake of Jesus Christ Thy Son, Who loved us and gave Himself for us. Amen.   (*Rev. Johann Arndt*, A.D. 1555.)

For Rest and Confidence in God.

COMPOSE, O God, our faculties and thoughts that we may be enabled worthily to thank Thee through Jesus Christ Thy Son for all the good with which Thou hast blessed us graciously to-day. This evening we commend our whole welfare and life and all other things to Thy guidance and keeping. Yea, we take refuge from all our enemies in the kindness of Thy Fatherly love, and in Thee only do we seek our rest, inasmuch as without Thee is no peace or calm in heaven or earth. Let us be Thine whether we wake or sleep, and work Thou Thyself in us whatever is well pleasing in Thy sight; through Jesus Christ and in the power of His Spirit. Amen.   (*Weimarischer Gesangbuch*, A.D. 1873.)

Benediction.

THE Lord Almighty grant us a quiet night and a perfect end: and the blessing of God Almighty, the Father, the Son, and the Holy Ghost, be with us this night and evermore. Amen.

Repentance.

O LORD our God, give unto us Thy servants the spirit of true repentance, and take away from us all that separates us from Thee. Assist us by Thy Holy Spirit to show true sorrow for our sins, and to form a sincere resolution to amend our lives according to Thy Holy Word. Have mercy on us, and succour us with Thy grace, make in us new and contrite hearts, and pardon all our offences; for the sake of our Redeemer Jesus Christ. Amen.

A Sacrifice of Praise.

HEAVENLY Father, receive our evening sacrifice of praise, and confession, and prayer, we beseech Thee. We thank Thee for all the known and unknown mercies of another day, for all the blessings of this life, for all the means of grace, for all the riches of Thy salvation, and for the hope of glory, that blessed hope, the coming of our Lord Jesus Christ and our gathering together unto Him. We are one day nearer to that day. Teach us to live every day as those whose conversation (citizenship) is in heaven, and who are looking from thence for a Saviour, the Lord Jesus Christ. Amen.

(Bishop H. C. G. Moule, Twentieth Century.)

An Evening Commendation.

INTO Thy Hands, O Lord, we commit ourselves, our spirits, soul and body. Thou hast created and Thou hast redeemed them, O Lord God of truth. And with us, we commend all our friends, and all our possessions. Thou, O Lord, hast graciously given them unto Thy servants. Preserve our down-sitting and our uprising from this time forth and even for evermore. That we may remember Thee upon our bed and diligently search out our spirit, and when we awake, be still with Thee. We will both lay us down in peace and sleep, for Thou, Lord, only makest us dwell in safety. Hear us and answer us, we humbly beseech Thee; for the sake of Christ Jesus our Lord. Amen.

(Bishop Andrewes, A.D. 1555.)

For Holiness.

O LORD, open our eyes that we may have a clear and uninterrupted sight of all the wonderful things which Thou hast done for us. Let us not live as if we were strangers to Thy commandments. Infuse into our hearts such an awe and fear to displease Thee, that nothing may seduce us from our obedience to Thee. Grant this, O heavenly Father, for the sake of Christ Jesus our Saviour. Amen.   *(Earl of Clarendon, A.D. 1757.)*

Calmness in Anxiety.

GRANT calmness and control of thought to those who are facing uncertainty and anxiety: let their heart stand fast, believing in the Lord. Be Thou all things to all men, knowing each one and his petition, each house and its need, for the sake of Jesus Christ. Amen.   *(Russian Liturgy.)*

For Faith.

O MOST loving Father, Who willest us to give thanks for all things, to dread nothing but the loss of Thee, and to cast all our care on Thee, Who carest for us, preserve us from faithless fears and worldly anxieties, and grant that no clouds of this mortal life may hide us from the light of that Love which is immortal, and which Thou hast manifested unto us in Thy Son Jesus Christ our Lord.   Amen.

(William Bright, A.D. 1824.)

For Those at Sea.

O LORD Jesus Christ, Who on the sea didst teach Thy disciples many heavenly things, and even in the storm didst come close to them, saying, "It is I, be not afraid," and didst bring their vessel swiftly to its haven; we pray Thee to shew the voice of Thy truth and the power of Thy presence to Thy Church upon the deep, and be Thou the Guide and Guardian of all that sail the seas; Who livest and reignest with the Father and the Holy Ghost, one God, world without end.   Amen.

(Source not found.)

For those "who sit in darkness."

O THOU God of infinite mercy and compassion, in Whose hands are all the hearts of the sons of men, look, we beseech Thee, graciously upon the darkened souls of the multitudes who know not Thee.   Enlighten them with the saving knowledge of the truth.   Let the beams of Thy Gospel break forth upon them, and bring them to a sound belief in Thee, God manifested in the flesh.   Bring in the fulness of the Gentiles; gather together the outcasts of Israel, and make Thy Name known over all the earth.   Grant this, through Jesus Christ.   Amen.

(Bishop Hall, A.D. 1574.)

A Memorial of Christ's Ascension.

O GOD, the King of Glory, Who hast exalted Thine only Son Jesus Christ with great triumph unto Thy Kingdom in heaven, we beseech Thee leave us not comfortless, but send to us Thine Holy Ghost to comfort us, and exalt us unto the same place whither our Saviour Christ is gone before ; Who livest and reignest with Thee and the Holy Ghost, One God, world without end.   Amen.

(Sarum Missal ; Book of Common Prayer, A.D. 1549. Used by Venerable Bede on his death-bed, A.D. 735.)

"In quietness and confidence shall be our strength."

L EAVING the things that are too high for us, in quietness and confidence may we find our strength.   We beseech Thee to inspire us with all the virtues of Thy children, and grant that by the doing of Thy will we may increase our light; through Jesus Christ our Lord. Amen. *(Professor Knight, Nineteenth Century.)*

For Pardon.

LOOK down from heaven, O Lord, with the eye of pity and compassion upon us, Thy humble servants, who now implore the pardon of our sins, and trust alone in Thy mercies; through Jesus Christ our Lord. Amen.   (*Gelasian Sacramentary.*)

For Protection.

O LAMB of God, Who takest away the sin of the world, look upon us and have mercy upon us; Thou Who art Thyself both Victim and Priest, Thyself both Reward and Redeemer, keep safe from all evils those whom Thou hast redeemed, O Saviour of the world. Amen.   (*Bishop Irenæus*, A.D. 130.)

For the Guidance of "the Good Shepherd."

O SHEPHERD of the sheep, Who didst promise to carry the lambs in Thine arms, and to lead us by the still waters, help us to know the peace which passeth understanding. Give us to drink that heavenly draught which is life, the calm patience which is content to bear what God giveth. Have mercy upon us, and hear our prayers. Lead us gently when we pass through the valley of the shadow of death. Guide us, till at last, in the assembly of Thy saints, we may find rest for evermore; for Thine own Name's sake. Amen.

(*Rev. George Dawson*, A.D. 1821.)

For Humility.

O LORD Jesus Christ, Who didst humble Thyself to become man, and to be born into the world for our salvation, teach us the grace of humility, root out of our hearts all pride and haughtiness, and so fashion us after Thy holy likeness in this world, that in the world to come we may be made like unto Thee; for Thine own Name and mercies' sake. Amen.

(*Bishop Walsham How*, A.D. 1823.)

An Evening Commendation.

O GOD, our heavenly Father, we would commit to Thy Fatherly care all whom we love, especially those who are far away. O Lord, remember them for good, be Thou with each one of them, keep them outwardly from all harm, and above all bless and strengthen them in their souls. Pour out Thy Holy Spirit upon them to guide them into all truth. Grant unto each one of us that we may be standing with our loins girded and our lamps burning, waiting for the coming of our Lord. And we also bless Thy holy Name for all Thy servants departed this life in Thy faith and fear, beseeching Thee to give us grace so to follow their good examples, that with them we may be partakers of Thy heavenly kingdom; grant this, O Father, for Jesus Christ's sake. Amen.

(*A. Wright. and E. S. Osmaston: Prayer Union*, A.D. 1889.)

For Forgiveness.

BEFORE we go to rest, we would commit ourselves to God's care through Christ, beseeching Him to forgive us for all our sins of this day past, and to keep alive His grace in our hearts, and to cleanse us from all sin, pride, harshness and selfishness, and give us the spirit of meekness, humility, firmness, and love. O Lord, keep Thyself present to us ever, and perfect Thy strength in our weakness. Take us and ours under Thy blessed care this night and evermore; through Jesus Christ our Lord. Amen.

(Dr. Arnold, A.D. 1795.)

A Prayer for the Sleepless.

WATCH Thou, dear Lord, with those who wake, or watch, or weep to-night, and give Thine angels charge over those who sleep. Tend Thy sick ones, O Lord Christ. Rest Thy weary ones. Bless Thy dying ones. Soothe Thy suffering ones. Pity Thine afflicted ones. Shield Thy joyous ones. And all, for Thy Love's sake. Amen.

(St. Augustine, A.D. 354.)

Preparation for Sunday.

WE would now dismiss the cares of the world with the week. May we rise in the morning with refreshed bodies and renewed strength, and be in the Spirit on the Lord's Day. And do Thou send out Thy Light and Thy Truth, that they may lead us and guide us, to Thy holy hill and to Thyself; through Jesus Christ our Lord. Amen. *(Rev. Fielding Ould, A.D. 1864.)*

For the Presence of the Holy Spirit.

ALMIGHTY God, Who art the Lord of our spirits, by Thy Holy Spirit the Comforter, shed abroad in our hearts at this time that quiet trust and constant faith, and sweet peace that passes all understanding; that so, we being duly fitted for the receiving of Thy Word, it may, as good seed, fall into good ground, and bring forth for us, for the world, and for Thy glory, abundantly. This we ask in the name of Jesus Christ our Lord. Amen.   *(Rev. George Dawson, A.D. 1821.)*

An Evening Thanksgiving.

WE thank Thee, O Lord and Master, for teaching us how to pray simply and sincerely to Thee, and for hearing us when we so call upon Thee. We thank Thee for saving us from our sins and sorrows, and for directing all our ways this day. Lead us ever onwards to Thyself; for the sake of Jesus Christ our Lord and Saviour. Amen.

(Father John of the Russian Church, Nineteenth Century.)

A Prayer for the Sick.

O OUR Master, Jesus Christ, visit the sick of Thy people and heal them. Amen.   *(Abyssinian Jacobite Liturgy.)*

That the lessons of the Day may bear Fruit in our Lives.

O ALMIGHTY God and Father, under Whose mighty and gracious protection all our days are spent, we thank Thee for all the mercies of the past day; for the continuance of our many and great blessings; for any good examples we may have seen; for any good words we may have heard or read; for all holy thoughts and right desires which Thy Holy Spirit has this day put into our minds. O Lord, grant that these may not be unfruitful in us, but may work in us that for which Thou didst send them; for Jesus Christ's sake. Amen.

(Rev. H. Stobart, Nineteenth Century.)

A Renewed Dedication.

O GOD, Who leadest us through seasons of life to be partakers of Thine eternity, the shadows of our evening hasten on. Quicken us betimes, and spare us that sad word, "The harvest is past, the summer is ended, and we are not saved." Anew we dedicate ourselves to Thee. We would ask nothing, reserve nothing for ourselves, save only leave to go whither Thou mayest guide, to live not far from Thee, to die into Thy nearer light. Content to accept the reproach of truth, we would take upon us the yoke of Christ, Whom it behoved to suffer ere He entered into His glory. We ask it in the Name and for the sake of the same Jesus Christ our Lord. Amen.

(James Martineau, Published A.D. 1891.)

An Evening Commendation.

TAKE us, we pray Thee, O Lord of our life, into Thy keeping this night and for ever. O Thou Light of lights, keep us from inward darkness; grant us so to sleep in peace, that we may arise to work according to Thy will; through Jesus Christ our Lord. Amen.   *(Bishop Andrewes, A.D. 1555.)*

That "we may be doers of the Word and not hearers only."

O LORD God of our life, Who hast given us the rest of this sacred day, grant that the benediction of its restfulness may abide upon us throughout the week. Enable us to carry the influence of its consecration into all that we do; let the praises of our lips rendered to Thee this day become praise in our lives. May the power of Thy love be with us in every duty, that by pureness, by knowledge, and by tenderness we may glorify Thee; through Jesus Christ. Amen.

(Bishop W. Boyd Carpenter, A.D. 1841.)

An Evening Blessing.

ABIDE with us, O good Lord, through the night, guarding, keeping, guiding, sustaining, sanctifying, and with Thy love gladdening us, that in Thee we may ever live, and in Thee may die; through Jesus Christ our Lord. Amen.

(Archbishop Benson, A.D. 1829.)

For Forgiveness.

O GOD, the Father of mercies, we, Thine unworthy children, who have erred and strayed from Thy ways, return unto Thee with contrite hearts, beseeching Thee to forgive and to deliver us from evil. Remembering our weakness, we ask Thee to help us to lay aside all evil thoughts, words, and works. May the power of evil be broken in us, and may the power of good be strengthened; through Jesus Christ our Lord. Amen.

(Original source not found.)

Thanksgiving and Prayer for Protection.

O LORD, our heavenly Father, by Whose Divine ordinance the darkness covers the earth and brings unto us bodily rest and quietness, we render Thee our hearty thanks for the loving-kindness which Thou hast shown, in preserving us during the past day, and in giving us all things necessary for our health and comfort. And we beseech Thee, for Jesus Christ's sake, to forgive us all the sins we have committed in thought, word, or deed, and that Thou wilt shadow us this night under the wings of Thy almighty power, and defend us from all power of the evil one. May our souls, whether sleeping or waking, wait upon Thee, delight in Thee, and evermore praise Thee, so that when the light of day returns, we may rise with pure and thankful hearts, casting away the works of darkness and putting on the armour of light; through Jesus Christ. Amen.

(Rev. T. Becon, A.D. 1512.)

Praise for All God's Good Gifts.

O LORD our God, Almighty and Eternal Father, Who givest to Thy children liberally and upbraidest not, we bless Thee this night for Thine infinite goodness to us and to all men. We give Thee thanks for the world and all the good things which are therein; for the sky above us and the earth beneath our feet; for the changing seasons, for our home and our friends. We bless Thee for Thy tender care which guards us, and for all Thy good gifts by which we are enriched. Most of all do we bless Thee for Jesus Christ our Saviour, and for all the means of grace and the hope of glory through Him. In Thy service may we live, and in Thy favour may we die; through the same Jesus Christ our Lord. Amen. *(Rev. H. Stobart, Nineteenth Century.)*

For Grace to live Prepared Lives.

A CCEPT, we beseech Thee, O Lord, our praises and supplications, and look graciously upon this household, that we may abide this night in peace and safety, under the shadow of Thy wings, and so assist us by Thy grace that we may be fitted for that Kingdom where there shall be no more sin, nor sorrow, neither any more pain, but all shall be joy and peace in the Holy Ghost; to Whom with Thee, O Father, and Thee, O blessed Jesus, be all glory, both now and evermore. Amen.

(Dean Goulburn, A.D. 1818.)

CONFESSION OF SIN AND SHORTCOMINGS.

FATHER, we Thy erring children humbly entreat Thy gracious pardon for all that is displeasing in us, for our many failings and failures, for our wilful sins and our sins of ignorance. We have no right to Thy forgiveness, but, taught by Thy Son, our Saviour, we ask for it as a gracious favour in His Name. Father, forgive us. Blot out the stains of past sin; cleanse us from it; impart to us Thy purity and righteousness. Look not, O Lord, upon our unworthiness, but upon the Face of Thine Anointed. Give us Thy Holy Spirit to inspire us to greater holiness and more worthy service; for the sake of Jesus Christ Thy Son. Amen.   (*Rev. C. J. N. Child, Twentieth Century.*)

"LIFT UP YOUR HEARTS UNTO THE LORD."

LET us not seek out of Thee what we can find only in Thee, O Lord, peace and rest, and joy and bliss, which abide only in Thine abiding joy. Lift up our souls above the weary round of harassing thoughts to Thy eternal Presence. Lift up our souls to the pure, bright, serene, radiant atmosphere of Thy Presence, that there we may breathe freely, there repose in Thy love, there be at rest from ourselves and from all things that weary us, and thence return arrayed with Thy peace to do and bear what shall please Thee; for the sake of Christ Jesus our Lord. Amen.   (*Canon E. B. Pusey,* A.D. 1800.)

FOR PROTECTION AND PEACE.

WATCH over us, we pray Thee, O Lord, this night, and keep our souls and bodies pure and holy. We pray Thee, if it be Thy will, to lighten our trials, and to prosper our endeavours; but we especially beseech Thee to give us that peace which the world can neither give nor take away, that our hearts may be established in Thy love. May we live calmly and contentedly here, striving to keep our conscience void of offence towards all men, and looking continually to Thee for grace to help us in every time of need. Bless all who are dear to us, and may they be partakers with us of eternal life; for the sake of our Lord and Saviour Jesus Christ. Amen.   (*O. H. C.,* A.D. 1880.)

CONFIDENCE IN GOD'S SAFE KEEPING.

"I WILL lay me down in peace and take my rest, for it is Thou, Lord, only that makest me dwell in safety."
            (*King David, Eleventh Century* B.C. ; *Ps.* iv. 8.)

FOR REST.

BE present, O merciful God, and protect us through the silent hours of this night, so that we who are wearied by the work and the changes of this fleeting world may rest upon Thy eternal changelessness; through Jesus Christ our Lord. Amen.
            (*An Ancient Collect.*)

Confession and Prayer for Pardon.

O LORD God, merciful and gracious, we come before Thee at the close of another day to praise Thee for Thy long-suffering and goodness to usward, and humbly to acknowledge our own unworthiness. We have done wickedly, we have offended Thee by evil thoughts and evil words. We have in many ways transgressed Thy righteous law, and wasted or misused our talents. We confess, O Lord, that we are unprofitable servants, we have provoked, and we deserve Thy wrath; yet we beseech Thee have compassion on our infirmities, and be not extreme to mark what is done amiss, but, according to the multitude of Thy mercies, do away our offences. Replenish us with the grace of Thy Holy Spirit, that we may truly repent of our sins past, and seek to serve Thee henceforward in newness of life, to Thy honour and glory; through Jesus Christ. Amen.

(Canon E. Hawkins, A.D. 1802.)

For Love.

O LORD, make us to love Thee and each other in Thee, and to meet before Thee to dwell in Thine everlasting love; through Jesus Christ our Lord. Amen.

(Canon E. B. Pusey, A.D. 1800.)

An Intercession for All Men.

HAVE mercy upon all, O Lord, this night, and protect us from all danger. Show mercy to those souls now passing away, and forgive their sins, for Christ's sake. Be near to all who are in special need or trouble; remember all at sea. We pray Thee to guard our King and Queen Elizabeth; we pray Thee to keep our friends and relations, and all who pray for us. Turn the hearts of all who are living a godless life, and renew a right spirit within them. Forgive the sins of the past day, and give us the blessing of sleep and health; for the sake of Christ Jesus our Lord. Amen. *(Bishop Boyd Carpenter, A.D. 1841.)*

An Evening Commendation.

INTO Thine arms we now commend ourselves this night. We will lay us down in peace, if Thou speak peace to us through Jesus Christ. May our last thoughts be of Thee. And when we awake, may Thy Spirit bring heavenly things to our mind. Pardon the imperfections of our prayers. Supply what we have omitted to ask for, and do for us exceeding abundantly above all that we ask or think; for the alone merits of Jesus Christ our Lord. Amen. *(Rev. Fielding Ould, A.D. 1864.)*

For God's Comfort at All Times.

GRANT, O Lord, that we may live in Thy fear, die in Thy favour, rest in Thy peace, rise in Thy power, reign in Thy glory; for the sake of Thy Son, Jesus Christ our Lord. Amen.

(Archbishop Laud, A.D. 1573.)

For Pardon.

O ALMIGHTY God, give us grace to approach Thee this evening with penitent and believing hearts. We confess that we have sinned against Thee in thought, word, and deed, and that we are not worthy to be called Thy children; yet, we beseech Thee, do Thou in mercy keep us as Thy children. Give us true repentance, and forgive us all our sins; through Jesus Christ our Lord. Amen.   (*Rev. H. W. Turner, Nineteenth Century.*)

For Submission to God's Will.

WE beseech Thee, O Lord, make us subject unto Thee with a ready will, and evermore stir up our wills to make supplication unto Thee; through Jesus Christ our Lord. Amen.
(*Gelasian Sacramentary.*)

A Prayer for Likeness to Christ.

A LMIGHTY and most merciful Father, in Whom we live and move and have our being, to Whose tender compassion we owe our safety in days past, together with all the comforts of this present life, and the hopes of that which is to come, we praise Thee, O God, our Creator; unto Thee do we give thanks, O God, our exceeding joy, Who daily pourest Thy benefits upon us. Grant, we beseech Thee, that Jesus our Lord, the hope of glory, may be formed in us, in all humility, meekness, patience, contentedness, and absolute surrender of our souls and bodies to Thy holy will and pleasure. Leave us not, nor forsake us, O Father, but conduct us safe through all changes of our condition here, in an unchangeable love to Thee, and in holy tranquillity of mind in Thy love to us, till we come to dwell with Thee, and rejoice in Thee for ever; through Jesus Christ our Lord. Amen.   (*Bishop Simon Patrick*, A.D. 1626.)

For those who tend the Sick.

O LORD Jesus Christ, Who hast said, "Inasmuch as ye do it unto one of the least of these, My brethren, ye did it unto Me," look upon those of Thy servants who have been called by Thee to tend Thy sick and suffering children. Give them patience and tenderness, wisdom and truthfulness, and the special guidance of Thy Holy Spirit in their work, so that they may faithfully minister to those to whom Thou shalt send them, in Thee and for Thee, and may be found worthy, at the last, to receive Thy eternal reward; through Thine own merit's sake. Amen.   (*Manual for Nurses, Nineteenth Century.*)

For Rest and Sleep.

O LORD our God, refresh us with quiet sleep when we are wearied with the day's labour, that, being assisted with the help which our weakness needs, we may be devoted to Thee both in body and mind; through Jesus Christ our Lord. Amen.
(*Leonine Sacramentary.*)

For Loyalty to Christ.

THOU, O Lord, Who commandest us to ask, grant that we may receive. Thou hast put us upon seeking, let us be happy in finding; Thou hast bidden us knock, we pray Thee open to us. Be graciously pleased to direct and govern all our thoughts and actions, that for the future we may serve Thee, and entirely devote ourselves to obeying Thee. Accept us, we beseech Thee, and draw us to Thyself, that we may henceforth be Thine by obedience and love, who are already all Thine own as Thy creatures—even Thine, O Lord, Who livest and reignest for ever and ever. Amen.   (*St. Augustine*, A.D. 354.)

For Loyal and Devoted Service.

O LORD our God, let our devout approach to Thee be that of the heart, not of the lips. Let it be in obedience to Thy spiritual law, not to any outward ritual. Thou desirest not temples nor offerings, but the sacrifice of a lowly and grateful heart Thou wilt not despise. Merciful Father, to all Thy dispensations we would submit ourselves, not grudgingly, nor merely of necessity, but because we believe in Thy wisdom, Thy universal rule, and Thy goodness. In bereavement and in sorrow, in death as in life, in joys and in happiness, we would see Thy Hand. Teach us to see it; increase our faith where we cannot see; teach us also to love justice and to do mercy, and to walk humbly with Thee our God. Make us at peace with all mankind, gentle to those who offend us, faithful in all duties, and sincere in sorrow when we fail in duty. Make us loving to one another, patient in distress, and ever thankful to Thy Divine power, which keeps, and guides, and blesses us every day. Lord, accept our humble prayer, accomplish in us Thy holy will. Let Thy peace reign in our hearts, and enable us to walk with Thee in love; through Jesus Christ our Lord. Amen.
(*Prof. Francis W. Newman*, A.D. 1805.)

For Unity.

O MERCIFUL God, bless Thy Church throughout all the world, and all those who love Thee in sincerity, although they follow not with us in all things. Heal all strife, divisions, and discord, and make us all Thine in willing devotion as we are all Thine by Redemption and Grace; for the sake of Jesus Christ our Lord. Amen. (*Rev. H. W. Turner, Nineteenth Century.*)

For Union with God.

O LORD our God, grant us grace to desire Thee with our whole heart, that so desiring, we may seek and find Thee; and so finding Thee we may love Thee; and loving Thee we may hate those sins from which Thou hast redeemed us; for the sake of Jesus Christ. Amen.   *St. Anselm*, A.D. 1033.)

For Protection.

BLESSED art Thou, Almighty Master, Who hast granted us to pass through this day and to reach the beginning of the night. Hear our prayers, and those of all Thy people, and forgive us our sins, voluntary and involuntary, and accept our evening supplications, and send down on Thine inheritance the fulness of Thy mercy and Thy compassion. Compass us about with Thy holy angels, arm us with the armour of Thy righteousness, fence us round with Thy Truth, guard us with Thy power. Deliver us from every assault and every device of the adversary, and grant us to pass this evening and the ensuing night, and all the days of our life, in fulness of peace and holiness, without sin and stumbling. For it is Thine to pity and to save, O Christ our God. Amen. (*Eastern Church Liturgy, Pentecost Vespers.*)

An Evening Commendation.

HEAVENLY Father, we commit ourselves to Thee; take us into Thy care this night. Cause us to lie down in peace and to rise in safety; let no evil come nigh us, nor plague about our dwelling. Defend us from all the terrors of night; let not Satan have any power over us to hurt us, but be Thou ever near—yea, close to us, in our souls, and bodies, and our dwelling. Be Thou the subject of our sleeping and waking thoughts, that when we awake, whether it be in this life or the next, we may still be with Thee. Cause us to lie down to sleep in the hope that, should we not awake again in this life, we may awake and rise in the morning of our Redeemer's coming in His Kingdom. And should we awake again here, grant that our souls may be enlightened by Thy Spirit, as our bodies by the returning sun. Be Thou the first object of our awakening thoughts and through the coming day. Enable us to keep it holy, not doing our own ways, nor finding our own pleasures, nor speaking our own words, but walking in Thy way; through Jesus Christ Thy Son, our Saviour. Amen. (*Rev. Thomas Dee, Nineteenth Century.*)

Preparation for Sunday.

O ALMIGHTY God, Who, after the creation of the world didst rest from all Thy works, and, as an image of Thine own, didst sanctify a day of rest for Thy creatures, grant us that, putting away all earthly cares and anxieties, we may be duly prepared for the services of Thy sanctuary; and that our rest here upon earth may be a preparation for the eternal Sabbath promised to Thy people in heaven; through Jesus Christ our Lord. Amen. (*Edward Benson, Archbishop of Canterbury, A.D. 1829.*)

For Restful Sleep.

SAVE us while waking, and defend us while sleeping, that when we awake we may watch with Christ, and when we sleep we may rest in peace. Amen. (*An Ancient Collect.*)

A Thanksgiving for the Day of Rest.

WE thank Thee, O Lord, for this Thy Day, and for all the ministrations and blessings which it has brought us; and we beseech Thee of Thy great goodness, that these days which bear Thy Name may never cease to be unto us as days of heaven upon earth, and lights to guide us from earth to heaven; to the praise and glory of Thy grace. Amen.

(Rev. H. Stobart, Nineteenth Century.)

Praise for God's Mercies.

O ETERNAL God, we praise Thee for Thine unceasing mercies, that, notwithstanding our sins and unworthiness, Thou continuest to us all the means of grace. Forgive our negligence and wandering thoughts, even in time of prayer. Give us grace, that we may become more worthy of Thy love; through Jesus Christ our Lord. Amen. *(Source not found.)*

For Confidence in God's Providence.

O MERCIFUL Lord God, heavenly Father, whether we sleep or wake, live or die, we are always Thine. Wherefore we beseech Thee heartily that Thou wilt vouchsafe to take care and charge of us, and not to suffer us to perish in the works of darkness, but to kindle the light of Thy countenance in our hearts, that Thy godly knowledge may daily increase in us through a right and pure faith, and that we may always be found to walk and live after Thy will and pleasure; through Jesus Christ our Lord. Amen. *(Edward VI. A.D. 1537. Primer.)*

For Peace.

MAKE Thy tranquillity, O Lord, to dwell amongst us, and Thy peace to abide in our hearts. May our voices proclaim Thy truth, and may Thy cross be the guardian of our souls. Account us worthy, O Lord, with the boldness which is of Thee, to offer unto Thee of Thy grace a pure and holy prayer through Jesus Christ our Lord. Amen. *(Liturgy of the Nestorians.)*

An Evening Commendation.

AND now, O blessed Redeemer, our Rock, our Hope, and only sure Defence, to Thee do we cheerfully commit both our soul and body. If Thy wise Providence see fit, grant that we may rise in the morning, refreshed with sleep, and with a spirit of activity for the duties of the day, but whether we wake here or in eternity grant that our trust in Thee may remain sure, and our hope unshaken, through Jesus Christ our Lord. Amen.

(Henry Kirke White, A.D. 1785.)

Darkness and Light.

THERE shall be no night there, where we shall be for ever with the Lord; and here also, if we follow Him, we shall not walk in darkness, but have the Light of Life. Let Thy peace, O Lord, be with us both now and evermore. Amen. *(Adapted.)*

Praise and Thanksgiving.

O LORD God Almighty, help us now to worship Thee in spirit and in truth. We desire to praise Thy holy Name for all the blessings of the past day, but above all for the free salvation promised us in Jesus Christ. We thank Thee that He died for our sins, and that He is even now pleading for us in heaven. O Lord, help us each to turn to Thee in all sincerity, to obey Thy voice, and to trust entirely to Thee and Thy finished work for us. May we lie down this night at peace with all men; and when the last night of our earthly life shall come, may we fall asleep in our Saviour, to wake up after His likeness—satisfied. May Thy peace abide with us, and Thy love rule in our hearts now and for ever. Amen.   (*O. H. C.*, A.D. 1880.)

For Illumination.

O HEAVENLY Father, the Author and Fountain of all truth, the bottomless Sea of all understanding, send, we beseech Thee, Thy Holy Spirit into our hearts, and lighten our understandings with the beams of Thy heavenly grace. We ask this, O merciful Father, for Thy dear Son our Saviour Jesus Christ's sake. Amen.   (*Bishop Nicholas Ridley*, A.D. 1500.)

Thanksgiving for the Knowledge of Heavenly Light.

ALMIGHTY God, our heavenly Father, we thank Thee for all that Thou unfoldest and revealest through the veil of earthly things, and for thoughts which have strengthened us to work patiently, to endure steadfastly, and to continue in the doing of Thy will. We also bless and praise Thee, O Lord our God, that when we are in darkness and we see Thee not, Thy heaven remaineth full of light, and we beseech Thee to help us at all times to remember that the darkness and the light are both alike to Thee; grant this through Jesus Christ our Lord. Amen.
            (*Original source not found.*)

An Evening Thanksgiving.

ACCEPT, we beseech Thee, our evening thanksgiving, O Thou Fountain of all good, Who hast led us in safety through the length of the day; Who daily blessest us with so many temporal mercies, and hast given us the hope of resurrection to eternal life; through Jesus Christ our Lord. Amen.
            (*From an Ancient Collect.*)

For a Quiet Night.

O LORD, the Maker of all things, we pray Thee now in this evening hour, to defend us through Thy mercy from all deceit of our enemy. Let us not be deluded with dreams, but if we lie awake keep Thou our hearts. Grant this petition, O Father, to Whom with the Holy Ghost, always in heaven and earth, be all laud, praise and honour. Amen.
            (*Henry VIII.*, A.D. 1491.)

For Forgiveness.

MOST gracious and merciful God, Who art of purer eyes than to behold iniquity, and hast promised mercy and forgiveness to all them who confess and forsake their sins. We come before Thee in an humble sense of our own unworthiness, acknowledging our manifold transgressions against Thy righteous laws, in thought, word, and deed. O gracious Father Who desirest not the death of a sinner, look upon us we beseech Thee in Thy Son Jesus Christ, and for the merits of His sufferings, be Thou merciful to us in the pardon of our sins. Accept, O Lord, as the testimony of our love, our hearty intercessions for all mankind. Let the glorious light of Thy Gospel shine upon all nations, and grant that all may come to the knowledge of Thy truth. O Lord, we beseech Thee to continue Thy gracious protection to us this night. Into Thy hands we commend ourselves and all we have, through Jesus Christ. Amen.

(Dean Stanhope, A.D. 1787.)

An Intercession.

REMEMBER again, Lord, them that have bidden us to remember them in the time of our prayer and our supplication wherewith we make request to Thee, O Lord our God. Give rest to them that have fallen asleep before us, heal speedily them that are sick, for Thou art the Life of us all, and the Hope of us all, and the Deliverer of us all, and the Raiser-up of us all, and to Thee we send thanksgiving unto the highest heaven, world without end. Amen. *(Ancient Abyssinian Jacobite Liturgy.)*

For Growth in Grace.

GIVE us, O Lord, an humble, quiet, peaceable, patient, tender and charitable mind, and in all our thoughts, words, and deeds have a taste of Thy Holy Spirit. Give us, O Lord, a lively faith, a firm hope, a fervent charity, a love of Thee. Take from us all lukewarmness in meditation, dullness in prayer. Give us fervour and delight in thinking of Thee and Thy grace, Thy tender compassion towards us. The things, good Lord, that we pray for, give us grace to labour for; through Jesus Christ our Lord. Amen. *(Sir Thomas More, A.D. 1478.)*

For Courage.

O MOST merciful Lord, we beseech Thee that Thou wilt give courage to Thy soldiers, wisdom to the perplexed, endurance to sufferers, fresh vigour and interest in life to those who have lost heart, a sense of Thy Presence to the lonely, and to bless and prosper all of this household; for the sake of Christ Jesus. Amen. *(Rev. A. McCheane, Nineteenth Century.)*

For a Sense of God's Presence.

ABIDE with us O Lord, until the Day-Star ariseth, and the Morning Light appeareth, when we shall abide with Thee, for ever. Amen. *(Rev. James Burns, Nineteenth Century.)*

For Forgiveness.

O GOD, Who wouldst not the death of a sinner, but that he should be converted and live, forgive the sins of us who turn to Thee with all our heart, and grant us the grace of eternal life, through Jesus Christ our Lord. Amen.

(Ancient Celtic Church Liturgy.)

For Love and Light.

O LORD, give us, we beseech Thee, in the Name of Jesus Christ Thy Son our Lord, that love which can never cease, that will kindle our lamps but not extinguish them, that they may burn in us and enlighten others. Do Thou, O Christ, our dearest Saviour, Thyself kindle our lamps, that they may evermore shine in Thy Temple, that they may receive unquenchable light from Thee that will enlighten our darkness, and lessen the darkness of the world. Lord Jesus, we pray Thee give Thy light to our lamps, that in its light the most holy place may be revealed to us in which Thou dwellest as the Eternal Priest, that we may always behold Thee, desire Thee, look upon Thee in love, and long after Thee, for Thy sake. Amen.

(St. Columba, A.D. 521.)

For Protection.

O LORD God, the Life of mortals, the Light of the faithful, the Strength of those who labour, the Repose of the dead; grant us a tranquil night, free from all disturbances; that after an interval of quiet sleep, we may, by Thy bounty, at the return of light, be endued with activity from the Holy Spirit, and enabled in security to render thanks to Thee, through Jesus Christ our Lord. Amen.   *(Mozarabic Liturgy.)*

God's Sovereignty.

ALMIGHTY and Eternal God, the Disposer of all the affairs in the world, there is not one circumstance so great as not to be subject to Thy power, nor so small but it comes within Thy care; Thy goodness and wisdom show themselves through all Thy works, and Thy loving-kindness and mercy appear in the several dispensations of Thy Providence. May we readily submit ourselves to Thy pleasure and sincerely resign our wills to Thine, with all patience, meekness, and humility; through Jesus Christ our Lord. Amen.   *(Queen Anne, A.D. 1665.)*

God's Unfailing Support.

O LORD support us (XVI Cent.) all the day long, till the shades lengthen, and the evening comes, and the busy world is hushed, and the fever of life is over, and our work done! Then in His mercy may He give us a safe lodging, and a holy rest, and peace at the last. Amen.   *(Author uncertain.)*

For Heavenly-Mindedness.

O MOST blessed Lord, deign to help us, and of Thy great mercy abolish our sins; detach our minds from earthly things, and raise them to the love of heavenly riches. Most merciful God, Who dost favour all true love, do Thou so aid and direct us that we may love Thee above all things, and recognizing Thine infinite benefits, may keep them in memory, and give Thee everlasting thanks for them. Finally, grant that ours may be the blessed life which shall enjoy Thy love for ever; through Jesus Christ our Lord. Amen.

(Raymond Jordanus, Fourteenth Century.)

For Manual Workers and Others.

O GOD, our Heavenly Father, we beseech Thee to hear us on behalf of all those who live by strength of arm or skill of hand. For men who face peril. For women who suffer pain. For those who till the earth; for those who tend machinery. For those whose business is in the deep waters, for sailors and seafarers. For those who work in offices and warehouses, for those who buy and sell. For those who labour at furnaces and in factories. For those who toil in mines. For those who keep house, for those who train children. For all who control, rule, or employ. For all who are poor, and broken and oppressed. For all whose labour is without hope; for all whose labour is without honour. For all whose labour is without interest. For those who have too little leisure. For those who are underpaid. We pray for all women-workers. We pray for all those who work in dangerous trades. For those who cannot find work, for those who have no home. For all prisoners and outcasts. For all who are sick, hungry, or destitute. We pray, O Father, for all men everywhere, that it may please Thee to comfort, sustain, protect and support these, and all others for whom we desire to pray, through Jesus Christ our Lord. Amen.

(Canon P. Dearmer, A.D. 1867.)

For a Knowledge of God's Will.

O ALMIGHTY God, Who having begun a good work in us, will perform it until the day of Jesus Christ; grant that our love may abound yet more and more in knowledge and in all judgment; that we may approve things that are excellent; that we may be sincere and without offence, till the day of Christ, being filled with the fruits of righteousness which are by Jesus Christ to the glory and praise of God. Amen.

(Adapted, St. Paul, First Century A.D.)

For Fitness on the Morrow.

LORD, when we sleep let us not be made afraid, but let our sleep be sweet, that we may be enabled to serve Thee on the morrow, through Jesus Christ our Lord. Amen.

(Archbishop Laud, A.D. 1573.)

For Forgiveness.

WE implore the mercy of Thy Majesty, that it may please Thee to give to us Thy servants, pardon of our sins, that we, being delivered from all the bonds of the enemy, may cleave to Thy commandments with our whole heart, and evermore love Thee alone, with all our strength, and one day be counted worthy to attain to the sight of Thy blessedness. Through Jesus Christ our Lord. Amen. *(Old Rheims M.S.)*

A National Confession.

O GOD of our fathers, we come before Thee to make a solemn act of penitence on behalf of our nation. We have sinned with our fathers, we have done amiss and dealt wickedly. We are truly sorry for all the past sins of this nation; it is with abasement that we look back on the sin, misery, crime, oppression, and immorality committed by us. We contemplate in deepest contrition the sins of which we are now guilty. We confess with shame that we have sinned, and deserve to be cut off in the midst of our prosperity. We have been ungrateful and faithless to Thee, O God; we have failed to carry out Thy purposes for us—we have neglected our opportunities; we have behaved ourselves arrogantly, we have trusted in human aid and neglected prayer, we have hasted to get rich, we have turned a deaf ear to the warnings of Thy prophets. But Thou, O God, hatest nothing that Thou hast made. We turn to Thee in weeping, fasting and prayer; we desire to amend our ways. Guide us, O God, into all truth; show us Thy mercy and grant us Thy salvation; through Jesus Christ our Lord. Amen.
(Rev. The Hon. James Adderley, A.D. 1861.)

For Holiness.

O HOLY Jesus, Who camest down from heaven and wast pleased to pay the ransom on the cross for us, on purpose that Thou mightest redeem us from all iniquity, and purify unto Thyself a peculiar people, zealous of good works. We beseech Thee to write Thy law in our hearts that we may see it, that we may know Thee, and the power of Thy resurrection, and express it in turning our foot from our iniquities. That Thou mayest rule in our hearts by faith, and that we, being dead unto sin and living unto righteousness, may have our fruit unto holiness, may grow in grace, and in the practical knowledge of Thee. Amen. *(Dr. Henry Hammond, A.D. 1605.)*

For a Lively Faith.

LET us not, O Lord, rest in a dead, ineffectual faith, but grant that it may be such as may show itself in good works, enabling us to overcome the world and to conform to the image of Christ on Whom we believe, by the same Lord Jesus Christ. Amen. *(Dean Lancelot Addison, A.D. 1632.)*

For Prepared Lives.

ALMIGHTY God, we give Thee thanks for the mighty yearning of the human heart for the coming of a Saviour, and the constant promise of Thy Word that He was to come. In our own souls we repeat the humble sighs of ancient men and ages, and own that our souls are in darkness and infirmity, without faith in Him Who comes to bring God to man, and man to God. We bless Thee for the tribute that we can pay to Him, from our very sense of need and dependence, and that our own hearts can so answer from their wilderness, the cry, "Prepare ye the way of the Lord." In us the rough places are to be made smooth, the crooked straight, the mountains of pride brought low, and the valleys of despondency lifted up. O God, prepare Thou the way in us now, and may we welcome anew Thy Holy Child. Hosanna! blessed be He Who cometh in the name of the Lord. Grant this, O heavenly Father, we humbly beseech Thee; through the same Jesus Christ Thy Son our Lord. Amen.

(Rev. Samuel Osgood, A.D. 1812.)

For Bishops and Pastors.

O LORD Jesus Christ, most true Pastor and Shepherd of our souls, we most humbly beseech Thee mercifully to behold Thy poor and scattered flock, whom Thou hast purchased with Thy most precious blood, and to send them such shepherds as may diligently seek the lost sheep, lovingly lay them on their shoulders and faithfully bring them home again to the fold. Vouchsafe ever to continue in Thy Church good Bishops, learned preachers, faithful teachers, godly ministers, and diligent shepherds; even such as have a powerful and unfeigned zeal towards the setting forth of Thy glory and the health of Thy people. Endue them with Thy holy Spirit, that they may be faithful, wise, and discreet servants, giving Thy household meat in due season. Give them that wisdom which no man is able to resist, wherewith also they may be able to exhort with wholesome doctrine, and to convince and overcome them that speak against it. Finally grant, we pray Thee, most merciful Saviour, that in all things they may so behave themselves according to Thy blessed Will and Commandment, that when Thou, the Chief Shepherd, shall appear, they may receive the incorruptible crown of glory. Amen.   *(King Edward VI. A.D. 1537. Primer.)*

A Fourfold Prayer.

O LORD, cure our infirmities, pardon our offences, lighten our burdens, enrich our poverty; through Christ our Lord. Amen.   *(Rev. Dr. Christopher Sutton, A.D. 1565.)*

For Union with God.

O GOD, of Thy goodness, give me Thyself, for only in Thee have I all.   *(Lady Juliana of Norwich, A.D. 1343.)*

A Sunday Thanksgiving.

WE thank Thee, O God, for the special blessings of this sacred day; that we have been admitted to the privilege of joining in the assemblies of public worship to offer up our praises and prayers to Thy Divine Majesty, and to hear Thy Holy Word read and preached. Cause the great truths in which we have been instructed to sink deep into our hearts, and to bring forth in us fruits of a holy and religious life. Pardon, we beseech Thee, whatever Thou hast seen amiss in us this day. Enable us throughout the week, upon which we have this day entered, to keep Thy laws and obey Thy commandments. Let Thy blessing be upon our actions, and let Thy wisdom direct our intentions, so that all we do may be righteous in Thy sight, through Jesus Christ. Amen. (*Bishop John Pearson*, A.D. 1613.)

Confession.

O MOST merciful Father, we confess that we have unworthily celebrated this day of joy and thankfulness and praise. Pardon, we humbly beseech Thee, all our want of fervour, our deadness and carelessness in worshipping Thee. Our best service is nothing worth. O God, not for our worthiness, but for the precious merits of Him Who, as on this day, rose again for our justification, forgive us our shortcomings, and accept our faulty worship. Let us not quench the Spirit, nor forfeit Thy grace by our unworthiness. But let us by rising to Thy glory, and by the grace Thou dost vouchsafe to give us, ever gain more and more increase thereof, to the conquering of sin, and advancement in holiness of life; through Christ Jesus our Lord. Amen.
(*Bishop Walsham How*, A.D. 1823.)

Dedication.

O LORD, we have a busy world around us. Eye, ear, and thought will be needed for all our work to be done in the world. Now ere we again enter upon it on the morrow we would commit eye, ear and thought to Thee. Do Thou bless them and keep their work Thine, that as through Thy natural laws our hearts beat and our blood flows without any thought of ours for them, so our spiritual life may hold on its course at those times when our minds cannot consciously turn to Thee to commit each particular thought to Thy service; hear our prayer for our Redeemer's sake. Amen.
(*Dr. Arnold, used before he entered Rugby School every day*, A.D. 1795.)

For Christ's Companionship.

O CHRIST, our only Saviour, so dwell within us that we may go forth with the light of hope in our eyes, and the fire of inspiration on our lips, Thy Word on our tongue, and Thy love in our hearts. Amen.   (*Source not found.*)

An Evening Thanksgiving.

O LORD God, we humbly thank Thee for all the mercies of another day, for life, health and strength, and for all Thy manifold blessings of this day. Now as we go to rest, grant us Thy forgiveness for all the sins and short-comings in our service, for the sake of Jesus Christ, Thy Son, our Redeemer. Amen.

From Forgetfulness.

O LORD of all mercy and full of benignity, suffer us not by any unthankfulness or hardness of heart, to forget Thy wonderful benefits and singular deliverances that Thou hast bestowed upon us this and every day; but grant that we may be continually careful and mindful to consider all the days of our life Thy gifts incomparable, which Thou ever givest us through Jesus Christ our Lord. Amen. *An Ancient Scottish Prayer.*

For Steadfastness.

O GOD, Who hast taught us how good a thing it is to follow the holy desires which Thou manifoldly puttest into our hearts, and how bitter is the grief of falling short of whatever beauty our minds behold. Strengthen us, we beseech Thee, to walk steadfastly in the better path which we once chose, and give us wisdom to tread it prudently in Thy fear, as well as cheerfully in Thy love, so that having been faithful to Thee all the days of our life here, we may be able hopefully to resign ourselves into Thy hands hereafter, through Jesus Christ our Lord. Amen. (*Rev. Rowland Williams*, A.D. 1818.)

For Night-Workers.

O LORD, before we close our eyes in sleep, we would remember before Thee all who are dear to us but who are now far absent. Guard them from all evil, uphold them in temptation, and give them the victory when assailed by sin. In their weariness give Thy refreshment and peace, and vouchsafe to all this night, sleep and rest. For those who work by night, grant Thy special protection. Enfold them and us in Thine everlasting arms that are ever about Thy people. Whether we sleep or wake grant us Thy peace for Thine own Name's sake. Amen.

For Quietness of Mind.

GIVE unto us, O Lord, that quietness of mind in which we can hear Thee speaking to us.

Our Unbroken Union in Christ.

BLESSING Thee for all the Faithful who have entered into rest, and for our loved ones now in Thy Presence, we beseech Thee to keep us one with them and with Thee until we too, come to where the Night is gone, and the Eternal Morn has dawned. Amen. (*Anonymous* A.D. 1940.)

For the Remembrance of His Holiness.

GRANT, O God, that we may draw nigh to Thee in reverence and holy fear in such sort as to be heard for the sake of Jesus Christ. Give us a sense of the majesty of Thy Presence: Thou Whom we now seek, Thou Whom we now confess, Thou Whom we adore in faith, and worship in spirit, even Thou art our God, God most glorious. Holy, Holy, Holy, Lord God Almighty, God the Father, God the Son, God the Holy Ghost blessed for evermore. Amen. *(Bishop John Armstrong, A.D. 1813.)*

For Quietness of Mind.

O LORD our God, Thou Who art the Helper of the heavy-laden, grant us who now, at evening-tide, draw near to Thee, may find rest unto our souls, and in waiting upon Thee we may, as Thou Thyself hast promised, renew our strength so that with the return of a new day on the morrow, we may run and not be weary, to Thy praise and honour. Amen.

"I am with you Alway."

O GOD, the Father everlasting, Who in Thy wondrous grace, standest within the shadows, keeping watch over Thine own; grant that in every peril and perplexity, in our groping and weariness, we may know the comfort of Thy pervading Presence. When the day grows dark may we fear no evil because Thy hand is upon us. Lead us onwards through the darkness into Thy light, through the sorrows into the joy of the Lord, and through the Cross of Sacrifice into closer communion with Thy Son, even Jesus Christ our Lord. Amen. *(Rev. Dr. J. Hunter, A.D. 1849.)*

For Peace.

ALMIGHTY God, from Whom all thoughts of truth and peace proceed, kindle, we pray Thee, in the hearts of all men, the true love of peace, and guide with Thy pure and peaceable wisdom those who take counsel for the nations of the earth; that in tranquility Thy kingdom may grow, till the earth is filled with the knowledge of Thy love, through Jesus Christ our Lord. Amen.

For Stability.

O GOD Almighty, Father of our Lord Jesus Christ, grant us, we pray Thee, to be grounded and settled in Thy truth by the coming down of the Holy Spirit into our hearts. That which we know not, do Thou reveal; that which is wanting in us, do Thou fill up; that which we know, do Thou confirm; and keep us blameless in Thy service, through the same Jesus Christ our Lord. Amen. *(St. Clement of Rome, A.D. d. 95.)*

For Serenity.

SET free, O Lord, the souls of Thy servants from all restlessness and anxiety. Give us that peace and power which flow from Thee. Keep us in all perplexity and distress, that upheld by Thy strength and stayed on the rock of Thy faithfulness we may abide in Thee now and evermore. Amen.

Adoration and Thanksgiving.

O LORD, and Father, we are not worthy of the least of all Thy mercies which Thou hast showed to Thy servants, neither can we render due thanks and praise for them; but, O Lord, accept our evening sacrifice of praise and thanksgiving.

For all the known and for all the unobserved blessings, deliverances, visitations and opportunities of doing good, and the graces of Thy Holy Spirit granted unto us, we bless and praise Thy holy Name.

Pardon, we beseech Thee, our ingratitude in that we have passed so many days without observing and acknowledging Thy wonderful goodness to us. Accept, we humbly pray Thee, our thanksgiving for all Thy gifts. We acknowledge our dependence upon Thee, for life, health of body and peace of mind, and for our general welfare—the grace and comfort of Thy Holy Spirit, salvation wrought for us by Jesus Christ, and the hope given us of everlasting life.

Glory be to Thee, O God our Creator. Glory be to Thee, O Jesus our Redeemer. Glory be to Thee, O Holy Spirit, our Sanctifier, our Guide and Comforter, both now and through the ages of the ages. Amen. *(Bishop Thomas Wilson, A.D. 1663.)*

For Concentration of Thought in Research.

O LORD, our Maker and Protector, Who hast graciously sent us into this world to work out our own salvation, enable us to drive from us all such unquiet and perplexing thoughts as may mislead or hinder us, in the practice of those duties which Thou hast required. When we behold the works of Thy hands, and consider the course of Thy Providence, give us grace always to remember that Thy thoughts are not our thoughts, nor Thy ways our ways. And while it shall please Thee to continue us in this world where much is to be done, and so little is known, teach us by Thy Holy Spirit to withdraw our mind from unprofitable and dangerous inquiries, from difficulties vainly curious, and doubts impossible to be solved. Let us rejoice in the light which Thou hast imparted. Let us serve Thee, O God, with active zeal and humble confidence, and wait with patient expectation for the time in which the soul which Thou receivest shall be satisfied with knowledge. Grant this, O Lord, for the sake of Jesus Christ our Lord. Amen.

(Dr. Samuel Johnson, A.D. 1709–1784.)

In God's Keeping.

NOW as the day draws to an ending, let Thy peace descend upon us, and on our homes. Take from us all irksome and doleful thoughts: still every fear; that we may trustfully give ourselves into Thy keeping, and say, "I will lay me down and sleep; for Thou, Lord, only makest me to dwell in safety." Amen.

(Rev. Dr. James Ferguson, A.D. 1873.)

"Unto God's gracious keeping we commit you."

LIGHTEN our darkness, we beseech Thee, O Lord; and by Thy great mercy defend us from all perils and dangers of this night; for the love of Thy only Son, our Saviour, Jesus Christ. Amen. (*Gelasian Sacramentary : Book of C.P.*, A.D. 1549.)

ABIDE with us, O most blessed and merciful Saviour, for it is toward evening and the day is far spent. As long as Thou art present with us, we are in the Light. When Thou art present all is brightness, all is sweetness. We discourse with Thee, watch with Thee, live with Thee and lie down with Thee. Abide then with us, O Thou Whom our soul loveth, Thou Sun of righteousness with healing under Thy wings arise in our hearts; make Thy Light then, to shine in darkness as a perfect day in the dead of night. (*Henry Vaughan*, A.D. 1622.)

OH! give Thy servants patience to be still and hear Thy will. Courage to venture wholly on Thine arm that will not harm. The wisdom that will never let us stray out of our way, the love that now afflicting knoweth best when we should rest.
(*John Neale*, A.D. 1818.)

AND now, O God, we turn our thoughts wholly from the world and all worldly objects to look up to Thee. Thou hast dealt hitherto with us so preciously, that we cannot mistrust Thy Providence but cast ourselves wholly upon Thee. We dedicate ourselves afresh to Thee. Give us the joys of Thy salvation. Let us find that whatever trials Thou dost put us to Thou art with us. Lead us, if Thou wilt, through the valley of the shadow of death, for even there Thou art with us. Bring us at last where Thou art, O our God, and our All. We are Thine, O our God, do with us what seems good in Thy sight—our God and our Portion for ever. (*Bishop Gilbert Burnet*, A.D. 1643.)

O SAVIOUR Divine, into Thy loving and merciful hands we commend the souls of the dying. By Thy most precious death which was our life, forsake not Thy servants who have now none other helper beside Thee. Receive their spirits, and bring them into Thy Presence, that the darkness may be Light about them, and that they may behold Thy face in righteousness and be satisfied when they awake with Thy likeness. Hear our cry we humbly beseech Thee, O Lord Christ. Amen.
(*Anonymous* A.D. 1940.)

INTO Thy hands, O Lord, we commend the spirit of our loved one, now passing from us into Thy Eternal Presence. Lord Jesus receive him [her] into Thy holy keeping. In the name of the Father and of the Son and of the Holy Ghost. Amen.
(*Queen Elizabeth* A.D. 1533 ; *Liturgical Service*.)

Praise and Thanksgiving.

O GOD, Who art the Giver of all good gifts, and the Father of mercies, we Thine unworthy servants entirely desire to praise Thy Name for all the expressions of Thy bounty towards us this day. We thank Thee for Thy love in giving Thy Son to die for our sins, for the covenant of mercy confirmed by His most precious Blood, for the means of grace instituted by Him here, and the hopes of glory through His merits hereafter.

We also bless Thee that Thou still hast patience with us, and hast added this one day more to our lives, that we may finish the work Thou hast set us to do, and renew and perfect our repentance. Pardon, good Lord, all the sins of this day for which we are now sorry at heart, and give us grace to lead a more holy life. Make Thyself always present to our minds, and let Thy love and fear rule in our souls, and so fit us for that pure and perfect bliss, which Thou hast prepared for them that love and fear Thee, in the glories of Thy eternal kingdom, and bring us all to Thy everlasting glory, through Jesus Christ our Lord. Amen.

(Rev. John Kettlewell, A.D. 1653.)

For Rest and Support.

O ALMIGHTY Father, Who in Thy Divine mercy dost cover the earth with the curtain of night that all the weary may rest. Grant to us, and to all men, rest in Thee this night. Let Thy grace, we beseech Thee, comfort and support all that are to spend it in sorrow, in loneliness, affliction, or in fear. We commend into Thy hands ourselves with all who are dear to us. Strengthen and confirm Thy faithful people, arouse the careless, relieve the sick, give peace to the dying that Thy holy Name may be glorified in Christ Jesus, Thy Son, our Lord. Amen.

(Rev. H. Stobart, Nineteenth Century.)

For Light in Darkness.

THINE is the day, O Lord, and Thine is the night. Grant that the Sun of Righteousness may abide in our hearts to drive away the darkness of evil thoughts. *(Gelasian Sacramentary.)*

For a humble walk with God.

O GOD and merciful Father, the day is past and we come to the foot of the Cross, to thank Thee for all the mercies Thou hast shewn to us to-day, for the deliverance from countless ills, for Thy forbearance and pity, for Thy blessing and protection. O our God, notwithstanding our desire to do right, we have failed again and again, but Thou hast raised us up with fresh hope, and faith, in Thy boundless mercy to pardon. Grant us Thy grace, O Lord, ever to contend for the right, and to live upheld by Thy Divine strength, and in humble dependence upon Thee to Thy honour and glory. Amen.   *(Source unknown.)*

A Thanksgiving.

HONOUR and praise be unto Thee, O Lord our God, for all Thy tender mercies again bestowed upon us throughout another week.

Continual thanks be unto Thee for creating us in Thine own likeness; for redeeming us by the precious blood of Thy dear Son when we were lost; and for sanctifying us with the Holy Spirit.

For Thy help and succour in our necessities, Thy protection in many dangers of body and soul; Thy comfort in our sorrows, and for sparing us in life, and giving us so large a time to repent. For all the benefits, O most merciful Father, that we have received of Thy goodness alone, we thank Thee; and we beseech Thee to grant us always Thy Holy Spirit, that we may grow in grace, in steadfast faith, and perseverance in all good works, through Jesus Christ our Lord. Amen. (*John Knox*, A.D. 1505?)

For Rest and Peace.

O LORD, Who art as the shadow of a great rock in a weary land, Who beholdest Thy weak creatures weary of labour, weary of pleasures, weary of heart from hope deferred, and weary of self. In Thine abundant compassion and unutterable tenderness bring us, we pray Thee, unto Thy rest, through Jesus Christ, Thy Son, our Saviour. Amen. (*C. G. Rossetti*, A.D. 1830.)

For a Renewal of Strength.

FATHER of peace, Grant us this night a sound repose, or if we awake, let us escape from ourselves and from all things that vex us; that in the morning we may rise, if it please Thee, with fresh vigour, resolved in all things to seek Thy glory and one another's good, through Jesus Christ our Lord. Amen.

(*Source not found.*)

For Courage and Assurance.

ALMIGHTY and Merciful God, to Whom the light and the darkness are both alike, and without Whom nothing befalls Thy children. Strengthen us to meet all the experiences of life with a steadfast and undaunted heart, help us to go on our way bravely whether it be rough or smooth, and when the mists hide Thy face, to continue patiently till they are dispersed by the Sun of Thy unchanging love, through Jesus Christ our Lord. Amen.

For those Far Absent.

UNITE them with us, O Lord—in the love of Thy Name and in the service of Thy Kingdom.

(*From a Memorial in a Village Church.*)

Preparation for Worship.

O GOD, the Author of Eternal Light, do Thou shed forth continual day upon us who watch for Thee, that our lips may praise Thee, our lives may bless Thee, and our meditations on the morrow glorify Thee, through Jesus Christ our Lord. Amen.

(*Sarum Missal.*)

CHILDREN'S PRAYERS.

"Lord, teach us to Pray."

O GOD, our Father, Thou hast promised to hear Thy children when they pray to Thee. Help us now to pray, teach us what to ask for, help us to mean what we say, and give us grace to love Thee more, and to love the people for whom we pray, for Jesus Christ's sake. Amen.

A Morning Prayer.

O MOST loving Saviour Jesus Christ, Who didst suffer little children to come unto Thee, and didst lay Thy hands upon them and bless them, look upon us also Thy children, and bless us. We thank Thee that Thou hast kept us safe through the night, and we pray Thee to take care of us this day. Bless our father and mother, our brothers and sisters, and all our friends; help us to love and serve Thee more and more. Amen.

A Prayer for Sunday Morning.

O HEAVENLY Father, we thank Thee for taking care of us during the past night, and now help us to remember that this is Thine own day. May we love Thy day, and never do anything which we know to be wrong. When we go to Thy House of Prayer may we be able to sing Thy praises, and understand Thy Word, and try to worship Thee. So may we be helped to be better in the week days, for Jesus Christ's sake. Amen.

For Father and Mother.

O LORD, we ask Thee to bless and keep dear father and mother, and our brothers and sisters. Watch over them every day and night. Help us to try and help them, and grant that we may all love and serve Thee more and more, that at last we may come to live with Thee in heaven; through Jesus Christ. Amen.

For King and Country.

O GOD our Heavenly Father, bless our King and our Country, and may all rulers remember Thee. Guard and keep our sailors, soldiers and airmen from harm and evil in times of peace, and hide them in war under the shelter of Thy wings. Bless our Church and all who minister to Thy people. Comfort all who are lonely and be with little children everywhere, through Jesus Christ our Saviour. Amen.

A Prayer for Missions.

O LORD Jesus Christ, Who at the time when Thou didst leave the earth and go back to heaven, told Thy disciples to go into all the world and teach people to believe in Thee, we pray Thee to bless all those who in distant lands are now obeying Thy commands; hasten the time when all shall become Christians and love and serve Thee for Thy sake. Amen.

CHILDREN'S PRAYERS

For Forgiveness.

FORGIVE us, O merciful Father, all our sins, and of Thy loving-kindness watch over us through the day. Keep us safe from all dangers, and help us in all temptations. Keep us from all evil thoughts, from all careless words, and from all wrong actions. Make us diligent in our work, unselfish and patient with all with whom we have to do. Help us to remember the example of the Lord Jesus, and try at work and at home to be like Him, for His sake we ask it. Amen.

For Kindness to Animals.

O LORD Jesus Christ, Who has taught us that without our Father in heaven no sparrow falls to the ground, help us to be very kind to all animals, and our pets. May we remember that Thou wilt one day ask us if we have been good to them. Bless us as we take care of them; for Thy sake. Amen.

For Help at Lessons.

O SAVIOUR of the world, help us not to be lazy to-day. Help us to follow Thy example and work with all our might at anything we have to do. Let us look on our lessons as work for Thee, which we must do well, to fit us for our after-life. And if we have any other tasks, let us do them as Thou didst do Thy work, cheerfully, willingly, and earnestly. And so bless all we do, dear Lord, that our work may please Thee and those who give it us to do, for Thy sake. Amen.

On Returning to School.

ONCE more, O Lord, have we left our home. We thank Thee for the blessings and happiness of the holidays just over. O heavenly Father, grant Thy blessing this term on all who live and work in this school. Grant us grace to be obedient, thoughtful, and civil. Help us to be kind to the new-comers. May no thoughts of past happiness or future trials distract our minds, but may we cheerfully and hopefully settle down to school life again, determined by Thy help to do our best in all things. O God, hear our prayer for the sake of Jesus Christ our Lord. Amen.

During Illness.

O GOD our heavenly Father, Who knowest our weakness and wilt not lay upon us more than we can bear, help us to bear it patiently. May we through suffering learn to love Thee better, for Jesus Christ's sake. Amen.

An Evening Prayer.

FORGIVE us, O Father in heaven, for all the wrong we have thought or spoken and done this day. Give us strength to fight more bravely to-morrow against our sins. Bless all whom we love, and keep them safe this night; for the sake of Jesus Christ our Saviour. Amen.

CHILDREN'S PRAYERS

For a Birthday.

IT is my birthday, Lord Jesus, my Saviour, and I thank Thee for giving me the wonderful gift of Life. I pray Thee that I may use my life rightly, that I may try to grow braver, kinder, wiser and truer year by year. I thank Thee for all the joys of the past year, and pray Thee to bless me through the coming one. Help me to conquer my faults and live more to Thy glory. Grant me Thy grace to help all those around me, and to try and make them happy. Be with me step by step all through this new year, and keep me safe unto the end; for Thy sake. Amen.

When in Trouble.

O LORD Jesus, our Saviour and Friend, we pray Thee shelter us in all these troubles. Give us strength to bear them, and grant that we may never complain but try to bear our cross as Thou didst Thine for us, till Thou callest us to dwell with Thee for ever and ever. Amen.

When Reading the Bible.

O LORD Jesus, Who hast told us in Thy Holy Word that Thou lovest us, and gavest Thy life for us, keep us in that love, and help us more and more to read, love, and understand Thy Word, that we may learn of Thee and of the Holy Spirit of Thy Father in Heaven. Amen.

In Remembrance of what Christ has Done.

O GOD our Heavenly Father, help us never to forget what Jesus Christ has done for us. We thank Thee for His wonderful love in coming as a little Child into this world. May we remember too that He died for us to save us from sin, and that on Easter Day He rose again from the dead, that He is now living in heaven with Thee our Father, but will come again to this world. O God, we thank Thee for all Thy love, help us to love Thee more; through Jesus Christ our Saviour. Amen.

A Prayer for the New Year.

ANOTHER year has gone, O our Father, and as we look back we see how full of faults it has been. We are truly sorry, and wish that we had tried harder to do well. We thank Thee that we have another chance to try again, and we pray Thee that Thou wilt give us the strength to do better. Help us, no matter what comes in this new year, to do our best. If illness comes, let us bear it bravely; if disappointment comes, let us learn to go to Thee for comfort. If joy comes, let it make us all the more ready to try and give joy to other people. Bless us now, O Lord, and all through the year, through Jesus Christ our Lord. Amen.

THE MINISTRY AND LAY WORKERS

O HOLY and Eternal Lord Jesus Christ, Thou great Shepherd and Bishop of our souls, send down upon Thy servants, the bishops and pastors of Thy Church, Thy heavenly blessing. Give them the Spirit of wisdom and holiness, patience and charity, zeal and watchfulness, that they may faithfully declare Thy will, boldly rebuke vice, rightly and duly administer Thy Holy Sacraments, and intercede with Thee acceptably for Thy people. Support and comfort them under all suffering and opposition for the cause of Thy truth, and grant that, after turning many to righteousness, they may shine as the stars for ever and ever, for Thy tender mercy's sake. Amen.

(Treasury of Devotion, A.D. 1872.)

O GOD, great in power, unsearchable in understanding, wondrous in counsels towards the children of men, do Thou fill with the gift of Thy Holy Spirit those whom Thou dost will to undertake the degree of the priesthood that they may be worthy to stand before Thy holy altar unblameably, to announce the Gospel of Thy kingdom, to administer the Word of Thy Truth, to offer gifts and spiritual sacrifices unto Thee, and to renew Thy people in the laver of regeneration; that at the second coming of our great God and Saviour Jesus Christ, Thine only begotten Son, they may go forth to meet Him, and by the multitude of Thy mercies receive their reward; for Thy venerable and majestic Name is blessed and glorified. Amen.

(Eastern Church Liturgy.)

G RACIOUSLY cast Thy light, O Lord, upon Thy Church, that Thy flock may everywhere go on and prosper, and its pastors, by Thy governance, may become acceptable to Thy Name; through Jesus Christ our Lord. Amen.

(Leonine Sacramentary.)

O GOD, Who providest for Thy people with tenderness, and rulest over them in love; give the Spirit of wisdom to those to whom Thou hast given the authority of government; that from the well-being of the holy sheep may proceed the eternal joy of the pastors; through Jesus Christ our Lord. Amen.

(Gregorian Sacramentary.)

A LMIGHTY and everlasting God, look mercifully upon Thy servants everywhere who visit the poor and the suffering, the needy and the distressed, in their homes; that, guarded by Thy protection, and kept by Thy power, they may carry on their work for Thee with joy and patience, through Jesus Christ our Lord. Amen. *(Rev. A. L. Illingworth,* A.D. 1878.)

FOR THE MEDICAL AND NURSING PROFESSIONS.

GOD of prayer, we would remember the infirm, in Thy Presence. Bless all our hospitals, where the lame and pain-ridden are brought under loving and beneficent care. May their ailments bind us all into a deeper and more fruitful fellowship, through Jesus Christ our Lord. Amen. *(Rev. J. Jowett, A.D. 1864.)*

O LORD Jesus Christ, Who alone hast power over life and death, over health and sickness, give power, wisdom and gentleness to all Thy ministering servants, our doctors and nurses, that always bearing Thy Presence with them, they may not only heal but bless, and shine as lamps of hope in the darkest hours of distress and fear, Who with the Father and the Holy Ghost livest and reignest ever one God, world without end. Amen.
(Society for the Propagation of the Gospel, A.D. 1701.)

O MOST merciful and loving Jesus, who camest into the world to teach us the glory of self-sacrifice and service, grant to all those who are called to the sacred office of nursing and caring for the sick, that they may always remember that they are fellow-workers with Thee. Give to them such patience, gentleness, tact, and love, that they may by the beauty of their lives win many sick and dying souls to Thee, Who livest and reignest with the Father and the Holy Ghost now and ever. Amen.
(Source not found.)

O LORD, the great Healer and good Physician both of body and soul: Bless all whether Doctors or Nurses, whom Thou hast called to minister to the sick and suffering in our hospitals with skill and power; that they may exercise their art for the well-being of Thy servants, and to Thy glory, Who livest and reignest with the Father and the Holy Spirit, world without end. Amen. *(Bishop W. W. Webb, Nineteenth Century.)*

O ALMIGHTY God, Who didst send Thy Blessed Son to be the great Physician of souls and bodies, look, we beseech Thee, upon Thy servants, to whom Thou hast committed the care of the sick. Bless, Lord, the remedies which they employ, help them ever to remember that in ministering to others, they minister to Thee; give them grace to be tender and patient, in all their work and service, and being mindful of their own last hours may their hearts be filled with sympathy and love, for the sake of Christ Jesus our Lord. Amen.
(Rev. A. McCheane, Nineteenth Century.)

NOTE.—See also St. Luke's Day, p. 240, and Medical Missions, p. 243.

PRISONS AND INSTITUTIONS.

MOST gracious Father, we beseech Thee to bless with Thy special care all penitentiaries and homes of refuge. Look down in pity on those who are sheltered in them. Guide and protect those who have again gone into the world. Give them all true contrition for their past sins. Strengthen them in their good resolutions. Lead them onward from grace to grace, that by Thy Holy Spirit guiding them, they may persevere in the paths of obedience and humility, and in striving against evil thoughts and desires. And to those engaged in teaching and training them, give Thy Holy Spirit, that they may have a right judgment; and that in deep humility and singleness of purpose, purity of heart and life, and real zeal for Thy glory and the salvation of souls, they may labour for the love of Thee. Give them faith and hope to sustain them in disappointment, love and patience towards those under their charge, and in Thine own good time crown their labour with an eternal reward. Grant this, we beseech Thee, for the sake of Christ Jesus our Lord. Amen. *("St. Cyprian's Bethesda.")*

DELIVER, O most merciful God, those little ones of Thy flock who have fallen into sin. Remember not their offences, but set them free from the snare of the enemy. Prosper with the help of Thy Holy Spirit the endeavours of all who are seeking to train them for good. Grant that following after humility and being made partakers of Thy heavenly wisdom, they may be strengthened to the performance of Thy will and may be restored to the perfect fellowship of Thy saints; through Jesus Christ our Lord. Amen. *(Archbishop Leighton, A.D. 1611.)*

ROOT out, O Lord, all the seeds of evil wheresoever they have been sown in youthful hearts. Prosper all that is done to reform young offenders in the Institutions, Reformatories, and Homes, of our land; that, being apart from the surroundings and companions of vice, they may learn to live as befits Thy children, and may be imbued and strengthened with habits of obedience and piety; through Jesus Christ our Lord. Amen. *(Sursum Corda, A.D. 1898.)*

VOUCHSAFE, we beseech Thee, O Lord, unto all such as are under sentence of punishment a true sense of their crimes, true repentance for them and Thy gracious pardon, that their souls may be saved in the day of the Lord Jesus, for His sake, Who underwent for us the death of the Cross, Who now liveth and reigneth with Thee and the Holy Ghost, One God world without end. Amen. *(Bishop Wilson, A.D. 1663.)*

PRAYERS FOR SPECIAL SEASONS OF THE CHRISTIAN YEAR.

ADVENT

O ALMIGHTY Father, Source of all being, Fountain of light and salvation, we adore Thy infinite goodness in sending Thy only begotten Son into the world, that, believing in Him, we may not perish, but have everlasting life; and we pray Thee that, through the power and grace of His first Advent to save the world, we may be made ready to meet Him at His second Advent to judge the world; through the same Thy Son, Jesus Christ our Lord. Amen.

(Bishop Walsham How, A.D. 1823.)

O GOD, Father of mercies, Who didst so love the world that Thou didst give Thine only begotten Son to take our nature upon Him for us men and for our salvation, grant to us who, by His first coming, have been called into Thy Kingdom of grace, that we may always abide in Him, and be found watching and ready when He shall come again to call us to Thy Kingdom of glory; through Jesus Christ. Amen.

(Rev. H. Stobart, Nineteenth Century.)

O LORD Jesus Christ, Who hast warned us that "in such an hour as we know not the Son of man cometh," make us so watchful every day that we may be truly prepared when it shall please Thee to call us hence, and grant us then a share in those eternal joys which Thou hast prepared for Thy faithful servants, O Lord, Thou Lover of souls. Amen.

(Rev. G. H. Sharpe, Nineteenth Century.)

BE Thou to us, O Lord, a crown of glory in the day when Thou shalt come to judge the world by fire; that Thou mayest graciously clothe us here with the robe of righteousness, and hereafter with the perfection of a glorious liberty; through Thy mercy, Who with the Father and Holy Spirit livest and reignest, one God, world without end. Amen. *(Mozarabic Liturgy.)*

O LORD Jesus Christ, Who at Thy first coming didst warn us to prepare for the day when Thou shalt come to be our Judge, mercifully grant that, being awake from the sleep of sin, we may be always watching and intent upon the work Thou hast given us to do; Who livest and reignest with the Father and the Holy Ghost, ever one God, world without end. Amen.

(Rev. W. E. Scudamore, A.D. 1813.)

STIR up, we beseech Thee, O Lord, our hearts to prepare the ways of Thine only begotten Son; that by His advent we may be enabled to serve Thee with purified minds; through the same Jesus Christ our Lord. Amen.

(Gelasian Sacramentary.)

ADVENT

MAKE us, we beseech Thee, O Lord our God, watchful and heedful in awaiting the coming of Thy Son, Christ our Lord; that when He shall come and knock He may find us not sleeping in sin, but awake, and rejoicing in His praises; through the same Jesus Christ our Lord. Amen.

(Gelasian Sacramentary.)

VOUCHSAFE to us, though unworthy, a plenteous out-pouring of Thy Spirit to refresh Thy heritage, for Thy Kingdom is now at hand, and Thou art standing at the door. Hear us, we beseech Thee, O Lord. Amen. *(John Milton, A.D. 1608.)*

ALMIGHTY God, Who in Thy Providence hast made all ages a preparation for the Kingdom of Thy Son, we beseech Thee to make ready our hearts for the brightness of Thy glory. Awaken us from our slumbers. Quicken us, O Thou Who art the Eternal Life. Revive and deepen our faith in the spiritual realities. Kindle our affections and restore us to hope. Our eyes wait for the glorious and blessed Dawn. Let us behold that Dayspring from on high, that we may live in peace; through Jesus Christ, our Saviour and Redeemer. Amen.

(Rev. Dr. John Hunter's Collection, A.D. 1892.)

O GOD, Who didst look on man when he had fallen down into death, and resolve to redeem him by the advent of Thine only begotten Son; grant, we beseech Thee, that they who confess His glorious Incarnation may also be admitted to the fellowship of Him their Redeemer; through the same Jesus Christ our Lord. Amen. *(St. Ambrose, A.D. 340.)*

O CHRIST our God, Who wilt come to judge the world in the manhood which Thou hast assumed, we pray Thee to sanctify us wholly, that in the day of Thy coming our whole spirit, soul, and body may so revive to a fresh life in Thee, that we may live and reign with Thee for ever, to Thy honour and glory; Who with the Father and the Holy Spirit livest and reignest, ever one God. Amen. *(Mozarabic Liturgy.)*

O LORD, Who hast revealed to us that "the night is far spent, the day is at hand," grant that we may ever be found watching like servants who wait for the coming of their Lord; that, when He cometh and knocketh, we may open to Him immediately. Save us from all love of this world, that we may wait with patient hope for the day of the Lord, and abide in Him, that when He shall appear, we may have confidence, and not be ashamed before Him at His coming; through Jesus Christ our Lord and Saviour. Amen.

(Rom. xiii. 12; Luke xii. 36; 1 John ii. 28; adapted.)

AMEN, Come Lord Jesus. *(St. John, First Century A.D.)*

MAY God Almighty, Who by the Incarnation of His only begotten Son drove away the darkness of the world, and by His glorious Birth enlightened this day, drive away from us the darkness of sins, and enlighten our hearts with the light of Christian graces. And may He who willed that the great day of His most holy Birth should be told to the shepherds by an angel, pour upon us the refreshing shower of His blessing, and guide us, Himself being our Shepherd, to the pastures of everlasting joy. And may He, Who through His Incarnation united earthly things with heavenly, fill us with the sweetness of inward peace and goodwill, and make us partakers with the heavenly host; for the glory of His great Name. Amen.

(Treasury of Devotion, A.D. 1869.)

ALMIGHTY God, bestow upon us, we beseech Thee, such love and charity as were His, to Whom it was more blessed to give than to receive, and Who came not to be ministered unto, but to minister. May the same mind be in us which was also in Christ Jesus, while we keep the festival of His Divine humility, consecrating ourselves to the service of all who are in need; for the sake of Jesus Christ our Lord. Amen.

(Original source not found.)

O GOD, Who makest us glad with the yearly remembrance of our redemption, grant that, as we joyfully receive Thine only begotten Son as our Redeemer, we may also see Him without fear when He cometh as our Judge; even our Lord, Who with Thee and the Holy Spirit ever liveth, one God, world without end. Amen.   *(Gelasian Sacramentary; American Book of Common Prayer, A.D. 1789.)*

O ETERNAL God, Father Almighty, Who, as at this time, didst give Thine only Son to be born of a woman and to be made the Son of man, that we might be made the sons of God, grant to us to be indeed Thy children; and be Thou now and ever our Father, through the same Jesus Christ our Lord. Amen.

(Rev. H. Stobart, Nineteenth Century.)

GRANT us, O God, such love and wonder that with humble shepherds, wise men, and pilgrims unknown, we may come and adore the Holy Babe, the Heavenly King; and with our gifts, worship and serve Him our Lord and Saviour Jesus Christ. Amen.

(Rev. James Ferguson, D.D., A.D. 1873.)

O GOD, Who hast made this most sacred night to shine with the illumination of the True Light, grant, we beseech Thee, that, as we have known the mystery of that Light upon earth, we may also perfectly enjoy it in heaven; through the same Jesus Christ our Lord. Amen.

(Gelasian Sacramentary: American B. of C.P., A.D. 1789.)

GLORY be to God in the highest, and on earth peace, goodwill towards men: for unto us is born this day a Saviour, Who is Christ the Lord. We praise Thee, we bless Thee, we glorify Thee, we give thanks unto Thee, for this greatest of Thy mercies, O Lord God, Heavenly King, God the Father Almighty. O Lord, the only begotten Son Jesus Christ, O Lord God, Lamb of God, Son of the Father, Who wast made man to take away the sins of the world, have mercy upon us by turning us from our iniquities. Thou Who wast manifested to destroy the works of the devil, have mercy upon us by enabling us to renounce and forsake them. Thou Who art the great Advocate with the Father, receive our prayer, we humbly beseech Thee. Amen.

(Bishop Ken, A.D. 1637.)

GRANT, O Lord, we beseech Thee, to Thy people firmness of faith, that as we confess Thine only begotten Son, the ever-lasting partaker of Thy glory, to have been born in our very flesh of the Virgin Mother, we may be delivered from present adversities, and admitted into joys that shall abide; through the same Jesus Christ Thy Son, our Lord and Saviour. Amen.

(St. Leo, Leonine Sacramentary.)

O ALMIGHTY God, Who by the Birth of Thy holy Child Jesus hast given us a great Light to dawn upon our dark-ness, grant, we pray Thee, that in His light we may see light to the end of our days; and bestow upon us, we beseech Thee, that most excellent Christmas gift of charity to all men, that so, the likeness of Thy Son may be formed in us, and that we may have the ever-brightening hope of everlasting life; through Jesus Christ our Lord. Amen.

(Professor Knight, Nineteenth Century.)

O GOD, Who of Thy compassion and tenderness towards the human race didst send Thine only begotten Son, that He might take upon Him our flesh and dwell amongst us; we desire to worship before the infinite greatness of Thy love. Our hearts are filled with joy, our tongues with praise. O blessed Jesus, Who as on this day wast born in Bethlehem, and didst lie a weak and helpless Child, whilst yet Thou wast the Eternal Son of God, look upon us, we beseech Thee, and make us willing to be partakers of Thy meekness and humility. O Thou Who art the Prince of Peace, grant us that inward peace which Thou alone art able to bestow, and enable us to live at peace with all men. Grant this, O heavenly Father, for the sake of Jesus Christ Thy Son, our Lord and Saviour. Amen.

(Rev. G. Calthrop, Nineteenth Century.)

ALMIGHTY and everlasting God, the brightness of faithful souls, Who didst bring the Gentiles to Thy light, and made known unto them Him Who is the true Light, and the bright and morning Star, fill, we beseech Thee, the world with Thy glory, and show Thyself by the radiance of Thy Light unto all nations; through Jesus Christ our Lord.   Amen.

(Gregorian Sacramentary.)

O CHRIST, the Sun of Righteousness, Who didst manifest Thyself in our flesh at this season, shine graciously into our hearts, that, walking as children of light, we may glorify Thee before men, and being always ready to obey Thy call, may, in our place and measure hold up the light of life to them that sit in darkness and the shadow of death.   Hear us, O Lord, for Thy great mercies' sake, who livest and reignest with the Father and the Holy Ghost, now and for ever.   Amen.

(Rev. H. Stobart, Nineteenth Century.)

ALMIGHTY and everlasting God, Who hast made known the Incarnation of Thy Son by the bright shining of a star, which, when the wise men beheld, they presented costly gifts and adored Thy Majesty; grant that the star of Thy Righteousness may always shine into our hearts; and that, as our treasure, we may give ourselves and all we possess to Thy service; through Jesus Christ our Lord.   Amen.   *(Gelasian Sacramentary.)*

O GOD, Who didst manifest Thy only begotten Son to the Gentiles, and hast commanded Thy Church to preach the Gospel to every creature, bless all Thy servants who are labouring for Thee in distant lands.   Have compassion upon the heathen and upon all who know Thee not.   Lead them by Thy Holy Spirit to Him Who is the Light of the world, that walking in the light they may at length attain to the light of everlasting life; through Jesus Christ our Lord.   Amen.   *(Robert Nelson, A.D. 1656.)*

ABIDE with us until the Day-Star ariseth, and the Morning Light appeareth, when we shall abide for ever with Thee. Amen.   *(Rev. James Burns, Nineteenth Century.)*

O BLESSED Jesus, Who by the shining of a star didst manifest Thyself to them that sought Thee, show Thy heavenly light to us, and give us grace to follow until we find Thee; finding to rejoice in Thee; and rejoicing, to present to Thee ourselves, our souls and bodies, for Thy service for evermore; for Thine honour and glory.   Amen.   *(Canon E. Hawkins, A.D. 1802.)*

MAY Thy heavenly Light, we humbly beseech Thee O Lord, go before us always, and in all places.   Amen.

(Roman Missal.)

O LORD, Almighty God of our fathers, we have sinned above the number of the sands of the sea. We have done evil before Thee, we have not done Thy will. Now therefore we bow the knee of our heart and beseech Thee forgive us, O Lord, Thou art the God, even the God of them that repent, and in us Thou wilt show all Thy goodness, for Thou wilt save us that are unworthy according to Thy great mercy. Therefore we will praise Thee for ever all the days of our life; for all the powers of the heavens do praise Thee, and Thine is the glory for ever and ever. Amen. *(King Manasseh, Seventh Century B.C.)*

O GOD, our heavenly Father, we humbly pray Thee for Thy dear Son's sake, to bless abundantly at this time whatever efforts may be made to turn the hearts of Thy children to more sincere repentance and more living faith. Give a double portion of Thy Holy Spirit to all who minister and work for others. Prepare all hearts to receive the seed of Thy Word. Grant that it may take deep root, and bring forth fruit to Thy glory. Alarm the careless, humble the self-righteous, kindle the lukewarm, soften the hardened, encourage the fearful, relieve the doubting, and bring many souls in loving faith to Thyself. Remember us, O Lord, according to the favour that Thou bearest unto Thy people; O visit us with Thy salvation. Give more than we can desire or deserve; for the sake of Thy Son Jesus Christ our Lord. Amen. *(Dean Goulburn, A.D. 1818.)*

O GOD, Who by Thy Word dost marvellously work out the reconciliation of mankind, grant, we beseech Thee, that by this holy fast we may both be subjected to Thee with all our hearts, and be united to each other in prayer to Thee; through Jesus Christ our Lord. Amen. *(Gelasian Sacramentary.)*

O GRACIOUS Saviour, we beseech Thee of Thy love and goodness to remember our manifold infirmities; give us full pardon of our sins and a new spirit. Give us grace, that we may always imitate Thy humility, resignation, purity, patience, charity, and all virtues, that we may be well-pleasing to Thee may become daily more like Thee, and may hereafter dwel with Thee for ever. For Thine own Name's sake we ask it Amen. *(Treasury of Devotion, A.D. 1872.)*

L ET Thy Spirit, O Lord, come into the midst of us, and washing us with the pure water of repentance, prepare us to be alway a living sacrifice unto Thee; Who livest and reignest, ever worl without end. Amen. *(Mozarabic Liturgy.)*

O LORD, Thou knowest the weakness and misery of Thy creatures. We have nothing, but what matter—so long as we have Thee, so long as we can seek Thee with certainty of finding all that is not to be found in ourselves. So help us, Lord, to seek; through Jesus Christ. Amen.

(Archbishop Fénélon, A.D. 1651.)

BLESSED by Thy glorious Name, which is exalted above all blessing and praise. Thou, even Thou, art Lord alone. Thou hast made heaven, the heaven of heavens, with all their host, the earth and all things that are therein; the seas and all that is therein; and Thou preservest them all, and the host of heaven worshippeth Thee. Thou art a God ready to pardon, gracious and merciful, slow to anger, and of great kindness, and forsakest not Thy people. Now, therefore, our God, the great, the mighty, and the terrible God, Who keepest covenant and mercy, let not all our weariness seem little before Thee, that hath come upon us, but hear us and bless us; for Thy Name's sake. Amen. *(Nehemiah: Fifth Century B.C.; Neh. ix.)*

WE beseech Thee, our most gracious God, preserve us from the cares of this life, lest we should be too much entangled therein; also from the many necessities of the body, lest we should be ensnared by pleasure; and from whatsoever is an obstacle to the soul, lest, being broken with troubles, we should be overthrown. Give us strength to resist, patience to endure, and constancy to persevere; for the sake of Jesus Christ our Lord and Saviour. Amen. *(St. Thomas à Kempis, A.D. 1379.)*

BLESSED Lord, Who for our sakes wast content to bear sorrow and want and death, grant unto us such a measure of Thy Spirit that we may follow Thee in all self-denial and tenderness of soul. Help us by Thy great love to succour the afflicted, to relieve the needy and destitute, to comfort the feeble-minded, to share the burdens of the heavy-laden, and ever to see Thee in all that are poor and desolate; through Jesus Christ our Lord. Amen. *(Bishop Westcott, A.D. 1825.)*

OUR God, may we lay hold of Thy Cross, as of a staff that can stand unshaken when the floods run high. It is this world and not another, this world with all its miseries—its ruin and its sin—that Thou hast entered to redeem by Thine Agony and Bloody Sweat. Amen. *(Canon H. Scott Holland, A.D. 1847.)*

HEAR us, O Lord, we beseech Thee, and in our tribulations pity us, grant unto us spiritual gladness, and give us everlasting peace; through Jesus Christ our Lord. Amen.

(Sarum Breviary.)

CONFESSION AND PRAYER FOR FORGIVENESS

O THOU Who hearest prayer, unto Thee shall every soul come which mourns over its own sin, and struggles against its besetting temptation. Many a time do we go astray through negligence, or through weakness, or through wilfulness. Renew our souls, lead us in the paths of righteousness, so that we may run in them and not faint. Work in us every noblest virtue, the fruit of Thy abounding grace. So make us blessed, and a blessing to others. Father of all men, Father of the most sinful children, out of sin, we would rise into holiness by the power of Thy Holy Spirit, out of failure, let us be consecrated to Thee. Draw us unto Thee for the sake of Him who loved us and died for us, even Jesus Christ Thy Son, our Lord and Saviour. Amen.
(Rev. Fielding Ould, 1864.)

A LMIGHTY God, Father of our Lord Jesus Christ, we humbly acknowledge our manifold sins and offences against Thee, by thought and deed. We have neglected opportunities of good which Thou in Thy love gavest unto us. We have been overcome by temptations, from which Thou wast ready to guard us. We have looked unto men, and not unto Thee, in doing our daily work. We have thought too little of others, and too much of our own pleasure in all our plans. We have lived in forgetfulness of the life to come. But Thou art ever merciful and gracious to those who turn to Thee. So we now come to Thee as those whom Thou wilt not cast out. Hear, O Lord, and have mercy upon us, O Almighty God, heavenly Father, Who forgivest iniquity and transgression. O Lord Jesus Christ, Lamb of God, Who takest away the sin of the world; O Holy Spirit, Who helpest the infirmities of those who pray, receive our humble confession. Give us true repentance and sincere faith in Thee. Do away our offences, and give us grace to live hereafter more worthily of our Christian calling; for the glory of Thy great Name. Amen. *(Bishop Westcott, A.D. 1825.)*

O FATHER of mercies and God of all comforts, Who by Thy Blessed Son hast declared that all sins shall be forgiven unto the sons of men upon their true repentance, let this most comfortable word support us Thy servants against the temptations of the devil. Though our sins are great, they cannot be too great for Thy mercy, which is infinite. O give us true repentance for all the errors of our life past, and steadfast faith in Thy Son Jesus Christ, that our sins may be done away by Thy mercy; through the merits of the same Jesus Christ our Lord. Amen.
(Bishop Thomas Wilson, A.D. 1663.)

L ORD, we pray not for tranquillity, nor that our tribulations may cease; we pray for Thy Spirit and Thy Love, that Thou grant us strength and grace to overcome adversity; through Jesus Christ. Amen. *(Girolamo Savonarola, A.D. 1452.)*

PRAYERS FOR HOLY WEEK AND EASTER

SUNDAY NEXT BEFORE EASTER—PALM SUNDAY

AS on this day we keep the special memory of our Redeemer's entry into the city, so grant, O Lord, that now and ever He may triumph in our hearts. Let the King of grace and glory enter in, and let us lay ourselves and all we are in full and joyful homage before Him; through the same Jesus Christ our Lord. Amen. *(Bishop Handley C. G. Moule, A.D. 1841.)*

O MOST merciful Father, Who by the mouth of our Saviour Jesus Christ hast said, "Ask, and it shall be given you," receive, we beseech Thee, our supplication, and for Thy Truth's sake hear us in Thy righteousness. We make our prayers unto Thee, most blessed Father, not trusting in our own righteousness, but in Thy manifold mercies. Have mercy upon us, Thy sinful children. Soften our hard hearts with the dew of Thy grace. Fulfil Thy promise made unto us by Thy prophet. Take away from us our stony heart, and put a new spirit within us, and make us to walk after Thy commandments. Lighten, O Father of lights, our blind hearts, blinded with error and ignorance. Lighten them with the true light of Thy holy Word, that we may know Thy will, love it, and live thereafter. Give us grace, O heavenly Father, to feel in our hearts Thine infinite goodness and mercy and Thine exceeding kindness set forth unto us in and by our Saviour Jesus Christ, Whom Thou hast given up to death to redeem us from everlasting death, and to make us Thy children and heirs, brethren and inheritors together with Thine only Son, our Lord Jesus Christ. Amen.
(Primer of Henry VIII., A.D. 1545.)

O GOD, who by the Passion of Thy blessed Son hast made the instrument of shameful death to be unto us the means of life and peace: grant us so to glory in the Cross of Christ that we may gladly suffer shame and loss; for the sake of the same Thy Son our Lord. Amen. *(Revised Prayer Book, A.D. 1928.)*

ALMIGHTY Father, we most humbly thank Thee for the unspeakable mercy which we commemorate at this season in the redemption of the world by the Blood of Jesus Christ, which cleanseth from all sin; and heartily we pray Thee so to shed abroad Thy love in our hearts that we may joyfully follow Thy blessed Son in His wondrous patience and humility. As He has trodden the way of death before us, so let us not fear death; and whensoever the time of our departure shall come, may we in faith commend our spirits into Thy hands, and so be with our Lord in Paradise until the glorious consummation of the last day; through Jesus Christ Thy Son our Lord. Amen.
(Bishop Walsham How, A.D. 1823.)

O GOD, Who hast brought us to this holy time, wherein we renew the memory of our Redeemer's Passion, hear us, we beseech Thee, and enable us to observe it in the spirit of holiness and piety, of humility and penitence, of love, and adoration and gratitude. Grant that His sufferings may show us the grievousness of sin, and the punishment due to it, while they give us comfort in showing to us the ground of our hope. That so, putting our whole trust in Him, Who is the Sacrifice and Ransom for our sin, we may enter into the fellowship of His sufferings, and dying unto the world, may live evermore with Him, our Saviour and Redeemer, even Jesus Christ Thy Son our Lord. Amen. *(Rev. H. Stobart, Nineteenth Century.)*

O LORD, Who in Thy righteous zeal didst, as on this day, cast out the profaners of Thy Father's house, enter with power into the temple of our hearts, and so cleanse them from all sinful thoughts and vain imaginations, that we may henceforth be holy unto Thee, Who with the Father and the Holy Ghost, livest and reignest, one God, world without end. Amen. *(Rev. W. E. Scudamore, A.D. 1813.)*

O LORD God, Who didst give Thine only Son as at this time to suffer and to die for us, give us grace to humble ourselves before Thee in heartfelt sorrow for sin. Help us to deny ourselves, and to take up our cross and follow our Lord. Have mercy on all men and draw them to Thyself by the power of the Cross. Bless all the services of this week, and grant that we may have such trust and confidence in Thy mercy towards us in Christ our Lord, that we may find in Him all pardon and peace. Prepare our hearts for the joyful worship of Easter Day; for His merits, Who died, and was buried, and rose again for us, Thy Son Jesus Christ our Lord. Amen. *(Rev. A. F. Thornhill, Nineteenth Century.)*

BE Thou Thyself, O Lord, the Sanctifier and the Shepherd of Thy people, that we, who are strengthened by Thy help, may in our daily life walk with Thee, and in all quietness of spirit serve Thee; through Jesus Christ our Master. Amen. *(Roman Breviary.)*

WE beseech Thee, O Lord, in Thy forgiving love, turn away what we deserve for our sins, nor let our offences prevail before Thee ; but let Thy mercy alway rise up to overcome them; through Jesus Christ our Lord. Amen. *(Leonine Sacramentary.)*

O ALMIGHTY and everlasting God, Who hast given us Thy Son Jesus Christ, that by His holy life, passion and death, He might redeem us from the curse of sin, we beseech Thee to grant to us Thy Holy Spirit, that we may heartily believe in this Thy great love and mercy, and believing may receive and hold fast the spirit of sonship while time shall endure, till Thou givest us the eternal heritage which Thou hast promised to all who believe in Thee; through Jesus Christ Thy Son, our Lord. Amen. *(Original source not found.)*

ALMIGHTY and most merciful God, Who gavest Thine only begotten Son to die for our salvation, grant unto Thy servants who following Him in devout remembrance and affection of His Cross and grave, that being with Him crucified unto sin, we may henceforth abide and live in Him; through the same Jesus Christ our Lord. Amen. *(Canon E. Hawkins, A.D. 1802.)*

LORD Jesus Christ, Son of the living God, Who for our redemption willedst to be born, and on the Cross to die the most shameful of deaths, do Thou by Thy death and passion deliver us from all sins and penalties, and by Thy holy Cross bring us, miserable sinners, to that place where Thou livest and reignest with the Father and the Holy Spirit, ever one God, world without end. Amen. *(Pope Innocent III., A.D. d. 1216.)*

SEARCH us, O God, and try our hearts; prove us and know our thoughts, and see if there be any wickedness in us, and lead us in the way everlasting. We know not what a day may bring forth, but Thou art the same yesterday, to-day, and for ever. O Thou Who art the everlasting refuge of the sons of men, in Thee do we put our trust. Hear us and help us, we beseech Thee; for the sake of Jesus Christ our Lord. Amen.
(Professor Knight, Nineteenth Century.)

O THOU Who in almighty power wast meek, and in perfect excellency wast lowly, grant unto us the same mind, that we may mourn over our evil will. Our bodies are frail and fading; our minds are blind and froward; all that we have which is our own is naught; if we have any good in us it is wholly Thy gift. O Saviour, since Thou, the Lord of heaven and earth, didst humble Thyself, grant unto us true humility, and make us like Thyself; and then, of Thine infinite goodness, raise us to Thine everlasting glory; Who livest and reignest with the Father and the Holy Ghost for ever and for ever. Amen.
(Archbishop Cranmer, A.D. 1489.)

O FATHER, most merciful, Who in the beginning didst create us, and by the Passion of Thine only begotten Son hast created us anew, work in us now, we beseech Thee, both to will and to do of Thy good pleasure. And forasmuch as we are weak, and can do no good thing of ourselves, grant us Thy grace and heavenly benediction, that in whatsoever work we engage we may do all to Thy honour and glory; and that, being kept from sin and daily increasing in good works, so long as we live in the body we may ever show forth some service to Thee; and after our departure may receive pardon of all our sins, and attain eternal life; through Him Who, with Thee and the Holy Ghost, liveth and reigneth for ever and ever. Amen.

(*St. Anselm*, A.D. 1033.)

O GOD, heavenly Father, Who to redeem us didst deliver up Thine only Son to be betrayed by one of His disciples and sold to His enemies, take from us, we beseech Thee, all covetousness and hypocrisy, and so help us, that loving Thee and Thy Truth above all things, we may remain steadfast in our faith even unto the end, and cleaving to Thee with all our hearts, may at last attain to the inheritance of the saints in light; through Him Who ever liveth to make intercession for us, Jesus Christ our Lord. Amen. (*Rev. L. Tuttiett*, A.D. 1825.)

B Y all the sufferings of Thine early years, Thy fasting and temptation, Thy nameless wanderings, Thy lonely vigils on the mount, by the weariness and painfulness of Thy ministry among men—good Lord, deliver us.

By Thine unknown sorrows, by the mysterious burthen of the Spiritual Cross, by Thine agony and bloody sweat—good Lord, deliver us.

O Lord Jesus Christ, Who wast lifted up from the earth that Thou mightest draw all men unto Thee, draw us also unto Thyself; for Thine own Name's sake. Amen.

(*Hon. Mrs. Lyttelton Gell, Nineteenth Century*.)

F ORGIVE us, O our Father, for we have sinned; pardon us, O our King, for we have transgressed, for Thou art ever ready to pardon and forgive. Blessed art Thou, the Eternal God, Who is gracious and doth abundantly pardon. Look upon our afflictions, we beseech Thee. Redeem us speedily, for Thou art a mighty Redeemer. Amen.

(*Rabbi of Lissa, Sixteenth Century*.)

O BLESSED Saviour, draw us; draw us by the cords of Thy love; draw us by the sense of Thy goodness; draw us by Thyself; draw us by the unspotted purity and beauty of Thy example; draw us by the merit of Thy precious death and by the power of Thy Holy Spirit; draw us, good Lord, and we shall run after Thee; for Thy Name's sake. Amen.

(Rev. Dr. Isaac Barrow, A.D. 1630.)

O LORD Jesus Christ, the Son of God, and Saviour of the world, Who didst foretell to Thine Apostles that at the time of Thy sufferings they should weep and lament, while the world rejoiced, and that they should be sorrowful, but their sorrow should be turned into joy, grant that, during this time wherein Thou didst suffer and wast afflicted for the sins of the whole world, we Thine unworthy servants may so weep and lament and be sorrowful for our sins, the cause of all Thy sorrows and sufferings, that on the day of Thy triumphant Resurrection we may rejoice with that joy which no man can take from us; grant this, O blessed Lord and Saviour, Who didst die for our sins, rise again for our justification, and now livest and reignest with the Father, in the Unity of the Holy Ghost, world without end. Amen. *(Bishop Walsham How*, A.D. 1823.)

O ALMIGHTY Saviour, Who hast taught us by Thine example to bear mocking and evil speaking, grant that we may never be ashamed of Thee and of Thy service. Grant that the fear of Thee may deliver us from all the sinful fear of man, so that we may never be turned aside from doing what is right, either by the violence of the wicked or through their false enticements. Give us grace manfully to confess Thee before men, that Thou mayst acknowledge us for Thine own when Thou shalt come to judge the world in righteousness. And to Thee, O Lord, with the Father and the Holy Ghost, be all honour and glory, world without end. Amen. *(Canon E. Hawkins*, A.D. 1802.)

O LORD Jesus Christ, Who, when about to suffer, didst institute the Holy Sacrament of Thy Body and Blood, and bid us observe it as a memorial of Thy death, and as a means of union and communion with Thyself, grant, we beseech Thee, that neither Thy great love, nor this last command, may ever fade from our forgetful hearts, but that in all things following Thee, and ever hasting unto Thy coming, we may at last be found of Thee in peace; Who livest and reignest with the Father and Holy Ghost one God for ever and ever. Amen.

(Rev. W. E. Scudamore, A.D. 1813.

O LORD Jesus Christ, our merciful and loving Saviour, Who didst bear Thy cross for us, help us to take up our cross daily and follow Thee. O Thou Who wast lifted up for us, draw us unto Thee, that we may love Thee better for Thy great love to us. Lord, we love Thee; help Thou our want of love. O heavenly Father, make us to bear in our body the marks of the Lord Jesus by a pure and holy life. O Saviour of the world, Who by Thy Cross and precious Blood hast redeemed us, save us and help us, we humbly beseech Thee, O Lord, both now and evermore. Amen. *(Dean Goulburn, A.D. 1818.)*

O THOU Prince of Peace, Who, when Thou wast reviled, reviledst not again, and on the cross didst pray for Thy murderers, implant in our hearts the virtues of gentleness and patience, that we may overcome evil with good, for Thy sake love our enemies, and as children of our heavenly Father seek Thy peace, and evermore rejoice in Thy love; through Jesus Christ our Saviour. Amen. *(Treasury of Devotion, A.D. 1869.)*

O BLESSED Jesus, our Lord and our Master, Who wast pleased to thirst for our souls, grant that we may not be satisfied with the pleasures of this lower life, but even thirst for the salvation of the souls Thou didst die to save, and, above all, to thirst for Thee; grant this for Thine own Name's sake. Amen. *(Edward King, Bishop of Lincoln, A.D. 1829.)*

O CHRIST, give us patience, and faith, and hope as we kneel at the foot of Thy Cross, and hold fast to it. Teach us by Thy Cross, that however ill the world may go, the Father so loved us that He spared not Thee. Amen. *(Rev. Charles Kingsley, A.D. 1819.)*

O LORD God, Who didst send down Thine only Son to redeem the world by His obedience unto death; grant, we humbly beseech Thee, that the continual memory of His bitter Cross and Passion may teach us so to crucify the flesh with the affections and lusts thereof that, dying unto sin and living unto Thee, we may, in the union and merits of His Cross and Passion, die with Him, and rest with Him, and rise again with Him, and live with Him for ever; to Whom with Thee and the Holy Ghost be all honour and glory, world without end. Amen. *(Bishop Hamilton, A.D. 1561.)*

L ORD Christ, Thou gavest Thyself for me; behold here I am and here I give myself to Thee. *(Rev. Jeremiah Dyke, d. A.D. 1620 ?)*

ALMIGHTY God, Who, of Thy great love to man, didst give Thy dearly beloved Son to die for us upon the cross as at this time, grant us grace ever to bear in mind His most precious sufferings and death, and to deny ourselves and to take up our cross and follow Him. May we die unto sin, and crucify the flesh with the affections and lusts thereof. Give unto us a living faith in our Redeemer and a thankful remembrance of His death. Help us to love Him better for His exceeding love to us, and grant that our sins may be put away, and nailed to the cross, and buried in His grave, that they may be remembered no more against us; through the same, Thy Son, Jesus Christ our Lord. Amen. *(Bishop Walsham How, A.D. 1823.)*

HAVE mercy upon us, O Lord; for though we are weak and evil, we are still Thy creatures. O Lord our God, we have put our trust in Thee. Be Thou our Saviour, and loosen, remit, and forgive all our sins, and turn, preserve, and deliver our soul; save us for Thy mercy's sake. Where sin hath abounded, there let grace much more abound; for Thou art the God of the penitent, and the Saviour of the sinner. Amen.
(Father John of the Russian Church, Nineteenth Century.)

O MOST loving Saviour, Who hast loved us and washed us from our sins in Thine own blood, we love Thee for all Thou hast done for us, and we desire to love Thee more and more with all the powers of our heart and soul. Help our weakness, and pour Thy grace into our hearts, that we may henceforth love Thee above all things, and seek to do Thy will; for Thine own Name's sake. Amen. *(The Narrow Way, A.D. 1869.)*

WE implore Thee, by the memory of Thy Cross's hallowed and most bitter anguish, make us fear Thee, make us love Thee, O Christ. Amen. *(St. Bridget, A.D. 453.)*

O LORD, Who dost wash out our offences, do Thou comfort us who faithfully call upon Thee; and, we beseech Thee, that Thou wouldest blot out our transgressions, and restore us from death to the land of the living; through Christ our Lord. Amen.
(Sarum Breviary.)

NOW the God of hope fill us with all joy and peace in believing that we may abound in hope, through the power of the Holy Ghost; through Jesus Christ our Lord. Amen.
(St. Paul, First Century A.D.; Rom. xv. 13.)

CHRIST is risen from the dead, and become the firstfruits of them that slept. For as in Adam all die, even so in Christ shall all be made alive. Glory be to Thee, O God most high. Amen.

(St. Paul, First Century, A.D.)

BLESSED be the God and Father of our Lord Jesus Christ, which, according to His abundant mercy, hath begotten us again unto a lively hope, by the resurrection of Jesus Christ from the dead, to an inheritance incorruptible and undefiled, and that fadeth not away, reserved in heaven for us. Keep us this day, O God, by Thy power unto salvation; through Jesus Christ our Lord and Saviour, Who with the Father and the Holy Ghost, even one God, liveth and reigneth, world without end. Amen. *(St Peter, First Century A.D. 1 Peter i. 3–5, adapted.)*

O MERCIFUL God, the Father of our Lord Jesus Christ, Who is the Resurrection and the Life; in Whom whosoever believeth shall live, though he die; and whosoever liveth and believeth in Him shall not die eternally. We bless Thy Holy Name for all Thy servants departed this life in Thy faith and fear; beseeching Thee to give us grace so to follow their good examples that with them we may be partakers of Thy heavenly Kingdom. Grant this, O Father, for Jesus Christ's sake, our only Advocate and Redeemer. Amen.

(Sarum Missal; B. of C. P., A.D. 1552–1662.)

WE adore Thee, O Christ, Son of the living God, Who didst rise in great triumph from the grave, and didst bear in Thy pierced Hands the keys of hell and death. We rejoice, O Lord our God, in Thy almighty power and glory. Raise Thou us up with Thee, O blessed Saviour, above all earthly desires. Inspire us with thoughts of joy, of hope, and love. Enter Thou within the chamber of our hearts and say unto us, "Peace be unto you." Give us the grace to see Thee, Blessed Saviour, the eyes of our understanding being enlightened, that we may know Thee walking by our side, in this our earthly pilgrimage. Come unto us, O our Lord, and dwell within us. Abide with us through our night of weeping. Make Thyself known to us in the Breaking of Bread. Teach us, O blessed Lord God most High, to look and see Thee beyond this dark, tempestuous sea, standing on the everlasting shore of peace; and suffer us to come unto Thee through the waters. Give us grace, O Lord our God, to arise with Thee, to leave all for Thee, that we may be made like unto Thee, that we may follow Thee, O Thou Blessed Lamb of God whithersoever Thou goest. Amen.

(Treasury of Devotion, A.D. 1872.)

O GRACIOUS Lord, Who as at this time didst raise Thy Son Jesus Christ with power from the grave, raise us up, we beseech Thee, from the death of sin to the life of righteousness. Revive our faith, and make us followers of Him Who hath taken away the "sin of the world; Who by His death hath destroyed death, and by His rising to life again hath restored to us everlasting life." Hear us, O merciful Father, we pray Thee, for the sake of our risen Saviour, to Whom, with Thee and the Holy Ghost, be all honour and glory, world without end. Amen.

(Bishop William Boyd Carpenter, A.D. 1841.)

O MERCIFUL God, the Father of our Lord Jesus Christ, Who is the Resurrection and the Life, we meekly beseech Thee to raise us from the death of sin unto the life of righteousness, that we may be found acceptable in Thy sight; through Jesus Christ our Lord. Amen.

("The Cloud of Witness," Hon. Mrs. Lyttelton Gell, Nineteenth Century.)

O ALMIGHTY God, Whose only begotten Son, as at this time, did burst the bonds of death, because it was not possible that He should be holden of it, raise us, we pray Thee, from the death of sin unto the life of righteousness, that, at the last day, when He shall come again in glory, we may be quickened in our mortal bodies, through the same Spirit that quickened Him, Who was the first-born from the dead, and is now alive for evermore; in Whose Name we beseech Thee to hear us, O merciful and gracious Lord. Amen. *(Rev. W. E. Scudamore,* A.D. 1813.)

O LORD Jesus Christ, our Redemption and our Salvation, we praise Thee and give Thee thanks; and though we be unworthy of Thy benefits, and cannot offer unto Thee due devotion, yet let Thy loving-kindness fill up that which our weakness endeavoureth. Before Thee, O Lord, is all our desire, and whatsoever our heart rightly willeth, it is of Thy gift. Grant that we may attain to love Thee even as Thou commandest. Let not Thy gift be unfruitful in us. Perfect that Thou hast begun, give that which Thou hast made us to long after, convert Thou our lukewarmness into fervent love of Thee; for the glory of Thy holy Name. Amen. *(St. Anselm,* A.D. 1033.)

NOW unto the King eternal, immortal, invisible, the only wise God, be honour and glory for ever and ever. Amen.

(1 Tim. i. 17; *St. Paul, First Century* A.D.)

O GOD, Who for our redemption didst give Thine only begotten Son to the death of the Cross, and by His glorious Resurrection hast delivered us from the power of the enemy, grant us to die daily to sin, that we may evermore live with Him, in the joy of His Resurrection; through the same Jesus Christ our Lord. Amen.

(*St. Gregory*, A.D. 590; *American Prayer Book*, A.D. 1789.)

GRACIOUS Lord, we remember that Thou didst accompany Thy two disciples as they journeyed to Emmaus. We, too, have a journey, we have a weary pilgrimage to perform. Our Emmaus is a distant though happy land. Do Thou go with us, O Lord: be our Fellow-traveller; guide us, uphold us, strengthen us, make our hearts to burn within us, and evermore manifest Thou Thyself to our souls in gracious and in heavenly power; for Thy own Name's sake we ask it. Amen.

(*Archdeacon of Raphoe, Nineteenth Century.*)

O LORD, Who by triumphing over the power of darkness, didst prepare our place in the New Jerusalem, grant us, who have this day given thanks for Thy Resurrection, to praise Thee in that City whereof Thou art the Light, where with the Father and the Holy Spirit Thou livest and reignest, world without end. Amen. (*Dr. William Bright*, A.D. 1824.)

O ETERNAL God, the very God of peace and all consolation, which broughtest again from the dead our Lord Jesus, the great Shepherd of the sheep, through the everlasting covenant, make us fruitful in all good works to do Thy will, and work in us that which is acceptable in Thy sight; sanctify us throughout, and keep our whole spirit, soul and body faultless unto the coming of Thy dear Son, our Lord Jesus Christ. Thou art faithful, O Father, Who hast promised this, Who also shalt bring it to pass; to Thee, therefore, be given everlasting praise, honour and glory. Amen. (*The Writer of the Epistle to the Hebrews, First Century* A.D. ; *Heb.* xiii. 20.)

O HEAVENLY Father, Whose blessed Son has "risen from the dead, and become the firstfruits of them that slept," grant that we may so live and die in Him, that when He shall appear again in His glory we may rise to everlasting life. We pray also for all our brethren in Christ, especially for our relations and friends and neighbours, that we may all share in a joyful resurrection and be partakers of Thy heavenly Kingdom; through Jesus Christ our Lord. Amen.

(*Bishop Walsham How*, A.D. 1823.)

OTHER SEASONS OF THE CHRISTIAN YEAR

ROGATION DAYS

WE beseech Thee, O Lord, that it may please Thee to give and preserve to our use the kindly fruits of the earth, so as in due time we may enjoy them.

(Litany, Archbishop Cranmer, A.D. 1489.)

O ALMIGHTY and everlasting God, Ruler of the Universe, Who hast commanded us to till the land with our labour for the support of mankind and the sustenance of the body, we humbly beseech Thee that Thou wouldst graciously look upon whatsoever good seed is sown or planted in the fields; give us temperate weather, make the crops plentiful, and grant that they may arrive at full perfection, that we Thy servants, thankfully receiving the abundant fruit of Thy gift, may pay due and acceptable praise to Thy Name; through Jesus Christ our Lord. Amen. *(Rev. H. Stobart, Nineteenth Century.)*

REMEMBER, O Lord, to crown the year with Thy goodness (Ps. lxv. 11). For the eyes of all wait upon Thee, and Thou givest them their meat in due season (Ps. cxlv. 15). Thou openest Thine hand and fillest all things living with plenteousness. Vouchsafe unto us, O Lord, the precious things from Heaven, the dew from above, the blessing of the fountains of the deep from beneath, the courses of the sun, the circuit of the moon, the heights of the mountains of the East, of the ancient hills, the blessing of the earth and the fulness thereof. Thou Who art the Maker and Sustainer of all things, hear us, we humbly beseech Thee, O Lord. Amen. *(Bishop Andrewes, A.D. 1555.)*

ALMIGHTY God, Who hast promised in Thy mercy that seed-time and harvest, cold and heat, summer and winter, day and night, shall not cease, and hath blessed the earth that it should be fruitful and bring forth everything that is necessary for the life of man, bless all farmers in all their labours, and grant such seasonable weather that they may gather the fruits of the earth and ever rejoice in Thy goodness, to the praise of Thy holy Name; through Jesus Christ our Lord. Amen.

(Original source not found.)

HAVE mercy, O Lord, upon all those who labour in the cultivation of the earth, and grant that by the power of Thy grace their own souls may be made fruitful unto all good works; through Jesus Christ our Lord. Amen.

(The Rev. R. M. Benson, A.D. 1824.)

O LORD Jesus Christ, Who after Thy Resurrection from the dead didst gloriously ascend into heaven, grant us the aid of Thy loving-kindness, that, according to Thy promise, Thou mayest ever dwell with us on earth, and we with Thee in heaven, where with the Father and the Holy Ghost, Thou livest and reignest one God for ever and ever. Amen.

(Gelasian Sacramentary.)

O GOD, Whose most dearly beloved Son was, by Thy mighty power, exalted into the heavens, that He might prepare a place in Thy Kingdom of glory for them that truly love Thee, so lead and uphold us, O merciful Lord, that we may both follow the most holy steps of His life here on earth, and may enter with Him hereafter into Thy everlasting rest; that where He is, we may be also; through the merits of the same Jesus Christ our Lord. Amen. *(Rev. W. E. Scudamore, A.D. 1813.)*

O GOD, Who hast inspired Thy Church to celebrate this day the memory of our Saviour's Ascension, when, having finished on earth the great work of our redemption, He carried up His glorified humanity above the clouds to its eternal rest, grant, we humbly beseech Thee, that, taking off our eyes from the vanities here below, we may stand continually looking after Him into heaven; and, heartily expecting His appearance thence again at the last day, may be always ready to obey His call, and meet Him in the clouds, and follow Him into those blissful mansions which He went to prepare for us at Thy right hand for evermore; through the same, our Lord Jesus Christ, Who with Thee and the Holy Ghost liveth and reigneth ever one God, world without end. Amen. *(Bishop George Hickes, A.D. 1642.)*

O BLESSED Jesus, Who art ascended up on high, and hast overcome death and hell, and entered victorious into heaven, raise our hearts, we beseech Thee, above all that is sinful, above all worldly cares and sorrows, and fears and joys, and remember us who remain in this vale of tears, and give us Thy blessing, the blessing of faith and of patience, the blessing of a sincere and humble heart, the blessing of purity and charity, and the blessing of peace; for Thy merit's sake, Who with the Father and the Holy Ghost, art one God, world without end. Amen.

(Rev. H. Stobart, Nineteenth Century.)

O LORD Jesus Christ, Who hast left us for a while giving us the promise that Thou wilt come again and receive us to be with Thee for ever; Grant us such communion with Thyself, that our souls may thirst for that time, when we shall behold Thee in Thy glory; Who livest and reignest with the Father and the Holy Spirit world without end. Amen.

(Liturgy of the Catholic Apostolic Church, A.D. 1861.)

WHIT SUNDAY

O GOD, Who as at this time didst send down Thy Holy Spirit from above upon Thine Apostles, and dost evermore send Him to renew Thine image in our souls, mercifully grant that by the effectual working of His grace we may be preserved from all sin, and may glorify Thee both in our bodies and in our spirits, which are Thine; through the merits and mediation of Thy Son, our Saviour Jesus Christ, Who liveth and reigneth with Thee in the unity of the same Spirit, one God, world without end. Amen. *(Rev. W. E. Scudamore, A.D. 1813.)*

O GOD, Who purifiest the heart of man from sin, and makest it more white than snow, pour down upon us the abundance of Thy mercy; renew, we beseech Thee, Thy Holy Spirit within us, that we may show forth Thy praise, and, strengthened by Thy grace, may obtain rest in the eternal mansions of the heavenly Jerusalem; through our Lord Jesus Christ. Amen.
(Sarum Breviary.)

BREATHE into our souls, O heavenly Father, the love of whatsoever is true and beautiful and good. May we fear to be unfaithful and have no other fear. Help us to remember that we are Thy children, and belong to Thee. In Thy service may we live and in Thy favour may we die; through Jesus Christ our Lord. Amen. *(Professor Knight, Nineteenth Century.)*

O GOD, Who wast pleased to send on Thy disciples the Holy Spirit in the burning fire of Thy love, grant to Thy people to be fervent in the unity of faith, that, abiding in Thee evermore, they may be found both steadfast in faith and active in work; through Jesus Christ our Lord. Amen.
(Gelasian Sacramentary.)

O HOLY Spirit of God, very God, Who didst descend upon Christ at the River Jordan, and upon the Apostles in the upper chamber, we have sinned against heaven and before Thee; purify us again, we beseech Thee, with Thy Divine fire, and have mercy upon us; for Christ's sake. Amen.
(St. Nerses of Clajes, Fourth Century.)

L ORD Jesus, all power is given to Thee in heaven and earth. Transform our understandings and our wills; cleanse our hearts; send Thy Holy Spirit into our souls; subdue us unto Thyself, so that our flesh may be brought into subjection to the Spirit, and our affections made obedient to Thy pure and holy law, to the praise and glory of Thy sovereign grace. Amen.
(Ludovicus Vives, A.D. 1492.)

O THOU true Light, that lightest every man that cometh into the world, do Thou in Thy mercy touch the hearts and lighten the understanding of all who are preparing for Thy ministry, that they may readily acknowledge and cheerfully obey all that Thou wouldst have them believe and practise, to the benefit of Thy people and their own salvation; Who livest and reignest God for ever and ever. Amen.

(Cuddesdon Manual, Nineteenth Century.)

O GOD, the Pastor and Ruler of Thy faithful people, look down in mercy, we beseech Thee, upon Thy servants, the Bishops and Pastors of Thy Church in this land. Uphold and guide them in their labours; defend, comfort, and sanctify them; and grant them so to go before Thy people in word and good example that, with the flocks committed to their charge, they may attain to everlasting life. Vouchsafe also, O Lord, we beseech Thee, the help of Thy grace to all Thy ministering servants who are in all the world, and give them strength to perform their work. Stir up the hearts of more of Thy people to desire a share in this office and work, and remove whatever deters them from seeking it, that the ranks of the ministry, being filled with holy, prudent, and zealous labourers, Thy glory may be promoted in the saving of the lost and the building up of the faithful, and Thy Kingdom hastened in the joyous submission of all wills to Thine; through Jesus Christ our Lord. Amen.

(Dean Goulburn, A.D. 1818.)

O MOST merciful God, incline Thy loving ears to our prayers, and illuminate the hearts of those called by Thee, with the grace of the Holy Spirit, that they may be enabled worthily to minister to Thy mysteries, and to love Thee with an everlasting love, and to attain everlasting joys; through Jesus Christ our Lord. Amen. *(Emperor Charlemagne, A.D. 742. Gallican Collect).*

O HOLY Lord God, carry onward in us the gifts of Thy grace, and mercifully bestow by Thy Spirit what human frailty cannot attain—through Jesus Christ our Lord. Amen.

(Leonine Sacramentary.)

WE pray always for you, that our God may count you worthy of your calling, and fulfil every desire of goodness, and every work of faith and power; that the name of our Lord Jesus may be glorified in you, and you in Him, according to the grace of our God and the Lord Jesus Christ. Amen.

(S. Paul; First Century A.D.; 2 Thess. i. 11-12.)

O MOST Holy, Almighty, Eternal, Divine Spirit, Who art of one Authority and Dominion with the Father and the Son, set up Thy Throne in our hearts, dwell within us, gather us into Thine obedience, reign over us. Thou Who art Lord and Giver of Life, grant us life, a long life, even life for evermore. Thou Who art a loving Spirit, ever willing to give Thyself to whosoever will receive Thee, give Thyself to us, give Thyself to us more and more, and never withdraw Thyself from us. Thou Who art Purity, purify us; Thou Who art Light, enlighten us; Thou Who art Fulness and Refreshment, make us Thine, keep us Thine, fill us, refresh us. Thou Who lovest us, grant us grace to love Thee. O Lord God Almighty, most Holy Trinity, Jesus Christ, Who is our sole plea for any gift, for any grace, for His sake grant this prayer. Amen.

(Christina G. Rossetti, A.D. 1830.)

K EEP us, O Lord, from the vain strife of words, and grant to us a constant profession of the truth. Preserve us in the Faith, true and undefiled; so that we may ever hold fast that which we professed when we were baptized into the Name of the Father, and of the Son, and of the Holy Ghost; that we may have Thee for our Father, that we abide in Thy Son, and in the fellowship of the Holy Ghost; through the same Jesus Christ our Lord. Amen. *(S. Hilary, Bishop of Poitiers,* A.D. 300.)

M AY the infinite and glorious Trinity, the Father, the Son, and the Holy Ghost, direct our life in good works, and after our passage through this world, grant to us eternal rest with the righteous. Grant this, O Eternal and Almighty God. Amen.

(Mozarabic Liturgy.)

M OST blessed and glorious Trinity, Three Persons in one God, teach us to worship and adore that absolute Trinity, that perfect Unity. And that we may adore Thee, that our worship may not be a mockery, make us to know that we are one in Christ, as the Father is one with the Son, and the Son with the Father. Suffer us not to look upon our sectarianism as if it were a destiny. Help us to regard it as a rebellion against Thee. Help us to see all distinctions more clearly in the light of Thy everlasting love. Help us to recognize the truth of every effort to express something of that which passes knowledge. Help us to feel and confess the feebleness of our own efforts. So may Thy holy Name embrace us more and more. So may all creatures in heaven and earth and under the earth at last glorify Thee throughout all ages. Amen.

(Rev. Frederick D. Maurice, A.D. 1805.)

O LORD, the Healer of all our diseases, Who knowest how the sick have need of a physician; bless all Whom Thou hast called to be sharers in Thine own work of healing with health alike of body and soul, that they may learn their art in dependence upon Thee, and exercise it always under Thy sanction, and to Thy honour and glory, Who livest and reignest with the Father and the Holy Spirit, ever one God, world without end.   Amen.

(*Sursum Corda*, A.D. 1898.)

O LORD Jesus Christ, Who art the Eternal Wisdom of the Father, we beseech Thee to assist us with Thy heavenly grace, that we may be blessed in our work this day, and above all things may attain the knowledge of Thee, Whom to know is life eternal; and that, according to Thy most holy example, we may ever be found going about amongst our fellow-men, doing good, healing the sick, and preaching the Gospel of the Kingdom of Heaven; through Jesus Christ our Lord.   Amen.

(*Family Prayers of the Church of Ireland*, A.D. 1895.)

A LMIGHTY and everlasting God, Who didst send Thine only Son Jesus Christ to be the Saviour and Healer of men, we pray Thee to bless the work of all Hospitals and Medical Missions.   Help all those who minister both in this and other places to have ever present to their minds the example of our Lord and of His tenderness and sympathy for all human suffering. Give us all grace and patience faithfully to fulfil our holy calling —doing all as unto Thee; and do Thou, O Lord, we pray Thee, crown all work with success and happiness.   We commend, O God, all patients to Thy loving care, soothe their pain, relieve their anxiety, help them to cast all their care upon Thee, and to know that around them are the Everlasting Arms.   Give them patience under their sufferings and a happy ending to all their trouble.   Grant this, we humbly beseech Thee, for the love of Thy Son Jesus Christ our Lord.   Amen.

(*Adapted from a Prayer in use at the London Hospital, Nineteenth Century.*)

O LORD Jesus Christ, we would give ourselves up to Thee to be led by Thee in all things.   Give us greater energy and zeal in the performance of our temporal duties.   Enable us to please and help those amongst whom we work and minister, and yet please and honour Thee; for Thy own Name's sake.   Amen.

(*Captain Hedley Vicars*, A.D. 1826.)

NOTE.—See also p. 215, "The Medical and Nursing Professions" and p. 243, "Medical Missions."

ALMIGHTY and everlasting God, Who dost enkindle the flame of Thy love in the hearts of the Saints, grant to our minds the same faith and power of love; that as we rejoice in their triumphs, we may profit by their examples; through Jesus Christ our Lord.   Amen.   (*Gothic Missal*, A.D. 1680.)

OUR Father, unto Thee, in the light of our Saviour's blessed life, we would lift our souls.   We thank Thee for that true Light shining in our world with still increasing brightness.   We thank Thee for all who have walked therein, and especially for those near to us and dear, in whose lives we have seen this excellent glory and beauty.   May we know that in the body and out of the body they are with Thee, and that when these earthly days come to an end, it is not that our service of Thee and of one another may cease, but that it may begin anew. Make us glad in all who have faithfully lived; make us glad in all who have peacefully died.   Lift us into light and love, and purity, and blessedness, and give us at last our portion with those who have trusted in Thee and sought, in small things as in great, in things temporal and things eternal, to do Thy holy Will. Amen.   (*Rev. Rufus Ellis*, A.D. 1819.)

ALMIGHTY and everlasting God, Who adornest the sacred body of Thy Church by the confessions of holy Martyrs; grant us, we pray Thee, that both by their doctrines and their pious example, we may follow after what is pleasing in Thy sight; through Jesus Christ our Lord.   Amen.
                              (*Leonine Sacramentary.*)

O THOU Lord of all worlds, we bless Thy Name for all those who have entered into their rest, and reached the Promised Land, where Thou art seen face to face.   Give us grace to follow in their footsteps, as they followed in the footsteps of Thy Holy Son.   Encourage our wavering hearts by their example, and help us to see in them the memorials of Thy redeeming grace, and pledges of the heavenly might in which the weak are made strong.   Keep alive in us the memory of those dear to ourselves, whom Thou hast called out of this world, and make it powerful to subdue within us every vile and unworthy thought.   Grant that every remembrance which turns our hearts from things seen to things unseen, may lead us always upwards to Thee, till we too come to the eternal rest which Thou hast prepared for Thy people; through Jesus Christ our Lord.   Amen.
                    (*Rev. F. J. A. Hort, D.D.*, A.D. 1828.)

WE beseech Thee to hear us, O God, for all who profess and call themselves Christians, that they may be led to the right understanding and practice of their holy faith; for all who preach the Gospel of Jesus Christ; for all missionaries, evangelists, and teachers, and for all who are seeking and striving in other ways to bless their fellows, and to build up the Kingdom of God, in the world, that they may be steadfast and faithful, and that their labour may not be in vain; through Jesus Christ Thy Son our Lord. Amen. *(Rev. Dr. J. Hunter, 1849.)*

BE merciful, O Lord, to all our brethren and sisters that suffer any kind of persecution or affliction, whether in mind or body, especially such as suffer for Thy Name, and Gospel; give them patience, constancy, and steadfast hope, till Thou send them full and good deliverance of all their troubles; through Jesus Christ our Lord. Amen. *(Christian Prayers, A.D. 1566.)*

O BLESSED Lord and God, Who hast never left Thyself without witnesses of Thy goodness and power, we beseech Thee now and evermore to choose the vessels of Thy grace to bear Thy Name before nations and kings, and the children of Israel; sanctify them, we pray Thee, with the Holy Ghost; teach them to endure hardness; give them perfect mastery over the flesh, a sanctified spirit, and a ready desire to do Thy Will; gird them with Thy Truth; make their hearts burn with Thy Word; and arm them with faith as a shield; that watching for Thee, and labouring for Thee till Thou return again, they may enter with the crown of their rejoicing into the joy of their Lord; to Whom with the Father and the Holy Ghost, be all honour and glory, world without end. Amen.
(Church Missionary Society, A.D. 1799.)

O LORD Jesus Christ, Who art the Way, the Truth, and the Life, have mercy upon those who are wandering in darkness and error; bring them to the knowledge of Thy truth, unite them to Thee by the Sacraments of Thy Love, that partaking of the blessedness of Thy grace in this life, they may dwell with Thee in the life everlasting; for Thy Name's sake. Amen.
(Rev. Dr. J. Oldknow, A.D. 1809.)

O THOU Who didst command Thy Apostles to go into all the world, and to preach the Gospel to every creature; let Thy Name be great among the Gentiles from the rising up of the sun unto the going down of the same. Amen.
(Bishop Andrewes, A.D. 1555.)

MEDICAL MISSIONS

O THOU Who didst send forth Thine only begotten Son to heal all manner of sickness and all manner of disease, both of body and soul, and hast received Him again unto Thine own right hand, where He ever liveth to make intercession for us, we beseech Thee ever to regard with Thy mercy those who are gathered together in our Mission Hospitals to seek the blessing of renewed health at Thy hand. Grant unto them all, O Lord, forgiveness of all their sins, and heal and deliver them from all infirmity of body or soul; through Jesus Christ our Lord, Who livest and reignest in the unity of the Holy Spirit, one God, world without end. Amen. *(Rev. H. Stobart, Nineteenth Century.)*

O LORD Jesus Christ, to Whom all the sick were brought that they might be healed, and Who didst send none of them away without Thy blessing; look in pity upon all who come to Thee for healing of heart and soul; send them not away without Thy blessing, but now and evermore grant them Thy healing grace. Amen. *(Rev. G. H. Sharpe, Nineteenth Century.)*

O ALMIGHTY and merciful Saviour, the Great Physician of our souls and bodies, send down, we humbly beseech Thee, Thy blessing on all the Hospitals and Dispensaries of our missions. Prosper the work of those who labour therein, and grant that whatsoever they do, they may do it as unto Thee. Give relief and comfort to those who lie on beds of sickness and of death, and incline their hearts to receive the message of salvation. Heal all the diseases of their souls, and bring them to life everlasting, through Thy merits and mediation, Who art the Resurrection and the Life. Amen. *(S.P.G., A.D. 1701.)*

O LORD Jesus Christ, Who dost rule Thy creatures in love, bow down Thine ear to our prayers, and look with Thy favour upon all those who are sick and dying. Comfort them with the light of Thy Presence, strengthen them with Thy power, and grant them healing by Thy mercy, for Thy honour and glory. Amen. *(William Maskell, A.D. 1814.)*

MEDICAL STUDENTS.

O MERCIFUL Father, Who hast wonderfully fashioned man in Thine image, and hast made his body to be a temple of the Holy Ghost, sanctify, we pray Thee, all those whom Thou hast called to study and practise the arts of healing the sick, and the prevention of disease and pain. Strengthen them in body and soul, and bless their work, that they may themselves live as members and servants of Christ, and give comfort to those whom He lived and died to save; through Him Who now liveth with Thee in the unity of the Holy Ghost, one God, world without end. Amen. *(Source not found.)*

NOTE.—See also p. 240, "St Luke's Day," and p. 215, "Medical and Nursing Professions."

NATIONAL PRAYERS

THE KING AND QUEEN, AND ALL THE ROYAL FAMILY

O LORD our heavenly Father, high and mighty, King of kings and Lord of lords, the only Ruler of princes, Who dost from Thy throne behold all the dwellers upon earth: most heartily we beseech Thee with Thy favour to behold our most gracious Sovereign Lord, King George; and so replenish him with the grace of Thy Holy Spirit, that he may alway incline to Thy will, and walk in Thy way: Endue him plenteously with heavenly gifts; grant him in health and wealth long to live; strengthen him that he may vanquish and overcome all his enemies; and finally, after this life, he may attain everlasting joy and felicity; through Jesus Christ our Lord. Amen.

(Book of Common Prayer, A.D. 1559.)

A LMIGHTY God, Who rulest over all the kingdoms of the world, and dost order them according to Thy good pleasure; we yield Thee unfeigned thanks, for that Thou wast pleased to set Thy Servant our Sovereign Lord, King George, upon the throne of this Realm. Let Thy wisdom be his guide, and let Thine arm strengthen him; let truth and justice, holiness and righteousness, peace and charity, abound in his days. Direct all his counsels and endeavours to Thy glory, and the welfare of his subjects; give us grace to obey him cheerfully for conscience' sake, and let him always possess the hearts of his people; let his reign be long and prosperous, and crown him with everlasting life in the world to come; through Jesus Christ our Lord. Amen. *(Book of Common Prayer, A.D. 1704, Accession Service.)*

A LMIGHTY God, the Fountain of all goodness, we humbly beseech Thee to bless our gracious Queen Elizabeth, Mary the Queen Mother, Princess Elizabeth, and all the Royal Family: Endue them with Thy Holy Spirit; enrich them with Thy heavenly grace; prosper them with all happiness; and bring them to Thine everlasting kingdom; through Jesus Christ our Lord. Amen. *(Archbishop Whitgift, A.D. 1530; Book of Common Prayer, A.D. 1604.)*

O GOD, Who providest for Thy people by Thy power, and rulest over them in love; Vouchsafe so to bless Thy servant our King, that under him this nation may be wisely governed, and Thy Church may serve Thee in all godly quietness; and grant that he being devoted to Thee with his whole heart, and persevering in good works unto the end, may, by Thy guidance, come to Thine everlasting kingdom; through Jesus Christ Thy Son our Lord, Who liveth and reigneth with Thee and the Holy Ghost, ever one God, world without end. Amen.

(Accession Service, Book of Common Prayer.)

O LORD, Who by Thy holy Apostles hast commanded us to make prayers and intercessions for all men, we implore Thy blessing more especially upon this our country, upon its Government and upon its people. May Thy Holy Spirit be with our rulers, with the King, and all who are in authority under him. Grant that they may govern in Thy faith and fear, striving to put down all evil, and to encourage and support all that is good. Give Thy Spirit of wisdom to those whose business it is to make laws for us. Grant that they may understand and feel, how great a work Thou hast given them to do, that they may not do it lightly or foolishly, or from any evil passion, or in ignorance; but gravely, soberly, and with a godly spirit, enacting always things just, and things wise, and things merciful, to the putting away of all wrong and oppression, and to the advancement of the true welfare of Thy people. Give peace in our time, O Lord. Preserve both us and our Government from the evil spirit of ambition and pride, and teach us to value and to labour with all sincerity, to preserve peace at home and peace with all nations, showing forth a spirit of meekness, as becomes those who call themselves Christ's servants. Save us from all those national sins which expose us most justly to Thy heavy judgments. From unbelief and profaneness, from injustice and oppression, from a careless and worldly spirit, working and enjoying, with no thought of Thee; from these, and all other sins, be pleased to preserve us, and give us each one for himself a holy watchfulness, that we may not by our sins add to the guilt and punishment of our country, but may strive to keep ourselves pure and holy, and to bring down Thy blessing upon ourselves, and all who belong to us. These things and all else which may be good for our temporal, and for our spiritual welfare, we humbly beseech Thee to grant, in the name and for the sake of Thy dear Son, Jesus Christ our Lord. Amen.

(Dr. Thomas Arnold, A.D. 1795.)

O LORD God of hosts, Who didst give grace to Thy servant, St. George, to lay aside the fear of man and to confess Thee even unto death; grant that all our countrymen who bear office in the world, may think lightly of earthly place and honour, and seek rather to please Thee, the Captain of our salvation, Who hath chosen them to be His soldiers; to Whom with Thee and the Holy Ghost be thanks and praise from all the armies of the saints, now and for evermore. Amen.

(Bishop John Wordsworth, A.D. 1844.)

BE gracious, O Lord, to the peoples that trust in Thee. And stretch forth the right hand of Thy protection to guard the British Dominions, that our realm, being always devoted to Thy glory, may ever be defended by Thy power, through Jesus Christ our Lord. Amen. *(Ancient Collect, adapted.)*

THE KING AND THE GOVERNMENT

THOU Wonderful, Counsellor, King of kings and Lord of lords, send Thy blessing on our Royal Sovereign in his care. Strong in counsel, patient in action, pure in motive, striving for the welfare of his people, may his great kingdom ever be Thy kingdom, Thy law his law, Thy glory his renown. And for us who are his subjects grant us so to walk worthy of his royal command that our humble service may never be his shame; through Jesus Christ our Lord. Amen.

(J. E. W., A.D. 1914.)

MOST gracious God, we humbly beseech Thee, as for this kingdom in general, so especially for the High Court of Parliament, under our most religious and gracious King at this time assembled: That Thou wouldest be pleased to direct and prosper all their consultations to the advancement of Thy glory, the good of Thy Church, the safety, honour, and welfare of our Sovereign and his Dominions; that all things may be so ordered and settled by their endeavours, upon the best and surest foundations, that peace and happiness, truth and justice, religion and piety, may be established among us for all generations. These and all other necessaries, for them, for us, and Thy whole Church, we humbly beg in the name and mediation of Jesus Christ, our most blessed Lord and Saviour. Amen.

(Archbishop Laud, A.D. 1573; *Book of Common Prayer,* A.D. 1662.)

GRANT and continue unto us legislators and rulers who have themselves been taught the wisdom of the Kingdom of Christ. Endow all Members of Parliament with a right understanding, a pure purpose, and sound speech; enable them to rise above all self-seeking and party zeal into the larger sentiments of public good and human brotherhood. Cleanse our political life of every evil; subdue in the nation all that is evil. Inspire us with calmness and self-restraint, and the endeavour to do Thy will on earth as it is done in heaven; through Jesus Christ our Lord. Amen.   *(Rev. Dr. John Hunter,* A.D. 1849.)

O GOD most High, Who alone rulest in the kingdom of men, grant, we beseech Thee, to all Members of Parliament the inspiration of Thy Holy Spirit, that they may labour faithfully for the advancement of Thy kingdom upon earth; through Jesus Christ our Lord. Amen.   *(Original source not found.)*

O LORD God Almighty, guide, we pray Thee, our Sovereign and all those to whom thou hast committed the government of our nation and empire; and grant to them at this time special gifts of wisdom and understanding, of counsel and strength; that upholding what is right, and following what is true, they may obey Thy holy will, and fulfil Thy Divine purpose; through Jesus Christ our Lord. Amen.

(Archbishop Davidson, A.D. 1848.)

O GOD, Who hast made us members of the British Empire, and hast bound us together by one King and one Flag, may we ever live in remembrance of our great responsibilities, and be mindful that "righteousness exalteth a nation." Help us to seek to excel in the practice of faith, courage, duty, self-discipline, fair dealing, even justice, and true sympathy, that, as loyal patriots and good citizens, we may each individually aid in elevating the British character, and as a God-fearing and a God-loving people glorify Thee, the King of kings and Lord of lords; through Jesus Christ Thy Son. Amen.

(The Earl of Meath, the Empire Movement, A.D. 1905.)

O LORD our God, Who hast ever been a gracious Helper and Friend to our country, our Refuge and Strength from one generation to another, we beseech Thee of Thy mercy to bless our Sovereign Lord, King George, with Thy heavenly grace, that in all his many and great anxieties for the peace and welfare of his Realm, he may find rest and strength in Thee, and be alway consoled by the loyalty and love of his people. We pray that it may please Thee to spare him to us for many years yet to come, and to make us worthy of so great a privilege by faithful allegiance to his person and his throne, by following him in the steps of his and our Divine Master, even Jesus Christ our Lord. Amen.   *(Archbishop Laud, A.D. 1573, adapted.)*

FATHER, we would remember before Thee all those who in this great world have need of Thee. All nations and peoples whom Thou hast made and whom Thou dost desire to serve Thee. We would have them to know Thee as we know Thee, by the revelation of Thy Son. Grant Thy blessing upon all missionary efforts for the extension of Thy Kingdom. We pray especially for our own country and Empire, that its rulers may be faithful to the Christian ideal, that the Truth may be more and more firmly established among us, and that all that is false or base may be destroyed from the hearts of the people. May the Empire be great in righteousness, wisdom, and peace; may its strength be used honourably for the good of mankind, in succouring the oppressed, and defending the right. We commend to Thee these our desires, through Him Who taught us to pray, Thy Son, our Lord and Saviour Jesus Christ. Amen.

(Rev. C. J. N. Child, Twentieth Century.)

O GOD, save all England, and bless it with Thy holy hand. Amen.   *(Lawrence Minot, A.D. 1300.)*

KEEP us securely in Thy way of righteousness and truth, O God. Amen.   *(Anon.)*

O CHRIST, Ruler and Lord of the world, to Thee we consecrate this land, its sceptre and its power. Guard Thy land, guard it from every foe. Amen. *(Emperor Constantine the Great, A.D. 288?)*

NOTE.—See also p. 251, "Civil Service."

O ETERNAL Lord God, Who alone spreadest out the heavens and rulest the raging of the sea; Who hast compassed the waters with bounds until day and night come to an end; be pleased to receive into Thy Almighty and most gracious protection the persons of Thy servants and the Fleet in which they serve. Preserve them from the dangers of the sea, and from the violence of the enemy, that they may be a safeguard unto our most gracious Sovereign Lord, King George and his Dominions, and a security for such as pass on the seas upon their lawful occasions; that the inhabitants of our Island may in peace and quiet serve Thee our God; and that they may return in safety to enjoy the blessings of the land, with the fruits of their labours, and with a thankful remembrance of Thy mercies to praise and glorify Thy holy Name; through Jesus Christ our Lord. Amen.

(Bishop Sanderson, A.D. 1587.)

O ALMIGHTY God, the Sovereign Commander of all the world, protect our sailors and the Fleet in which they serve from the dangers of the sea and the violence of the enemy. Nerve them to meet the strain of waiting and of their great responsibility for the welfare of the nation. Make them alert in watching and resistless in fighting; through Jesus Christ our Lord. Amen.

(Source not found.)

O ETERNAL Lord God, Who alone spreadest out the heavens and rulest the raging of the seas, be pleased to receive into Thy almighty and most gracious protection the persons of our sailors now fighting our battle upon the seas. Let Thy Fatherly hand be over them; give them sure trust in Thee, and victory over our enemies, that the homes Thou hast given us may be safe, and that peace may be restored to us in Thy good time. Let the healing benediction of Thy pardon be with them as they go into battle; in the hour of need succour and defend them and enable them to know and feel Thee near, and be Thou unto them a strong defence against the face of the enemy. Be Thou their Saviour and mighty deliverer; through Jesus Christ our Lord. Amen.

(A.D. 1798, adapted.)

MAY the great God Whom I worship grant to my country, and for the benefit of Europe in general, a great and glorious victory; and may no misconduct in anyone tarnish it; and may humanity after victory be the predominant feature in the British Fleet. For myself, individually, I commit my life to Him that made me, and may His blessing alight on my endeavours for serving my country faithfully. To Him I resign myself and the just cause which it is entrusted to me to defend. Amen. Amen. Amen. *(Lord Nelson, A.D. 1758 (On the eve of the Battle of Trafalgar, A.D. 1805.)*

THE ARMY

O ALMIGHTY Lord God, King of all kings, and Governor of all things, that sittest in the Throne judging right, we commend to Thy Fatherly goodness the men who through perils of war are serving this nation, beseeching Thee to take into Thine own hand, both them, and the cause wherein their King and country send them. Be Thou their tower of strength where they are set in the midst of so many and great dangers. Make all bold through death or life to put their trust in Thee, Who art the only giver of all victory, and canst save by many or by few; through Jesus Christ our Lord. Amen.

(Archbishop E. W. Benson, for the Egyptian War, A.D. 1885.)

G RANT that our soldiers may be brave in battle, high-hearted in hardships, dauntless in defeat, gentle in victory. Remember those who have trained themselves in peace to help their country in war; and give them skill and courage, endurance and self-control, in the work now set them. We ask it in the Name and for the sake of Christ Jesus our Lord. Amen.

(Source not found.)

O LORD God of Hosts, stretch forth, we pray Thee, Thine Almighty arm to strengthen and protect the sailors and soldiers of our King in every peril, both of land, and sea, and air; shelter them in the day of battle, and in time of peace keep them safe from all evil; endue them ever with loyalty and courage, and grant that in all things they may serve as seeing Thee Who art invisible; through Jesus Christ our Lord. Amen.

(Prayer Book of the Church of Scotland, A.D. 1912.)

R EMEMBER, O Lord, all whom Thou hast called to minister to the souls of those engaged in warfare. Give to them great gifts and holiness, that with wisdom and charity, diligence and zeal, they may open the eyes of the blind, comfort those who suffer, and speak peace to the dying. Grant them Thy grace to strengthen the weak, and to confirm the strong, that in all their ministrations, in all their life and conversation, they may shepherd the souls committed to their care, and advance the honour of Our Saviour and His Kingdom, through Jesus Christ our Lord. Amen.

(Bishop Taylor Smith, Nineteenth Century.)

O LORD God, our Father—our Saviour—our Might, we commend to Thy keeping all those who are venturing their lives on our behalf: that whether by life or by death they may win for the whole world the fruits of their sacrifice, and a holy peace: through Jesus Christ our Lord. Amen.

(Day of National Prayer called by H.M. King George VI, May 26, 1940.)

THE ROYAL AIR FORCE

A S on unseen pinions, bear
Our devoted men who dare
All the perils of the air.
            Keep them, we beseech Thee.
                        (*F. W. S.*, A.D. 1915.)

L OOK in Thy mercy, we beseech Thee, O Lord, on those
who are called to tasks of special peril, in the air or beneath
the sea. Even there also shall Thy hand lead them, and Thy
right hand shall hold them. Help them to do their duty with
prudence and with fearlessness, confident that in life or in death
the Eternal God is their refuge, and underneath them are the
Everlasting Arms. Grant this, for Jesus Christ's sake, thy Son
our Lord. Amen.
        (*Randall Davidson, Archbishop of Canterbury*, A.D. 1848.)

O THOU Who bringest the winds out of Thy Treasury, let
Thy guiding and protecting Hand be about our airmen: and
help those who love them to feel that underneath are the Everlasting Arms; through Jesus Christ. Amen.
                        (*Source not found*, A.D. 1915.)

H E Who directs the sparrow's tender flight,
And sees him safely reach the heartless ground,
Guide thee in all thy passages aright,
And grant thy course be sure, thy resting sound.
                        (*Richard Zouche*, A.D. 1590–1661.)

O LORD God Almighty, Who inhabitest Eternity, Who created
the heavens and the earth, have mercy, we humbly beseech
Thee, on all our airmen. Give unto them the assurance of Thy
protection when they are amidst the clouds and wonders of the
sky, that, whether in the calm sunshine, or surrounded by the
thick mists of darkness and storm, they may feel Thy Spirit
and Thy presence ever around them. Sustain them, O Lord,
in all their perils, and give them a perfect trust in Thee, Who
art the only source of all knowledge and power, through Jesus
Christ our Lord. Amen.   (*F. O. A.*, A.D. 1915.)

O GOD of our fathers, under Whose wings we are come to
trust, be merciful unto all those who fly in the air, for Thy
loving-kindness is great. Yea, in the shadow of Thy wings will
we make our refuge until these calamities be overpast. Uphold
them lest they fall, O God of our righteousness, for Thy mercy
is unto the heavens and Thy truth unto the clouds; through
Christ Jesus our Lord. Amen.
            (*Hon. Mrs. Lyttelton Gell, Nineteenth Century.*)

THE CIVIL SERVICE

GRANT, O Lord, that all those who shall be called to legislate or give judgment in any matters touching the interest of Thy people may ever act with justice, truth, and reverence; so that they may not add to the guilt of our nation by commands at variance with the Laws of Thy Sanctuary, but may acknowledge Thee as the only Fountain of authority; through Jesus Christ our Lord. Amen.

("Office of Intercession," Twentieth Century.)

THAT it may please Thee, O God, to give wisdom, strength, and courage to all who are placed in authority and in posts of special responsibility; to the Government, the members of Parliament, to all leaders in our spiritual and social life, for the sake of Christ Jesus our Lord. Amen.

(Bishop Winnington-Ingram, A.D. 1858.)

GIVE wisdom, O Lord, we pray Thee, to all those who are concerned in the correction of the unruly, especially the magistrates of our country. Enable them so to be diligent in investigation and impartial in judgment, that their word may tend to the diminution of vice and the removal of the principal occasions of evil; and grant that their responsibility for others may lead them to anxious preparation for that sentence which they shall themselves receive from Thee, the Judge of all; through Christ Jesus our Lord. Amen.

(Rev. R. M. Benson, A.D. 1824.)

GUIDE, O Lord, we pray Thee, the Mayor and Councillors of our cities with all those who share in the ordering of our towns; give strength, honour, and charity to all our fellow-citizens, that all their work may be done as in Thy sight, and seeking not the good of party, may ever see before them the vision of that free city perfect in the heavens whose builder and maker is God; through Jesus Christ our Lord. Amen.

(Canon Percy Dearmer, A.D. 1867.)

O GOD, Almighty Father, King of kings and Lord of all our rulers, grant that the hearts and minds of all who go out as leaders before us, the statesmen, the judges, the men of learning, and the men of wealth, may be so filled with the love of Thy laws, and of that which is righteous and life-giving, that they may serve as a wholesome salt unto the earth, and be worthy stewards of Thy good and perfect gifts; through Jesus Christ our Lord. Amen.

(Prayer from the Service of the Knights of the Order of the Garter, Fourteenth Century.)

FOR A GENERAL ELECTION

O ALMIGHTY Lord and Heavenly Father, we beseech Thee to guide and govern the minds of Thy people in wisdom, sincerity, and judgment, that they being called to elect just legislators and faithful counsellors to our Sovereign, on behalf of all conditions of men in many nations, they may understand both the sacredness of the trust which Thy providence commits to each of them, and also the greatness of the interests which thereon depend for Thy world and Church, for virtue and Thy true religion. To Thee, O Lord, we commend this whole land, for which thou hast done so great things of old. Abolish all mean desire and unworthy motive, let none be deceived through wilfulness or vain words. Cleanse all thoughts, uplift all minds, enable them to consider all things diligently, and in singleness of heart to fulfil Thy will; through Jesus Christ our Lord. Amen. *(Archbishop Benson, A.D. 1829.)*

ALMIGHTY God, Who orderest all things, and to Whom all hearts are subject, we beseech Thee at this time to look upon our Country, and to give Thy grace and guidance to those who are to take part in the coming election of Members of Parliament. We thankfully acknowledge Thy goodness to our land; and we beseech Thee to overrule this election to the advancement of Thy glory, and the good of this Nation and People; through Jesus Christ our Lord. Amen. *(Source not found.)*

GOVERN, O Lord, the minds of all who are called to choose faithful men into the Great Council of the Nation; that, considering their sacred trust and the great issues thereof, they may exercise the same in all godliness and honesty; through Jesus Christ our Lord. Amen.
(Sanctioned for Use in the Diocese of Southwark, A.D. 1910.)

ALMIGHTY God, Who rulest in the affairs of men, and givest power to whomsoever Thou wilt, grant that those who are appointed to any high office, whether in Church or State, may with such purity of faith and singleness of intention devote themselves to Thy glory, that they may prosper in the work entrusted to them, and while they adorn by their own conversation the doctrine of our Saviour Jesus Christ, they may win others to the love of Thy most holy Name and the exercise of Thy holy religion; through the same Jesus Christ our Lord. Amen. *(Rev. R. M. Benson, A.D. 1824.)*

RAISE up, O God, politicians who will fear Thee and Thee alone, and will Thy Will, and work Thy work, fearless and faithful unto death in the Name of Jesus Christ. Amen.
(General Election Pamphlet, A.D. 1910.)

FOR PEACE

O GOD, Who art the Father of all, and Who alone makest men to be of one mind in a house, we beseech Thee, at this time of strife and unrest, to grant to us, by the inspiration of Thy Holy Spirit, a fuller realization of our brotherhood, man with man in Thee; allay all anger and bitterness, and deepen in us a sense of truth and equity in our dealings one with another; for the sake of Thy Son, our Lord Jesus Christ. Amen.

(Dr. Randall Davidson, Archbishop of Canterbury, A.D. 1848.)

GRACIOUS Lord, thou art not the God of confusion or discord, but the God of concord and of peace, unite our hearts and affections in such sort together, that we may as brethren walk in Thy House, in brotherly charity and love, and as members of the body of Christ. Let the oil of sanctification, that is Thy Holy Spirit inflame us, and the dew of Thy blessing continually fall upon us, that we may obtain life eternal; through the same Jesus Christ Thy Son. So be it. *(Scottish Psalter, A.D. 1595.)*

O OUR God, amidst the deplorable division of Thy Church let us never widen its breaches, but give us universal charity to all who are called by Thy Name. O deliver us from the sins and errors, from the schisms and heresies of the age. O give us grace daily to pray for the peace of Thy Church, and earnestly to seek it and to excite all we can to praise and to love Thee; through Jesus Christ, our one Saviour and Redeemer. Amen. *(Bishop Ken, A.D. 1637.)*

O GOD, Who callest the peacemakers Thy children, we beseech Thee that as Thou didst send Thy Son with the heavenly voice of peace on earth to be the Prince of Peace to men, so Thou wilt keep our hearts and minds in His peace, and make us both to love and defend the same. Guide the counsels of the King, and of all princes and governors, in equity and steadfastness, to establish unity and concord among the nations, that all mankind may render Thee the fruits of peace and righteousness; through Jesus Christ our Lord. Amen.

(Diocese of Canterbury, A.D. 1885.)

THOU hast quieted those which were in confusion. Praise to Thy calmness! O Lord make quiet in Thy Churches; and blend and unite, O Lord, the contentious sects; and still and rule also the conflicting parties, and may there be at every time one true Church, and may her righteous children gather them-selves together to confess Thy graciousness. Praise to Thy reconciliation, O Lord God. Amen.

(St. Ephraim the Syrian, A.D. 306.)

IN TIME OF WAR

O LORD, who lovest not the wrath and strife of men, and yet wouldest have Thy servants to contend earnestly for the Faith. Grant us so to labour in seeking Thy truth as never to forget to obey it; and so to contend for it as never to despise our brethren and cause them to offend; through Jesus Christ our Lord. Amen. (*Charles Marriott*, A.D. 1811.)

O LORD God Almighty, Who from Thy Throne dost behold all the dwellers upon earth, look down with pity upon those on whom have fallen the miseries of war. Have compassion on the wounded and dying; comfort the broken-hearted; assuage the madness of the nations; make war to cease; give peace in our time, O Lord; we ask it in the Name of Him Who is the Prince of Peace, even Thy Son Jesus Christ our Lord. Amen.
(*Adapted.*)

O THOU that slumberest not nor sleepest, protect, we pray Thee, our sailors from the hidden perils of the sea, from the snares and assaults of the enemy. In the anxious hours of waiting, steady and support those on whom the burdens of responsibility lie heavily; and grant that in dangers often, in watchings often, in weariness often, they may serve Thee with a quiet mind; through Jesus Christ our Lord. Amen.
(*Archbishop Davidson*, A.D. 1848.)

WE do instantly beseech Thee of Thy gracious goodness to be merciful to the Church militant here upon earth, and at this time compassed about with most strong and subtle adversaries.

O! let Thine enemies know that Thou hast received England, which they most of all for Thy Gospel's sake do malign, into Thine own protection. Set a wall about it, O Lord, and evermore mightily defend it. Let it be a comfort to the afflicted, a help to the oppressed, and a defence to Thy Church and people persecuted abroad. And, forasmuch as this cause is now in hand, direct and go before our armies, both by sea and land.

Bless them and prosper them, and grant unto them honourable success and victory.

Thou art our help and shield. O! give good and prosperous success to all those that fight this battle against the enemies of Thy Gospel.
(*Prayer of Queen Elizabeth before the Armada*, A.D. 1588.)

ALMIGHTY and merciful God, we beseech Thee to give us rest from the storm of war, for Thou wilt bestow on us all good things if Thou givest us peace both of soul and body; through Jesus Christ our Lord. Amen. (*Leonine Sacramentary*.)

DELIVER us from our enemies, we beseech Thee, and defend us from all dangers to soul and body, that at length we may come to Thine eternal rest; through Jesus Christ our Lord. Amen. (*St. Bernard*, A.D. 1091.)

IN TIME OF WAR

HAVE mercy, O Lord, upon the wounded and the suffering, whether of our own people or of the enemy. Let Thy grace be their comfort, although natural friends be far away. Raise them to health, if it be good, but chiefly give them such faith and patience that they may glorify Thee upon the earth, and escaping the assaults of Satan, may rest in peace, and rise to partake of Thy glory; through Jesus Christ our Lord. Amen.

(Rev. R. M. Benson, A.D. 1824.)

O LORD God of our Salvation, Who orderest all things by Thy unsearchable Wisdom, Thou hast been our merciful God from generation to generation. We have trusted in Thee, and we have been holpen. Without Thee the wisdom of the wise is vain, and the multitude of an host is weak. Vouchsafe to continue to us, O Lord, in such manner, Thy guidance and support, that the enemies of our peace may see that Thine Arm, stretched out to save, can crush the mightiest force, and bring to nought the most subtle designs of human policy; and that the man of earth, who lifteth up his banner against Thee, shall ever be humbled under Thy Almighty Hand. Hear us, O merciful God, for the sake and through the merits of our only Saviour, Jesus Christ, Thy Son our Lord. Amen. *(A.D. 1798.)*

O GOD Almighty, Lord of Hosts, look down we beseech Thee with favour upon our troops now engaged in war, and crown them with victory. Cover their heads in the day of battle; give them valour that comes of Faith, and the mercy which beseems Christian soldiers. Have compassion on those who suffer—the sick, the wounded, the dying—and the mourners for the fallen. Bring the war, if it please Thee, to a right and lasting peace; and overrule all things in this world of sin and sorrow, to the enlargement of Thy blessed Kingdom, for the sake of Him Who is our peace, Jesus Christ our Lord. Amen.

(Archbishop J. B. Crozier, A.D. 1858.)

O GOD, Who never sleepest, and art never weary, have mercy upon those who watch to-night; on the sentry, that he may be alert; on those who command, that they may be strengthened with counsel; on the sick, that they may obtain sleep; on the wounded, that they may find ease; on the faint-hearted, that they may hope again; on the light-hearted, lest they forget Thee; on the dying, that they may find peace; on the sinful, that they may turn again. And save us, O good Lord. Amen.

(Canon Newbolt, A.D. 1844.)

WE trust to the great Disposer of all events, and to the justice of our cause. I thank God for this great opportunity of doing my duty.

([Admiral] Horatio Lord Nelson, A.D. 1758.)

BE Thou unto us at this time of need a tower of strength, a place of refuge, and a defence against the enemy. Let Thy comfort support and strengthen us, Thy mercy keep us, and Thy grace guide us; and then receive unto Thyself, O Lord God the Father, that which Thy power hath shapen; receive, O Lord the Son, that which Thou has bought with Thy precious blood; receive, O Lord the Holy Ghost, that which Thou hast kept and preserved so lovingly in this evil world; and to Thee, Who art over all, Three Persons and One God, be praise and honour for ever and ever. Amen. (*Primer of Henry VIII.*, A.D. 1545.)

MOST gracious God, Who hast in all ages shown Thy mighty power in protecting righteous Kings and States, we humbly beseech Thee with Thy favour to look in mercy upon us Thy servants at this time of anxiety and distress. Deliver us, we pray Thee, from the great and imminent dangers which threaten the welfare of our Church and Country. Accept our contrition of heart and humility of service, and grant that all that is said and done may tend to the glory of Thy great Name, and the welfare of Thy Church and people, so that truth and justice, religion and piety, may be established among us for all generations; through Jesus Christ our Lord. Amen. (*Dr. Crozier*, A.D. 1858.)

GRANT, we beseech Thee, Almighty God, that we, who in our tribulation are yet of good cheer because of Thy loving-kindness, may find Thee mighty to save from all dangers; through Jesus Christ. Amen. (*Roman Breviary.*)

TAKE from us, O God, all pride and vanity, all boasting and forwardness, and give us the true courage that shows itself by gentleness; the true wisdom that shows itself by simplicity; and the true power that shows itself by modesty; through Jesus Christ our Lord. Amen. (*Rev. Charles Kingsley*, A.D. 1819.)

SEND Thy blessing, O heavenly Father, on this our beloved Land. Increase in our own and in every nation, the Spirit of truth and justice, peace and godly love. Turn the hearts of all men unto Thee, and so hasten the blessed time when the kingdoms of the world shall become the Kingdom of our Lord Jesus Christ, in Whose Name we offer these petitions, even the same Christ Jesus Thy Son our Lord. Amen.
(*Century National Prayer Union*, A.D. 1900.)

FATHER of all men and God of Peace, hear our prayers, we beseech Thee, and grant that at this time those in authority may so faithfully conduct all negotiations between this Country and . . . that peace may be maintained. Grant that all concerned may have a single eye to Thy glory, and that while no injustice may be left unredressed they may honestly labour for peace as Thy sons, from whom every family in heaven and on earth is named; through Jesus Christ our Lord. Amen.
(*Rev. The Hon. James Adderley*, A.D. 1861.)

NATIONAL CONFESSION AND INTERCESSION

O HEAVENLY Father, Who sendest trials and afflictions upon Thy children to humble them and prove them, and to know what is in their hearts, help us in our time of trial to see Thy Fatherly hand, and to believe in Thy purposes of love. We confess before Thee with shame and sorrow that we have lived too much without Thee in the world, that we have depended for our success and for our prosperity, upon ourselves as a nation. We would desire to thank Thee for calling us so mercifully to repentance. May we humble ourselves now under Thy mighty hand, and see that Thou of very faithfulness hast caused us to be troubled. Above all may we come back to Thee as to a loving Father, and trust Thee for the future, casting our care upon Thee, for that Thou carest for us. And may it please Thee to make this and every trial work for our everlasting good, so that we may be established in righteousness, strengthened and settled, and may abide in Thee; through Jesus Christ our Lord. Amen. *(Rev. F. P. Wickham, A.D. 1871.)*

O LOOK graciously, and speedily have compassion upon Thy people in Thy abundant mercy, for the sake of Thy Name, O Eternal God. Pity, compassionate, and save the sheep of Thy pasture; suffer not wrath to prevail against us, for our eyes are directed towards Thee. Save us, then, for the sake of Thy Name. Have mercy upon us. Regard and answer us in time of trouble, for unto Thee belongeth salvation, in Thee is our hope, O God of forgiveness. O pardon us, Thou good and forgiving God, for Thou, Omnipotent King, art most gracious and compassionate. Hear us, we humbly beseech Thee, for the glory of Thy great Name. Amen.

(Jewish Daily Services, Jewish Calendar, 5671.)

O LORD, the great and dreadful God, keeping the covenant and mercy to them that love Thee, and to them that keep Thy commandments; we have sinned, and committed iniquity, and have done wickedly, and have rebelled even by departing from Thy precepts and from Thy judgments. O Lord, righteousness belongeth unto Thee, but unto us confusion of face, as at this day, because of our trespass that we have trespassed against Thee. To the Lord our God belong mercies and forgivenesses, though we have rebelled against Him; neither have we obeyed the voice of the Lord our God, to walk in His laws, which He set before us. O Lord, according to all Thy righteousness, we beseech Thee, let Thine anger be turned away from us. Now, O God, hear the prayer and supplications of Thy servants, and cause Thy face to shine upon us. O Lord, hear; O Lord, forgive; O Lord, hearken and do; defer not, for Thine own sake, O our God. Amen. *(Daniel; Sixth Century B.C; Dan. ix.)*

ETERNAL God, Who art constantly adored by thrones and powers, by Seraphim and Cherubim, we confess that Thou art most worthy to be praised, but we of all others are the most unworthy to be employed in showing forth Thy praise. How can we praise Thee, the pure and holy Majesty of Heaven? Yet how can these bodies which Thou hast wonderfully formed, and these souls which Thou hast inspired, which owe entirely to Thine unmerited favour all that they are, all that they possess, and all that they hope for, forbear praising Thee, their wise and bountiful Creator and Father. Let our souls, therefore, and all that is within us, bless Thy holy Name; yea, let us say, O Lord, who is like Thee, who is like unto Thee? Far be it, most gracious Father, from our hearts to harbour anything that is displeasing to Thee; let them be, as it were, temples dedicated to Thy service, thoroughly purged from every idol, from every object of impure love and earthly affection. Let our most gracious King and Redeemer dwell and reign within us; may He take full possession of us by His Spirit, and govern all our actions. May He extend His peaceable and saving Kingdom throughout the whole habitable world, from the rising of the sun till the going down thereof. Let the nations acknowledge their King, and the isles be glad in Him, particularly that which we inhabit, with those in its neighbourhood; and that they may be truly blessed in Him, may they duly submit more perfectly and dutifully to His golden sceptre and the holy laws of His Gospel. Bless this nation and this city; may it be continually watered with the dew of Thy Spirit, and plentifully produce fruit acceptable in Thy sight; through Jesus Christ our Lord. Amen.

(Archbishop Leighton, A.D. 1611.)

O LORD our God, we cried unto Thee in trouble, and Thou heardest us; we put our trust in Thee, and were not confounded. Thou hast turned our heaviness into joy, and girded us with gladness; therefore will we praise Thee with all our heart, and give thanks unto Thy holy Name for ever. Hear us and accept us; for the sake of Jesus Christ our Lord. Amen.

(Rev. L. Tuttiett, A.D. 1825.)

WE beseech Thee, O Lord our God, that the relief from anxiety which Thy mercy has bestowed upon us may not make us negligent, but rather cause us to become more acceptable worshippers of Thy Name; through Jesus Christ our Lord. Amen. *(Leonine Sacramentary.)*

WE give Thee humble thanks, most merciful Father, that Thou dost graciously hear the prayers of Thy servants who call upon Thee, and hast done for us great things whereof we rejoice; we desire to thank Thee, O most loving Father, for all Thy goodness vouchsafed unto us, through Jesus Christ our Lord. Amen.

(Bishop W. W. Webb, Nineteenth Century.)

O GOD, our Heavenly Father, we bless Thee again for the remembrance of this day, when by Thy Providence, and by the might of Thine arm, Thou madest wars to cease; accept our praise and thanksgivings.

As on this day we remember before Thee all those who fought and died that we might live, accept our gratitude, and make us, we humbly beseech Thee, more worthy of their sacrifice even unto death, and help us to follow more closely in the steps of Thy blessed Son, that at last, we with them, may stand in Thy Presence, where with the Father and the Holy Ghost, all praise, thanksgiving, honour and might be ascribed, world without end. Amen.

WE bless Thy holy Name, O God, for all Thy servants who, having finished their course, do now rest from their labours. Give us grace, we beseech Thee, to follow the example of their steadfastness and faithfulness, to Thy honour and glory, through Christ Jesus our Lord. Amen.

IN remembrance of those who made the great sacrifice, O God, make us better men and women, and give peace in our time, through Jesus Christ Thy Son our Saviour. Amen.

ALMIGHTY and everlasting God, we give Thee humble thanks for the memory and good example of Thy servants who have laid down their lives in the service of our country. We bless Thee for their courage and devotion. Accept their sacrifice we pray Thee, let it not be in vain that they have died in the cause of righteousness and honour. And of Thy mercy, O heavenly Father, vouchsafe that we, who now serve Thee here on earth, may at last, together with them be found meet to be partakers of the inheritance of the saints in light, for the sake of Jesus Christ Thy Son our Lord and Saviour. Amen.

AS we bless Thy holy Name for those Thy servants departed this life in Thy faith and love, so we beseech Thee to give to us who remain, grace to follow their good example, and to carry on the work which they began. Grant, O Lord, we pray Thee, that the offering of their lives may not have been made in vain; that we and all Thy people may hear the call to nobler living which sounds in our ears from the graves of those who have died that we might live; that we may dedicate our lives anew to the work of bringing in Thy Kingdom upon earth; that so out of these years of sin, and misery and loss, there may arise a better world through Jesus Christ our Lord. Amen.

REMEMBER, O Lord, what Thou hast wrought in us and not what we deserve; and, as Thou hast called us to Thy service, make us worthy of our calling; through Jesus Christ our Lord Amen. *(From a form of humble prayer to Almighty God on behalf of the Nation and Empire. A.D. 1914.)*

THE DAY OF REMEMBRANCE

O FATHER of Spirits, we have joy at this time in all who have faithfully lived, and in all who have triumphantly died. We thank Thee for all fair memories and all aspiring hopes, for the sacred ties that bind us to the unseen world, for the dear and holy dead who encompass us like a cloud of witness, and make the unseen heaven a home to our hearts. May we be followers of those who through faith and patience now inherit the promises. In this hour of quiet thought and solemn joy, may the meditation of our hearts and the answer of our lips be from Thee, through Jesus Christ our Saviour Who is the Resurrection and the Life. Amen.

O GOD, the strength of those who suffer, and the repose of them that triumph, we rejoice in the Communion of Saints. We remember all who have faithfully lived, all who have passed on into Heaven (especially those most dear to us). May we have the assurance of their continual fellowship in Thee, and realize that though converse be no longer possible according to the flesh, there is no separation in the realm of love. Lift us into that light and love, where the Church on earth is one with the Church in Heaven; through Jesus Christ our Lord. Amen.

O GOD, our heavenly Father, we would especially remember before Thee on this Day of Remembrance all those who have suffered and been maimed, disabled, or blinded. Those whom the war has left weakened in body or mind. Grant that they may never be forgotten, but that they may live brave, cheerful, and so far as may be, useful lives amid grateful regard and deserved honour. Give them, O Lord, Thy peace and the abiding sense of Thy sustaining power, and enable us, each one, to do our part for their comfort and help, through Him Who is the Burden Bearer, even Jesus Christ Thy Son our Lord. Amen.

O GOD of all mercy and comfort, accept the heartfelt praises and thanksgivings of those whose dear ones after having fought a good fight, returned to them in safety. In the greatness of their joy may they ever be mindful of those whose lives are shadowed with abiding sorrow, for the sake of Christ Jesus our Saviour. Amen.

O GOD our Father, on this Day of Remembrance, look upon the unrest of the world and be pleased to complete the work of Thy healing hand. Send peace upon the earth, a deeper and more lasting peace than the world has ever known. Draw all men unto Thyself, and to one another by the bonds of love. Grant understanding to the Nations with an increase of sympathy and mutual good will, that they may be united in a sacred Brotherhood wherein justice, mercy and faith, truth and freedom may flourish, so that the sacrifice of those who died may not have been made in vain, for the sake of Christ Jesus our Lord. Amen.

EVENTS OF THE HOME

A WEDDING IN THE HOME

O GOD, bless Thy servants who are about to be joined together this day in holy matrimony; keep them, we beseech Thee, under the protection of Thy good providence, and make them to have a perpetual fear and love of Thy holy name. Look, O Lord, mercifully upon them from heaven, and bless them; that they obeying Thy will and always being in safety under Thy protection, may abide in Thy love unto their lives' end; through Jesus Christ our Lord. Amen.
(Family Prayer Book of the Church of Ireland, A.D. 1895.)

O LORD Jesus Christ, Who hast vouchsafed to be the Husband of Thy Church, binding Thy people unto Thyself in the mysterious unity of a nature renewed by the Holy Ghost; have mercy upon those who are recently married, and grant that they, realizing that mutual love which Thou hast ordained to be an image of the love between Thyself and Thy people, may be found each to the other a comfort in sorrow, a strength in need, a counsellor in perplexity, a companion in every enjoyment; and having shared together Thy blessings upon earth, may attain to the blessing of Thy Heavenly Feast in the satisfaction of Thy perfect love, Who livest and reignest with the Father and the Holy Ghost, one God, world without end. Amen.
(Rev. R. M. Benson, A.D. 1824.)

O LORD God of our fathers, Giver of life and love, give Thy blessing to those whom Thou hast drawn together in love; surround them with Thy protecting care; build Thou for them their home; make it to be the abode of light and love. May all that is pure, tender and true, grow up under its shelter; may all that hinders godly union and concord, be driven far from it. Make it the centre of fresh, sweet, and holy influence. Give them wisdom for life, and discretion in the guidance of their affairs. Let Thy Fatherly hand ever be over them, and Thy Holy Spirit ever be with them. O Lord, bless them and theirs, and grant them to inherit Thine everlasting Kingdom; through Jesus Christ our Lord. Amen.
(Bishop William Boyd Carpenter, A.D. 1841.)

O THOU, Who by Thy presence in Cana of Galilee, didst sanctify the holy estate of matrimony, send Thy blessing upon Thy servants who have this day entered upon this holy estate, and so fill them with all spiritual benediction and grace, that, living together in perfect love and holy peace in this world, in the world to come they may obtain life everlasting; through Jesus Christ our Lord. Amen. *(A. L. Illingworth, A.D. 1878.)*

FOR A BIRTHDAY

ALMIGHTY and everlasting God, the Maker of all creation, mercifully hear our prayers, and grant many and happy years to Thy servant whose birthday it is, that *he* may spend all *his* life so as to please Thee; through Jesus Christ our Lord. Amen. (*Gelasian Sacramentary.*)

ETERNAL Father, the Giver of life, Who as on this day didst cause Thy servant, ——, to be born into this world; we thank Thee, O Lord, for all Thy mercies vouchsafed to *him* from that time unto this present, humbly beseeching Thee to continue Thy gracious favour and protection unto *his* life's end. Assist *him* in every time of trial, shield *him* in danger, relieve and comfort *him* in trouble, succour *him* in temptation, defend *him* from the assaults of the enemy, that *his* days here may pass away in peace, and when *he* dies, *he* may attain unto the everlasting rest that remaineth for Thy people; through Jesus Christ our Lord. Amen. (*Rev. W. E. Scudamore*, A.D. 1813.)

MAY God, before Whom our fathers did walk, God Who hast fed us from our youth even unto this hour, the Angel which redeemeth us from all evil—"Bless the *lad*." (*From Gen.* xlviii. 15, 16; *Jacob, Twentieth Century* B.C.)

WE beseech Thee, Lord, open Thy heavens; from thence may Thy gifts descend to *him*. Put forth Thine own hand from heaven and touch *his* head. May *he* feel the touch of Thy Hand, and receive the joy of the Holy Spirit, that *he* may remain blessed for evermore. Amen. (*St. Æthelwold*, A.D. 925.)

ON THE BIRTH OF A CHILD

O LORD God, in Whose hands are the issues of life, we thank Thee for Thy gifts to us at this time. We thank Thee for the life given, and the life preserved. And as Thou hast knit together life and love in one fellowship, so we pray Thee to grant that with this fresh gift of life to us, there may be given an increase of love one to another. Grant that the presence of weakness may awaken our tenderness, enable us to minister to the little one that has been given to us in all lovingness, wisdom, and fidelity; and grant that *he* may live as Thy child, and may serve this generation according to Thy will; through Jesus Christ our Lord. Amen.

(*Bishop William Boyd Carpenter*, A.D. 1841.)

"O THAT *my son* might live before Thee, O God." (*Gen.* xvii. 18; *Abraham, Twentieth Century* B.C.)

FOR OUR CHILDREN

BLESS our children with healthful bodies, with good under-standings, with the graces and gifts of Thy Spirit, with sweet dispositions and holy habits; and sanctify them through-out in their bodies, souls, and spirits, and keep them unblame-able to the coming of our Lord Jesus.   Amen.

(Bishop Jeremy Taylor, A.D. 1613.)

ALMIGHTY God and Heavenly Father, we thank Thee for the children which Thou hast given us; give us also grace to train them in Thy faith, fear, and love, that as they advance in years they may grow in grace, and may hereafter be found in the number of Thine elect children; through Jesus Christ our Lord.   Amen.   *(Bishop Cosin, A.D. 1595.)*

GOOD Shepherd, Who carriest the lambs in Thine arms, give Thy Spirit, we beseech Thee, to all those engaged in training the young; make them patient, grant them tenderness, sincerity, and firmness, and enable them to lead the young hearts to Thee, for Thy Name's sake.   Amen.   *(Source not found.)*

LOOK down from heaven, O Lord, upon Thy flock and lambs; bless their bodies and their souls; and grant that they who have received Thy sign, O Christ, on their foreheads may be Thine own in the day of judgment; through Jesus Christ our Lord.   Amen.   *(Archbishop Egbert, A.D. 734.)*

O LORD Jesus Christ, Who didst take little children in Thine arms and bless them; bless, we beseech Thee, all little children dear to us.   Take them into the arms of Thy ever-lasting mercy, keep them from all evil, and bring them into the company of those who ever behold the face of Thy Father which is in heaven—to the glory of Thy Holy Name.   Amen.

(Priest's Prayer Book, A.D. 1870.)

MERCIFUL Father, regard with Thy tender love and favour Thy children.   Grant that as they have been admitted by Baptism into the fellowship of Thy People, so they may ever-more grow in grace and in the knowledge of our Lord Jesus Christ.   Keep them in all temptation; teach them Thy truth; and grant that they may early give their hearts to Thee; through Jesus Christ our Lord.   Amen.

(Rev. W. Bellars, Nineteenth Century.)

ALMIGHTY God, Giver of all good things, mercifully behold this Thy child now going forth in Thy Name to school, so replenish *him* with the truth of Thy doctrine and adorn *him* with innocency of life, that both by word and good example *he* may faithfully serve Thee to the glory of Thy Name and the edification of Thy Church; through Jesus Christ our Lord. Amen.   *(Gelasian Sacramentary.)*

O LORD, Holy Father, Almighty Author of the eternal universe, God unto Whom all things live, Who givest life to the dead, and callest those things which are not, as those which are; mercifully perform Thy accustomed work, Thou Who art the Maker, in this Thy child; through Jesus Christ our Lord. Amen.

(*Ancient Celtic Church.*)

O GOD, Who through the teaching of Thy Son Jesus Christ, didst prepare the disciples for the coming of the Comforter; make ready, we beseech Thee, the hearts and minds of Thy servants who at this time are seeking the gifts of the Holy Ghost through the laying on of hands, that drawing near with penitent and faithful hearts, they may be filled with the power of His Divine Presence; through the same Jesus Christ our Lord. Amen. (*Prayer Book of the Scottish Church*, A.D. 1912.)

STRENGTHEN, O Lord, we pray Thee, by Thy Holy Spirit, Thy servants who are now preparing to seek Thy help in the sacred rite of Confirmation; and grant that all they who bear the Cross upon their foreheads may bear it also in their hearts, so that boldly confessing Thee before men, they may be found worthy to be numbered among Thy Saints; through Jesus Christ our Lord. Amen. (*Source not found.*)

O MERCIFUL Lord, we beseech Thee so abundantly to strengthen these Thy servants with the sevenfold gift of Thy Holy Spirit, that they who are admitted by Thine ordinance to the perfection of Christian graces, may grow unto the perfection of Christian life, in the exercise of the power which Thou hast given them, through Thy Son Jesus Christ, our Mediator and Redeemer. Amen. (*Rev. R. M. Benson*, A.D. 1824.)

O LORD, my Heavenly Father, I thank Thee that Thou hast called me, Thy child, to be a candidate for Confirmation. Incline me to attend regularly the lectures and classes, and to listen with a serious mind and an honest heart to the instruction, so that I may receive much blessing during these weeks of preparation and an abundant outpouring of Thy Holy Spirit on the day of my Confirmation. May I learn to know Thee better and love Thee more than in the past, and to prove my love by giving up all that is wrong and doing the things that please Thee. Bless those who are preparing us for Confirmation, and give Thy grace, I pray Thee, to myself and all the other candidates, that this season, which will never come again, may fit us all to become faithful Communicants in Thy Church on earth, and hereafter partakers together in the Communion of Thy Saints above, through Jesus Christ our Lord. Amen.

(*Bishop Blunt*, A.D. 1833.)

BEFORE HOLY COMMUNION

TAKE away from us, we beseech Thee, O Lord, all our iniquities, and the spirit of pride and arrogance, which Thou resistest and fill us with the spirit of fear, and give us a contrite and humbled heart, which Thou dost not despise, that we may be enabled with pure minds to enter into the Holy of Holies; through Jesus Christ our Lord. Amen. (*Leonine Sacramentary.*)

WE pray Thee let Thy Spirit purify our hearts, lest we come unworthily to the heavenly feast, that Thou being shed abroad in our hearts, we may grow up into Thee, and become strong in spiritual growth, so that we may persevere in the blessed society of Thy mystical Body, which it is Thy will should be so one with Thee as Thou art one with the Father in the unity of the Holy Ghost, to Whom be praise and thanksgiving for ever. Amen. (*Desiderius Erasmus*, A.D. 1467.)

O THOU Who art of purer eyes than to behold iniquity, canst Thou bear to look on us conscious of our great transgressions? Yet hide not Thy face from us, for in Thy light alone shall we see light. Forgive us for the sins which crowd into the mind as we realize Thy Presence. Not for pardon only, but for cleansing, Lord, we pray; through Jesus Christ. Amen.
(*Rev. Dr. W. E. Orchard*, A.D. 1877.)

ALMIGHTY and most merciful Father, we are about to commemorate the death of Thy Son Jesus Christ our Saviour and Redeemer. Grant, O Lord, that our whole hope and confidence may be in His merits and Thy mercy. Enforce and accept our imperfect repentance, make this commemoration available to the confirmation of our faith, the establishment of our hope, and the enlargement of our love, and make the death of Thy dear Son Jesus Christ effectual to our redemption. Have mercy upon us, and pardon the multitude of our offences. Bless our friends. Have mercy upon all men. Support us by Thy Holy Spirit throughout our life, and receive us at last into everlasting happiness, for the sake of Jesus Christ our Lord. Amen. (*Dr. Samuel Johnson*, A.D. 1709.)

VOUCHSAFE to us, O Lord God, that having our hearts sprinkled we may be accounted worthy to enter into the Holy of Holies, to stand before Thine altar high and exalted, and to present unto Thee a reasonable and spiritual sacrifice; through Jesus Christ our Lord. Amen. (*Liturgy of the Syrian Jacobites.*)

O GOD the Father, bestow upon us such a measure of Thy Spirit as may sanctify for ever our body and soul which we offer to Thee, and may likewise help us to perform those services which we do now promise; through Jesus Christ our Lord. Amen. (*Dean Brevint*, A.D. 1616.)

AFTER HOLY COMMUNION

WE thank Thee, O Lord, holy Father, Almighty, everlasting God, Who hast satisfied the hunger and thirst of our souls with the spiritual food of the Body and Blood of Thy Son Jesus Christ our Lord; and we beseech Thee, O merciful Lord, that this Sacrament may be the washing away of our iniquities, the strength of our weakness and our defence against the dangers of the world. O Lord, let this Communion cleanse us from sin, and prepare us to be partakers of heavenly joys; through Jesus Christ our Lord. Amen.

(Bishop of Salisbury, Nineteenth Century.)

AND now, O Loving Father, we go forth, we leave this holy place, to do the work that Thou hast taught us, to use the strength that Thou hast given. Be Thou with us henceforth in all Thy love and power, and establish the thing that Thou hast wrought in us; through Jesus Christ our Lord. Amen.

(Original source not found.)

GO forth with us, O Lord, from this Thy holy house; cast about us the fence which the evil one cannot pass, and clothe us in the armour which his darts cannot pierce. Send down upon us Thy love and light and calm, wherein, as in a cloud, we may continually dwell and worship Thee for evermore; through Jesus Christ our Lord. Amen.

(W. E. Gladstone, A.D. 1809.)

GRANT, we beseech Thee, merciful Lord, that the designs of a new and better life, which by Thy grace we have formed, may not pass away without effect. Incite and enable us by Thy Holy Spirit to improve the time which Thou shalt grant us; to avoid all evil thoughts, words, and actions, and to do all the duties which Thou shalt set before us. Hear our prayer, O Lord, for the sake of Jesus Christ. Amen.

(Dr. Samuel Johnson, A.D. 1709.)

ALMIGHTY God, Who hast given Thine only Son to die for us, grant that we who have this day been united in the Communion of His most precious Body and Blood, may be so cleansed from our past sins, and so strengthened to follow the example of His most Holy Life, that we may hereafter enjoy everlasting fellowship with Thee in heaven, through Him Who loved us and gave Himself for us, Jesus Christ. Amen.

(Bishop Westcott, A.D. 1825.)

O GOD, Who hast so greatly loved us, long sought us, and mercifully redeemed us; give us grace that in everything we may yield ourselves, our wills and our works, a continual thank-offering unto Thee; through Jesus Christ our Lord. Amen.

(Westminster Confession of Faith, A.D. 1647.)

LORD, be with those who at this season will be taking needful rest and change from daily toil. Let Thy Presence brighten their holiday. May sin have no power to spoil enjoyment, and grant to them on their return renewed strength in body and mind for life's daily duties; for the sake of Jesus Christ our Lord. Amen. *(Source not found.)*

O GOD of life and love, Who art the true rest of the soul, sanctify to us our hours of rest. Keep us from all harm and evil, and draw us nearer to Thyself. Enlighten our eyes that we may see Thee in the beauties of Thy creation, and find Thee in all the ways of happiness. Grant that, strengthened in body and purified in soul by the vital energies of Thy indwelling Spirit, we may serve Thee faithfully in the life to which Thou hast called us, through Jesus Christ our Lord. Amen.

O FATHER, Who givest life and health, and blessest recreation as our relief from labour, make happy to-day the hearts and lives of the holiday-makers of our land; that in taking their pleasures they may bear in mind that for Thy pleasure they exist and were created; that in spending time and money they may not forget that they themselves have been bought for Thee by the precious Blood of Christ; that in time of temptation they may themselves be kept true, and by winning ways may draw others to Thee; so may our streets be filled, like the streets of Zion, with the merriment of boys and girls at play, and our whole country re-echo with the gladsome mirth of Thy people, rejoicing in the light of Thy countenance, Who alone art the God of our joy and of our gladness; through Jesus Christ. Amen.
(Federation of Working Girls Clubs, Twentieth Century.)

O GOD the Father, Who alone satisfiest the desire of every living thing, Who ordainest our strength for Thy service, and grantest us intervals of rest for the renewal of our strength. Sanctify, we beseech Thee, to Thy glory, our labour and our rest, our seriousness and our mirth, our sorrow and our joy; and dismiss us now with Thy blessing, that we may go on our way rejoicing; through Jesus Christ our Lord. Amen.
(George 4th Lord Lyttelton, 1817.)

WE give thanks unto Thee, the Doer of good and the merciful Father, the Father of our Lord Jesus Christ, for He hath sheltered us, He hath kept us, He hath redeemed us unto Himself; He hath spared us, He hath helped us; He hath brought us to this hour. Keep us, we pray Thee, this day and all the days of our life in peace; through Jesus Christ our Lord. Amen.
(Liturgy of Coptic Jacobites.)

ON ONE LEAVING THE HOME

O GOD, Who art in every place beholding the evil and the good, take into Thine own keeping our dear one now going into the world of strangers. Give *him* courage, prudence, self-control. Grant *him* a right judgment in all things. Raise up for *him* friends, if it be Thy will, and deliver *him* from the snares and sorrows of loneliness by the power and joy of Thy Presence. Grant that in every place *he* may find the House of God and the gate of heaven. Safeguard *him* with the ministry of Thy never-failing Providence, now and always; for the sake of Jesus Christ our Lord. Amen. (*Dr. S. Johnson*, A.D. 1709.)

O GOD, Who art the Strength and the Protector of Thy people; we humbly place in Thy hands the *member* of this family who is to-day about to leave us, and to enter a new sphere of life and work. Keep and preserve *him*, O Lord, as it seemeth best to Thy Divine wisdom and love, in all health and safety, both of body and soul; through Jesus Christ our Lord. Amen. (*Canon E. Hawkins*, A.D. 1802.)

O LORD God Almighty, bless, we beseech Thee, with Thy grace the child of this family about to leave the shadow of home, for the discipline and companionship of school. Keep *him* from all dangers of body and soul. Grant *him* perfect truth and purity in thought, word, and deed. May *he* daily grow in favour with Thee and with man, and be prepared to serve Thee faithfully all the days of *his* life; through Jesus Christ our Lord. Amen. (*Rev. H. Stobart, Nineteenth Century.*)

O OUR God, Who openest Thy hand, and fillest all things living with plenteousness, unto Thee we commit all those who are dear to us; watch over them, we beseech Thee, and provide all things needful for their souls and bodies, from this time forth for evermore; through Jesus Christ our Lord. Amen. (*St. Nerses of Clajes, Fourth Century.*)

O JESUS, Master, stay with us as we travel on. Suffer us not to set out on any search, or to go to any work, or trust ourselves in any conflict, without Thy Light to accompany us, and Thy Presence to be our strength. Amen. (*Rev. James Ferguson*, D.D., A.D. 1873.)

WE humbly commend unto Thy Fatherly care, O Lord, Thy servant about to leave this house and family, beseeching Thee that Thy grace and mercy may never fail *him*. Succour *him* in temptation, preserve *him* in danger, assist *him* in every good work, and further *him* continually in the right way; and grant unto us all, O God our Saviour, that by Thy merciful aid we may one day meet again in Thy eternal Kingdom; through Jesus Christ our Lord. Amen. (*Rev. W. E. Scudamore*, A.D. 1813.)

FOR TRAVELLERS BY LAND, SEA, AND AIR

O GOD, Who bestowest Thy mercy at all times on them that love Thee, and in no place art distant from those that serve Thee, direct the ways of Thy servants in Thy will, that, having Thee for their Protector and Guide, they may walk without stumbling in the paths of righteousness; through Jesus Christ our Lord. Amen. *(Gelasian Sacramentary.)*

PRESERVE, O Lord, from all dangers those who are travelling, whether by land, sea, or air. Prosper them with all necessary things, and grant them ever steadfastly to abide in the way of Thy commandments, and attain the end of their faith, even the salvation of their souls, in the home which Thou hast provided for Thy children; through Jesus Christ our Lord. Amen.
(Rev. R. M. Benson, A.D. 1824.)

O GOD, Who didst call Abraham to leave his home, and didst protect him in all his wanderings, grant to those who now travel by land, sea, or air, a prosperous journey, a quiet time, and a safe arrival at their journey's end. Be to them a shadow in the heat, a refuge in the tempest, a protection in adversity, and grant that when life's pilgrimage is over, they may arrive at the heavenly country; through Jesus Christ our Lord. Amen.
(Priest's Prayer Book, A.D. 1870.)

O LORD, be merciful to all travellers, and grant them a safe return, that they, beholding Thy mercy, and praising Thee for Thy goodness here, may the more be quickened with a desire for the full enjoyment of their privileges as fellow-citizens with the saints in Thy heavenly household; through Jesus Christ. Amen. *(Gothic Missal.)*

TO Thy Fatherly protection, O Lord, we commend ourselves and those about to travel. Bless, guide, and defend us, that we may so pass through this world as finally to enjoy in Thy Presence everlasting happiness, for Jesus Christ's sake. Amen. *(Dr. S. Johnson, A.D. 1709.)*

O ALMIGHTY God, Whose way is in the sea and whose paths are in the great waters. Be present, we beseech Thee, with our brethren in the manifold dangers of the deep; protect them from all its perils, prosper them in their course; and bring them in safety to the haven where they would be with a grateful sense of Thy mercies; through Jesus Christ our Lord. Amen.
(Prayer Book, Church of Scotland, A.D. 1912.)

FOR ABSENT FRIENDS

O LORD our God, Who art in every place, from Whom no space or distance can ever separate us, we know that those who are absent from each other are present with Thee, and we therefore pray Thee to have in Thy holy keeping those dear ones from whom we are now separated, and grant that both they and we, by drawing nearer unto Thee, may be drawn nearer to each other, bound together by the unseen chain of Thy love, in the communion of Thy Spirit, and in the holy fellowship of Thy Saints, so that, whether or not, as seemeth best to Thy Divine Providence, we meet again here on earth, we may surely meet again at the Resurrection of the just, and go in together to that Home of many mansions, which Thou hast prepared for them that unfeignedly love Thee; through Jesus Christ our Lord. Amen.
(*Sir William Martin, Chief Justice of New Zealand*, A.D. 1807.)

ALMIGHTY God, by Whose goodness we were created, and Whose mercies never fail; we commend to Thee all who have a place in our hearts and sympathies; all who are joined to us by the sacred ties of kindred, friendship, and love; all little children who are dear to us; all who help us to a faithful life and whose spirits turn our duties into love; keep them both outwardly in their bodies and inwardly in their souls, and pour upon them the continual dew of Thy blessing; through Jesus Christ our Lord. Amen.

(*Rev. J. Hunter*, A.D. 1849.)

BE pleased, O Lord, to remember our friends, all that have prayed for us, and that have done us good. Do Thou good to them and return all their kindness double into their bosom; rewarding them with blessings, sanctifying them with Thy graces, and bringing them to glory; through Jesus Christ our Lord. Amen. (*Bishop Jeremy Taylor*, A.D. 1613.)

O LORD, we bless Thy Holy Name, and thank Thee for Thy good gift, the gift of Friendship.
(*Rev. E. D. Jarvis, Nineteenth Century*.)

ALMIGHTY, Everlasting God, have mercy on Thy servants our friends. Keep them continually under Thy protection, and direct them according to Thy gracious favour in the way of everlasting salvation; that they may desire such things as please Thee, and with all their strength perform the same. And forasmuch as they trust in Thy mercy, vouchsafe, O Lord, graciously to assist them with Thy heavenly help, that they may ever diligently serve Thee, and by no temptations be separated from Thee; through Jesus Christ our Lord. Amen.
(*St. Thomas à Kempis*, A.D. 1379.)

FOR ABSENT FRIENDS

O LORD of Love, Who art not far from any of Thy children, watch with Thy care those who are far away from us; be Thou about their path; be Thou within their hearts; be Thou their defence upon their right hand; give them unfailing trust in Thee; grant them power against temptation; qualify them for whatever task Thou givest them to do; deliver them from the snares of setting duty aside; make it their joy to do Thy will. Let not distance break the bonds of love which bind them to us and to Thee, but knit us closer in Thy love; for the sake of Jesus Christ our Lord. Amen.

(Bishop William Boyd Carpenter, A.D. 1841.)

O BLESSED Lord and Saviour, Who hast commanded us to love one another, grant us grace that, having received Thine undeserved bounty, we may love every man in Thee and for Thee. We beseech Thy blessing for all; but especially for the friends whom Thy love hast given to us. Love Thou them, O Thou fountain of love, and make them to love Thee with all their heart, with all their mind, and with all their soul, that those things only which are pleasing to Thee they may will, and speak, and do. And though our prayer is cold, because our charity is so little fervent, yet Thou art rich in mercy. Measure not to them Thy goodness by the dulness of our devotion; but as Thy kindness surpasseth all human affection, so let Thy hearing transcend our prayer. Do Thou to them what is expedient for them, according to Thy will, that they, being always and everywhere ruled and protected by Thee, may attain in the end to everlasting life; and to Thee, with the Father and the Holy Spirit, be all honour and praise for ever and ever. Amen.

(St. Anselm, A.D. 1033.)

B LESS all, O Lord, who are connected with us, especially those who may be in trouble or adversity; helping them to possess their souls in patience, and giving them, if it be Thy will, a happy issue out of trouble; through Jesus Christ our Lord. Amen.

(Professor Knight, Nineteenth Century.)

A LMIGHTY God, Who hast given us the comfortable assurance that Thou art present in every place to hear the prayers of such as fear Thee, and to protect those for whom we pray; we commit all our friends to Thy favour and care; pardon their sins, preserve them from all dangers to body and soul; and grant that we may ever dwell with Thee in Thy glory; through Jesus Christ our Lord. Amen.

(Prebendary Berdmore Compton, Nineteenth Century.)

271

LORD Jesus Christ, our sympathizing Saviour, Who for man didst bear the agony and the Cross, draw Thou near to Thy suffering servants in their pain of body or trouble of mind, *especially* ———. Hallow all their crosses in this life, and crown them hereafter where all tears are wiped away, where with the Father and the Holy Ghost Thou livest and reignest, ever world without end. Amen. *(William Bright, A.D. 1824.)*

O BLESSED Jesus, Who in Thy wise providence, thinkest fit sometimes to call Thy faithful servants to bear their cross of suffering. Bring *him* not to suffer till Thou hast fitted and prepared *him* for it, and lay no more upon *him* than Thou wilt enable *him* to bear. Give *him* patience, and let the graces and comforts of Thy Holy Spirit abound in *him*. Blessed Jesus. Amen. *(Rev. John Kettlewell, A.D. 1653.)*

LORD, behold *he* whom Thou lovest is sick, but come and lay Thine hand upon *him* and *he* shall live. Look, O merciful Lord of life and health, upon our loved one now sick. Renew *his* strength and restore *him* to health, if it be Thy gracious will. Give *him* in the time of bodily weakness the renewal of Thy Spirit, and the upholding power of Thy love; and as all things work together for good to them that love Thee, so do Thou shed abroad in *his* heart Thy love, that out of this weakness *he* may grow stronger in Thee, and in Thy love; for the sake of Jesus Christ our Lord. Amen.

(Bishop W. Boyd Carpenter, A.D. 1841.)

O LORD God, we cry unto Thee in behalf of the child of this family whom Thou hast visited with sickness. To Thee in faith and trust we wholly resign *him*, for from Thee alone come healing and comfort and strength. O Lord, deliver *him* from all fretfulness and impatience, strengthen *him* in weakness, sustain *him* in pain, and soothe *him* in restlessness. If it be Thy good pleasure to spare *his* life, hasten, we beseech Thee, *his* recovery, and bless all means that are used thereto. But, above all, O Thou who didst give Thy life for the sheep, keep ever by Thy side this lamb of Thine own redeeming, that, living or dying, *he* may be Thine; Lord, have mercy upon *him*, support, cheer, and bless *him*, now and evermore. Amen.

(Rev. L. Tuttiett, A.D. 1825.)

O LORD, forasmuch as it is an easy thing with Thee to give life to the dead, restore, we pray Thee, to the sick their former health, and grant that they who seek the healing of Thy heavenly mercy, may also obtain the remedies necessary for the body; through Jesus Christ our Lord. Amen.

(Gothic Missal.)

O HOLY spirit, bless all who have sleepless nights, and grant them patience, and fill their hearts with peace, for Jesus' sake. Amen. *(S. B. Macey, Nineteenth Century.)*

O GOD, Who makest cheerfulness the companion of strength, but apt to take wings in time of sorrow, we humbly beseech Thee that if, in Thy sovereign wisdom, Thou sendest weakness, yet for Thy mercy's sake deny us not the comfort of patience. Lay not more upon us, O heavenly Father, than Thou wilt enable us to bear; and since the fretfulness of our spirits is more hurtful than the heaviness of our burden, grant us that heavenly calmness which comes of owning Thy hand in all things, and patience in the trust That Thou doest all things well; through Jesus Christ. Amen. *(Rev. Rowland Williams, A.D. 1818.)*

MAY Jesus Christ, the King of Glory, help us to make the right use of all the myrrh (*i.e.*, suffering) that God sends, and to offer to Him the true incense of our hearts; for His Name's sake. Amen. *(John Tauler, A.D. 1300.)*

WEARIED by the conflict of life, worn by the burden of the day, we seek Thee as our resting-place. May Thy eternal calm descend upon our troubled spirits and give us all Thy peace. Amid the treacherous sands of time Thou standest still, the Rock of Ages. In life's desert places Thou, O Christ, art a spring whose waters never fail; hear us, we beseech Thee, O Lord Christ. Amen. *(Rev. Dr. Orchard, A.D. 1877.)*

MOST merciful God, the Helper of all men, so strengthen us by Thy power that our sorrow may be turned into joy, and we may continually glorify Thy holy Name; through Jesus Christ our Lord. Amen. *(Sarum Breviary.)*

O JESU, Who hast known what troubles and sorrows are, have compassion upon us in our trouble. Thou Who wast despised and rejected of men; Whose life was sought for of Herod; Who wast tempted by the devil; Who wast hated by the world which Thou camest to save, and set at nought by Thine own people; Who wast called a deceiver and a dealer with the devil; Who wast driven from one place to another, and hadst not where to lay Thy head; Who wast betrayed by one disciple and forsaken by all the rest; wast falsely accused, spitted on and scourged; set at nought by Herod and his men of war; given up by Pilate to the will of the Jews; hadst a murderer preferred before Thee; wast condemned to a most shameful death; crucified betwixt thieves; reviled by those that passed by; hadst gall and vinegar given Thee to drink; and sufferedst a most bitter death, submitting with patience to the will of Thy Father. O Jesu, Who now sittest at the right hand of God, to succour all those who suffer for righteousness' sake, be Thou our advocate with God for grace that in all our sufferings and trials we may follow Thy example, and be supported in all difficulties and discouragements with which God shall see fit to exercise the patience and fidelity of us His servants; for Thine honour and glory. Amen.

(Thomas Wilson, Bishop of Sodor and Man, A.D. 1663.)

OUR God, we desire to bless and praise Thee for Thy unspeakable mercy for restoring *him* who was sick to health. In the time of sickness Thou wast indeed gracious unto us. Thy chastening hand was upon us, but it was a hand of love. Grant that this visitation may never be forgotten by us. May it have left many a blessing behind it. May our future life be marked by more devotedness to our Saviour, more humility, more love, more earnestness of heart and life. O Holy Spirit, deepen Thy work in our souls. Sanctify us wholly, so that we may be more entirely Thine than we have ever been before. Take up Thine abode with us. Comfort us with Thine indwelling Presence. May we live henceforth only to Thy glory; grant this for Jesus Christ's sake. Amen.

(Bishop Ashton Oxenden, A.D. 1808.)

O FATHER of mercies, we thank Thee in behalf of the member of this family whom Thou hast restored to health. We cried unto Thee, and Thou hast healed *him.* We trusted in Thee, and Thou hast helped us. Therefore will we praise Thy Name together. Grant, O Lord, that the life which Thou hast saved may be more entirely devoted to Thy service, and that we may learn to love Thee, and trust in Thee more and more; through Jesus Christ our Lord. Amen.

(Rev. L. Tuttiett, A.D. 1825.)

O ALMIGHTY and merciful God, the Author and Giver of life and health and all good things, we most humbly bless Thee that Thou hast been pleased to deliver from *his* bodily sickness Thy servant. We now desire to return our thanks unto Thee for Thy great mercies vouchsafed to *him.* Impress our hearts with a sense of Thy goodness; and grant us grace to devote our lives to Thy service, walking before Thee in holiness and righteousness all our days; through Jesus Christ our Lord. Amen. *(Family Prayers of the Church of Ireland,* A.D. 1897.)

O MOST merciful Father, we thank Thee for having heard our prayers and hast continued to us Thy gift of the friendship of Thy servant our dear ——. Let (him) yet abide with us awhile, for the strengthening of our faith and joy, and for the furtherance of Thy honour and glory, through Jesus Christ our Lord. Amen. *(Rev. Nicholas Ferrar,* A.D. 1592.)

O GOD, the Father of lights, from Whom cometh down every good and perfect gift; mercifully accept our thanksgivings, and look upon our frailty and infirmity, and grant us such health of body as Thou knowest to be needful for us; that both in body and soul, we may evermore serve Thee with all our strength and might; through Jesus Christ our Lord. Amen. *(Bishop Cosin,* A.D. 1595.)

A DEATH IN THE HOME

WE commend unto Thee all those about to depart this life, beseeching Thee to grant unto them the spirit of tranquillity and trustfulness. May they put their hope in Thee and having passed through the valley of the shadow in peace, may they enter into the rest that remaineth for the people of God; through Jesus Christ our Lord. Amen.

(Professor Knight, Nineteenth Century.)

O GRACIOUS Father, enable us Thy servants to bow before Thee in humble submission to Thy Divine appointment. Draw us, we pray Thee, unto Thyself, that while we mourn the loss of *him* we have so much loved, we may obtain consolation in the fuller knowledge of that love of Thine which at the first provided for us so great an earthly blessing, and is effectual to supply the place of every gift which Thy wisdom removes; and grant us, when this life of trial is ended, to find with *him* who has been taken from us a merciful judgment in the last day and a joyful entrance into Thy glory; through the merits of Jesus Christ our Lord. Amen. *(Rev. R. M. Benson, A.D. 1824.)*

MAY we become as this little child who now follows the Child Jesus, that Lamb of God, in a white robe whithersoever He goes; even so, Lord Jesus. Thou gavest *him* to us, Thou hast taken *him* from us. Blessed be the Name of the Lord. Blessed be our God for ever and ever. Amen. *(John Evelyn, A.D. 1620.)*

GRANT, O Lord, that the soul of our *brother* here departed may rest in Thy peace and protection, and reign in Thy Kingdom in heaven; through the merits and mediation of Jesus Christ Thy Son our Lord. Amen. *(Rev. Martin J. Routh, A.D. 1755.)*

WE remember with thanksgiving, those near and dear to us whom Thou hast taken unto Thyself.

Grant us, like them, to follow Christ unto the end. Grant unto all who have entered upon the path of Thy commandments, neither to look back, nor to err from the way; but hasting to Thee without stumbling, finally to attain eternal blessedness with all Thy saints; through the merits of Thy Son, our Lord Jesus Christ, unto Whom, with Thee, and the Holy Ghost, be the glory and the praise, both now and evermore. Amen.

(Rev. James Ferguson, D.D., A.D. 1873.)

O LORD, by Whom all souls live; we thank Thee for those whom Thy love has called from the life of trial to the life of rest. We trust them to Thy care; we pray Thee that by Thy grace we may be brought to enjoy with them the endless life of glory; through Jesus Christ our Lord. Amen. *(Source not found.)*

NOW, our Lord Jesus Christ Himself, and God, even our Father, which hath loved us and hath given us everlasting consolation and good hope through grace, comfort our hearts and establish us in every good word and work. Amen.

(2 Thess. ii. 16; St. Paul, A.D. First Century.)

NOTE.—See Thursday in 4th Week Evening Prayer, p. 208.

FOR THOSE IN SORROW

HEAVENLY Father, hear our voice out of the deep sorrow which Thou in Thy mysterious wisdom hast brought upon us. We know that Thou art with us, and that whatsoever cometh is a revelation of Thine unchanging love. Thou knowest what is best for us. Thy will be done. Thou gavest and Thou hast taken away, blessed be Thy Name. O keep our souls from all the temptations of this hour of mourning, that we may neither sorrow as those without hope, nor lose our trust in Thee; but that the darker this earthly scene becometh the lighter may be our vision of that eternal world where all live before Thee. And grant that the remnant of this our family, O Lord, still being upon earth, may be steadfast in faith, joyful through hope, and rooted in love, and may so pass the waves of this troublesome world, that finally we may come to the land of everlasting life, there to reign with Thee, world without end; through Jesus Christ our Lord. Amen. *(Rev. L. Tuttiett, A.D. 1825.)*

O LORD, our heavenly Father, without Whom all purposes are frustrate, all efforts are vain, grant us the assistance of the Holy Spirit, that we may not sorrow as those without hope, but may now return to the duties of our present life with humble confidence in Thy protection, and so govern our thoughts and actions that no business or work may ever withdraw our minds from Thee, but that in the changes of this life we may fix our hearts upon the reward which Thou hast promised to them that serve Thee, and that whatsoever things are true, whatsoever things are honest, whatsoever things are just, whatsoever things are pure, whatsoever things are lovely, whatsoever things are of good report, wherein there is virtue, wherein there is praise, we may think upon and do, and obtain mercy, consolation, and everlasting happiness. Grant this, O Lord, for the sake of Jesus Christ. Amen. *(Dr. S. Johnson, A.D. 1709.)*

LORD, do not permit our trials to be above our strength; and do Thou vouchsafe to be our strength and comfort in the time of trial. Give us grace to take in good part whatever shall befall us, and let our hearts acknowledge it to be the Lord's doing, and to come from Thy Providence, and not by chance. May we receive everything from Thy hand with patience and with joy; through Jesus Christ our Lord. Amen.
(Bishop Thomas Wilson, A.D. 1663.)

LET the cry of widows, orphans, and destitute children enter into Thine ears, O most loving Saviour. Comfort them with a mother's tenderness, shield them from the perils of this world, and bring them at last to Thy heavenly home. Amen.
(Bishop Cosin, A.D. 1595.)

NEW YEAR'S EVE

ALMIGHTY and most merciful Father, Who hast given us grace in times past, and hast mercifully brought us to see the end of another year, grant that we may continue to grow in grace and in the knowledge of Thy dear Son. Lead us forward by Thy Spirit from strength to strength, that we may more perfectly serve Thee, and attain a more lively hope of Thy mercy in Christ Jesus. Quicken our dull hearts, inspire us with warmer affections for Thee, O God, and for Thy heavenly Truth. Stir up the gift that is in us, and pour down from above more abundant gifts of grace, that we may make progress in heavenly things. Increase our faith as Thou dost increase our years, and the longer we are suffered to abide on earth, the better may our service be, the more willing our obedience, the more consistent our daily lives, the more complete our devotion to Thee. Grant this our prayer, O gracious Father, which we humbly offer at the throne of grace, in the name and for the sake of Jesus Christ Thy Son, our Lord and Saviour. Amen.

(Tracts for Christian Seasons, Nineteenth Century.)

IF we have found favour in Thy sight, show us now Thy ways, that we may know Thee; but if Thy Presence go not with us, carry us not up hence. O Lord Jehovah, show Thy servants Thy greatness and Thy strong hand.

(Moses; Fifteenth Century B.C; Exod. xxxiii.; Deut. iii.)

O LORD, our only Saviour, we cannot bear alone our load of responsibility; up-bear us under it. We look without seeing unless Thou purge our sight; grant us sight. We read without comprehending, unless Thou open our understanding; give us intelligence. Nothing can we do unless Thou prosper the work of our hands upon us; "O prosper Thou our handiwork." We are weak; out of weakness make us strong. We are in peril of death; come and heal us. We believe; help Thou our unbelief. We hope; let us not be disappointed of our hope. We love; grant us to love much, to love ever more and more, to love all and most of all to love Thee. Grant this, we humbly beseech Thee, for the sake of Christ Jesus our Lord. Amen.

(Christina G. Rossetti, A.D. 1830.)

LET us be diligent in Thy service, O Lord, day by day. Let all labour be our delight, which is for Thee; and all rest weary us which is not in Thee; and may every undertaking be begun, continued, and ended in Thee; to the glory of Thy holy Name. Amen. *(Hon. Mrs. Lyttelton Gell, Nineteenth Century.)*

O THOU Who art ever the same, grant us so to pass through the coming year with faithful hearts, that we may be able in all things to please Thy loving eyes; through Jesus Christ our Lord. Amen. *(Mozarabic Liturgy.)*

MOST gracious God, Who hast been infinitely merciful to us, not only in the year past, but through all the years of our life, be pleased to accept our most unfeigned thanks for Thine innumerable blessings to us; graciously pardoning the manifold sins and infirmities of our life past, and bountifully bestowing upon us all those graces and virtues which may render us acceptable to Thee. And every year which Thou shalt be pleased to add to our lives, add also, we humbly implore Thee, more strength to our faith, more ardour to our love, and a greater perfection to our obedience; and grant that, in a humble sincerity and constant perseverance, we may serve Thee most faithfully the remainder of our lives; for Christ's sake. Amen.

(Charles How, A.D. 1661.)

WE render unto Thee our thanksgiving, O Lord our God, Father of our Lord and Saviour Jesus Christ, by all means, at all times, in all places. For that Thou hast sheltered, assisted, supported, and led us on through the time past of our life, and brought us to this hour. And we pray and beseech Thee, O God and loving Lord, grant us to pass this day, this year, and all the time of our life without sin, with all joy, health, and salvation. But all envy, all fear, all temptation, all the working of Satan, do Thou drive away, O God, from us, and from Thy holy Church. Supply us with things good and profitable. Whereinsoever we have sinned against Thee, in word, or deed, or thought, be Thou pleased in Thy love and goodness to forgive, and forsake us not, O God, who hope in Thee, neither lead us into temptation, but deliver us from the evil one and from his works; by the grace and compassion of Thine only begotten Son, Jesus Christ. Amen.

(Liturgy of St. Mark.)

ALMIGHTY God, have mercy upon us, who, when troubled with the things that are past lose faith, and life, and courage, and hope. So have mercy upon us, and uphold us, that we, being sustained by a true faith that Thou art merciful and forgiving, may go on in the life of the future to keep Thy commandments, to rejoice in Thy bounty, to trust in Thy mercy, and to hope in the eternal life. Grant unto all of us, whatsoever may betide us, to remember ever, that it is all of Thy guidance, under Thy care, by Thy will; that so, in darkest days, beholding Thee, we may have courage to go on, faith to endure, patience to bear, and hopefulness to hold out, even unto the end; through Jesus Christ. Amen. *(Rev. George Dawson, A.D. 1821.)*

O GOD of time and eternity, Who makest us creatures of time, to the end that when time is over we may attain to Thy blessed eternity. With time, which is Thy gift, give us also wisdom to redeem the time lest our day of grace be lost, for the sake of Christ Jesus our Lord. Amen.

(Christina G. Rossetti, A.D. 1830.)

HARVEST THANKSGIVING

O ALMIGHTY God and Heavenly Father, we glorify Thee that Thou hast again fulfilled to us Thy gracious promise, that while the earth remaineth, seed-time and harvest shall not fail. We bless Thee for the kindly fruits of the earth, which Thou hast given to our use. Teach us, we beseech Thee, to remember that it is not by bread alone that man doth live, and grant us evermore to feed on Him Who is the true Bread from heaven, even Jesus Christ our Lord, to Whom with Thee, and the Holy Ghost, be all honour and glory, world without end. Amen.

(Prayer Book of the Church of Ireland, A.D. 1877.)

ALMIGHTY God, Who givest to all life and breath and all things, and bringest forth food out of the earth for the use of man, keep us ever in mind that this world, with all the glory of it, fadeth, and the fashion thereof passeth away. Grant that we may so use the fruits of the ground which Thou hast now given us, and all other Thy temporal blessings wherewith Thou crownest the year, as we abuse them not, but may evermore serve Thee in Christian temperance and sobriety, as it becometh those who, living on earth, have their conversation (citizenship) in heaven, that at the last we may be admitted into Thy heavenly Kingdom, where we shall never hunger nor thirst again, being satisfied with the plenteousness of Thy house, and filled with the abundance of Thy pleasures for evermore; grant this, O heavenly Father, for Jesus Christ's sake, our Lord. Amen.

(Bishop Cosin, A.D. 1595.)

O HEAVENLY Father, Which art the fountain and full treasure of all goodness, we beseech Thee to show Thy mercies upon us Thy children, and sanctify these gifts which we receive of Thy merciful liberality, granting us grace to use them soberly and purely, according to Thy blessed will, so that hereby we may acknowledge Thee to be the Author and Giver of all good things, and above all, that we may remember continually to seek the spiritual food of Thy Word, wherewith our souls may be nourished everlastingly; through our Saviour Christ, Who is the true Bread of life which came down from heaven, of Whom whosoever eateth shall live for ever, and reign with Him in glory, world without end. Amen. *(Christian Prayers, A.D. 1566.)*

THE eyes of all things do look up and trust in Thee, O Lord. Thou givest them their meat in due season, Thou dost open Thy hand and fillest with Thy blessing everything living. Good Lord, bless us and all Thy gifts, which we receive of Thy bounteous liberality; through Jesus Christ our Lord. Amen.

(Queen Elizabeth's Primer, A.D. 1558.)

FOR FRUITFUL SEASONS AND FAVOURABLE WEATHER

O LORD God, Whose mighty word all things in heaven and earth obey, we confess that Thou art justly displeased with us, and that our sins have withholden good things from us. Turn again, O Lord of Hosts, and visit us with Thy mercy. Grant us now such weather that the labours of harvest may not be hindered, nor the fruits of the earth fail. And give us all grace seriously to lay to heart Thy judgments, that we may truly repent of our sins and seek to live holier lives to Thy honour and glory; through Jesus Christ our Lord and Saviour. Amen.

(Rev. L. Tuttiett, A.D. 1825.)

THOU God of Providence, grant to farmers and keepers of cattle good seasons; to the fleet and fishers fair weather; to tradesmen not to overreach one another; to mechanics to pursue their business lawfully, even down to the meanest workman, even down to the poor; for Christ's sake. Amen.

(Bishop Lancelot Andrewes, A.D. 1555.)

ALMIGHTY God, Lord of heaven and earth, in Whom we live and move and have our being, Who doest good unto all men, making Thy sun to rise on the evil, and on the good, and sending rain on the just and on the unjust, favourably behold us, Thy servants, who call upon Thy Name, and send us Thy blessing from heaven, giving us fruitful seasons, and filling our hearts with food and gladness, that both our hearts and mouths may be continually filled with Thy praise, giving thanks to Thee in Thy holy Church; through Jesus Christ our Lord. Amen.

(Bishop Cosin, A.D. 1595.)

BLESS this year for us, O our God, and bless every species of its fruits for our benefit. Bestow a blessing upon the face of the earth, and satisfy us with Thy goodness. O bless our years, and make them good years; for Thine honour and glory. Amen.

(Polish Jewish Prayer Book, Jewish Calendar, 5671.)

ALMIGHTY God, Who hast blessed the earth that it should be fruitful and bring forth everything necessary for the life of man, and hast commanded us to work with quietness and eat our own bread; bless us in all our labours, and grant us such seasonable weather that we may gather in the fruits of the earth, and ever rejoice in Thy goodness, to the praise of Thy holy Name; through Jesus Christ our Lord. Amen.

(American Prayer Book, A.D. 1789.)

FOR BLESSING ON NEW ENTERPRISES

LORD, we desire to place ourselves and what we are about to undertake in Thy hands. Guide, direct, and prosper us, we beseech Thee; and if Thou seest that this undertaking will be for Thy glory, grant us good success. Make us and those who act with us to feel that, unless Thy blessing is with us, we cannot succeed, and that, except the Lord build the house, their labour is but lost that build it. Prevent us, then, O Lord, in this and all our doings with Thy most gracious favour, and further us with Thy continual help, that in all our works begun, continued, and ended in Thee, we may glorify Thy Name; through Jesus Christ. Amen. *(Bishop Ashton Oxenden, A.D. 1808.)*

O LORD, Who by Thy holy Apostle hast taught us to do all things in the Name of the Lord Jesus and to Thy glory; give Thy blessing, we pray Thee, to this our work, that we may do it in faith, and heartily, as to the Lord, and not unto men. All our powers of body and mind are Thine, and we would fain devote them to Thy service. Sanctify them and the work in which we are engaged; let us not be slothful, but fervent in spirit, and do Thou, O Lord, so bless our efforts that they may bring forth in us the fruit of true wisdom. Strengthen the faculties of our minds, and dispose us to exert them for Thy glory and for the furtherance of Thy Kingdom. Save us from all pride and vanity and reliance upon our own power or wisdom. Teach us to seek after truth, and enable us to gain it; while we know earthly things may we know Thee, and be known by Thee through and in Thy Son Jesus Christ, that we may be Thine in body and spirit, in all our work and undertakings; through Jesus Christ. Amen. *(Dr. Arnold, A.D. 1795.)*

TEACH us, O gracious Lord, to begin our works with fear, to go on with obedience, and to finish them in love, and then to wait patiently in hope, and with cheerful confidence to look up to Thee, Whose promises are faithful and rewards infinite; through Jesus Christ. Amen. *(Bishop George Hickes, A.D. 1642.)*

ALMIGHTY God, the Giver of wisdom, without Whose help resolutions are vain, without Whose blessing study is ineffectual, enable us, if it be Thy will, to attain such knowledge as may qualify us to direct the doubtful, and terminate contentions. And grant that we may use that knowledge which we shall attain, to Thy glory and our own salvation; for the sake of Jesus Christ our Lord. Amen. *(Dr. S. Johnson, A.D. 1709.)*

OUR God and Father Himself, and our Lord Jesus Christ, direct our ways; and the Lord make us to increase and abound in love one toward another, and toward all men, to the end that He may establish our hearts unblameable in holiness before God, even our Father, at the coming of our Lord Jesus Christ with all His saints. Amen. *(S. Paul, First Century A.D.; 1 Thess. iii. 11–13.)*

BEFORE AND AFTER THE STUDY OF GOD'S WORD

O LORD, Thy Word is before us, give us a meek, and reverent, and teachable mind, whilst we read and study it. Open to us its sacred truths, and enable us to receive it, not as the word of men, but as the Word of God, which liveth and abideth for ever. Be Thou, O Blessed Spirit, our teacher. Enlighten our minds and prepare our hearts. Shine, O Lord, upon Thine own sacred page, and make it clear to us. What we see not show us, and where we are wrong correct us. Bring home some portion to our soul, and thus make us wise unto salvation; through Jesus Christ our Saviour. Amen.

(Ashton Oxenden, Bishop of Montreal, A.D. 1808.)

O LORD Jesus Christ, Who art the Truth Incarnate, and the Teacher of the faithful, let Thy Spirit overshadow us in reading Thy Word, and conform our thoughts to Thy Revelation, that, learning of Thee with honest hearts, we may be rooted and built up in Thee, Who livest and reignest with the Father, ever One God, world without end. Amen.

(William Bright, A.D. 1824.)

LORD, give us a heart to turn all knowledge to Thy glory, and not to our own. Keep us from being deluded with the lights of vain philosophies; keep us from the pride of human reason; let us not think our own thoughts, nor dream our own imaginations, but in all things acting under the good guidance of the Holy Spirit, may we find Thee everywhere, and live in all simplicity, humility, and singleness of heart unto the Lord. Amen. *(Henry Kirke White, A.D. 1785.)*

IN times of doubts and questionings, when our belief is perplexed by new learning, new teaching, new thought, when our faith is strained by creeds, by doctrines, by mysteries beyond our understanding, give us the faithfulness of learners and the courage of believers in Thee; give us boldness to examine, and faith to trust all truth; patience and insight to master difficulties; stability to hold fast our traditions with enlightened interpretations, to admit all fresh truth made known to us, and in times of trouble to grasp new knowledge and to combine it loyally and honestly with the old. Save us and help us, we humbly beseech Thee, O Lord. Amen.

(Bishop Ridding, A.D. 1828.)

O THOU Who art the everlasting Essence of things beyond space and time and yet within them; Thou Who transcendest yet pervadest all things, manifest Thyself unto us, feeling after Thee, seeking Thee in the shades of ignorance. Stretch forth Thy hand to help us, who cannot without Thee come to Thee; and reveal Thyself unto us, who seek nothing beside Thee; through Jesus Christ our Lord. Amen.

(John Scotus Erigena A.D. 813.)

FOR GUIDANCE

O GOD, for Jesus Christ's sake give us Thy Holy Spirit.
(Catherine Marsh, A.D. 1818.)

O GOD, by Whom the meek are guided in judgment, and light riseth up in darkness for the godly; grant us, in all our doubts and uncertainties, the grace to ask what Thou wouldst have us to do, that the spirit of wisdom may save us from all false choices, and that in Thy light we may see light, and in Thy straight path may not stumble; through Jesus Christ our Lord. Amen.
(William Bright, A.D. 1824.)

GOD, Who as at this time didst teach the hearts of Thy faithful people by the sending to them the light of Thy Holy Spirit, grant us by the same Spirit to have a right judgment in all things, and evermore to rejoice in His holy comfort; through the merits of Christ Jesus our Saviour, Who liveth and reigneth with Thee in the unity of the same Spirit, one God, world without end. Amen.
(Gregorian Sacramentary; Book of Common Prayer, A.D. 1549.)

ALMIGHTY and most merciful God, as we need Thy help, illumination, and guidance, grant these things unto us, we beseech Thee; that so we may attain unto a fuller knowledge of Thy will, that we may increase in spiritual wisdom, and being inwardly strengthened with all might, may work patiently unto the end, through Jesus Christ our Lord. Amen.
(Professor Knight, Nineteenth Century.)

VOUCHSAFE unto us clear and distinct perceptions of things, for Christ's sake. Amen. *(W. Wollaston, A.D. 1660.)*

BLESSED are all Thy Saints, O God and King, who have travelled over the tempestuous sea of this mortal life, and have made the harbour of peace and felicity.

Watch over us who are still in our dangerous voyage; and remember such as lie exposed to the rough storms of trouble and temptations.

Frail is our vessel, and the ocean is wide; but as in Thy mercy Thou hast set our course, so steer the vessel of our life toward the everlasting shore of peace, and bring us at length to the quiet haven of our heart's desire, where Thou, O our God, are blessed, and livest and reignest for ever and ever. Amen.
(St. Augustine, A.D. 354.)

GRANT us, O Lord, to know that which is worth knowing, to love that which is worth loving, to praise that which pleaseth Thee most, to esteem that highly which to Thee is precious. Give us the right judgment to discern between things visible and spiritual, and above all, to seek after the good pleasure of Thy will; through Jesus Christ Thy Son. Amen.
(Ladies' College, Cheltenham, Nineteenth Century.)

IN Thee would we lose ourselves utterly; do in us what Thou wilt. *(Jakob Boehme, A.D. 1575.)*

MISCELLANEOUS PRAYERS AND INTERCESSIONS

For a Deeper Sense of God's Presence.

O LORD God and Father, Thou knowest how blind we are to Thy presence, how dead to Thy purpose and deaf to Thy call, grant us to feel Thy guiding hand through all the scattered details of our daily life, in all the tumult to hear Thy still small voice, and in all dimness of our spirits to have a sense of Thine everlasting arms upbearing us, so that, being willing to spend and be spent in Thy service, we may accomplish all that Thou wouldest have us do, and at the last find fulfilment in the perfect freedom of Thy sole sovereignty, through Jesus Christ Thy Son our Lord. Amen.

The Hallowing of Work.

O BLESSED Lord, Who by the example of Thy work at Nazareth hast sanctified our daily toil, and by Thy teaching hast revealed the sympathy of God in our common task, grant that in the midst of our work we may find rest and peace in Thy presence and may take joy in all that ministers to Thy service, Who art ever our Refuge, our Strength and our exceeding great Reward. Amen.

For Daily Needs.

THOU knowest, O heavenly Father, the duties that lie before us this day, the dangers that may confront us, the sins that most beset us. Guide us—strengthen us—protect us. Give us Thy Life in such abundance that we may go on from strength to strength. Give us Thy Power that we may become a power for righteousness among our fellow men. Give us Thy Love that all lesser things may have no attraction for us. Let us find Thy Power, Thy Love, Thy Life in all mankind and thus may we know Thee our Father in Heaven. Amen.

Reprisals.

HELP us, O Divine Lord of Life, to train our hearts, as servants of God, to mercy, kindness, humbleness of mind, long-suffering, forbearance, and gentleness. Give us the largeness and depth of character whereby we may forgive one another if any man have a quarrel against us, even as God, for Christ's sake, forgives us, so help us to forgive others. And above all things, give us love, which is the bond of perfectness, and may the peace of God dwell in our hearts, through Jesus Christ our Lord. Amen.

Strength for Duty.

GIVE us now, O merciful Father, Thy Holy Spirit, that we may be strengthened for the work of this day, through Jesus Christ Thy Son our Lord. Amen. (*Father John of Cronstadt.*)

Guidance in Committee Meetings.

RULE over our deliberations we beseech Thee, O Lord; Direct us by Thy Holy Spirit, and sanctify us by Thy Presence, O Lord Christ. Amen. (*B.M.M.*, A.D. 1904.)

MISCELLANEOUS PRAYERS AND INTERCESSIONS

For Those amongst Whom we Live.

O MAKER of us men, Who hast set us in no strange land, but surrounded our life with familiar things and well-known faces, we pray for all those amongst whom we live, our neighbours and acquaintances and those amongst whom we work. We commit them all to Thy favour and care; preserve them from all dangers of body and soul, pardon all our sins, and grant that we and they may ever dwell with Thee; through Jesus Christ our Lord. Amen.

(J. Leslie Johnston, Twentieth Century.)

For our Friends and Others.

MAY Thy Spirit hallow, and Thy Grace fortify, O blessed Lord, friends and others for whom we would seek Thine aid: those of closest tie, those of greatest need.

May Thy Divine Power protect and provide for them. May Thy Peace comfort them. May Thy Pardon reassure them, and Thy precious Blood redeem them. May Thy prosperity attend them. May daily progress be theirs in the heavenly way; through Christ Jesus our Lord. Amen.

An Intercession For all Men.

ALMIGHTY God, our Heavenly Father, Who lovest all and forgettest none, we bring to Thee our supplications for all Thy creatures and all Thy children. For all whom we love and for whom we watch and care. For all who have blessed us with kindness and led us with patience, restored us with their sympathy and help.

We remember before Thee all on whom Thou hast laid the cross of suffering, the sick in body and the weak in mind. All who have been bereaved of relations or friends, all who are troubled by the suffering or sin of those they love; all who have met with worldly loss, that in the dark and cloudy day they may find assurance and peace in Thee. We pray for all who are absorbed in their own grief, that they may be raised to share the sorrows of their brethren, and know the secret and blessed fellowship of the Cross. For all who are lonely and sad in the midst of others' joys, that they may know God as their Friend and Comforter. Remember, O Lord, the aged and infirm, all who are growing weary with the journey of life, all who are passing through the valley of shadows, that they may find that Christ the risen of the dead is with them, and that there is light at evening time.

O God our Father, hear our intercessions, answer them according to Thy will, and make us the channels of Thine infinite pity and love, for the sake of Jesus Christ Thy Son our Saviour and Redeemer. Amen. *(Rev. Dr. John Hunter, A.D. 1849.)*

For Unity.

O GOD of peace, Who through Thy Son Jesus Christ didst send forth one faith for the salvation of mankind, send Thy grace and heavenly blessing upon all Christian people who are striving to draw nearer to Thee and to each other, in the unity of the spirit and in the bond of peace. Give us penitence for our divisions, wisdom to know Thy Truth, courage to do Thy will, love which shall break down the barriers of pride and prejudice, and an unswerving loyalty to Thy holy Name. Suffer us not to shrink from any endeavour, which is in accordance with Thy will, for the peace and unity of Thy Church. Give us boldness to seek only Thy glory and the advancement of Thy Kingdom. Unite us all in Thee as Thou O Father with Thy Son and the Holy Ghost, art one God, world without end. Amen.

(Bishop Anderson, Nineteenth Century.)

Prayer for the New Era.

O LORD Jesus Christ, Son of God the Father, Who hast redeemed us by Thy blood, the fountain of peace, and source of pure love, grant, we beseech Thee, that God may be exalted in this new age, that He may be the First and the Last, the Beginning and the End of all our thoughts, plans, and actions. Let the love of God be spread abroad in all hearts, kindling the fire of true religion. May the Church of God be filled with the one spirit, united, and uniting men in the one Body, able with great power to give its witness and draw the world to Thee. Fill all men and women with the ardour of true service, that they may look not to their own things but to the things of others and live by Thy example, Who didst not please Thyself but came, not to be ministered unto, but to minister, and wentest about doing good. Draw, attract, arouse, constrain all men in all nations to come unto Thee and be saved and grant them in Thy light to see light.

Bind together all classes and professions in the State, teaching each and all to do loyally and honourably the work that Thou hast assigned, that they may regard themselves as members of one great family, working together for the good of all and growing into unity of affection.

Purify the world till it becomes Thy Kingdom, knowing no King but Thee, obeying no law but Thy law, and moving with the consent of every will in the accomplishment of Thy will, to the glory of Thy great Name. Amen.

(Adapted from a form of Prayer authorized in India.)

For Social Stability.

O THOU Who hast ordained love to be the bond and basis of true life, so fill Thy Church with love towards mankind, that by Thy light, all men and nations may walk in sacred fellowship, and in secure and righteous peace; through Jesus Christ our Lord. Amen. *(Rev. E. A. L. Clarke, Twentieth Century.)*

MISCELLANEOUS PRAYERS AND INTERCESSIONS
For All Mankind.

O ALMIGHTY and most merciful God, in the name of Jesus Christ Thy Son, our Redeemer, we would pray Thee for all men everywhere. That Thou wouldest have mercy upon Thy Church throughout the world so as it may be cleansed, defended, perfected in Thee. That with sanctity of life and spiritual might, those who minister Thy gifts may unweariedly convey Thy grace to human need: upon those in adversity—those who suffer wrongfully—upon those who are in any grief or pain— upon the fearful and the anxious—upon the tempted and the despairing—upon those stricken by worldly misfortune—the widow and the fatherless children, the destitute and down-trodden—upon the helpless and the weak, the deceived and the embittered, the wayward and the erring—upon the overworked and weary, the unemployed and careworn—upon this realm in every estate that it may prosper in Thy righteousness, and be ordered after Thy will. We beseech Thee Almighty God, for Christ Thy Son our Saviour's sake, to have mercy upon all; to pity and pardon all, to assist and protect all, to guide and quicken all, to ransom and perfect us all for Thine own glory; by way of the Cross and through the same Thy Son Jesus Christ our Lord. Amen. *(Adapted from The People's Missal, Rev. E. A. L. Clarke, Twentieth Century.)*

Prayer for King and Empire.

O ALMIGHTY God, Who rulest over all the earth, and guidest the affairs of men, we humbly beseech Thee to govern and bless all connected with our land and nation. We pray for our King, Queen, and all the members of the Royal Family. We pray for the Prime Minister, the Cabinet, and Ministers of State, that Thy wisdom may be their guide in foreign and domestic policy, for the maintenance of high principle, and the advancement of justice, truth, holiness, peace, and love. We pray for the Legislature, both the Lords and Commons, that Thou wilt direct and prosper their deliberations to the advancement of Thy glory and the welfare of the realm, giving them freedom from party spirit and a hearty desire for the good of their country. We pray especially for all Christian members of Parliament that they may not be ashamed to confess the faith of Christ crucified, but may speak out and vote manfully on the side of righteousness. We also pray for the Bishops in the House of Lords, that they may show themselves in all things an example of good works to others; and finally we pray that all righteous reforms may be pressed forward and passed by Parliament, and that all Thy Christian people may learn to pray more earnestly for Thy guidance in all political matters, and that all things may be done with a single eye to Thy glory, through Jesus Christ our Lord. Amen.

(Lady Margaret Hall, Lambeth, A.D. 1902.)

FOR GUIDANCE IN INDUSTRIAL PROBLEMS

O GOD, help us to know and believe in Thee as our Father, and ourselves as Thy children.

O Saviour Christ, Thou Who art the Son of the Father, draw us the heavy-laden to Thee, that we may learn the depth of Thy love and the need of our own redemption.

O Holy Spirit, come as the fire into our hearts, that we may be purified from wickedness and may be aflame with zeal for the service of God and our fellow men.

O God of Love, fill us with Thine own Self and help us all to face the difficulties and injustices of human life in the spirit of Christ crucified for others.

Lift up Thine hand and help us to be mindful of the needs of others. Give us the will and the strength to arise in Thy great might and to maintain Thine own cause by seeing that all who are in need and necessity have right, and that the many who are defenceless before organized tyranny, whether from employers or employed, may be treated with justice and consideration; through Jesus Christ Thy Son our Lord. Amen.

(Adapted from Litany of Christian Industry.)

ALMIGHTY God, our heavenly Father, bless our Country and Empire that it may be a blessing to the world; grant that our ideals and aspirations may be in accordance with Thy will, and help us to set Thee ever before us. Keep us from hypocrisy in feeling or action. Grant us sound government and just laws, good education, a clean press, simplicity and justice in our relations one with another, and above all a spirit of service which will abolish all pride of place and inequality of opportunity; through Jesus Christ our Lord. Amen.

O GOD, Who dost command all hearts, and dost teach the joys of obedience and of self-denial for others' sake, deliver us in this our realm and our brethren in other realms, from the dangers, or the presence of anarchy and social upheaval. Guide the minds of all classes to a fuller realization of interdependence and brotherhood, and give victory to Thy law of love and consideration between man and man; through Him Who sacrificed Himself for us, even Jesus Christ our Lord. Amen.

O GOD our Father, Whose will is our satisfaction, grant we beseech Thee, that we as a people may found our policy in both social and international relations upon Thy eternal laws of love, brotherhood, and right. Remove from us all pride, self-seeking, and a desire of unfair gain. Grant that labour may be done honestly as in Thy sight and rewarded justly as before Thee our Judge. Create a new spirit of mutual confidence between nations, classes and individuals, that with clean hands and hearts, we may dwell together in unity and brotherhood, through Him Who is One with Thee and with us, even Jesus Christ Thy Son our Lord. Amen.

FOR GUIDANCE IN INDUSTRIAL PROBLEMS
The Realm and Empire.

O GOD our Heavenly Father, we remember before Thee all estates of this Realm, all men, women and children of this Commonwealth of Nations. Grant, O God, that this Empire may be ruled in Thy faith, fear and love. That our king may be directed by Thy Holy Spirit and upheld by Thy Divine power. May our people everywhere be taught and inspired by Thy laws. Bless all who take up the Cross, and battle for the right. May Thy love shed abroad break down every barrier that separates man from man, and man from God. We humbly pray Thee that Thy Spirit of goodwill and brotherhood may abound amongst us, until at last we come in the Unity of the one Spirit to worship Thee, the One and only God, through Jesus Christ Thy Son our Lord. Amen.   (*Contributed* A.D. 1941.)

CREATOR and Ruler of mankind, we pray Thee this day for our country, that her new life may be established and built up in Thyself, that all hatred and malice, all indifference to the sufferings of others, all narrow exclusiveness and selfish greed, may be swept away by the breath of Thy Spirit, and that public spirit, honour and justice, co-operation in service, self-sacrifice for the good of the whole people, may flourish abundantly amongst us. Purify us from all baseness, fill us with Thy divine passion to uplift the weak, to sweep away oppression and wrong, to give to every man even to the lowest and most degraded, the opportunity of a full life that may be lived to Thy glory and to the service of mankind; through Jesus Christ Thy Son our Lord. Amen.

ALMIGHTY and Everlasting God, we humbly beseech Thee to help us in these times of anxiety, and overrule all the unrest that is prevalent in the Industrial world. Defeat all selfish aims, that each may labour for the good of all. Grant to all men a wide outlook and a strong faith in Thy Son Jesus Christ. Bless, we pray Thee, all conferences between employers and workers, and guide all in authority by Thy Holy Spirit that all things may be ordered according to Thy will, for the well-being of our people and the prosperity of our country, through Jesus Christ our Lord. Amen. (*Rev. A. Wilkinson Markby.*)

O GOD, Thou mightiest Worker of the universe, Source of all strength and Author of all unity, we pray Thee for our brothers the industrial workers of the nation. As their work binds them together in toil and danger, may their hearts be knit together in a strong sense of their common interests and so fulfil the law of Christ by bearing the common burdens. Grant the organizations of labour quiet patience and prudence in all disputes. Raise up leaders of able mind and large heart, and give them grace to follow wise counsel. Bless all classes of our nation and build up a great body of workers strong of limb, clear of mind, glad to labour, striving together for the final Brotherhood of all men; through Jesus Christ our Lord. Amen.
(*W. Rauchsenbusch, Twentieth Century.*)

ALMIGHTY and Eternal God, glorious in holiness and power, we thank and praise Thy holy Name for all the manifold wonders of Thy grace with which Thou hast enriched our lives. For the fellowship of Thy Holy Spirit, for all the ministrations of Thy holy Church, for the revelation of Thy Holy Word, for the souls of men sustained in suffering and redeemed from sin, and for all Thy miracles of love and power. Marvellous are Thy works, Thy mercy is greater than the heavens, Thy truth reacheth unto the clouds, Thou art great and doest wondrous things, Thou O God art God alone. We give thanks and praise unto Thee, O Lord our God, with all our hearts, through Jesus Christ Thy Son our Lord. Amen. *(Rev. F. W. Drake, 19th Cent.)*

ALL glory, thanks, and praise be to Thee, O Lord our God and Saviour, for those who take up their cross and follow bravely after Thee. For those who tread the way of sorrow in the calm of faith. For those who battle for the right, in Thy strength. For those who bear physical pain with sweet and sanctifying grace. For those who endure petty slights forgivingly. For those who rise above still greater wrongs. For those who continue their duties conscientiously whether so recognized or not. For those, who by Thy heavenly wisdom are enabled to teach the way of life. For those who tend Thy flock with diligent care. For those who love others unselfishly in Thee. All glory be to Thee O Lord most high. Amen.

(Rev. E. A. L. Clarke, Twentieth Century.)

O GOD, I thank Thee for my life—I thank Thee for my body, for the strength of my limbs, and for my mind. I thank Thee for my Soul—for the perception that feels Thee near to me, and knows that my body is even now the temple of Thy Holy Spirit. I thank Thee for my surroundings, for the fresh air and the sweet earth, and the love of friends. I thank Thee also for my pains and difficulties both of body and soul, because they are the means whereby I shall attain to a clearer light and truer understanding. And above all, I thank Thee for the life and death of Thy holy Son, Jesus Christ, through Whom by Thy power we are brought to peace everlasting. Amen.

ALMIGHTY God, Who above all Thy gifts hast given the crowning mercy that we are called to know, and love, and serve Thee in Jesus Christ; we render thanks and praise unto Thee for Him, the Light of light, Who reveals the heart of Thy grace. Help us to rise to a fit gratitude for the overflowing blessings which Thou dost ever mingle even in the darkest lot: the temporal felicities, the Divine comforts, the Eternal hopes. That all things are of Thy mercy and by Thy mercy, we thank Thee. Make us to sing Thy song in the daytime, and in the night to touch Thy hand and be at peace. Grant us, we pray Thee, with all other blessings, thankful and trustful hearts, that Thou mayest be our Lord and King for evermore. Amen. *(Rev. H. W. Foote, D. 1889.)*

THOU hast given so much to us, give one thing more, a grateful heart; for Christ's sake. Amen. (*George Herbert*, A.D. 1593.)

WE thank Thee, O Lord our Lord, for our being, our life, our gift of reason; for our nurture, our preservation and guidance; for our education, civil rights and religious privileges; for Thy gifts of grace, of nature, of this world; for our redemption, regeneration, and instruction in the Christian Faith; for our calling, recalling, and our manifold renewed recallings for Thy forbearance and long suffering. Thy prolonged forbearance many a time and many a year. For all the benefits we have received, and all the undertakings wherein we have prospered; for any good we may have done; for the use of the blessing of this life; for Thy promise, and our hope of the enjoyment of good things to come; for good and honest parents, gentle teachers, benefactors ever to be remembered, congenial companions, intelligent hearers, sincere friends, faithful servants; for all who have profited us by their writings, sermons, conversations, prayers, examples, reproofs, injuries. For all these, and also for all other mercies, known and unknown, open and secret, remembered by us or now forgotten, kindnesses received by us willingly or even against our will. We praise Thee, we bless Thee, we thank Thee, and will praise and bless and thank Thee all the days of our life; through Jesus Christ our Lord. Amen.
(*Bishop Lancelot Andrewes*, A.D. 1555.)

WE praise Thee and thank Thee, O Lord our God, for all that Thou hast done for us in the time that is past. We thank Thee for Thy love to us, for the gift of Thy Son to be our Saviour and Redeemer, and for the gift of the Holy Spirit to lead our thoughts to Thee and to direct our way through life. We praise and thank Thee for all the innumerable blessings that Thou hast showered upon us, and we rejoice in the calm assurance of Thy presence, and in every measure of attainment that Thou hast granted. We rejoice, O Lord, in Thee who art the giver of life and light, accept our thanksgiving and our praise for all that Thou hast done, and make us worthy of Thy Service. Through Jesus Christ our Lord who with Thee and the Holy Spirit, liveth and reigneth now and for ever more. Amen. (*Twentieth Century*.)

HONOUR and glorie Vnto the Father bee:
    And to his Sonne Quhilk is in heuin sahie,
And right also Vnto the holie Spreit,
Of troubled heartes the Comforter most svveit.
As it vvas euer Before in the beginning,
Is novv, and shall Be Warld without ending.
(*Ancient Scottish Prayers*, A.D. 1595.)

BENEDICTIONS

THE Lord bless us and keep us. The Spirit of the Lord cleanse and purify our inmost hearts, and enable us to shun all evil. The Lord enlighten our understandings and cause the Light of His Truth to shine into our hearts. The Lord fill us with faith and love towards Him. The Lord be with us day and night in our coming in and going out, in our sorrow and in our joy. And bring us at length into His eternal rest. Amen.

UNTO God's gracious mercy and protection we commit ourselves. The Lord bless us and keep us. The Lord make His face to shine upon us and be gracious unto us. The Lord lift up the light of His countenance upon us, and give us peace, both now and evermore. Amen.

(Num. vi. 24-26; *the Aaronic Blessing.)*

MAY our Lord Jesus Christ be near us to defend us, within us to refresh us, around us to preserve us, before us to guide us, behind us to justify us, above us to bless us. Who liveth and reigneth with the Father and the Holy Ghost, God for evermore. Amen.

GOD Almighty, bless us with His Holy Spirit; guard us in our going out and coming in; keep us ever steadfast in His Faith, free from sin and safe from danger; through Jesus Christ our Lord. Amen.

MAY the Blessing of God Almighty, the Father, the Son, and the Holy Ghost, rest upon us and upon all our work and worship done in His Name. May He give us Light to guide us, Courage to support us, and Love to unite us, now and for evermore. Amen.

MAY the Lord lead us when we go, and keep us when we sleep, and talk with us when we wake; and may the peace of God, which passeth all understanding, keep our hearts and minds in Christ Jesus our Lord. Amen.

THE peace of God which passeth all understanding, keep our hearts and minds in the knowledge and love of God, and of His Son Jesus Christ our Lord, and the blessing of God Almighty, the Father, the Son, and the Holy Ghost, be amongst us and remain with us always. Amen.

(Book of Common Prayer, A.D. 1549.)

AND now may the blessing of the Lord rest and remain upon all His people in every land of every tongue. The Lord meet in mercy all that seek Him. The Lord comfort all that suffer and mourn. The Lord hasten His coming, and now give us and all His people peace by all means. Amen.

BENEDICTIONS

MAY God the Father bless us. May Christ the Son take care of us. The Holy Ghost enlighten us, all the days of our life. The Lord be our defender and keeper of body and soul both now and for ever and to the ages of ages. Amen.

(An Ancient Blessing.)

MAY the right hand of the Lord keep us ever in old age, the grace of Christ continually defend us from the enemy. O Lord, direct our heart in the way of peace; through Jesus Christ our Lord. Amen.

(From the Book of Cerne, the Prayer-book of Aedelwald, Saxon Bishop, Ninth Century.)

MAY God, the Lord, bless us with all heavenly benediction, and make us pure and holy in His sight.
May the riches of His glory abound in us.
May He instruct us with the word of truth, inform us with the Gospel of salvation, and enrich us with His love,
Through Jesus Christ, our Lord. Amen.

(Gelasian Sacramentary.)

GO forth into the world in peace; be of good courage; hold fast that which is good; render to no man evil for evil; strengthen the faint-hearted; support the weak; help the afflicted; honour all men; love and serve the Lord; rejoicing in the power of the Holy Spirit. Amen. *(Revised Prayer Book, 1928.)*

MAY the Lord Jesus Christ fill us with spiritual joy, may His Spirit make us strong and tranquil in the truths of His promises. And may the blessing of the Lord come upon us abundantly. Amen.

MAY God, the Fountain of all blessing, fill us with the understanding of sacred knowledge. May He keep us sound in faith, steadfast in hope and persevering in patient charity. And may the blessing of the Father, the Son, and the Holy Spirit, and the peace of the Lord be with us always. Amen.

MAY our blessed Lord be with us, the love of the Eternal Father embrace and follow us. The Mighty Saviour be our Shepherd and defence. The Holy Ghost, sanctify, counsel and confirm us, For the praise of Him Who called us into His marvellous Light, and into the footsteps of Him Who is the Way, the Truth, and the Life, even Jesus Christ our Lord. Amen.

THE grace of our Lord Jesus Christ, and the love of God, and the fellowship of the Holy Ghost, be with us all, evermore. Amen.
(Eastern Church Liturgy, Book of Common Prayer, A.D. 1559.)

GIVE unto us, O Lord, that quietness of mind in which we can hear Thee speaking to us, for Thine own Name's Sake.

"YE shall receive power after that the Holy Ghost is come upon you, and ye shall be witnesses unto ME." (*Acts* i. 8.)

SPEAK to us, O Lord, in the silence of this day.

Reveal to us, O Lord, how to help Thee in Thy work in the world.

Feed our souls, O Lord, that we may take the Bread of Heaven to others.

Pour upon us, O Lord, the Spirit of wisdom and understanding, and fill us with the spirit of Thy holy fear.

Give strength and hope to all who are labouring for Thee.

Grant to us all an increased compassion to those who know Thee not, that we may both give and be given for their sakes.

Fill us with Thy Love toward all men, and grant to us all, thankful hearts, through Jesus Christ our Lord.

"HERE we offer and present unto Thee, O Lord, ourselves, our souls, and bodies, to be a reasonable, holy, and lively sacrifice unto Thee."

TO the surrender of ourselves to Thee, O Lord Christ,
We consecrate ourselves.

To the surrender of ourselves to the Service of God,

To the preaching of the good tidings of Salvation,

To the teaching of Jesus—the Way, the Truth, and the Life,
We consecrate our gifts.

To the service of Thy holy Church in all the world,

To the helping of the needs of those around us,

To the healing and care of broken lives,

To the sharing with others the privileges which we enjoy,
We consecrate our gifts.

"SPEAK, Lord, for Thy servant heareth."
(1 *Sam.* iii. 9.)

"I HEARD the voice of the Lord saying, 'Whom shall I send, and who will go for Us?' Then said I, 'Here am I, send me'." (*Isa.* vi. 8.)

O GOD, show us Thy will and give us Thy strength to do it. Amen.

LORD, inspire us with Thy love, that we may work for Thy glory, through Jesus Christ our Lord. Amen.

LITANIES
A MORNING DEDICATION.

O GOD, the Father of Heaven,
  O God, the Son, Redeemer of the world,
  O God, the Holy Ghost, the Sanctifier of Thy People:
    Hear us, we beseech Thee, O Lord.

We, in communion with all Thy saints in all ages, with patriarchs and prophets, with apostles and martyrs, with all who have passed from us into Thy Presence,

We, who are still striving to do and to bear Thy blessed will on earth,

Adore Thee, and offer to Thee our praises, thanksgivings and supplications. Hear us, we beseech Thee, O Lord.

Make us of quick and tender conscience, that we may follow every suggestion of Thine indwelling Spirit.
    Hear us, we beseech Thee, O Lord.

We pray Thee to reveal to us
  The beauty of Thy perfect will,
  The gladness of Thy service,
  The power of Thy Presence in our hearts.
    Hear us, we beseech Thee, O Lord.

May no perplexity create in us an impatient spirit, no temptation lead us into sin, no sorrow hide Thy loving will from us. Hear us, we beseech Thee, O Lord.

Teach us all to feel the need of Thy grace and to seek it, to know Thy will and to do it; and to abide in peace in our appointed lot. Hear us, we beseech Thee, O Lord.

Calm our passions,
  Repress the waywardness of our wills, and
  Direct the motions of our affections.
    Hear us, we beseech Thee, O Lord.

Help us to forgive as we would be forgiven, dwelling neither in speech nor thought upon offences committed against us, but loving one another as Thou lovest us.
    Hear us, we beseech Thee, O Lord.

Help us with all diligence to keep our hearts, and to conform ourselves to Thy will in things both small and great.
    Hear us, we beseech Thee, O Lord.

Gracious Father, Who willest us to cast our care on Thee Who carest for us, preserve us from all faithless fears and selfish anxieties, and grant that no clouds of this mortal life may hide from us the light of the love which is immortal and which Thou hast manifested to us in Jesus Christ our Lord, but that we may this day walk in the Light of Thy Countenance, be guided by Thine eye, sanctified by Thy spirit, and be enabled to live to Thy glory.

Hear us, we beseech Thee, O Lord.

Blessing.

May the rich blessing of the Lord attend us, and grant us all, remission of our sins.

May the Lord graciously protect us from all evil and mercifully preserve and keep us in all good, and

May He Who created and redeemed us preserve us for Himself unspotted to the end. Amen. (*Mozarabic Psalter.*)

A LITANY OF THANKSGIVING.

IT is a good thing to give thanks unto the Lord, and to sing praises unto the name of the Most High. Offer unto Him sacrifices of thanksgiving and utter the memory of His great goodness.

O Lord, open Thou our lips,
And our mouth shall show forth Thy praise.

Almighty God, our Heavenly Father, from Whom cometh every good and perfect gift, we call to remembrance Thy loving kindness and Thy tender mercies which have ever been of old, and with grateful hearts we would lift up to Thee the voice of our thanksgiving.

For all the gifts which Thou hast bestowed upon us and our race,

For the life Thou hast given us, and the world in which we live: We praise Thee, O God.

For the work we are enabled to do, and
For the truth we are permitted to learn;
For whatever of good there has been in our lives,
For all the hopes and aspirations which lead us onwards to better things: We praise Thee, O God.

For the order and constancy of nature;
For the beauty and bounty of the world;
For day and night, summer and winter, seedtime and harvest;
For the varied gifts of loveliness and use which every season brings: We praise Thee, O God.

For the Autumn with all its glories;
For the Harvest with its boundless store;
For all the fruits of the earth that gladden and sustain the life of man; We praise Thee, O God.

For all the comforts and gladness of life;
For our homes and all our home-blessings;
For our friends and all the pure pleasures of social inter-
course:
                 We praise Thee, O God.

For all true knowledge of Thee and Thy love—and the world
in which we live;
For the life of truth and righteousness and Divine communion to which Thou hast called us:
                 We praise Thee, O God.

For Prophets and Apostles, and all earnest seekers after truth;
For all lovers and helpers of mankind and all godly and gifted
men and women: We praise Thee, O God.

For all the blessings of civilization, wise government and
legislation;
For education, and all the privileges we enjoy through
literature, science, and art;
For the help and counsel of those who are wiser and better
than ourselves: We praise Thee, O God.

And most of all and above all:
For the gift of Thy Son Jesus Christ, and all helps and hopes
which are ours as His disciples;
For His life and death—His resurrection and ascension for
our redemption;
For the presence and inspiration of Thy Holy Spirit and for
all the ministries of Thy truth and grace:
                 We praise Thee, O God.

For communion with Thee, the Father of our spirits;
For the light and peace that are gained through trust and
obedience to Thy laws:
                 We praise Thee, O God.

For the desire and power to help others;
For every opportunity of serving our generation according
to Thy will, and manifesting the grace of Christ to men:
                 We praise Thee, O God.

For all the discipline of life;
For the tasks and trials by which we are trained to patience,
self-knowledge and self-conquest;
For all the circumstances which bring us into closer sympathy
with our suffering brethren;
For troubles which have lifted us nearer Thee and drawn us
into deeper fellowship with Jesus Christ:
                 We praise Thee, O God.

For the sacred and tender ties which bind us to the unseen world;

For the faith which dispels the shadows of earth, and fills the saddest, and the last moments of life with the light of an immortal hope: We praise Thee, O God.

God of all grace and love, we have praised Thee with our lips; Grant that we may also praise Thee in consecrated and faithful lives, to Thy honour and glory, through Jesus Christ our Lord. Amen. (*Adapted from Rev. Dr. J. Hunter*, A.D. 1849.)

Our Father which art in heaven . . .

LENT.

Part I.—A Litany of Repentance.

TURN away, O Lord, the fierceness of Thy wrath, and in pity spare Thy people:
And have mercy.

Grant a favourable and speedy answer to the prayers of all, we beseech Thee:
And have mercy.

Do Thou, O Christ, look upon our groanings, loose the bands of death, and grant us life:
And have mercy.

Behold our tears—consider our sighs, and now at length in pity forgive our sins:
And have mercy.

Though none of us be worthy to be heard, do Thou, O Christ, for Thine own self help us:
And have mercy. (*Mozarabic Breviary.*)

Part II.—For Forgiveness.

We cry to Thee, O Lord, do Thou have mercy upon us:
And grant forgiveness.

O King of Heaven, and everlasting Lord, receive the prayers which we pour forth:
And grant forgiveness.

Visit the sick—bring forth the captives, help the widow and the orphan:
And grant forgiveness.

We have sinned and have departed from Thee, do Thou, Who art the Redeemer of all, save us:
And grant forgiveness.

Have mercy on the penitent, and wash away the stains of sin:
And grant forgiveness. (*Mozarabic Breviary.*)

LITANIES ON THE PASSION (1).

L ET us all with one voice cry:
Lord, have mercy.

Thou Who wert led as a sheep to be crucified:
Lord, have mercy.

Thou Who from the Cross didst look upon Thy mother and
Thy disciple, look with pity from heaven upon us:
Lord, have mercy.

Thou Who by Thy blood-shedding hast redeemed the world:
Lord, have mercy.

Thou Who didst commend Thy spirit to the Father:
Lord, have mercy.

Make us by Thy Cross to obtain forgiveness:
Lord, have mercy.   (*Mozarabic Breviary.*)

Show us Thy mercy, O Lord, grant pardon, grant remission:
And have mercy graciously.

Thou Who, coming to save the world, wert brought to
judgment, when Thou comest as Judge, deliver us not up with
the ungodly:
And have mercy graciously.

Thou, Who wert hung upon the Cross, bear on Thy shoulders
the death due to our guilt:
And have mercy graciously.

Thou Who didst once suffer for the ungodly, and diest no more,
mortify our vices in us, and heal us by the wound of the Cross:
And have mercy graciously.

That in the judgment Thy face may not be turned on us for
punishment, but may shine on us with pardon:
And have mercy graciously.
                        (*Mozarabic Breviary.*)

Blessing.

May God the Father bless us, Who created all things in the
beginning.
May the Son bless us, Who for our salvation came down from
His throne on high.
May the Holy Ghost bless us, Who rested as a Dove on the
Christ in Jordan.
May He sanctify us in the Trinity Whose coming to judgment
all nations look for.   Amen.
                        (*Gallican Missal.*)

O GOOD Shepherd, Who didst lay down Thy life for the sheep, remember us:

> Be propitious, and have mercy upon us.

O Everlasting Power and Wisdom of the most High God, Thou Word of the Father, remember us:

> Be propitious, and have mercy upon us.

O Thou Maker of the world, the Life of all, the Lord of Angels, remember us:

> Be propitious, and have mercy upon us.

O Lamb of God, Who for us wast led as a sheep to the slaughter, remember us:

> Be propitious, and have mercy upon us.

O Thou Who wast seized, though guiltless, buffeted, given over to robbers, remember us:

> Be propitious, and have mercy upon us.

Thou Who alone hast by Thy death overcome the death of our guilt, remember us:

> Be propitious, and have mercy upon us.

(Mozarabic Breviary.)

DOXOLOGY.

BLESSING and honour, thanksgiving and praise
more than we can utter be unto Thee,
O most adorable Trinity, Father, Son, and Holy Ghost,
by all angels, all men, all creatures
for ever and ever Amen and Amen.
To God the Father, Who first loved us,
and made us accepted in the Beloved:
To God the Son, Who loved us,
and washed us from our sins in His own blood:
To God the Holy Ghost,
Who sheds the love of God abroad in our hearts
be all love and all glory for time and eternity. Amen.

(Bishop Ken, A.D. 1637.)

INDEX OF AUTHORS AND SOURCES*

(Revised 1947.)

---

* NOTE—All dates are A.D. with the exception of those marked B.C. When date of birth or death is uncertain, the nearest century is indicated.

INDEX OF AUTHORS AND SOURCES

INDEX OF AUTHORS AND SOURCES

INDEX OF SUBJECTS

INDEX OF SUBJECTS

INDEX OF SUBJECTS

INDEX OF SUBJECTS

INDEX OF SUBJECTS

318

INDEX OF SUBJECTS

INDEX OF SUBJECTS

PRINTED IN GREAT BRITAIN BY
WYMAN & SONS, LIMITED, LONDON, FAKENHAM AND READING.